The Characterization of an Empire

The Characterization of an Empire

The Portrayal of the Assyrians in Kings and Chronicles

MARY KATHERINE YEM HING HOM

⌖PICKWICK *Publications* · Eugene, Oregon

THE CHARACTERIZATION OF AN EMPIRE
The Portrayal of the Assyrians in Kings and Chronicles

Copyright © 2018 Mary Katherine Yem Hing Hom. All rights reserved. Except for brief quotations in critical publications or reviews, no part of this book may be reproduced in any manner without prior written permission from the publisher. Write: Permissions, Wipf and Stock Publishers, 199 W. 8th Ave., Suite 3, Eugene, OR 97401.

Pickwick Publications
An Imprint of Wipf and Stock Publishers
199 W. 8th Ave., Suite 3
Eugene, OR 97401

www.wipfandstock.com

PAPERBACK ISBN: 978-1-5326-4661-4
HARDCOVER ISBN: 978-1-5326-4662-1
EBOOK ISBN: 978-1-5326-4663-8

Cataloging-in-Publication data:

Names: Hom, Mary Katherine Y. H., author.

Title: The characterization of an empire : the portrayal of the Assyrians in Kings and Chronicles / Mary Katherine Yem Hing Hom.

Description: Eugene, OR: Cascade Books, 2018. | Includes bibliographical references and indexes.

Identifiers: ISBN: 978-1-5326-4661-4 (paperback). | ISBN: 978-1-5326-4662-1 (hardcover). | ISBN: 978-1-5326-4663-8 (epub).

Subjects: LCSH: Assyria in the Bible. | Bible. OT. Kings—Criticism, interpretation, etc. | Bible. OT. Chronicles—Criticism, interpretation, etc. | Assyrians.

Classification: BS1335.52 H67 2018 (print). | BS1335.52 (epub).

Manufactured in the U.S.A.   07/06/18

Contents

Permissions | vii
Preface | ix
Abbreviations | xi

1 General Introduction | 1

2 Downfall and Agency: The Characterization of the Assyrians through the Fall of the Northern Kingdom (2 Kings 15–17) | 9

3 Sennacherib and YHWH at War: Assyrian Attack, Prophetic Oracles, and YHWH's Deliverance of Jerusalem and Hezekiah (2 Kings 18–20) | 65

4 Ancestors and Aggressors: The Portrayal of the Assyrians in 1 Chronicles (1 Chronicles 1:17; 5:6, 22b–26) | 124

5 The Failure of Assyria as an "Alternative" to YHWH (2 Chronicles 28) | 139

6 Covenant Broken and Restored through the Intermediaries of the Assyrians: Two Brief References to the Assyrians in the Early Chapters of Chronicles' Hezekiah Account (2 Chronicles 29:9; 30:6–9) | 149

7 YHWH is Greater than Assyria: The Characterization of the Assyrians in 2 Chronicles 32 through Chiastic and Linear Readings (2 Chronicles 32) | 163

8 A Unique Chiasmus and the Assyrians as the Pivotal Intensifying Factor and Instrument of YHWH (2 Chronicles 33:1–20) | 199

9 Conclusions | 217

Appendix 1: The "Twenty Years" Reign of Pekah
in 2 Kings 15:27 | 237

Appendix 2: Diagram for the Relational Complex
in 2 Chronicles 30:6-9 | 241

Appendix 3: The Absence and Minimization of Assyria
in Kings and Chronicles (1 Kings 16:21-28, 29-22:40;
19:16-17; 2 Kings 9-10; 14:23-29; 21:1-18; 19-26;
22:1—23:30; 2 Chronicles 33:21-25; 34-35) | 242

Bibliography | 261
Index of Subjects | 277
Index of Hebrew Terms | 281
Index of Ancient Documents | 283

Permissions

Scripture quotations marked (NIV) are taken from the Holy Bible, New International Version®, NIV®. Copyright © 1973, 1978, 1984, 2011 by Biblica, Inc.™ Used by permission of Zondervan. All rights reserved worldwide. www.zondervan.com. The "NIV" and "New International Version" are trademarks registered in the United States Patent and Trademark Office by Biblica, Inc.™

Scripture quotations marked (NRSV) are from New Revised Standard Version Bible, copyright © 1989 by the National Council of the Churches of Christ in the United States of America. Used by permission. All rights reserved worldwide.

Scripture quotations marked (NJPS) are reprinted from *Tanakh: The New JPS Translation according to the Traditional Hebrew Text*. Copyright © 1985, 1999 by The Jewish Publication Society with the permission of the publisher.

Chapters 5, 7, and 8 incorporate parts of "Chiasmus in Chronicles: Investigating the Structures of 2 Chronicles 28:16–21; 33:1–20; and 31:20–32:33," *AUSS* 47/2 (2009) 163–79, reprinted with permission of the editor of *Andrews University Seminary Studies*.

Preface

THE CHARACTERIZATION OF AN *Empire: The Portrayal of the Assyrians in Kings and Chronicles* is a substantially updated edition of my heretofore mostly unpublished PhD work. In a way, it is the sequel to my published PhD dissertation, *The Characterization of the Assyrians in Isaiah: Synchronic and Diachronic Perspectives*, and indeed was researched and initially drafted alongside said dissertation. This book has received the double benefit of the keen oversight of my supervisor, Professor Robert P. Gordon, through its various stages, in addition to the experienced and kind guidance of Professor Gordon McConville in its more advanced phases of development.

As always, I am very grateful to several entities and individuals for their assistance during this project: Tyndale House Library and staff; Lucy Emerton and Simon and Jean Barrington-Ward for their gracious and generous hospitality; the excellent team at Wipf and Stock, especially Ian Creeger, Matt Wimer, and Shannon Carter, with whom it has been a true joy to work; and especially: Joanne Boisvert, Anne-Marie Ellithorpe, Lukas Emmert, Dianne and Brad Green, Gary and Diane Gretzinger, Zach Holmgren, Christine and Satoshi Kojima, Polly Long, Abi and Matt Lynch, Patrick McClure, Katy and Pete Myers, Ulrich Paquet, Blaise Thomson, Christine Yajima, the weekly group that meets in the home of Ron and Sherry Beams, Alice Parente and the gals, and Donte Cuellar, Judy Sowa, and friends at AFA. Special thanks goes to Auntie Muriel and Uncle Ron, Auntie Marlene and Uncle Gordon, Kyungmin, Ashlyn, Menemsha, and Laura for their care and service to my mother when life had its challenges and this book pulled through its last stages, by the grace of God.

This study is dedicated to three people whose lives converged during its inception: my Uncle Al, who lived a long and very full life; my incredible mother, Christina Fong Hom, who in her battle against cancer has redefined and truly demonstrated life; and Abigail Grace McAllister and Isaac Benon Mwesigwa Bishanga, wee ones who each began theirs at just the same time as the birthing of this book.

Abbreviations

AB	Anchor Bible
ABD	Anchor Bible Dictionary
ABRL	Anchor Bible Reference Library
ANEM	Ancient Near Eastern Monographs
ANET	*Ancient Near Eastern Texts Relating to the Old Testament.* 3rd ed. Edited by James B. Pritchard. Princeton: Princeton University Press, 1969
ANEP	*The Ancient Near East in Pictures Relating to the Old Testament.* 2nd ed. Edited by James B. Pritchard. Princeton: Princeton University Press, 1994
AOAT	Alter Orient und Altes Testament
ARAB	*Ancient Records of Assyria and Babylonia.* Daniel David Luckenbill. 2 vols. Chicago: University of Chicago, 1926–1927
ARI	*Assyrian Royal Inscriptions.* A. K. Grayson. 2 vols. RANE. Wiesbaden: Otto Harrassowitz, 1972–1976
ASV	American Standard Version
ATD	Das Alte Testament Deutsch
ATM	Altes Testament und Moderne
AUM	Andrews University Monographs
AUSS	*Andrews University Seminary Studies*
BA	*Biblical Archaeologist*
BDAG	Walter Bauer, Frederick William Danker, W. F. Arndt, and F. W. Gingrich. *A Greek-English Lexicon of the New Testament and Other Early Christian Literature.* 3rd ed. Chicago: University of Chicago, 2000
BDB	Francis Brown, S. R. Driver, and Charles A. Briggs. *The New Brown–Driver–Briggs–Gesenius Hebrew and English Lexicon:*

	With an Appendix Containing the Biblical Aramaic. Peabody, MA: Hendrickson, 1979
BDF	R. Blass, A. Debrunner, and Robert W. Funk, *A Greek Grammar of the New Testament and Other Early Christian Literature.* Chicago: University of Chicago; London: Cambridge University Press, 1961
BETL	Bibliotheca ephemeridum theologicarum lovaniensium
Bib	*Biblica*
BibOr	Biblica et orientalia
BIS	Biblical Interpretation Series
BKAT	Biblischer Kommentar, Altes Testament
BN	*Biblische Notizen*
BSac	*Bibliotheca sacra*
BWANT	Beiträge zur Wissenschaft vom Alten und Neuen Testament
BZAW	Beihefte zur Zeitschrift für die alttestamentliche Wissenschaft
CAD	*The Assyrian Dictionary of the Oriental Institute of the University of Chicago.* Chicago: Oriental Institute, 1956–
CAH	*Cambridge Ancient History*
CANE	*Civilizations of the Ancient Near East.* Edited by Jack M. Sasson. 4 vols. New York: Schribner, Macmillan, 1995
CBET	Contributions to Biblical Exegesis and Theology
CBQ	*Catholic Biblical Quarterly*
CC	Continental Commentaries
CHANE	Culture and History of hte Ancient Near East
ConBOT	Coniectanea biblica: Old Testament Series
DCH	*Dictionary of Classical Hebrew.* Edited by David J. A. Clines, Philip R. Davies, J. Cheryl Exum, John W. Rogerson, et al. 9 vols. Sheffield: Sheffield Academic and Sheffield Phoenix, 1993–2016
DDD	*Dictionary of Deities and Demons in the Bible.* 2nd ed. Edited by Karel van der Toorn, Bob Becking, and Pieter W. van der Horst. Leiden: Brill, 1999
DSB	Daily Study Bible
EBib	*Etudes bibliques*
EJ	*Evangelical Journal*
EvQ	*Evangelical Quarterly*

ExpTim	*Expository Times*
EHZAT	Exegetisches Handbuch zum Alten Testament
FAT	Forschungen zum Alten Testament
FOTL	Forms of the Old Testament Literature
FRLANT	Forschungen zur Religion und Literatur des Alten und Neuen Testaments
GAT	Grundrisse zum Alten Testament
HAT	Handbuch zum Alten Testament
HALAT	*Hebräisches und aramäisches Lexikon zum Alten Testament.* 3rd ed. Edited by Ludwig Koehler, Walter Baumgartner, and Johann Jakob Stamm. 5 vols. and Supplement. Leiden: Brill, 1967–1996
HALOT	*The Hebrew and Aramaic Lexicon of the Old Testament.* Translated and edited under the supervision of M. E. J. Richardson. 5 vols. Leiden: Brill, 1993–2000
HCOT	Historical Commentary on the Old Testament
HKAT	Handkommentar zum Alten Testament
HSAT	Die Heilige Schrift des Alten Testamentes
HSM	Harvard Semitic Monographs
ICC	International Critical Commentary
Int	*Interpretation*
JAOS	*Journal of the American Oriental Society*
JBL	*Journal of Biblical Literature*
JBQ	*Jewish Bible Quarterly*
JCS	*Journal of Cuneiform Studies*
JSOT	*Journal for the Study of the Old Testament*
JSOTSup	Journal for the Study of the Old Testament: Supplement Series
JNES	*Journal of Near Eastern Studies*
JNSL	*Journal of Northwest Semitic Languages*
JSS	*Journal of Semitic Studies*
KAT	Kommentar zum Alten Testament
LCL	Loeb Classical Library
LHBOTS	Library of Hebrew Bible/Old Testament Studies
LTQ	Lexington Theological Commentary
LXX	Septuagint

NCB	New Century Bible
NCBC	New Century Bible Commentary
NICOT	New International Commentary on the Old Testament
NIDOTTE	*New International Dictionary of Old Testament Theology and Exegesis*
NIBC	New International Bible Commentary
NIV	New International Version
NJB	New Jerusalem Bible
NJPS	New Jewish Publication Society Translation
NRSV	New Revised Standard Version
NSK-AT	Neuer Stuttgarter Kommentar–Altes Testament
OBO	Orbis biblicus et orientalis
OBT	Overtures to Biblical Theology
OTL	Old Testament Library
OtSt	*Oudtestamentische Studiën*
PMIRC	Penn Museum International Research Conferences
PTMS	Pittsburgh Theological Monograph Series
RB	*Revue biblique*
RlA	*Reallexikon der Assyriologie und Vorderasiatischen Archäologie.* Edited by Erich Ebeling, Bruno Meissner, Ernst Weidner, Wolfram von Soden, Dietz Otto Edzard, and Michael P. Streck. 11 volumes. Berlin: Walter de Gruyter, 1928–
RSR	*Recherches de science religieuse*
SBLDS	Society of Biblical Literature Dissertation Series
SBLMS	Society of Biblical Literature Monograph Series
SBLSCS	Society of Biblical Literature Septuagint and Cognate Studies
SBLSPS	Society of Biblical Literature Seminar Paper Series
SBLSS	Society of Biblical Literature Semeia Studies
SBS	Stuttgarter Bibelstudien
SBT	Studies in Biblical Theology
SJOT	*Scandinavian Journal of the Old Testament*
SJT	*Scottish Journal of Theology*
SPCK	Society for Promoting Christian Knowledge
SSN	Studia Semitica Neerlandica
SUNY	State University of New York

TB	Theologische Bücherei: Neudrucke und Berichte aus dem 20. Jahrhundert
TDOT	*Theological Dictionary of the Old Testament*
TLOT	*Theological Lexicon of the Old Testament*
TNIV	Today's New International Version
TOTC	Tyndale Old Testament Commentaries
TQ	*Theologische Quartalschrift*
Transeu	*Transeuphratène*
TWOT	*Theological Wordbook of the Old Testament*. Edited by R. Laird Harris, Gleason L. Archer, and Bruce K. Waltke. 2 vols. Chicago: Moody, 1980
TZ	*Theologische Zeitschrift*
VT	*Vetus Testamentum*
VTSup	Vetus Testamentum Supplements
WBC	Word Biblical Commentary
WMANT	Wissenschaftliche Monographien zum Alten und Neuen Testament
WTJ	*Westminster Theological Journal*
ZAW	*Zeitschrift für die alttestamentliche Wissenschaft*
ZBK	Zürcher Bibelkommentare

1

General Introduction

THE PORTRAYAL OF THE very first ancient Near Eastern empire—that grand, notorious, and commandeering superpower known as Assyria—remains a relatively neglected sector in biblical studies. While the portrayal of the Egyptians and Babylonians has long been popular and given attention, the "middle person" and strangely quiet, almost missing link in the typological development of the national/imperial oppressor in the Old Testament has been left to the wayside, along with many of the biblical texts concerning it. Undoubtedly, this should no longer be the case, and the relatively recent ravages of ancient Assyrian imperial sites in the Middle East compounds the necessity—indeed, the present urgency—of recognizing the significant contribution of the Assyrians to history, culture, the development of empires, and for our purposes, the impact of all this on biblical literature.

Thus, it is a primary aim of this book to attend to those neglected passages concerning the Assyrians and, moreover, to the manners, ways, appearances, actions, effects, roles, etc. of the Assyrians they describe. Relatedly, texts in which the Assyrians may have been expected to appear, but did not, are also discussed. And so, this work is a systematic compilation of rigorous, careful exegetical study of the literary aspect of these biblical texts as well as focused discussion and distillation of the characterization of the Assyrians in individual passages in Kings and Chronicles. In this way, the research gathered here contributes to ancient Near Eastern literary studies, biblical studies, ethnology, and imperialism studies. There is also much in this work to offer in future comparative studies with Assyriology. But most importantly, this volume contributes yet another step forward in filling the gap left by the near-missing link of research concerning the once inescapable Assyrians in the Old Testament. As that gap is in critical danger of increasing through the modern destruction of Middle Eastern antiquities and sites—bearers of material history and societal memory—textual witnesses and attention to the Assyrians in general have become more important and timely. While warfare and extremism may threaten to erase Assyrian history, the studies in this monograph elevate and engage with the Assyrians from the perspectives of the biblical historical books.

METHOD AND PROCEDURE

The approach of this book is fairly straightforward: this is a literary, exegetical investigation of the characterization of the Assyrians in Kings and Chronicles. In view of that purpose, I primarily explore for this study the final, received form of the MT and approach each individual passage by utilizing a synchronic approach in order to apprehend the overall narrative artistry that may be present. While my focus is on the literary aspect of the text, related issues of social psychology and imperialism will also be touched upon as they pertain to the literary presentation of the passages.

Thus, every explicit and implicit mention of the Assyrians in Kings and Chronicles is analyzed in canonical order. Explicit references to the Assyrians are in 2 Kings 15; 16; 17; 18–20; 23:29; 1 Chr 1:17; 5:6, 22b–26; 2 Chr 28; 29:9; 30:6–9; 32; 33:1–20; implicit—or curiously silent—incidences concerning the Assyrians are explored in 1 Kgs 16:21–28; 16:29—22:40; 2 Kgs 9–10; 14:23–29; 21:1–18, 19–26; 22:1—23:30; 2 Chr 33:21–25; 34–35.

Although the presentation of this book may seem straightforward, extensive discussion necessarily has been given to chapters involving two related passages that have historically engendered much analysis and debate in scholarship: the discussion of the portrayal of the Assyrians in the full text of 2 Kgs 18–20 (by way of contrast to the analysis of Isaiah 36–39 in *The Characterization of the Assyrians in Isaiah*,[1] which focussed on distinctives of the Isaianic version) and the examination of the portrayal of the Assyrians in 2 Chr 32 with regard to not only its narratival-linear presentation, but also its chiastic form and nuanced, rich comprehension of communication. At the same time, may the reader find that every text—long or short, complex or not-so-complex (none are quite simple!)—yields a wealth of literary and ideological meaning involving the Assyrians.

---

1. Mary Katherine Y. H. Hom, *The Characterization of the Assyrians in Isaiah: Synchronic and Diachronic Perspectives*, LHBOTS 559 (New York: Bloomsbury, 2012).

Previous Research and Related Material

Simply by virtue of the dearth of research in this specific area, it must again be emphasized that there are very few works treating at length the characterization of the Assyrians in the Old Testament, apart from this work and its predecessor, *The Characterization of the Assyrians in Isaiah: Synchronic and Diachronic Perspectives*.[2] Danna Nolan Fewell's article "Sennacherib's Defeat: Words at War in 2 Kings 18.13–19.37," conducts in short form the careful and perceptive literary analysis with attention to characterization that I have pursued in both volumes.[3] Her excellent work here, in fact, makes one eager for further exploration of characterization, especially with regard to that unusual "other," Assyria. There are several works that attend to similar texts, but focus on the portrayal of a narratologically primary character, who is usually an Israelite or Judean king—e.g., Hezekiah in David Bostock's *A Portrayal of Trust: The Theme of Faith in the Hezekiah Narratives*; Hezekiah and his representatives in Paul S. Evans' *The Invasion of Sennacherib in the Book of Kings: A Source-Critical and Rhetorical Study of 2 Kings 18-19*; Ahaz in Klaas A. D. Smelik's "The Representation of King Ahaz in 2 Kings 16 and 2 Chronicles 28"; and Manasseh in Klaas A. D. Smelik's "Portrayal of King Manasseh: A Literary Analysis of 2 Kings 21 and 2 Chronicles 23."[4] Each of these works is, of course, a contribution in its own right, but again for the purposes of our study—namely, the portrayal of the foreign and developing empire called Assyria—they are of related, but not principal, interest.

With regard to method for the elucidation of the remarkable chiastic structure of 2 Chr 32 (as well as 2 Chr 28:16–21 and 33:1–20), I am obliged to note Mike Butterworth's critical and engaging methodology in "Investigating Structure: In Search of a Reliable Method."[5] As discussed further in my chapter on the portrayal of the Assyrians in 2 Chr 32, his work refined

2. Hom, *Characterization of the Assyrians in Isaiah*, 161–85.

3. Danna Nolan Fewell, "Sennacherib's Defeat: Words at War in 2 Kings 18.13–19.37," *JSOT* 34 (1986) 79–90.

4. David Bostock, *A Portrayal of Trust: The Theme of Faith in the Hezekiah Narratives*, Paternoster Biblical Monographs (Milton Keynes, UK: Paternoster, 2006); Paul S. Evans, *The Invasion of Sennacherib in the Book of Kings: A Source-Critical and Rhetorical Study of 2 Kings 18-19*, VTSup 125 (Leiden: Brill, 2009), 123–65; Klaas A. D. Smelik, "The Representation of King Ahaz in 2 Kings 16 and 2 Chronicles 28," in *Intertextuality in Ugarit and Israel*, ed. Johannes C. de Moor, OTS 40 (Leiden: Brill, 1997), 142–85; Klaas A. D. Smelik, "Portrayal of King Manasseh: A Literary Analysis of 2 Kings 21 and 2 Chronicles 23," in *Converting the Past: Studies in Ancient Israelite and Moabite Historiography*, OTS 28 (Leiden: Brill, 1992), 129–89.

5. Mike Butterworth, "Investigating Structure: In Search of a Reliable Method," ch. 1 of *Structure and the Book of Zechariah*, JSOTSup 130 (Sheffield: Sheffield Academic, 1992), 18–61.

my discernment of proper chiasmuses, which were unexpectedly present and significant in Chronicles.

Concerning my somewhat empire-conscious approach, with its resemblance to the first of Sugirtharajah's five hermeneutical agendas for postcolonial biblical criticism, I am glad to say that I have been preceded in this by David Janzen's monograph, *The Necessary King: A Postcolonial Reading of the Deuteronomistic Portrait of the Monarchy*.[6] Janzen's work utilizes an interdisciplinary combination of approaches that is overall different than this study, but remains an interesting and thoughtful contribution to biblical studies, demonstrating the fruitfulness of focussed attention on this single aspect of the postcolonial optic. Uriah Y. Kim's *Decolonizing Josiah: Toward a Postcolonial Reading of the Deuteronomistic History* delivers insightful and thought-provoking commentary on a wide diversity of related topics. Most relevant to my work here is his discussion on the absence of Assyria in the Kings narratives concerning Manasseh, Amon, and Josiah.[7] Finally, Leo Perdue and Warren Carter's *Israel and Empire: A Postcolonial History of Israel and Early Judaism* attempts to apply more explicit postcolonial terminology to a much broader purview of Israelite history than my study.[8] Although Perdue's book differs in topical scope, genre-focus, and extent of engagement with explicit postcolonial concepts, it provided some helpful introduction and background to the topic of the Israelite monarchy in relation to the Assyrian empire.

COMPOSITIONAL HISTORY

While this study concentrates on characterization, particularly that which is conveyed through the final, received form of the text, a few provisional comments concerning the compositional history of Kings and Chronicles are apropos here. First, with regard to Kings, the hypotheses concerning its compositional history since Noth have been multitudinous,[9] generally falling into either a double-redaction model (pre-exilic and exilic stages, with a pre-exilic emphasis on Hezekiah or Josiah) or a triple-redaction model (the "Göttingen school" model of an original further redacted by

---

6. David Janzen, *The Necessary King: A Postcolonial Reading of the Deuteronomistic Portrait of the Monarchy*, HBM 57 (Sheffield: Sheffield Phoenix, 2013), see 11–12.

7. Uriah Y. Kim, *Decolonizing Josiah: Toward a Postcolonial Reading of the Deuteronomistic History*, BMW 5 (Sheffield: Sheffield Phoenix, 2005).

8. Leo Perdue and Warren Carter, *Israel and Empire: A Postcolonial History of Israel and Early Judaism*, ed. Coleman A. Baker (London: Bloomsbury, 2015).

9. Martin Noth, *The Deuteronomistic History*, JSOTSup 15 (Sheffield: JSOT Press, 1981).

stages characterized by prophecy and law, respectively; or developments of Weippert's hypothesis of a pre-exilic, Hezekian stage, followed by a Josianic stage and an exilic stage).[10] After consideration of the possibilities, the current position of this work adopts the basic perspective of McKenzie on the matter of Kings' compositional history, which for the most part follows a two-stage development of Kings with recognition of several evident pre-DtrH sources. The following chart summarizes my tentative position concerning the stage and date of composition for individual passages discussed in this study.

Text	Pre-Dtr	DtrH, primarily Josianic (late 7th-c.)	Exilic, post-Jehoiachin's release in 561 BCE
1 Kgs 16:21-28		•	
1 Kgs 16:29—22:40		•	
1 Kgs 19:16-17		•	
2 Kgs 9-10	•		
2 Kgs 14:23-29		•	
2 Kgs 15		•	
2 Kgs 16		•	
2 Kgs 17:1-7aa, 18a, 21-34a		•	•
2 Kgs 17:7ab-41, minus 18a, 21-34a			•
2 Kgs 18-20:11		•	
2 Kgs 20:12-19			•
2 Kgs 21:1-7, 17-18		•	
2 Kgs 21:8-16			•
2 Kgs 21:19-26		•	

---

10. Rudolph Smend, "Das Gesetz und die Völker: Ein Beitrag zur deuteronomistichen Redaktionsgeschichte," in *Probleme biblischer Theologie: Gerhard von Rad zum 70. Geburtstag*, ed. Hans Walter Wolff (Munich: Kaiser, 1972), 494-509, and Walter Dietrich, *Prophetie und Geschichte*, FRLANT 108 (Göttingen: Vandenhoeck & Ruprecht, 1972), 134-48: DtrG/DtrH —> DtrP —> DtrN; Helga Weippert, "Die 'deuteronomistischen' Beurteilungen der Könige von Israel und Juda und das Problem der Redaktion der Königsbücher," *Bib* 53 (1972) 301-9: Dtr(hez) —> Dtr(jos) —> Dtr(x).

| 2 Kgs 22:1–14;
23:1–15, 19–25 | | | • | |
| 2 Kgs 22:15–20;
23:16–18, 26–30 | | | | • |

The compositional history of Chronicles is much more difficult to ascertain, as consensus has evaded scholarly opinion regarding the date of Chronicles. Modern theories for the date of the final form of Chronicles range from the late-sixth century to the second century BCE, and may be classed into four periods: restoration; post-Ezra-Nehemiah; late Persian; and Greek.[11] Various issues may impinge on one's evaluation of these possibilities, including the relation or non-relation of Chronicles to Ezra-Nehemiah,[12] the discernment of reference to Chronicles in Sirach or other post-biblical literature, the apparent lack of Greek influence, the genealogy of Zerubbabel (who we know operated in the sixth-century BCE; 1 Chr 3:19–24), and time-sensitive references to possible Persian circumstances (the most clear case being the 1 Chr 29:7 reference to the Persian daric, which was introduced and named after Persian emperor Darius I). The working hypothesis of this work regarding the date of composition for Chronicles is sometime in the fourth-century BCE, during the Persian period and before significant Greek influence in the region (Yehud).

As for the development itself of Chronicles, it is clear that one of its primary *Vorlagen* is a version of Samuel-Kings,[13] which bore resemblance at points with 4QSam^a and the Lucianic LXX (L).[14] Positing precise sources beyond this is, as has been often recognized by scholars, a venture into the realm of conjecture or informed conjecture, at best.[15] Though Chronicles

---

11. Martin J. Selman, *1 Chronicles: An Introduction and Commentary*, TOTC (Leicester, UK: Inter-Varsity Press, 1994), 70.

12. Despite the Talmud's claim that Ezra and Nehemiah were the authors of Chronicles, this seems unlikely. Cf. *b. Baba Bathra* 15a. For a proposed and nuanced redactional explanation of the relation between Ezra–Nehemiah and Chronicles, see H. G. M. Williamson, *Ezra, Nehemiah*, WBC 16 (Waco: Word, 1985), xxxiii–xxxv.

13. Contra the Shared Text theses of A. Graeme Auld, "What Was the Main Source of the Books of Chronicles?" in *The Chronicler as Author: Studies in Text and Texture*, eds. M. Patrick Graham and Steven L. McKenzie, JSOTSup 263 (Sheffield: Sheffield Academic, 1999), 91–99 (93); and Raymond F. Person, *The Deuteronomic History and the Book of Chronicles: Scribal Works in an Oral World*, Ancient Israel and its Literature 6 (Atlanta: SBL, 2010), 163–69.

14. See discussion in Gary N. Knoppers, *1 Chronicles 1–9: A New Translation with Introduction and Commentary*, AB 12 (New York: Doubleday, 2003), 70; and Selman, *1 Chronicles*, 74.

15. H. G. M. Williamson, *1 and 2 Chronicles*, NCBC (London: Marshall, Morgan & Scott, 1982), 19–21; Gwilym H. Jones, *1 & 2 Chronicles*, Old Testament Guides

makes reference to apparently eighteen separately-titled works, the identity of these works and whether they are indeed distinct from one another beyond title, refer to a unified extra-biblical source, or refer to Samuel-Kings remains an open question;[16] that Chronicles itself merits recognition as a unified and distinctive whole is less so, and most likely the final form was composed by a single author (or perhaps a tightly-knit group of scholars).[17] The following chart reflects my current positions regarding the source of texts discussed in this study.

Text	Gen	Josh	2 Kgs	Isa	Chr	Note also
1 Chr 1:17	Gen 10:22-23					
1 Chr 5:6, 22b-26		Josh 13:8-32				
2 Chr 28			2 Kgs 16:2-20		2 Chr 28:6-15	
2 Chr 29:9					2 Chr 29:9	
2 Chr 30:6-9					2 Chr 30:6-9	
2 Chr 32			2 Kgs 18:13-20:21	Isa 36-39		Cf. 2 Chr 32:32
2 Chr 33:1-20			2 Kgs 21:1-18			Cf. Jer 15:4
2 Chr 33:21-25			2 Kgs 21:19-26			
2 Chr 34-35			2 Kgs 22:1-23:30			Cf. 35:25

(Sheffield: Sheffield Academic, 1993), 69.

16. See, e.g., discussion in Sara Japhet, *1 and 2 Chronicles: A Commentary*, OTL (London: SCM, 1993), 20-23; and Steven L. McKenzie, *1 and 2 Chronicles*, Abingdon Old Testament Commentaries (Nashville: Abingdon, 2004), 35-43.

17. While the unity and distinctive authorship of Chronicles has been generally commonly agreed upon, it has been especially popularized more recently by Isaac Kalimi, *The Reshaping of Ancient Israelite History in Chronicles* (Winona Lake, IN: Eisenbrauns, 2005), 406-9; Steven L. McKenzie, "The Chronicler as Redactor," in *The Chronicler as Author: Studies in Text and Texture*, eds. M. Patrick Graham and Steven L. McKenzie, JSOTSup 263 (Sheffield: Sheffield Academic, 1999), 70-90 (esp. 88-90).

In this work, concerning both Kings and Chronicles, I will employ the term "author," with the recognition that final authorship of either book may have been corporate.

2

Downfall and Agency
The Characterization of the Assyrians through the Fall of the Northern Kingdom (2 Kings 15–17)

A NARRATOLOGICAL-THEOLOGICAL BACKGROUND TO THE PERICOPAE OF 2 KINGS 15–17

WITH REGARD TO THE kingdom of Israel, the dynasty of Jehu has ended—as one may expect—with Zechariah's death, fulfilling the word of YHWH that " . . . your sons to the fourth generation shall sit on the throne of Israel" (10:30; 15:12). Meanwhile, the accumulation of evil behaviour among the kings of Israel, including the favoured dynasty of Jehu (10:31; 13:2–3; 14:24; cf. 15:29), has prepared the reader to expect a post-Zechariah downward spiral for the Northern Kingdom. As Provan comments regarding vv. 8–12, "We have the impression of accumulated wrath, ready to burst in upon Jehu the moment the blockage to the normal flow of events is removed."[1] The surprisingly brief reign of Jehu's descendant Zechariah ("six months," v. 8), truncated in comparison to its precedessors, reinforces this ominous expectation.

The narrator then presents the final kings of Israel in quick succession. A total of six Israelite reigns are presented within three chapters. As well, the Judean reign of Azariah is presented before the whirlwind run of Israelite

---

1. As Iain W. Provan, *1 and 2 Kings*, NIBC (Peabody, MA: Hendrickson, 1995), 241. Similarly, Burke O. Long, *2 Kings*, FOTL 10 (Grand Rapids: Eerdmans, 1991), 171–73.

kings, and then the reigns of Judean kings Jotham and Ahaz (15:32—16:20) appear between the final and penultimate reigns of Israel. To the modern reader, the placement of the Jotham and Ahaz accounts may seem like an "interruption" in the narrative flow, but it is unremarkable and consistent in the light of Kings' presentation. It may be easily observed that Kings synchronizes the commencement of reigns and presents an individual reign in its entirety before shifting to another reign and/or kingdom.[2] Moreover, closer attention to detail and the Kings author's implicit and explicit themes throughout the work demonstrate a synergy and dynamic of complementarity within his "history of the dual monarchies."[3] On one level, there are two separate storylines, the history of Israel and the history of Judah. At the same time, the stated synchronization of kings with their northern/southern contemporaries and the alternation between the histories of Judah and Israel explicitly indicate that the two histories are vitally related and may be comparable.[4] Further, content indicates a united story of a divided kingdom: the repeated motifs and themes of ideal Davidic fidelity, Jeroboam-like infidelity, and the resultant promises of each impinge on both Judah and Israel and unite the whole of Kings.[5] The overall effect of these themes throughout the Kings author's presentation is, in the words of Knoppers, to promote "the Deuteronomistic ideals of one cult, one sanctuary, and one king—all devoted to one deity."[6]

2. For further discussion on the synchronization of reigns in Kings, see Mordechai Cogan, *1 Kings: A New Translation with Introduction and Commentary*, AB 10 (New York: Doubleday, 2001), 100; T. R. Hobbs, *2 Kings*, WBC 13 (Waco: Word, 1985), xx, xxvii–xxviii; Simon J. DeVries, *1 Kings*, WBC 12 (Waco: Word, 1985), xlvi; Mordechai Cogan and Hayim Tadmor, *2 Kings: A New Translation with Introduction and Commentary*, AB 11 (Garden City, NY: Doubleday, 1988), 3; and Gwilym H. Jones, *1 and 2 Kings*, vol. I, *1 Kings 1–16:34*, NCBC (London: Marshall, Morgan & Scott, 1984), 9–28.

3. See Gary N. Knoppers, *Two Nations Under God: The Deuteronomistic History of Solomon and the Dual Monarchies*, vol. 2, *The Reign of Jeroboam, the Fall of Israel, and the Reign of Josiah* (Atlanta: Scholars, 1994), e.g., 106, 113–14; 237–46; Frank Moore Cross, "The Themes of the Book of Kings and the Structure of the Deuteronomistic History," chapter 10 in *Canaanite Myth and Hebrew Epic: Essays in the History of the Religion of Israel* (Cambridge: Harvard University Press, 1973), 274–89.

4. Basically agreeing with Julian Reade, "Mesopotamian Guidelines for Biblical Chronology," *Syro-Mesopotamian Studies* 4/1 (1981) 1–9 (6): "The apparent purpose of these synchronizations was to give an impression of essential unity to the history of two neighbouring but frequently hostile kingdoms." Consider also more recent discussion on this issue in Benjamin D. Thomas, *Hezekiah and the Compositional History of the Book of Kings*, FAT 2/63 (Tübingen: Mohr/Siebeck, 2014), 69–77.

5. Consider Knoppers, *Reign of Jeroboam*, and Cross, "Themes of the Book."

6. Knoppers, *Reign of Jeroboam*, 246, 238, 246. That said, the Deuteronomistic ideal of one human king was conditional and theologically nuanced. Consider J. G. McConville, *God and Earthly Power: An Old Testament Political Theology*, LHBOTS 454

Beyond this megastructure, the precise relationship between reports of Judean and Israelite reigns at a more detailed level (e.g., between individual reigns or pericopae) may be determined contextually and within units (in this case, the chapter divisions of chs. 15, 16, and 17). In the case of chs. 15–16, it appears that the reigns of Jotham and especially Ahaz conveniently provide a general contrast to those of the ill-fated kings of Israel.[7] As well, the wickedness attributed to Judaean monarch Ahaz's reign leads well into the inclusion of Judah in parts of the narrator's reflective condemnation in 17:7–23 (specifically, vv. 13, 18–20). In this book, the histories of Israel and Judah in chapters 15–17 are considered with respect to both levels: on the one hand, the history of Israel and the history of Judah evidence a continuity within themselves; on the other hand, the Kingly author has shaped his history in such a way that both continuous streams inform each other and together convey the message that the cultic ideals of the Davidic monarchy—cultic purity and unity in Jerusalem—effect hope and blessing (and as such are to be upheld; 2 Sam 7:5–16; 1 Kgs 8; 11:12–13, 34, 36) while the ways of Jeroboam effect punishment and termination (and as such are to be avoided; 1 Kgs 12:31–13:5, 33–34; 14:9, 15b–16). This serves to justify Israel's destruction and demonstrate the folly of abandoning the exclusivistic ideals of the Yahwistic cultus.

Returning to our particular discussion of 2 Kgs 15, recall that the narrative of the final Israelite kings presents the individual reports briefly and quickly. Whether a monarch's reign was "one month" (Shallum, v. 13) or "twenty years" (Pekah, v. 27), relatively little is told concerning these final Israelite kings, and the resultant impression is that, likewise, little concerning these particular kings was of significance for the final redactor's work.[8] However, the high degree of selectivity regarding details for these accounts

---

(London: T. & T. Clark, 2006), esp. 125–27, 132, 155–56, 166–67, 170, 172–73.

7. Peter Dubovsky, "Why Did the Northern Kingdom Fall According to 2 Kings 15?," *Bib* 95 (2014) 321–46, would add Judean king Azariah to this short list of kings contributing to a contrast here, though the success of Azariah's reign was compromised by the tragedy of his chronic skin disease.

8. This is especially so, given the general speed with which the narrative presents reigns in 2 Kings. E.g., Hobbs, *2 Kings*, xxvii–xxviii:

> Although the material dealing more specifically with the kings of Israel and Judah (chaps. 9–25) covers a much longer period of time and more complicated matters of internal and foreign politics, the swift pace is maintained, only to be slowed at those particular junctures in the narrative where an important point needs to be made with care. So the reader pauses over the activities of Jehu and their side-effects, the reign of Jezekiah and, above all, the reign of Josiah. As for most of the others, the reader is forced to be content with swift and predictable characterizations of various monarchs according to established patterns of behavior. A major impression that one receives from

of the final kings of Israel and their location between the especially theologically-explicit verses of 15:12 and 17:7–22 suggest that some broader structural and theological points are being made beyond just the individual accounts.

Where details may be spare, structure can speak more effectively. This may be the case with 2 Kgs 15, which Dubovsky perceives as organized into a broadly chiastic structure:

A: Judahite "legitimate successor," did-right-but-retained-high-places king: Azariah (vv. 1–7)

  B: Israelite "legitimate successor" king, followed by Israelite "usurper" king: Shallum: Zechariah and Shallum (vv. 8–15)

    C: Israelite "usurper" king: Menahem (vv. 16–22)

  B': Israelite "legitimate successor" king, followed by Israelite "usurper" king: Pekahiah and Pekah (vv. 23–31)

A': Judahite "legitimate successor," did-right-but-retained-high-places king: Jotham (vv. 32–38)[9]

This structure naturally reinforces the similarities between the two Judahite kings and draws attention to Menahem's reign in ch. 15.

Now, the individual reports themselves in ch. 15 generally consist of the usual regnal information and formulae (i.e., reign commencement, duration, and place; theological evaluation; further sources concerning the reign; and reign closure)[10] and one or two distinctive factors—either incidents of conspiracy (vv. 10, 14, 15, 25, 30) and/or Assyrian relations (15:19–20, 29). These distinctive factors reflect a state of internal discord and violence, often alongside external hostilities—in these cases, at the hands of the Assyrians. Together, these on-the-ground circumstances lead to the YHWH–determined demise of Israel. If we combine our observation of the overall structure of ch. 15 with the structure of the individual reports within ch. 15, the dominant structural emphases of the chapter are: the relative stability of Judah and, moreover and relatedly, the Davidic covenant (vv. 1–7, 32–38, which are the endpoints of the chiasmus);[11] Menahem's

---

the reading of 2 Kings is that of the speed with which the narrative proceeds, but coupled with this is the occasional 'retardation' . . . of the narrative.

9. Based on Dubovsky, "Why Did the Northern Kingdom," 335–36, 340.

10. See also Donald J. Wiseman, *1 and 2 Kings*, TOTC (Downers Grove: IVP, 1993), 46–52; Hobbs, *2 Kings*, xx; DeVries, *1 Kings*, xlvii; Burke O. Long, "Regnal Resume" definition, in *2 Kings*, 311–12.

11. Dubovsky, "Why Did the Northern Kingdom," 340–41, observes this emphasis with regard to the narrative frame, but not to the chiastic structure as a whole. However,

extreme cruelty in warfare (v. 16, a distinctive of the pivot section); and the invasion of the Assyrian king and Menahem's subsequent negotiations with him, which clearly drained the northern kingdom of financial resources (vv. 19–20, a second distinctive of the pivot section).[12]

We turn now to the theological commentaries in chs. 15–17, which are two of many brief, theological explanations provided by the narrator throughout Kings.[13] On the whole, this scattered commentary within Kings functions both to reinforce the understanding that YHWH is in control of history generally and to observe and interpret the action of YHWH in specific events. Second Kings 15:12 makes the transition from the end of Jehu's dynasty to the beginning of the final series of (illegitimate) kings with a clear statement on the fulfilment of YHWH's word: ". . . and it was thus." As well, 15:12 begins: "This was the word of YHWH spoken to Jehu . . .," "This" ultimately referring to the fact of the reign of Zechariah, fourth generation of Jehu. As I observed earlier regarding brief theological comments in Kings, the double affirmation of the fulfilment of YHWH's word in 15:12 demonstrates, in general, the certainty and power of YHWH's word and indicates, in particular, that the present change of tide moves under the intentions of YHWH.

Second Kings 17:7-22 is easily recognized as the theological commentary-reflection and conclusion to Kings' account of the northern kingdom.[14] The prominence of this passage both in content (reflection, in contrast to events) and structure (as the conclusion to Israel's account) contribute to its strong explanatory effect for all that precedes (note v. 7). The fall of Israel now having swiftly come (though perhaps belatedly, cf. 2 Kgs 10:30–31), the narrator breaks from his usual reporting of events to reflect theologically at length on the reasons for Israel's demise, reaching back to the ways of its first renegade king, Jeroboam (17:21–23). Second Kings 17:7, 13, 18–22 especially place the blame on the Israelites while attributing the responsive action to YHWH. The narrative makes clear here that Israel's end and the events leading up to it (v. 20) are the intentional work of YHWH. The retroactive force of 17:7-23 upon our passage of interest (15:13—17:6) perhaps

---

the endpoints of a narratival chiasmus often establish an important point.

12. Regarding the economic drain of the northern kingdom by Menahem's taxation during the Assyrian invasion, see Dubovsky, "Why Did the Northern Kingdom," 338–40.

13. Some other examples involving the divided monarchy (and not the Elijah–Elisha narratives, which merit their own study regarding theological representation and explanation) are 1 Kgs 12:15, 24; 15:4–5, 29–30; 16:1–4, 34; 2 Kgs 8:9; 10:30–32; 14:26–27; 15:5; 18:1–8; 12; 21:10–15; 23:25–27; 24:2–4, 13, 20.

14. E.g., Hobbs, *2 Kings*, 228; Long, *2 Kings*, 180; House, *1, 2 Kings*, 338; Provan, *1 and 2 Kings*, 247–48.

is facilitated by the exceptionally brief length of the reports of Israel's final five kings, in addition to the recent reminder of the power of YHWH's will (15:12). This broader context of the will of YHWH actively fulfilled must be borne in mind as one considers the accounts of the final reigns of Israel.

Thus, the otherwise matter-of-fact reports of the final kings derive additional meaning from both their wider and specific structures, as well as the surrounding theological commentaries.

CONCLUSION

In concluding this introduction, note again that, in addition to Israel's own internal instability, outside influences weaken the kingdom, and those outside influences appear in 2 Kgs 15–17 in the sole form of the first aNE imperial superpower, Assyria. The Assyrian presence explicitly appears in the narrative concerning Israel in the accounts of Menahem's reign (15:14–22), Pekah's reign (15:27–31), and Hoshea's reign (17:1–6), and in the theological reflection concerning the fall of Israel and the sinfulness of Israel and Judah (17:7–23). The sense of 15:12, with the ceasing of Jehu's lineage in accordance with the word of YHWH and the resultant downward spiral of Israel, combined with the explicit statements of 17:7–23, together imply that Assyria's destructive actions toward Israel in the nation's final, ill-fated days are ultimately the work of YHWH:

- Immediately following the report of the Assyrian exile (17:6), 17:7a continues: "And it was because the Israelites had sinned against YHWH their God . . . "
- 17:18: "So YHWH was very angry with Israel and he removed them from his presence [i.e., into exile by Assyria] . . . "
- 17:20: "YHWH rejected all the offspring of Israel; he afflicted them and gave them into the hands of plunderers [i.e., the Assyrians] until he had cast them from his presence [i.e., into exile by Assyria]."
- 17:23: " . . . until YHWH removed Israel from his presence, as he had spoken by the agency of all his servants, the prophets. Israel went into exile, from its land to Assyria, as is the case to this day."

Having seen that, to the Kings writer, Assyria is a significant, YHWH-ordained agent in the demise and punishment of Israel, one may now appreciate the details of that depiction, beginning with the reign of Menahem through to that of Hoshea.

ASSYRIA ACCELERATES ISRAEL'S OWN DEMISE (2 KINGS 15)

Shallum's Reign and the Rise of Menahem (2 Kings 15:13-16)

With the close of Jehu's dynasty in 15:12, the reader is prepared for catastrophe to fall on Israel. The unusually brief report of Shallum's unusually brief reign of "one month" (beginning and ending with conspiracy) reinforces the sense of an immediately deteriorating infrastructure.[15] The character Menahem enters, truncating Shallum's reign (15:14). Menahem's high ambitions for regal power may be suggested by the first word concerning him: ויעל ("and he went up"). His apparent choice of military headquarters, Tirzah, former capital of Israel (cf. 1 Kgs 14:17; 15:21, 33; 16:8, 15, 23-24; 2 Kgs 15:14, 16), also suggests his intent to challenge the present holder of the throne.[16] Within this first verse about Menahem (v. 14), five forceful verbs connoting invasion and power characterize his actions: "he went up," "he came," "he attacked," "he killed," "he reigned." Three times in vv. 14-16 the verb נכה, "to strike, attack," describe Menahem. His ruthless and bloodthirsty nature are exhibited beyond his usurpation of the throne. The narrative proceeds to describe Menahem's excessive and bloody massacre of Tiphsah and its vicinity for resisting him (v. 16). The grammar of v. 16 does seem awkward,[17] but this "jerkiness" may be suggestive of the violence it describes.[18] Menahem's attack on entire cities, even pregnant women, is "unparalleled" in brutality and inter-tribal warfare by Israelite-Judean standards.[19] Verse 16's

---

15. As Robert L. Cohn, *2 Kings*, Berit Olam (Collegeville: Liturgical, 2000), 107, comments: "His name is about all we know of him. There is not even time to castigate him for following in the sins of Jeroboam!"

16. Dubovsky, "Why Did the Northern Kingdom," 332, observes that the archaeological discovery in Tell el-Far'ah (North) of a palace that was comparable in size to the largest palaces in Israel during that period suggests its rise as a rival to Samaria. While this is quite likely since Tirzah was a former capital of Israel anyway, the question then becomes at what specific moments in time was Tirzah a serious rival to Samaria and to what degree. Either way, some degree of influence, resources, and social support would likely have existed in Tirzah during Menahem's time, given its history.

17. Agreeing with Hobbs, *2 Kings*, 196, though he dismisses the grammar as "clumsy" and does not consider possible narratological functions. Menahem Haran, "The Rise and Decline of the Empire of Jeroboam Ben Joash," *VT* (1967) 266-97 (289-90), attributes the phrase מתרצה in v. 16 as dittography from v. 14.

18. Various Greek, Targum, and Syriac versions smooth the grammar. Some G, T, and S manuscripts add the 3fs suffix to וַיַּךְ; some G, T, and S prefix a ו to אֶת; and MT apparatus suggests deleting the unnecessary definite article הָ in הֶהָרוֹתֶיהָ.

19. Wiseman, *1 and 2 Kings*, 253; John Gray, *1 and 2 Kings: A Commentary*, 2nd and rev. ed., OTL (London: SCM, 1970), 622.

description of the slaughter ends with the ringing reinforcement of בקע, a word expressing the forcefulness of a splitting action and, in the context of warfare, violence.[20] Furthermore, the description הריות/הרות + בקע ("to rip open pregnant women") is evidently a "uniform formulation ... employed to portray an unspeakable outrage."[21] Such unwarranted brutality indicates a moral low for Israelite leadership.[22] At the same time, Wiseman suggests, such violence "may mark the increasing influence of the surrounding nations ... It was a foreign practice inflicted on the Israelites themselves by Aram (2 Kgs 8:12), Ammon (Amos 1:13) and Assyria (Hos 13:8)."[23] Under Tiglath-Pileser III, Assyria especially had advanced the means of warfare to new and strategic heights, unattainable for any power but the empire.[24]

20. John N. Oswalt, "בקע," in *TWOT* 1:123–24, and Victor P. Hamilton, "בקע," in *NIDOTTE* 1:702–4 (702–3).

21. Mordechai Cogan, " 'Ripping open Pregnant Women' in Light of an Assyrian Analogue," *JAOS* 103 (1983) 755–57 (755, see also 756). The idiomatic nature of הריות/הרות + בקע is attested for the OT (also in 2 Kgs 8:12; Amos 1:13; Hos 14:1) and in one occurrence thus far in the Middle Assyrian corpus: *userriti libbi arati unappil lakuti* ("he slits the wombs of pregnant women; he blinds the infants"). P. Dubovsky, "Ripping Open Pregnant Arab Women: Reliefs in Room L of Ashurbanipal's North Palace," *Orientalia* 78 (2009) 394–419, suggests that the practice is depicted in the reliefs from Ashurbanipal's North Palace in Nineveh (668–627 BCE).

22. Agreeing with Paul R. House, *1, 2 Kings*, NAC (Nashville: Broadman & Holman, 1995), 330; and Dubovsky, "Why Did the Northern Kingdom," 338.

23. Wiseman, *1 and 2 Kings*, 253. Note that reading MT אָשׁוּר as אַשּׁוּר is a Greek-Syriac-Latin tradition. See discussion in Hans Walter Wolff, *Hosea*, trans. Gary Stansell, Hermeneia (Philadelphia: Fortress, 1974), 220; David Allan Hubbard, *Hosea: An Introduction and Commentary* (Leicester: Inter-Varsity, 1989), 217. That said, the implicit agent remains Assyria. See also Hobbs, *2 Kings*, 102 and 197; and Hos 13:15–14:1, in which it is apparent that Assyria is the agent (e.g., Hubbard, *Hosea*, 223–24; Wolff, *Hosea*, 228–29; Douglas Stuart, *Hosea–Jonah*, WBC [Waco: Word, 1987], 208).

24. Tiglath-Pileser III developed the Assyrian army from one of conscripted, seasonal farmers to a year-round composite of armies based around a core, royal standing army, all consisting of Assyrian and auxilary professional soldiers. Tiglath-Pileser III also implemented notably sophisticated logistics in military campaigns, and his army improved the already-extant weapons of the first and second millennium BCE (the Assyrians *improved*, but apparently did not invent wholly new weapons under Tiglath-Pileser III). See Raija Mattila, *The King's Magnates: A Study of the Highest Officials of the Neo-Assyrian Empire*, SAS 11 (Helsinki: Neo-Assyrian Text Corpus Project, 2000), 149–57; Peter Dubovsky, "Neo-Assyrian Warfare: Logistics and Weaponry During the Campaigns of Tiglath-Pileser III," in *Proceedings of the International Symposium: Arms and Armour through the Ages*, eds. M. Novotna, W. Jobst, M. Dufkova, K. Kuzmova, and P. Hnila (Trnava: Trnavaska Univerzita, 2006), 61–67 (61, 65, 67); Karen Radner, "The Assyrian army," *Assyrian empire builders*, University College London 2012 [http://www.ucl.ac.uk/sargon/essentials/soldiers/theassyrianarmy/]; and Karen Radner, "Tiglath-pileser III, king of Assyria (744–727 BC)," *Assyrian empire builders*, University College London, 2012 [http://www.ucl.ac.uk/sargon/essentials/kings/tiglatpileseriii/].

As Haran puts it: "The deed smacks of Assyrian-style atrocities and apparently it was Assyrian warfare that brought it into the Israelite environment."[25] Wiseman observes that "some find [foreign influence on Israel in v. 16] possible if Tiphsah is identified with the distant Thapsacus . . . "[26] Menahem himself indeed may have been influenced by the Assyrian military example in his own oppressive approach. The innerbiblical language of the excesses of warfare in v. 16 (as above, cf. 2 Kgs 8:12; Amos 1:13; Hos 13:8) likens Israel's cruelty to that of foreign nations. As well, the text makes clear that Menahem relies on the Assyrian strength to fortify his own in v. 19. Thirdly, if the MT's "Tiphsah" is correct in v. 16a, then the city was located on the west bank of the Euphrates and evidently in close geographical proximity to Assyrian and other non-Israelite influence. Thus, from a social-geographical perspective, Menahem may have utilized warfare methods more endemic to that area (i.e., from the Assyrians). From a strictly strategic cross-cultural, military perspective, this technique would be sensible—it would both communicate a known fear-inducing threat while also achieving objectives (i.e., conquest) towards a community.[27]

Thus, it appears that Menahem adopted a foreign military approach in confronting a foreign-influenced city (i.e., Menahem inflicts Assyrian-like vengeance on an Assyrian-like city).[28] This helps us understand the main point of v. 16, which is that Menahem inflicted a horrific degree of violence on his fellow Israelites, reminiscent of foreign, pagan cruelty, if not Assyria. Having said this, it should also be noted that the subaltern interest of minimizing the power and influence of the empire in this pericope is reflected

---

See also, e.g., Hobbs, *2 Kings*, 102 and 197; Philip J. King, "Warfare in the Ancient Near East," in *The Archaeology of Jordan and Beyond: Essays in Honor of James A. Sauer*, eds. Lawrence E. Stager, Joseph A. Greene, and Michael D. Coogan (Winona Lake, IN: Eisenbrauns, 2000), 266–76 (267):

> The Assyrian army, highly skilled in military organization and maneuvers as well as being professionally equipped, was without peer in its day. In fact no juggernaut had attained such military might and power. Neighboring peoples imitated but could not equal the Assyrians in tactics, weapons, and equipment. The Assyrians were notoriously cruel warriors, slaughtering, mutilating, and flaying their defeated enemies.

25. Haran, "The Rise and Decline," 288.

26. Wiseman, *1 and 2 Kings*, 253. Xenophon, *Anabasis*, trans. Carleton L. Brownson, LCL 90 (London: Heinemann, 1980), 40, 45 // I. 4. 11, 17.

27. Given the consistent borrowing and adaptations of innovations in all spheres of society (e.g., religion, law, economics, arts and crafts, language, etc.) throughout the aNE, this is not surprising.

28. Gwilym H. Jones, *1 and 2 Kings*, vol. 2, *1 Kings 17:1–2 Kings 25:30*, NCBC (Grand Rapids: Eerdmans, 1984), 524, suggests similarly that "it may be that Menahem emulated Assyrian practice in order to demonstrate his power and to stifle opposition."

in the absence of explicit mention of Assyria. Indeed, in this passage it is not the foreign empire that is acknowledged as the ultimate negative power entity, but one from within the oppressed people group of Israel itself, Menahem. His imperial-oppressor-like characteristics of exercising military force, fear, and—as shall be seen in the continued narrative of Menahem—extortionate taxation.

Menahem's Reign and the Invasion of "Pul" (2 Kings 15:17–22)

Next, the narrative launches into its official royal account of Menahem's reign. Consistent with the history of the kings of Israel, Menahem continues "the sins of Jeroboam son of Nebat," yet even more so, as suggested by the exceptional addition of "all his days" to this standard description (v. 18).

The reader is poised at this stage to expect the kingdom to disintegrate in some way, especially as the ill-fated sins of Jeroboam not only persist, but intensify. The appearance of Tiglath-Pileser III may not be surprising: "Then came Pul king of Assyria against the land . . . " (v. 19a). The action is confrontative: בא . . . על, woodenly translated "he came upon." The combination is more often translated, according to *DCH*, as "he came to/for/against";[29] according to BDB, as "he came against," with a sense of attack and hostility.[30] All major translations interpret with this sense (NIV, JPS, NEB, NASB, NRSV, and KJV). This is contrary to the argument of Hobbs that בוא "is not the regular language used to describe an invasion" and that עלה ("to go up") is a more appropriate term to convey invasion.[31] עלה may have a narrower semantic range and "to invade" may be a more dominant meaning for that root, but this does not negate the possibility of a confrontative sense for בוא—a possibility that is amply attested elsewhere (including in chapter 15 itself concerning another invasion of TP, see v. 29), as BDB and *DCH* confirm. As well, the context of 15:19–20 suggests a hostile "coming" on the part of the king of Assyria. Looking at both vv. 19 and 20, the language is not "reminiscent of a military alliance,"[32] but of an unwelcome invasion (see esp. v. 20b).

With regard to syntax, Cohn observes "the unusual and abrupt opening with the Hebrew verb in the perfect."[33] Na'aman suggests that this is part of a somewhat standard verbal pattern (*qatal* followed completely by

---

29. *DCH*, 2:113–14.
30. BDB, 98, 757.
31. Hobbs, *2 Kings*, 199.
32. Hobbs, *2 Kings*, 199.
33. Cohn, *2 Kings*, 107.

wayyiqtol forms) for episodes in Kings, including those referring to Assyrian campaigns (15:19-20; 29-30; 17:3-6; 18:13-15).[34] At the very least, this pattern signals a significant moment in the narrative. By virtue of its less frequent occurrence in narrative, the *qatal* form naturally draws the reader's attention (especially when beginning an episode). Thus, the dramatic impact regarding this episode through the use of the perfect may not only be intentional on the part of the Kingly author (as perceived by Cohn), but also on the part of the structural formula used more generally by the author for emphasis, delineation, and organization. 2 Kings 15:19-20 would be the first in a series of close episodes highlighting, through grammatical tense, the Assyrian invasions. Also, there may be a stylistic nuance or indication of reliable record through what Montgomery identifies as an "archival idiom" in the form of "the asyndetic statement of data, as against the prevailing Hebrew use of the conjunction."[35]

The Assyrian king is identified as "Pul" (a form also found in 1 Chr 5:26), apparently the Hebrew equivalent for Mesopotamian *Pulu* (or Pulu). The earliest known Mesopotamian attestation of Pulu for Tiglath-Pileser III is the Babylonian King List A, in which Tiglath-Pileser III and Shalmaneser V are both identified by alternative names Pulu and Ululaya, respectively.[36] These names also occur in the hellenistic "Ptolemaic Canon" (Πώρου [var.: Πόρου] and Ἰλουλαίου;[37] this source most probably used the Babylonian King List A tradition as a *Vorlage*)[38] and, for Ululaya alone, in the Aššur Ostracon (which dates to the mid-seventh century).[39] Though it has been implied that Pulu was a name Tiglath-Pileser III used distinctly as

---

34. Nadav Na'aman, "The Historical Background to the Conquest of Samaria (720 BCE)," in *Ancient Israel and Its Neighbors: Interaction and Counteraction: Collected Essays* (Winona Lake, IN: Eisenbrauns, 2005), 1:76-93 (81); repr. fr. *Bib* 71 (1990) 206-25.

35. James A. Montgomery, "Archival Data in the Book of Kings," *JBL* 53 (1934) 46-52 (50). Montgomery claims there are "some five cases" of this idiom, but 2 Kgs 15:19 is the only example he provides.

36. E.g., *ANET*, 272; *COS* 1:462.

37. J. A. Brinkman, *A Political History of Post-Kassite Babylonia, 1158-722 B.C.*, *AnOr* 43 (Rome: Pontificium Institutum Biblicum, 1968), 241, 243. Note that forms are in the genitive.

38. Agreeing with O. Loretz and W. Mayer, "Pulu-Tiglatpileser III. und Menahem von Israel: nach assyrischen Quellen und 2 Kön 15, 19-20," *UF* 22 (1990) 221-31 (228). Jones, *1 and 2 Kings*, 525, cites the name "Porosid" from "the king-list of Ptolemy." Either Jones is mistaken, or he refers to a list other than the commonly-known so-called "Ptolemaic Canon."

39. See Brinkman, *A Political History*, 22, 35, 62.

Babylonian sovereign,[40] this proposal must remain a possibility and not a strong probability. The occurrences of Pulu for Tiglath-Pileser III are both rare and late. At the same time, "contemporary and nearly contemporary documents in both Babylonia and Assyria—the king's own royal inscriptions, the Assyrian kinglists and eponym lists, economic texts coming from Babylon during his reign, and the Babylonian Chronicle—uniformly refer to him as 'Tiglath-Pileser.'"[41] Furthermore, Pulu is a well-attested Assyrian name,[42] the fact of which heightens the possibility that Pulu is a non-exceptional name for Tiglath-Pileser III. Exactly how and when Pulu came to be associated with Tiglath-Pileser III cannot be conclusively deduced. One may cautiously forward that it appears that the association arose relatively late—*terminus a quo* the date of Babylonian King List A (which Brinkman dates to ca. 6th or early 5th c. BCE).[43] As for the association itself, it remains an attractive hypothesis that Pulu is a quasi-hypocoristic derived from the second element of Tiglath-Pileser.[44] Given that the name's particular use for Tiglath-Pileser III is late, it seems more likely than not that Pulu was only a late designation for the Assyrian monarch, and that the use of Pul in 2 Kgs 15:19 is anachronistic.[45] Whether or not the use of this nickname has any further significance is conjectural. Given the likelihood of Pulu's late usage, if 15:19–20 is based on original royal records from the time of Menahem, then the use of "Pul" in v. 19 evidences a later working of the original record. This is not a particularly extraordinary conclusion, however, given the post-exilic provenance of the final form of Kings. At the very least, it appears that when Pulu was used in royal and biblical accounts, it was always understood

40. James A. Montgomery, *The Books of Kings*, ICC (Edinburgh: T. & T. Clark, 1951), 450; Wiseman, *1 and 2 Kings*, 254; House, *1, 2 Kings*, 331; Jones, *1 and 2 Kings*, 525; Hobbs, *2 Kings*, 198; William W. Hallo and William Kelly Simpson, *The Ancient Near East: A History*, 2nd ed. (Orlando: Harcourt Brace, 1998), 133—note also Hallo and Simpson's comments regarding Shalmaneser V/"Ululai." For a contrary argument, see Brinkman, *A Political History*, 61–62.

41. Brinkman, *A Political History*, 62.

42. Cogan and Tadmor, *2 Kings*, 172: "Pulu is a well-attested Assyrian name meaning 'limestone (block)' . . . "; Brinkman, *A Political History*, 62 n.316. See also C. H. W. Johns, *Assyrian Deeds and Documents: Recording the Transfer of Property; Including the so-called private contracts, legal decisions and proclamations preserved in the Kouyunjik Collections of the British Museum; Chiefly of the 7th Century B. C.*, vol. 1, *Cuneiform Texts*, 2nd ed. (Cambridge: Deighton, Bell and co., 1924), no. 281, rev. 8, no. 642, rev. 17.

43. Brinkman, *A Political History*, 16.

44. See ibid., 62 n.317; Cogan and Tadmor, *2 Kings*, 172.

45. Agreeing with Volkmar Fritz, *1 and 2 Kings*, trans. Anselm Hagedorn (Minneapolis: Fortress, 2003), 333; Loretz and Mayer, "Pulu-Tiglatpileser III. und Menahem von Israel," 228–29; House, *1, 2 Kings*, 331.

to be another name for Tiglath-Pileser III, not a different king. On the Babylonian side, the Babylonian King List A and the Babylonian Chronicle correlate the two names.⁴⁶ On the biblical side, 1 Chr 5:26 correlates Pul with Tiglath-Pileser III. Concerning 2 Kgs 15:19–20 in particular, Tiglath-Pileser III was clearly the only Assyrian king who could have performed such actions on Menahem—Aššur-Nirari's reign ended shortly after Menahem took the Israelite throne, and Tiglath-Pileser III was the one who made forays into Syria during Menahem's reign. The annals of Tiglath-Pileser III and the Iran Stela demonstrate that Menahem did give tribute to Tiglath-Pileser III. Whether or not one or both of those documents correspond directly with the events of vv. 19–20 is not certain, but they do demonstrate that Menahem and Tiglath-Pileser III represented a vassal-empire relationship and that payments were made by Menahem to Tiglath-Pileser III. Let us consider the biblical account of these interactions further.

The simple but dramatic statement of Pul/Tiglath-Pileser III's invasion is immediately followed by the plain and direct statement that Menahem gave Pul a thousand talents of silver—the Assyrian king's imperial action receives an immediate vassal-like response from Menahem. That said, while אלף ככר־כסף is matter-of-factly stated, the fact also remains that this was an exorbitantly high amount in that day. As Dubovsky elucidates:

> If this sum of money is translated into terms of real estate, then Menahem gave to the Assyrians a financial capital that would enable them to buy almost the entire land of Israel, its cattle, sheep, and goats. If this sum is translated into terms of human beings, then with this money the Assyrian king could acquire a good number of Israelites. In sum, by giving this money to the Assyrians Menahem enabled the Assyrian king to acquire almost the whole of Israel and its inhabitants.⁴⁷

---

46. As observed by C. F. Burney, *Notes on the Hebrew Text of the Books of Kings: With an Introduction and Appendix* (Oxford: Clarendon, 1903), 322; Brinkman, *A Political History*, 61, also n. 313; and Loretz and Mayer, "Pulu-Tiglatpileser III. und Menahem von Israel," 228–29. See also *ANET* 272//*COS* 1:462; and A. K. Grayson, *Assyrian and Babylonian Chronicles* (Locust Valley, NY: Augustin, 1975), 72. Brinkman adds that the identification of Pulu and Tiglath-Pileser III as the same person is also "made certain on the Assyrian side by the *limmu* lists, which state that Tiglath-Pileser performed the physical ceremony making him king of Babylonia."

47. Dubovsky, "Why Did the Northern Kingdom," 339. Dubovsky's point is to be taken, though the application of equivalents from Lev 27—which apply to the special dedication of people and property to YHWH—to the one thousand talents of silver in 2 Kgs 15:19 is arguably questionable. As touched on below regarding Lev 27, a different verb (ערך) is used and with a different sense.

Further, the narrator adds that this subservience to Assyria is for self-serving reasons (in contrast to acting for the sake of the Israelite people), "to be a support to him [Menahem] for strengthening his hold on the kingdom." Given Menahem's established history of merciless mass murder upon his own people for the sake of exalting himself to the throne, the narrator's insight on Menahem's motive in v. 19b contributes to the characterization of this Israelite king as consistently and ruthlessly self-ambitious and opportunistic, regardless of whether the pressures and opportunities are internal or external. He is not only submitting himself to the Assyrian imperial metanarrative by way of using his regional leadership to support the empire, but he goes about it with the character qualities of an oppressive colonizer. Menahem chose to become, in a sense, the representative of the empire, a sort-of close colonizer at the doorsteps of every Israelite.

As the reader has been prepared to expect of Menahem's character, v. 20 details the abusive way by which Menahem secured tribute for Assyria. Again, as if consorting with the enemy—the enemy empire, at that—in order to wield a stronger hold over his own country people was not enough, Menahem then imposes this levy on all of Israel's "men of means" (כל־גבורי החיל). The verb describing Menahem's action is ויצא (Hi. imp. 3ms of יצא, a root that basically means "to go/come out"). The Hiphil inflections of יצא are predictably causative, often meaning "to take/bring/lead out." While the nuances of יצא are acknowledged to be "manifold" and "various,"[48] the major translations' rendering of "exacted" (NIV, JPS, NASB, NRSV, and KJV/ASV; NEB has a similar sense with "laid a levy") is supported in the lexica by only this verse and sometimes 2 Kgs 12:12 (which itself appears to be an even more unusual usage).[49] For such reasons Hobbs reluctantly allows "exacted," though he prefers "paid out," arguing that the Hiphil of ערך is "the normal word for the verb 'tax.'"[50] However, that form occurs only six times in the OT (Lev 27:8, 12 [2x], 14 [2x]; 2 Kgs 23:35), five of which are in a particular cultic context in Leviticus and all of which may be argued to be better rendered "set the value of" instead of "tax." Klostermann (followed by Benzinger and Burney) also has difficulty with the unique use of יצא in 15:20 and proposes a textual emendation/solution (ויצו, 'he commanded'), though there are no textual traditions to support it.[51] Though the precise

---

48. E. Jenni, "יצא," in *TLOT* 2:561–66 (562, 563).

49. *DCH*, 4:261c; BDB, 425a; H. D. Preuss, "יצא," in *TDOT* 6:225–50 (237).

50. Hobbs, *2 Kings*, 199.

51. August Klostermann, *Die Bücher Samuelis und der Könige*, Kurzgefasster Kommentar zu den heiligen Schriften Alten und Neuen Testamentes sowie zu den Apokryphen (Nördlingen: Verlag der C. H. Beck'schen, 1887), 446, n. i, who observes a similar *Vermischen* of ואוצאה and ואצוה in the ketib-qere of Ezr 8:17 See also I. Benzinger,

sense of "forcibly drew out (payment)" may be rare for יצא, still it appears to qualify under the root's basic meaning. Very possibly the highly unusual nature of the situation—an extortionistic Israelite monarch appropriating his people's resources to deliver them to a third party of alarming growth and threat, the first empire in the aNE —led the Kings author to unique use of this root.[52] That said, obviously one or two dubious uses of יצא in the biblical corpus do not support an idiomatic or technical use of the word.[53] It appears more likely that the Kings author selected יצא to convey afresh that

---

Die Bücher der Könige (Kurzer Hand-Commentar zum Alten Testament (Freiburg i. B.: J. C. B. Mohr/Paul Siebeck, 1899), 168; Burney, *Notes on the Hebrew*, 322–23. Cogan and Tadmor (evidently following Bernhard Stade and Friedrich Schwally, *The Books of Kings: Critical Edition of the Hebrew Text*, in Haupt, et al., *The Sacred Books of the Old Testament: A Critical Edition of the Hebrew Text* [Leipzig: J. C. Hinrichs'sche, 1904; 1st ed. pub. 1888–1892 under title: *Geschichte der Hebräer*], 253), include Kittel among those who follow Klostermann, but I found no statements or discussion on that point in the one work of Kittel in their Select Bibliography (*Geschichte des Volkes Israel*, vol 2, *Das Volk in Kanaan: Geschichte der Zeit bis zum Babylonischen Exil* [Gotha: Leopold Klotz, 1925], see 351–54; similarly, its translation: *A History of the Hebrews*, vol. 2, *Sources of Information and History of the Period Down to the Babylonian Exile*, trans. Hope W. Hogg and E. B. Speirs [London: Williams & Norgate, 1896], 332–37).

52. Siegfried Herrmann, *A History of Israel in Old Testament Times*, tr. John Bowden, rev. ed. (London: SCM, 1981), 245, perhaps has this in mind when he states that Menahem "raised this sum [of a thousand talents of silver] by imposing a poll tax of a kind which we cannot find attested elsewhere." Similarly, Michael E. W. Thompson, *Situation and Theology: Old Testament Interpretations of the Syro-Ephraimite War* (Sheffield: Almond, 1982), 110.

53. Albert Šanda, *Die Bücher der Könige: Übersetzt und Erklärt*, vol. 2, *Das zweite Buch der Könige*, EHZAT (Münster: Aschendorffsche, 1912), 186, suggests a parallel with Arabic *haraj* ("land-tax") from *haraja* ("to go out") and meaning in the Xth form (which is causative reflexive) "to impose the land-tax." Such a supposed parallel is a stretch, however, because there is no noun designating "tax" from the root יצא. Furthermore, a nuance of "to impose a tax" for Hiphil יצא remains barely attested, if at all. Šanda's proposal remains possible, but neither conclusive nor well-supported. Similarly, Montgomery, *The Books of Kings*, 455, also cites LH and Haupt (more specifically, "Haupt"= Stade and Schwally, *Books of Kings*, 253, and the reference is to "post-Biblical Hebrew," not MH) for use of the verb as "to collect" and like usage in Jewish Aramaic of נפק, in addition to Arabic; Cogan and Tadmor, *2 Kings*, 172, find a parallel use in Akkadian *susu* ("to deliver, make payment"); Gary A. Rendsburg, *Israelian Hebrew in the Book of Kings*, Occasional Publications of the Department of Near Eastern Studies and the Program of Jewish Studies, Cornell University 5 (Bethesda, MD: CDL, 2002), 128, notes MH and Aramaic developments; see also Stade and Schwally, *Books of Kings*, 253; and Gray, *1 and 2 Kings*, 624. The difficulty in forwarding any of these arguments to support such a development in יצא remains the common sense and basic reality that the semantic development of a word in one language and/or period does not necessitate a like development of another word in another language and/or period; the possibility may exist, but it is not necessary and is more likely for an etymologically-related word than for a semantically-related one.

Menahem caused resources to come out from the leading members of the community in a way that was hostile to them (which is a more common use of עַל than BDB's "on behalf of" or the wooden sense of "from").[54] The translations' renderings "exacted" and "laid a levy" are adequate, communicating both ideas of an intentional causing to come out and that the action was hostile to the people. However, the author's deliberation in selecting these terms may be further appreciated when it is borne in mind that יצא is not used in an idiomatic or technical way (as the English translations imply), but that the action of imposed production is freshly conveyed by more novel and thoughtful terminology.

The translation of גבורי החיל has been frequently debated by scholars, though the English translations are nearly unanimous in their renderings. NIV, NEB, and NRSV have the same nuance—"every wealthy person," "all the men of wealth," and "all the wealthy." KJV/ASV and NASB emphasize the element גבורי: "all the mighty men of wealth." NJPS seems to emphasize גבורי less: "every man of means." The phrase occurs in the OT 41 times,[55] of which at least 12.5 % may be translated "man/men of standing" (1 Sam 9:1; 1 Kgs 11:28; Ruth 2:1) or "(cap)able man/men" (Neh 11:14; 1 Chr 9:13; 26:6, 31; possibly 28:1 [cf. 29:6]). De Vaux suggests that it is "almost synonymous" with *sarim*, *n^edibim*, *horim*, *z^eqenim*, and *g^edolim* and that these words on the whole denote "the ruling class of the monarchical period, administration and heads of influential families—in short, the men of position."[56] For גבורי החיל in particular, de Vaux asserts that the compound does not simply denote "a class of landed proprietors, a sort of squirearchy," but instead has developed over time and circumstances to stand for both its original designation of "brave warriors, fighting men" and its later referent of those bound to armed service and having the means to support themselves as such.

---

54. BDB, 425a (but BDB's second proposal regarding יצא + עַל in 2 Kgs 15:20, "imposed it, on [Israel]" is supportable by the context); *DCH*, 4:264c proposes "from," but qualifies it with "exacted money." If "from" is understood as indicating a hostile imposition (instead of locative movement) governed by יצא, then "from" also is supportable.

55. H. Eising, "חיל," in *TDOT* 4:348-55 (350), and Robin Wakely, "חיל," in *NIDOTTE* 2:116-26 (119), correctly count 41 occurrences for the phrase, but miscount the Chronicles occurrences, which are 27 in number (as J. Kühlewein, "גבר," in *TLOT* 1:299-302 [300], correctly reckons), not 25. OT distribution is as follows: 4x in Joshua (Josh 1:14, 6:2; 8:3; 10:7); 2x in Judges (Judg 6:12; 11:1); 2x in Samuel (1 Sam 9:1; 16:18); 4x in Kings (1 Kgs 11:28; 2 Kgs 5:1; 15:20; 24:14); 1x each in Ruth and Nehemiah (Ruth 2:1; Neh 11:14); 27x in Chronicles (1 Chr 5:24; 7:2, 5, 7, 9, 11, 40; 8:40; 9:13; 11:26; 12:8, 21, 25, 28, 30; 26:6, 31; 28:1; 2 Chr 13:3; 14:8; 17:13, 14, 16, 17; 25:6; 26:12; 32:21).

56. Roland de Vaux, *Ancient Israel: Its Life and Institutions*, trans. John McHugh (London: Darton, Longman & Todd, 1961), 69-70.

It seems that this term meant originally (and often does mean in the Chronicles) the valiant men, the brave warriors, the gallant knights, like *gibborim* on its own, even if they possess no property of their own (Jos 8:3; Judg 11:1). The term was then applied to those who were bound to armed service and, having to provide their own equipment, enjoyed a certain standard of living. This is the sense which best answers the text of 2 Ki 15:20, where there are sixty thousand of them, of 2 Ki 24:14, where they are contrasted with the poorest people of the land,[57] and of Ruth 2:1, where Boaz is simply a man of substance, like Saul's father in 1 Sam 9:1.[58]

57. The text is not clear in 2 Kgs 24:14, but it seems more likely that "fighting men, warriors" is intended. De Vaux's assertion that the גבורי החיל are contrasted with the poorest people of the land is misleading, because 1) a contrast is not necessarily posed in 2 Kgs 24:14; the author simply may be identifying the differing outcomes of different categories of people; 2) *if* a contrast is set-up in the verse, it is between not just the poor and the גבורי החיל, but between the poor and the substantial members of Jerusalem—those able to contribute to battle: the officers, the גבורי החיל, the craftsmen, and the smiths; and 3) syntactical cues suggest an active military role for the גבורי החיל in v. 14. The syntax of 2 Kgs 24:14 appears to pair officers and גבורי החיל, as it does craftsmen and smiths; and, the pseudo-resumptive v. 16 uses the parallel term אנשי החיל to denote, it seems, the officers and גבורי החיל of v. 14. Further, v. 16 more clearly appears to associate together the אנשי החיל, craftsmen, and smiths as "all the mighty ones ready for battle."

58. De Vaux, *Ancient Israel*, 70.

Eising makes a similar proposal, but seems to perceive a stronger military element persisting throughout the phrase's development. Also, Eising's starting point is the assumption that our usage in 2 Kgs 15:20 refers to those able to pay the imposed tax. While that may be a valid point, it is perhaps better at this stage to evaluate the use of גבורי החיל in 2 Kgs 15:20 after assessing other and clearer incidences of גבורי החיל as involving non-military aspects.

> If this term is used not only for warriors but also for able men in general, and especially men of wealth, the explanation may be found in 2 Ki 15:20. Here we read of a tax imposed by Menahem on all *gibbore hachayil*, presumably those able to pay it. What is true of Boaz could also be true of Saul's father (1 Sam 9:1): military ability and wealth go together, because the warrior had to arm and maintain himself. Such citizens could well be meant by the rather high number of people taxed as well as the ten thousand (2 Ki 24:14) carried into exile from Jerusalem, while "the poorest people of the land" were let stay behind. [As in two notes above, this assertion cannot necessarily be maintained.] This suggested explanation stops short of meaning that *chayil* can be translated "wealth" or "means" here. As is true of *gibbor*, the primary aspect of *chayil* is military: it would be hard to characterize the 30, 000 men led by Joshua against Ai (Josh 8:3) or Jephthah (Judg 11:1) as wealthy property owners. (Eising, "חיל," 351.)

The difference between de Vaux and Eising's explanations is a subtle one of the extent to which military activity is understood in later developments of the phrase. Essentially, however, de Vaux and Eising offer the same proposal, and thus far it best explains

Interestingly, the most common use of the phrase is to denote "fighting men" or "brave/valiant warriors," but few support such an interpretation for 15:20. Hobbs comes close in his interpretation as he defends "soldiers" for גבורי החיל and "because of" for its preposition, עַל.[59] With this reading, Menahem supposedly hires Assyrian "mercenaries" at a rate of 50 shekels a person.[60] While this interpretation is possible, it 1) has a slight grammatical difficulty; 2) makes less sense of the immediate context; and 3) would be an unusual historical arrangement. Firstly, עַל in relation to יצא and meaning "because of" is unattested in *DCH*.[61] The second point to note is that the introductory and conclusive statements regarding the coming and departure of Pul strongly indicate a hostile invasion by the Assyrians against the Israelites—not a supportive visit to the Israelite king. Finally, that the imperial forces would come to the aid of a submissive and obedient vassal state is understandable (e.g., 16:7–9), but that part of the Assyrian army—"mercenary" ("auxiliary" is a more fitting descriptor) or not—could be hired and used by petty nations on the brink of incorporation into the empire seems unlikely. Even if Tiglath-Pileser III were not invading in v. 19 (a la Hobbs' interpretation), more historical evidence should be required to support such a specific, per soldier hiring of the Assyrian army by a vassal (or rather, almost-vassal) people.

Thus, the major translations' rendering of גבורי החיל is more historically and contextually probable, as well as grammatically attested. With this reading, we may understand that an upper stratum with some degree of

---

the various uses and contexts of גבורי החיל, as well as similar terms (e.g., אנשי החיל, בני החיל). See Eising, "חיל," 349–50, and Wakely, "חיל," 118–19, for further discussion. Subsequent commentators usually adopt an abbreviated, if not oversimplified version of de Vaux and Eising's proposal that lacks the definitive military aspect sustained throughout the phrase's development. See Montgomery, *The Books of Kings*, 451; Mordechai (Morton) Cogan, *Imperialism and Religion: Assyria, Judah and Israel in the Eighth and Seventh Centuries B. C. E.*, SBLMS (Missoula, MT: Scholars, 1974), 97n4–98n4; and Cogan and Tadmor, *2 Kings*, 172. Wiseman is one step removed from their conclusion when suggesting that the גבורי החיל were "the leading class who would otherwise have had to furnish men of war." See Wiseman, *1 and 2 Kings*, 255. Others propose an upper stratum that may have included historically-established Israelite landowners, royal officials, and administrators (how exactly this stratum may have come to be known as גבורי החיל is not explained). See Herrmann, *History of Israel*, 245; and Jones, *1 and 2 Kings*, 526. Similarly, Cohn, *2 Kings*, 107.

59. Hobbs, *2 Kings*, 199–200.

60. Relatedly, Gray, *1 and 2 Kings*, 624, translates as "men of property," but still favors the view that "Menahem enlisted Assyrian support." H. J. Cook, "Pekah," *VT* 14 (1964) 121–35 (128) *might* also have this in mind when he states: "When Tiglath-Pileser III appeared in the west, Menahem took the opportunity to enlist his support by sending tribute…"

61. *DCH*, 4:264.

military and financial interests was imposed upon by Menahem to provide money to Assyria. Quite possibly these eighth-century גבורי החיל had a respected and somewhat elevated standing in Israelite society, in the same way that the גבורי החיל of old were honored. Evidently, they had the financial means to pay the tax, while presumably others did not. That said, the tax was still extortionate. Because the then-average price of a slave in Assyria was 50 shekels, Wiseman suggests that Menahem forced the Israelites to pay the same amount, effectively redeeming themselves.[62] Possibly the payments were in naturalia (e.g., wine, oil) assessed at silver value.[63] Either way, Menahem begins to deplete the resources of Israel's strength—its societal leadership—and thus Israel itself. Menahem responds to the external threat of Assyria by bowing to it and creating further internal vulnerability— perhaps more than as if he were not also "strengthen[ing] his hold on the kingdom."[64] That the giving of the one thousand talents of silver takes place under hostile pressure from Assyria is suggested by the literary context (as discussed above; and below, concerning v. 20c) and cognate literature.[65] The Assyrian "Calah Annals" and "Iran Stela," both from the reign of Tiglath-Pileser III, include "Menahem, the Samarian" in their lists of tribute-paying rulers sometime between 743 and 738 BC.[66]

62. D. J. Wiseman, "The Nimrud Tablets," *Iraq* 15 (1953) 135-60 (136 and n1); idem, *1 and 2 Kings*, 255.

63. Yigael Yadin, "Ancient Judaean Weights and the Date of the Samaria Ostraca," *Scripta Hierosolymitana* 8 (1961) 9-25 (23n69), in attempting to harmonize the Samaria Ostraca with Menahem's reign, asserts that "the fact that the Bible specifies the amount of the tax in silver sheqels, while the Ostraca record taxes in naturalia, does not create a difficulty, since even taxes in naturalia were assessed at their silver value." Though it appears that the Samaria Ostraca coincide better with Jeroboam II's reign, Yadin's equation of goods and silver likely extends beyond that particular reign.

64. Dubovsky, "Why Did the Northern Kingdom," 340, 345, suggests that Assyria taxed other lands both to bring resources into Assyria and to drain the resources and internal stability of the subject lands. Very likely Menahem's high tax lowered his popularity with the leading classes in Israel.

65. It is worth noting that the extrabiblical remains known as the Samaria Ostraca apparently do *not* coincide with the biblical account of Menahem, as Yadin suggested and Frank Moore Cross, Jr. affirmed. See Yadin, "Ancient Judaean Weights," 22-23; Frank Moore Cross, Jr., "Epigraphic Notes on Hebrew Documents of the Eighth-Sixth Centuries B.C.: II. The Murabba'at Papyrus and the Letter Found Near Yabneh-Yam," *BASOR* 165 (1962) 34-46 (35). Alternate and more recent proposals may be seen in Yohanan Aharoni, "The Use of Hieratic Numerals in Hebrew Ostraca and the Shekel Weights," *BASOR* 184 (1966) 13-19 (18); idem, *The Land of the Bible: A Historical Geography*, rev. and enl. ed., trans. A. F. Rainey (Philadelphia: Westminster, 1979), 356-68 (includes extensive editorial note by Rainey), 383n102; and Ivan T. Kaufman, "Samaria (Ostraca)," in *ABD* 5:921-26.

66. For further discussion, see Louis D. Levine, "Menahem and Tiglath-Pileser: A

Verse 20c records the practical and immediate effect of the payment. שָׁם ("there") appears to have an emphatic locative function.[67] Montgomery and Cogan and Tadmor propose that שָׁם is written from the perspective of the author (or, one might further specify, a late redactor), who apparently is not writing from within the northern kingdom (in the same way that the author anachronistically uses "Pul" instead of Tiglath-Pileser III).[68] While this could be the sense behind שָׁם, the locative emphasis can also be seen to function within the narrative's world, drawing attention to the fact that Assyria—the imperial, would-be colonizer—really had invaded and had been present in Israel. Perhaps the Kingly writer emphasized this point because of the lack of documented witnesses otherwise.[69]

That "the king of Assyria withdrew and did not remain there in the land" (v. 20c) demonstrates 1) the sobering proximity of the Assyrian threat—Tiglath-Pileser III and/or his imperial representatives are depicted as being "there in the land" such that the danger is not that the Assyrian king would come (cf. v. 19a), but that he would "remain"; and 2) that Tiglath-Pileser III was sufficiently appeased by the payment, which apparently initiated Israel's entry into vassal status into the empire.[70] The original audience of Kings, already familiar with Assyrian history such that the author could refer to Tiglath-Pileser III as "Pul," would have been well aware that this is only a brief and expedient respite from the imperial Assyrian threat. Moreover, the narrative indicates that the temporary relief comes at the expense of Israel's own resources. Bearing in mind the broader context of vv. 19-20, the narrator already has indicated Israel's impending demise (e.g., v. 11 and related verses, see discussion above), and even the forceful ways of Menahem cannot prevent it. It is not Menahem's oppressive manipula-

---

New Synchronism," *BASOR* 206 (1972) 40–42; Mordechai Cogan, "Tyre and Tiglath-Pileser III: Chronological Notes," *JCS* 25 (1973) 96–99. See also the texts themselves: Hayim Tadmor, *The Inscriptions of Tiglath-Pileser III, King of Assyria: Critical Edition, with Introductions, Translations and Commentary* (Jerusalem: Israel Academy of Sciences and Humanities, 1994), 68–69; 106–7 (chapter on "The Stele from Iran" in collaboration with Louis D. Levine); 276 (commentary); Wiseman, *1 and 2 Kings*, 256, supports the earlier date (c. 743 BCE) for the Iran Stela, linking it with Menahem's tribute; *ANET*, 283//*COS* 2:285; *COS* 2:287.

67. BDB, 1027a, notes emphatic uses of שָׁם. *HALOT*, 1547, suggests a few temporal uses of שָׁם, but they remain very rare and still interpretively uncertain.

68. Montgomery, *The Books of Kings*, 451; Cogan and Tadmor, *2 Kings*, 173.

69. Cogan and Tadmor, *2 Kings*, 173, observe that contemporary Assyrian sources do not attest to Tiglath-Pileser III or Assyrian forces in Israel during Menahem's reign.

70. Agreeing with Jones, *1 and 2 Kings*, 2:526. Also, as corroborated by cognate Assyrian literature cited in n. 66, above. The brief sketch in vv. 19–20 of the relationship begun between Assyria and Israel appears to comport with the boundaries and levels of obligation and autonomy presented in Cogan, *Imperialism and Religion*, 55–61.

tion and opportunism that ultimately direct the Assyrian king's steps, but YHWH's will (cf. 2 Kgs 17:7–23). In less than a generation, the futile nature of Menahem's strategy will be evident as most of Israel is carried away into Assyrian exile. It should also be pointed out that where Menahem could have sought YHWH, he bowed to Assyrian power instead. Thus, through the "distraction" of Assyria, the Israelite king continues to lead Israel away from her Lord (cf. v. 18).[71]

Just as it is important to keep in mind that each of these reigns is part of the larger story of Israel, so one should remain aware that vv. 19–20— which explicitly concern Assyria—are primarily part of the account about Menahem. Menahem's reign is characterized by unparalleled internal violence, regnal opportunism, and dubious external relations. The fact that Menahem's external relations are conducted with Assyria in particular renders the deeds more ignominious, for Assyria is not only the first major empire in the aNE—the new and more threatening replacement to Aram as "the great [foe/northern enemy]" and the soon-to-be destroyer of Israel[72]—but is also the most notorious and merciless of vanquishers to date. Menahem evidently tastes some of Assyria's bite (v. 19a), and chooses to ally himself with it rather than to resist it (v. 19b). In drawing upon Menahem's interactions with Assyria, the Kings author emphasizes Assyria's oncoming military prowess and threat. Assyria presents a challenge to Menahem that leads the Israelite king to respond with selfish intent (v. 19b) and through oppressive means (v. 20a) that evidently counter the ways of YHWH, resulting in explicit and implicit disapproval by the narrator (vv. 18, 22). Though ch. 15's emphasis is on Menahem's brutality and his response to the Assyrian empire, Assyria itself is still portrayed as an intimidatingly powerful and threatening enemy to Israel—the narrative presumes that it is in Israel's best interests not to align itself with Assyria and to submit to its demands, not simply for political reasons, but moreover for religious motivations. This implication will further inform the subsequent narrative concerning Judean king Ahaz and his interactions with Assyria in 2 Kgs 16.

---

71. As noted by House, *1, 2, Kings*, 331.
72. For the former epithet, see Provan, *1 and 2 Kings*, 242.

Pekahiah's Reign, the Rise of Pekah, and the Reign of Pekah (2 Kings 15:23–31, with Reference to 15:32–37; 16:5–9; and Related Passages)

The next reign, that of Pekahiah, is cut short in a manner that has now become the norm rather than the exception: conspiracy and assassination (15:25, cf. vv. 10, 14). Unlike Shallum, but like Menahem, the instigator of Pekahiah's assassination receives an extended account of his conspiracy and assassination of his predecessor that begins his characterization before his royal file. Pekah, a probable Gileadite (given the fifty Gileadites who accompany him in the coup) is not only chief conspirator and assassinator, but also a traitor (v. 25). Though the exact meaning of שליש is uncertain, its innerbiblical usage appears to suggest at least an officer of important and trusted rank "who could be appointed to direct attendance upon the king."[73] By the time the reader is informed that Pekah reigned "twenty years" (v. 27b)—twice the reign of Menahem—one may expect he will evince twice the ruthlessness and ambition of Menahem.[74] The by-now 'standard' Jeroboam formula is not expanded as it is for Menahem, however. Likewise, the narrative proceeds to depict Pekah differently from Menahem. Excessively violent and self-serving motives and deeds are not attributed to Pekah as they are to Menahem, though it could be argued that Pekah caused double the suffering that Menahem did. Israel is now not only oppressed and threatened by Assyria, but in large part conquered and exiled (v. 29). Further, not only does Israel suffer under Pekah's leadership, but Judah is attacked (v. 27; 16:5). What is suggested in the subtle, but significant nuances of these introductory formulae is demonstrated on the more complex stage of world history through the Kings author's selective presentation. In one respect, Pekah evidences the ambition and cold-heartedness of Menahem. That said, Pekah's callousness is evidently of a more deceptive, apostate type (in that

---

73. See Cook, "Pekah," 124–26, esp. 126. Also, Reade, "Mesopotamian Guidelines," 5; and Hobbs, *2 Kings*, 117, who articulates the etymological caution that "military terms, such as שליש 'third,' have a tendency to lose their original meaning quickly, and become simply designations of rank." Other common interpretations for שליש in 15:25 include captain/lieutenant (NRSV/Hobbs, *2 Kings*, 200, 117), chief officer/commander-in-chief (NIV; Wiseman, *1 and 2 Kings*, 255, 127), aide (JPS), and adjutant (Cogan and Tadmor, *2 Kings*, 173; Louis Jonker, "שליש," in *NIDOTTE* 4:126; see esp. B. A. Mastin, "Was the SALIS the Third Man in the Chariot?" in *Studies in the Historical Books of the Old Testament*, ed. J. A. Emerton, VTSup 30 (Leiden: Brill, 1979) 125–54, who concludes that the word did not designate a "third man" in a supposed-but-unsupportable standard Hittite-Palestinian chariot riding practice, but a man 'of the third rank' to the king and his senior officers.

74. Interpretation of the "twenty years" reign of Pekah has engendered both sizable debate and creative theories. See Appendix 1 for further discussion.

he deceived his former king and evidently resisted previously established Assyrian authority over the land), in contrast to Menahem's bloody mass destruction. At the same time, Pekah "doubles" the trouble of Menahem's days, oppressing Judah and, more deplorably, seeing the invasion and exile of large parts of Israel to Assyria.[75]

Still, Pekah is not regarded by either the formulae or by the passages concerning him to be as evil a monarch as was Menahem.[76] Though Pekah oppressed Judah, his action is explicitly and implicitly depicted as divine judgment towards Judah.[77] Pekah apparently could behave in YHWH-displeasing ways but still be used even in his wickedness for YHWH's purposes:

75. Consider also Dubovsky, "Why Did the Northern Kingdom," 332–34, which compares the themes of the Assyrian invasion reports in ch. 15 and thus perceives a decline in executive power from Menahem to Pekah. While I do not think that a strict comparision between the two invasion accounts is indicated by the text and so related conclusions should not be pressed, Dubovsky's point is worth considering:

> Comparing both invasion reports we can see the differences. In the first case the country is stripped of money; in the second case it is stripped of people. In the first case the country is ravaged by the Israelite king; in the second by the Assyrian king. In the first case the Assyrian king returned to Assyria, but the Israelites stayed in the land; in the second case the Israelites were deported to Assyria. In the first invasion Menahem is still an active protagonist able to negotiate with the invaders; in the second case Pekah becomes a passive observer silently witnessing the pillage of his country. The contrast between the two invasion reports points not only to increasing Assyrian power, but also to the gradual loss of executive power of the Israelite kings. During the second invasion the Israelite king had already lost any real power and had to put up with Assyrian whims. (334)

76. It may be perceived that the narrative indicates that the northern kingdom reached its zenith in terms of internal stability under Pekah. Dubovsky, "Why Did the Northern Kingdom," 326–31, compellingly observes that the location, origin of the assassinator, and narrative time across the first three accounts of *coups d'état* in ch. 15 indicate a gradual and increasing deterioration of Israel. One should note, however, that the fourth *coup d'état* in ch. 15 does not follow the observed pattern, though Dubovsky has a creative explanation for this (329–30).

77. Explicit in that Hiphil forms of שלח denote divine punishment, 15:37; implicit in that he causes trouble for Ahaz, who demonstrates as much displeasing behaviour to YHWH as do the kings of Israel, 16:2-4. See also C. John Collins, "שׁלח," in *NIDOTTE* 4:119–23 (121), observes that the Hiphil forms of שלח all share the same syntax and meaning, namely that of divinely-sent punishment:

> all five examples of the Hiphil [of שלח] have the same syntax: <A> שלח (אֶת) <B> "A sent B." All have the same semantics, too: God is subject, and the B-element is some punishment (insect swarm, Exo 8:21 [17]; wild beasts, Lev 26:22; Rezin, 2 Ki 15:37; famine, Ezek 14:13; Amos 8:11).

Montgomery, *The Books of Kings*, 456, makes a similar and attractive observation, but it is apparently selective and/or exaggerated: "The Hiphal [is] always used of plagues, e.g., Exo 8:17, Amos 8:11."

Pekah inflicts external pressure on Judah such that Ahaz is forced to appeal to a higher power (which he chooses to be Assyria instead of YHWH). As well, Pekah could still be punished by YHWH: Pekah's divinely-ordained attack on Judah brings punishment in the form of Assyria and Assyria's puppet vassal, Hoshea (15:29–30; suggested by 17:3).[78] Pekah enacts divine judgment and receives divine judgment. In both cases, Assyria plays a role. Assyria will take over—indeed, replace—Israel and Aram in their divinely-ordained oppression of Judah (16:8, 18; 19:25–26).[79] Meanwhile, Assyria also literally displaces Israel by invading and exiling significant portions of the northern kingdom (15:29).[80] Pekah perhaps had a role as YHWH's instrument of judgment (serving as a warning)[81] in that he functions along with Rezin/Aram and then Tiglath-Pileser III/Assyria to bring trouble to Ahaz/Judah. In Pekah/Israel's (other) role as the recipient of YHWH's judgment, Tiglath-Pileser III/Assyria functions as the intermediary. Logically and chronologically, one could say that Ahaz and then Assyria function instrumentally against Pekah/Israel, but the actual connection of Ahaz to the fate of Israel is carefully avoided by the narrative. Verse 29 makes no mention of Ahaz's part in summoning the Assyrian forces against Rezin and Pekah, and 16:5–9, which is clear about Rezin's fate, is completely silent on the complementary fate of Pekah such that the omission is blatant.[82] This

---

78. Second Kings 17:3 indicates Hoshea's early submission to the Assyrian throne. Beyond that, the biblical text does not explicitly state what is claimed by Tiglath-Pileser III in Summary Inscription 4:17'–18': "Pekah, their king [I/they killed] and I installed Hoshea [as king] over them." Thus Tiglath-Pileser III claims to have installed Hoshea and possibly also to have eliminated Pekah (the restoration of the verb could be either "I killed" or "they killed"). One could harmonize the two accounts and assert that Pekah was killed by the Israelites, and then Hoshea was installed with the support of Assyria. See *COS* 2:288–89 (289n11); and Tadmor, *The Inscriptions*, 141, note to 17'.

79. Provan, *1 and 2 Kings*, 242, perceives a similar development earlier in the account of Menahem's reign.

80. Israel is whittled down to the "rump state" of Ephraim (i.e., the Ephraimite hill country, the Assyrian province of Samaria)—e.g., as compiled in Aharoni, *The Land of the Bible*, 374–76.

81. Agreeing with Thompson, *Situation and Theology*, 88–89:

> This portrayal of judgment on Judah and Jerusalem for the sins of Ahaz [i.e., judgment by way of the coalition attacking and Judah's losing Elath] is only a token of what will happen in the future if such kings as Ahaz reign in Jerusalem. After all, Rezin and Pekah fail in their enterprise against Ahaz, so it cannot be claimed that a judgment is actually portrayed. Nevertheless there is surely in the account this element of warning, directed to the people of the southern kingdom in the aftermath of the catastrophe which befell the northern kingdom in 722 BC: the sort of thing that had happened in the north would happen in the south if kings such as Ahaz were to reign.

82. As perceived by Hayim Tadmor and Mordechai Cogan, "Ahaz and Tiglath-Pileser

narratological "denial" of the connection of Ahaz to Israel's punishment may be best explained as part of the author's efforts to depict Ahaz as being as distant from YHWH (and from obedience to him) as possible.[83]

Thus in the narratives concerning Pekah, either Pekah or Ahaz—not Tiglath-Pileser III or Assyria (or Rezin/Aram, for that matter)—is the primary interest of the passages. Pekah's characterization is especially complex in that he is explicitly and implicitly portrayed as YHWH's instrument of punishment or the recipient of YHWH's punishment. Assyria has an instrumental role in both dynamics, though it is minimized and subservient to that of Pekah and Ahaz in the narrative. Tiglath-Pileser III's campaign and deportation of most of Israel is not denied, but it is reported matter-of-factly and as briefly as possible (v. 29). As noted earlier, even Assyria's role in installing Hoshea on the throne is not mentioned by the Kings author. The capture and deportation of Damascus and the murder of Rezin by Tiglath-Pileser III are equally minimized, especially in comparison to the narrative space given to Ahaz's words and actions (Ahaz's deeds may be "smaller," but they are given over twice the number of words as Tiglath-Pileser III's; see 16:7–9). In reality, the Assyrian presence in Pekah's time would have been huge, undeniable, and expected to define significantly the success or failure of Pekah's reign. To the Kings author, however, Assyria is controllable and containable—it does not overwhelm or even dominate the narrative . . . (for now), nor is it allowed in the Scripture to be a significant part of the

---

in the Book of Kings: Historiographic Considerations," *Bib* 60 (1979) 491–508 (507–8); and Thompson, *Situation and Theology*, 150n45.

83. One may then ask whether Ahaz's role in Aram's destruction is justified. Thompson, *Situation and Theology*, 150n45, suggests that the determinative characterization regarding Israel's fate in 2 Kgs 16 is not that of Ahaz, but of Pekah: it is "because the Historian wishes to portray Israel at this period as being in the role of the agent of the divine judgement." This still does not solve the problem of the apparent distinction between Rezin/Aram and Pekah/Israel, however, since Rezin/Aram is also depicted as YHWH's instrument of punishment in 15:37. Cogan and Tadmor, "Ahaz and Tiglath-Pileser," 508, forward that 2 Kgs 15:29 was originally part of a fuller account concerning Ahaz (as seen or reflected in 2 Kgs 16:5–9) and that the Kingly author simply decided to move the verses concerning the fate of Israel to the account of Pekah, leaving "the apocopated ending of the Ahaz story." This assumes too careless a maneuver on the part of the Kingly author, however, to explain *why* he crafted the text as he did (though it might explain partly *how*). The detail and deliberation in the Kingly author's craft behooves the reader to consider a reason in the interest of the text for the Aram-Israel difference. Simply put, if one compares the general portrayals of Aram (a foreign, long-term archenemy to YHWH's people) and Israel (the most closely-related nation to Judah and also considered part of YHWH's chosen people), then the narrator's discrimination may be understood. One may only conjecture that the Kingly author was also aware of the events of 2 Chr 28:9–15 and thus wished not to condemn his merciful "brothers" (28:11, 15).

standard for evaluating the Israelite monarch. At present, Assyria functions only instrumentally, and that instrumental role is implicitly retributive and in the service of YHWH, whether it be inflicting deserving punishment on Israel (v. 29) or joining Aram and Israel in troubling Ahaz/Judah for their YHWH-displeasing ways.

One final note on the account of Pekah's reign: it has been often assumed that pro- and anti-Assyrian factions compose much of the background to the so-called Syro-Ephraimite War and related events. Menahem was apparently pro-Assyrian, and Pekah was anti-Assyrian. The Israelites' responses to Assyria facilitated various usurpations of the throne and even motivated Pekah to join Rezin's anti-Assyrian coalition/efforts. While Israel's relationship to Assyria apparently did play a role in its quickly deteriorating history, internal strife is reported as just that and no more. The narrator recognizes internal problems as the Israelites' own and attributes corruption on the part of the king and others precisely to themselves and not an external party. All that to say, in the narrative's presentation, Israel's relations to Assyria are important, but they are far from the whole portrayal of Israel.

Regarding the so-called Syro-Ephraimite War in particular, Oded points out that "the intervention of the Assyrians marks the end of this war, not its beginning," and wars within Syro-Palestine were "internal and regional, not external and international."[84] Hence, a smaller, more localized explanation is sought, and Oded proposes control of the Transjordan as the motivating factor. While this may have been a (if not the) motivating factor behind the Syro-Ephraimite War, such motivations are inessential to the narrative, which says nothing of either an anti-Assyrian coalition or control of Transjordania.[85] Isaiah 7 may be alluded to by the close likeness of 2 Kgs 16:5 to Isa 7:1,[86] but no further explanation for the Syro-Ephraimite War is given apart from 7:6, which states Rezin and Pekah's intent to install "the son of Tabeel" as king over Judah and possibly to expand their territories (which could be interpreted as a desire for Transjordania, but this remains conjectural until further evidence surfaces). At any rate, within his own history concerning the Syro-Ephraimite War, the Kingly author is not concerned with Rezin, Pekah, or Tiglath-Pileser III's purposes,[87] but with

---

84. B. Oded, "The Historical Background of the Syro-Ephraimite War Reconsidered," *CBQ* 34 (1972) 153–65 (153–55).

85. Similarly pointed out by Wiseman, *1 and 2 Kings*, 261.

86. Agreeing with Provan, *1 and 2 Kings*, 245, while also recognizing the particular emphases and distinctives of Kings in comparison with Isaiah. See Thompson, *Situation and Theology*, 88.

87. Ahaz is depicted as so effete that he does not even fight or have purposes other

YHWH's purposes (2 Kgs 15:37). In this way, the narrative emphasizes that the so-called Syro-Ephraimite War and its related Aram-Israel alliance serve a divine purpose and, implicitly, render a divinely-ordained warning to Judah,[88] especially when it is under the leadership of Ahaz.

ASSYRIA AS AN "ALTERNATIVE" TO YHWH (2 KINGS 16)

In this chapter we consider the characterization of the Assyrians in 2 Kings 16, the "Ahaz Chapter." Specifically, my focus here is the characterization of Tiglath-Pileser III, king of the Assyrians, who effectively represents the empire that he controls. As we shall see in further detail, the Assyrian king is depicted as an "alternative choice," contra YHWH for Ahaz's loyalty and dependence. This depiction of Tiglath-Pileser III is overall negative, but not in such a way as to detract from the greater burden of responsibility that Ahaz bears in the eyes of the narrator. The primary way the narrative achieves this is by depicting the Assyrian king as more passive than active in his influence towards Ahaz, and as less significant and more distant from the reader through repetitive use of only his official title, on the one hand, and noticably selective use of his personal name, on the other. Through these various means of literary minimization, the Assyrian emperor and his empire are yet again denied the dominance of their imperial metanarrative.

The Assyrians have already made a significant appearance in the Kings narrative, specifically in regard to the fortunes of the Northern Kingdom in 2 Kgs 15. Now in chapter 16, the Assyrians enter the Judahite scene. The main concern of the chapter is King Ahaz, whom the early verses establish as the most apostate king of Judah thus far (16:1–3a). The verses that follow support this evaluation. After quickly summarizing Ahaz's abhorrent pagan religious practices (vv. 3b–4), the majority of the chapter illustrates Ahaz's YHWH-displeasing reign by way of his international relations and related cultic alterations, particularly 1) Ahaz's appeal to Assyria in the midst of attack by Aram and Israel, and 2) Ahaz's new altar and removal of temple furnishings—changes which were apparently influenced, but not required, by Assyrian-Judahite relations. Let us consider further the role of Assyria in these verses.

Following several brief reports of reigns (14:23—15:38), the narrative pace slows down. Second Kings 16:5–6, which gains resumptive emphasis by the anticipatory comment of 15:37, provides the setting: Rezin of Aram

than survival, but calls for help from power-wielding Assyria.

88. Cf. Thompson, *Situation and Theology*, 82, 88–90.

and Pekah of Israel attack Jerusalem and Ahaz. The crisis was no doubt aggravated by the influx of Edomites into Elath (v. 6). The narrative then conveys Ahaz's response, an appeal to Tiglath-Pileser III for assistance. The appeal is the first instance of direct speech not only from Ahaz, but from any human since Jehoash in the early part of chapter 14, hence the words have additional impact.

Ahaz's direct speech (v. 7) immediately demonstrates the extent to which Ahaz has distanced himself from acknowledging YHWH as lord. His first words appeal for help not to YHWH, but Tiglath-Pileser III. Instead of the usual verbal form in the sentence-initial position, Ahaz's speech begins with self-descriptions that place himself under commitment and submission to the king of Assyria: "Your servant and your son I am." It is oft-noted that "servant" language is typical of aNE treaty and covenantal relations.[89] "Son" language is also usually thought to apply to covenantal circumstances such as those of v. 7. Elsewhere in 2 Kings, father-son language is used by a monarch towards the revered prophet Elisha (8:9), cf. 8:13; 13:14. It has been suggested that a quasi-familial sense is brought to the relationship by invoking the father-son relation.[90] Given the context of "son" in 2 Kgs 16:7, I would agree. Although it is true that the combination "your servant and your son" is rarely-attested in aNE documents and occurs in the OT only here,[91] that does not at all necessarily mean that the two concepts were incompatible. This should be apparent, but Cogan and Tadmor seem skeptical and further claim that "a vassal would not have dared to use the term 'son,' which expressed familial dependency." Earlier, however, Cogan interprets Ahaz's declaration to be "I am your vassal, your son."[92] Hence if Cogan and Tadmor maintain the earlier interpretation, then they must be interpreting

---

89. E.g., several times in the Amarna letters, and in Assyrian royal correspondence. For the latter, see sources in Cogan and Tadmor, *2 Kings*, 187. Similarly, James A. Montgomery, *Books of Kings*, 458.

90. See, e.g., Dennis J. McCarthy, "Notes on the Love of God in Deuteronomy and the Father-Son Relationship between Yahweh and Israel," *CBQ* 27 (1965) 144–47. See also Montgomery, *Books of Kings*, 458; Jones, *1 and 2 Kings*, vol. 2, 546 (apparently agreeing with McCarthy); Cogan, *Imperialism and Religion*, 66n4; Cohn, *2 Kings*, 113.

91. E.g., one or both relations referred to in Amarna letter 158.1–2 and 288.66; correspondence between Ashurbanipal and Ishtarduri in *KB* 2, 230 and *ARA* 2, §834. aNE sources as seen in *ANET*, 489; *ARA* 2, 320–21; and Cogan and Tadmor, *2 Kings*, 187. Other aNE examples are in David I. Owen, "An Akkadian Letter from Ugarit at Tel Aphek," *Tel Aviv* 8 (1981) 1–17 (7, line 6; 11); and Paul Kalluveettil, *Declaration and Covenant: A Comprehensive Review of Covenant Formulae from the Old Testament and the Ancient Near East*, AB 88 (Rome: Biblical Institute Press, 1982), 129, who notes that the combined formula has not yet been found in the covenant-making context, but it "is attested outside the pact-realizing scene."

92. See Cogan, *Imperialism and Religion*, 66n4.

"son" as used by the narrator to convey an aspect of the vassal-overlord relation (as they strongly later imply), though the historical reality, also from their perspective, did not include the precise use of "son."[93] That said, Cogan and Tadmor's historical argument is significantly undercut by the fact of extant aNE attestations (however rare), while the literary point persists. Whether one understands Ahaz's use of "son" to be historical or not, the narrative evidently uses it in combination with "servant" to convey a formal, filial-like submission and dependency assumed by Ahaz towards the king of Assyria.[94] Note that actual biological or adopted sonship among the Assyrian royals indicated not only subservience and devotion on the part of the son, but also status, honour, and privileges to the son.[95] Possibly Ahaz drew on this concept as well in identifying himself as the Assyrian king's "son." Politically-speaking, Ahaz's adoption of a "son" identification towards Assyria was the ultimate betrayal of Judah's independence and resistance to the Assyrian empire.

It is not clear whether or not the Kings author understood that Israel already had an alliance with Assyria,[96] but Ahaz's words in v. 7 at least introduce the reader to a significantly advanced step in Israel's dependency on Assyria. There certainly had been previous negotiations, interactions, and conquests involving Israel and Assyria (15:19-20, 29), but this is the first instance in Kings of a strongly-indicated alliance between Israel and the imperial superpower. Effectively, v. 7 reads as if the fatal move to align with Assyria has just occurred in the storyline.

Ahaz seeks salvation through obsequious submission to Assyria, which is, further, at the expense of YHWH's temple and the royal coffers. In appealing to Tiglath-Pileser, the Judean king uses the Hiphil form of the verb ישע, ("to save, rescue, deliver"), a term most often used with God as

93. Cogan and Tadmor, 2 Kings, 187: "Therefore one doubts the originality of the formula as used here by Ahaz; it just may be a combination coined by our storyteller." Similarly, Nadav Na'aman, "The Deuteronomist and Voluntary Servitude to Foreign Powers," JSOT 65 (1995) 37–53 (43).

94. Agreeing with Cogan and Tadmor, 2 Kings, 187; Cohn, 2 Kings, 113; McCarthy, "Notes on the Love," 147, implies. Na'aman, "Deuteronomist and Voluntary Servitude," 43–44, rejects a pejorative, religious sense for the combination because of the combination's uniqueness and his interpretation of "son" as an entirely political reference. "Ahaz at this stage was also a 'son,' that is, a minor independent political partner" (44).

95. See Pierre Villard, "La notion de famille royale à l'époque néo-assyrienne," in *La famille dans le Proche-Orient ancien: réalités, symbolismes, et images: Proceedings of the 55th Rencontre Assyriologique Internationale at Paris; 6-9 July 2009*, ed. Lionel Marti (Winona Lake, IN: Eisenbrauns, 2014), 515–23.

96. With reference to Isaiah 7, Kalluveettil argues convincingly that "2 Ki 16:5–9 . . . recounts the beginning of a covenant of vassalage" (127). See discussion in Kalluveettil, *Declaration and Covenant*, 124–27.

the subject, though military obligations between treaty partners involve ישע as well.⁹⁷ Sawyer understands the use of ישע in v. 7 as "addressing Tiglath-pileser as though he were a god."⁹⁸ This is certainly possible, though the secular, political-military sense would also naturally apply in v. 7. Both senses may be seen to operate for ישע here: in its immediate context of v. 7, Ahaz uses the verb for political-military reasons. However, in the overall context of chapter 16, which broadly concerns Ahaz's extreme apostasy, the root's more commonly-attested, theological sense comes into play and brings a self-incriminating irony to Ahaz's speech.⁹⁹

At this point, Ahaz remains simply "Ahaz," while Tiglath-Pileser is identified with his title and status as "king of Assyria." The former is presented in a more personally-accessible way while the latter retains a sense of hierarchical distance and otherness as "king" and "of Assyria." This use of names here encourages the reader to attend more to Ahaz's movements than to that of the king of Assyria.

The Assyrian king is the first object of Ahaz's efforts to overcome the Aramean-Israelite threat; Ahaz turns for help to him instead of YHWH. In this respect, v. 7 is primarily a comment on Ahaz's wayward dependencies. The Assyrian king and the empire that he represents function secondarily in v. 7 as an alternative to YHWH in the primary relationship of Ahaz::YHWH-as-lord. From the perspective of the YHWH-affirming narrator, the language that should have been directed to YHWH is given to a foreign power (i.e., "your servant and your son I am.... deliver me ... "). We should note what has not happened in the narrative: Tiglath-Pileser III has not been shown to demand anything from, nor to offer anything to, Ahaz. Instead, Ahaz takes the initiative and seeks out Assyria for protection and assistance. Thus far, the portrayal of Assyria is fairly colorless. Its role as an alternative to YHWH simply provides the litmus test for demonstrating Ahaz's allegiances. While it may be assumed that Assyria, in its previous attack and exiling of Israel, was generally depicted as being against the ultimate desires of YHWH (since Assyria successfully removed YHWH's people from their land), v. 7 contributes little to the moral-ethical characterization of Assyria in Kings so far. There is perhaps a yellow warning light in Ahaz's call to Assyria to fight not only Aram, but also Israel. Again, the greater responsibility is with Ahaz, who makes the request, but the reader is now poised to expect destruction in Israel at the hands of the Assyrians, and

---

97. Robert L. Hubbard, Jr., "ישע," in *NIDOTTE* 2:556–62 (556, 557); J. F. Sawyer and H.-J. Fabry, "ישע," in *TDOT* 6:441–63 (450–51; 453–54).

98. Sawyer and H.-J. Fabry, "ישע," 454.

99. See Hubbard, "ישע," 556; Sawyer and Fabry, "ישע," 445.

the retrospective allusion to 15:29 may be seen to render Ahaz's summons to Assyria in particular as ominous for the people of God.

Ahaz reinforces and substantiates his appeal to Tiglath-Pileser by appropriating silver and gold from the temple and royal treasuries (v. 8). While this could be viewed as a typical political gesture by a vassal state to its imperial lord,[100] the inclusion of the distinctive term שחד suggests more than a merely obligatory act or allegiance-reinforcing offering. Though scholars differ in the degree to which they perceive a manipulative sense inherent in the meaning of שחד, they do generally agree that שחד usually may be translated as "bribe."[101] Only three specific events involving שחד appear in the OT:[102] that of the corrupt sons of Samuel (1 Sam 8:3), of Judean King Asa (given to Ben-Hadad king of Aram; 1 Kgs 15:19), and of King Ahaz (given to Tiglath-Pileser king of Assyria; 2 Kgs 16:8). The correspondence between the reports of Asa and Ahaz suggests itself, and scholars since Kalluveettil

---

100. Some examples of religious-political obligations from subservient states to Assyria are in Steven W. Holloway, *Aššur is King! Aššur is King! Religion in the Exercise of Power in the Neo-Assyrian Empire*, CHANE 10 (Leiden: Brill, 2002), 100–108; 184–93; Cogan, *Imperialism and Religion*, 49–56.

101. On the more reserved end of the interpretive spectrum, one may place Greenfeld's comments: "[שחד] is different from *minḥā* in that it is the present used to interest a stronger power to intercede in one's behalf... The use of the verb *šḥd* in Eze 16:33 and Job 6:22 shows clearly that the *šoḥad* was a gift whose purpose was to initiate action."

The majority of scholars (e.g., Beyse, Grisanti and McCann, Hamilton) investigating this term defend a more dominant sense of "bribe" and often back-up their arguments with more support and apparent research than Greenfeld (and similarly, Ackroyd). See Jonas C. Greenfield, "Some Aspects of Treaty Terminology in the Bible," in *Fourth World Congress of Jewish Studies: Papers*, vol. 1 (Jerusalem: World Union of Jewish Studies, 1967), 117–19 (119); Peter R. Ackroyd, "The Biblical Interpretation of the Reigns of Ahaz and Hezekiah," in *In the Shelter of Elyon: Essays on Ancient Palestinian Life and Literature in Honor of G. W. Ahlström*, eds. W. Boyd Barrick and John R. Spencer, JSOTSup 31 (Sheffield: JSOT Press, 1984), 247–59 (249, 258n11); K.-M. Beyse, "שחד," in *TDOT* 14:555–57 (556); Michael A. Grisanti and J. Clinton McCann, "שחד," in *NIDOTTE* 4:75–76; Victor P. Hamilton, "שחד," in *TWOT* 2:914; *HALOT*, 4:1457 (observe that all three instances under "gift"—the reference to Isa 21:14 presumably a typo for Prov 21:14—may be interpreted as "bribe" or "manipulative gift"). Beyse's description/explanation seems most sound:

> Although the first meaning lexicons generally offer for the verb is "to give a present" and for the noun, "gift," closer examination shows that the reference is never to the unintentional or aimless giving of gifts... the idea is rather that of *do ut des*, "I give that you may give." The variously adduced passages show [below]... that the focus is on the second meaning, namely "to bribe; a bribe."

As well, see the excellent evidence and argumentation in Cogan and Tadmor, "Ahaz and Tiglath-Pileser," 491–508 (499–503).

102. Further, שחד is fairly infrequent in the OT, the verbal form occurring only twice and the nominal form occurring 23 times. Of those 23 instances, most are in legal, stipulative contexts and clearly denote "bribery."

have noted the similarity of vocabulary, phraseology, and circumstances.¹⁰³ In particular, both Judean kings sought to establish—through a declaration and a שחד taken from the temple and the royal treasuries—a covenant with a foreign, third party so as to receive military assistance in order to ward off an invading enemy. An allusion to the Asa story in 1 Kgs 15:16–20 surely informs the similar Ahaz story in 2 Kgs 16:5–9. Though the Kings account of Asa evaluates him at the beginning as a righteous and YHWH-committed king (1 Kgs 15:11–15), the function of the remaining verses seems to be to present the exceptional and contrasting lapse in Asa's commitment and trust in YHWH in the latter part of his reign. Not only do Asa's actions illustrate a lack of trust in YHWH (cf. 2 Chr 16:1–10), but the mention of an unfavourable condition as the final word on Asa's reign (namely, diseased feet)—even after the concluding formulae—signals a disturbing incongruity with the Asa of 1 Kgs 15:11–15. It is as if Asa's previously spotless record is sullied in the interim by his particular international relations, betraying a lack of trust in, and reverence for, YHWH (note especially the contrast between vv. 15 and 18). When a similar situation arises for Ahaz, one may assume that the Judean king's political maneuvers are just as self-condemning; further, when considered in the context of the rest of the Kings account of Ahaz, they are even more condemning, for Ahaz is clearly depicted as a faithless king. With regards to שחד specifically, in 1 Kgs 15:19 the term evidently denotes a "gift" understood by both parties in that would-be alliance as one with obligations attached; in all other instances of שחד, the term may be understood as meaning "bribe" or "manipulative gift." Common translational renderings of "present" (NRSV, TEV, NASB) and "gift" (NIV, NJPS) for 2 Kgs 16:8 mask the sense of criticism associated with the OT use of שחד. One should also bear in mind that the basic idea of "bribe"—the act of "hiring a third party in order to upset the balance in favour of one of two rivals[—] is considered a 'deviation' from the accepted rules of war."¹⁰⁴ Ahaz's "gift" to Assyria is unfavourably perceived by the narrator not so much for its manipulative intent as its unjust purpose, which is further incriminating in the case of Ahaz because the injustice is directed against part of the people of God, the kingdom of Israel. שחד is enacted on Ahaz's initiative, but Tiglath-Pileser III's "passive" acceptance of the "gift" effectively makes him an accomplice in the devious and destructive scheme. The primary responsibility remains on Ahaz, who issued the declaration formula (v. 7) and reinforced it with

---

103. Kalluveettil, *Declaration and Covenant*, 122, 128, 136; Stuart A. Irvine, *Isaiah, Ahaz, and the Syro-Ephraimitic Crisis*, SBLDS 123 (Atlanta: Scholars, 1990), 88–89; Na'aman, "Deuteronomist and Voluntary Servitude," 45–46; and Cogan and Tadmor, "Ahaz and Tiglath-Pileser," 499, 502–3.

104. Cogan and Tadmor, "Ahaz and Tiglath-Pileser," 503.

the שחד, but Tigalth-Pileser's consent to the treaty is evidently indicated in that he responds to Ahaz's request for help against Aram and Israel. As Kalluveettil understands it, שמע אל (v. 9) is a response

> to a request, and not to an assertion of relationship.... Tiglath-pileser's consenting to the entreaty and coming to the rescue implies that the pact has been already realized; these acts resulted from the covenant: the Assyrian king accepts the appeal and moves against the enemies, because he is bound to defend the cause of his ally.[105]

Thus Tiglath-Pileser III participates both in an alliance with the apostate Ahaz and in Ahaz's specific request for deliverance. Tiglath-Pileser III appears to take Ahaz's request several steps further in that the Assyrian king not only delivered Jerusalem from Aram and Israel, but put an end to Aram and its king and exiled significant portions of Israel (15:29). Assyria's destructive actions against Israel are probably not repeated in chapter 16 so much because repetition is to be avoided (cf. 17:3–7 and 18:9–12), but rather to avoid suggesting that Ahaz has an instrumental role in YHWH's punishment of Israel. This latter possibility would have given Ahaz a somewhat positive role. As well, the author may not have been comfortable associating Israel's fate closely with that of arch-enemy Aram. At any rate, the absence of explicit mention of Israel's outcome in v. 9 lessens the large damage with which Assyria could have been credited. Passively, the king of Assyria replaces YHWH in Judah's allegiances; actively, the king of Assyria takes part in Ahaz's agenda, evidently capitalizes on Ahaz's voluntary position of dependence upon him, and proceeds a step further than Ahaz's subtle request for deliverance in that he is reported as destroying Aram. This characterization of Assyria is negative on all counts, while still condemning Ahaz as the initiator. On the whole, the depiction of Assyria is remarkably minimized, especially in that it does not include an explicit description of Israel's fate at the hands of Tiglath-Pileser III.[106] From a post-colonial perspective, this functions to subvert the presumed priority and influence of the Assyrian empire by way of elevating the responsibility and influence of subaltern Judah.

As already noted, Tiglath-Pileser is always identified in chapter 16 with the title "king of Assyria," whereas Ahaz is simply referred to by his personal name in vv. 1–8, and then with the additional title "king" in vv. 10–17.

---

105. Kalluveettil, *Declaration and Covenant*, 138.

106. This is a more nuanced interpretation than that of Cohn, *2 Kings*, 113, who concludes a bit simplistically: "In all of this Tiglath-Pileser is given no voice, no demands, no quid pro quo. The focus is on the initiative of Ahaz."

One may apply here in Kings the general interpretive principles of Kalimi with regard to Chronicles.[107] In all cases in chapter 16, Ahaz may be seen to be rendered more personally-accessible than Tiglath-Pileser because his less-titled name creates less distance between him and the reader than the continuous reminder that Tiglath-Pileser is "the king of Assyria"— ultimate representative of an outside, invading entity who takes the agenda of Ahaz to new, destructive levels. The title "king of Assyria" serves to reinforce the otherness of the Assyrian representative. Kalimi observes that the use of a personal name (in addition to the formal title) in difficult situations is likely to create further distance, if not a sense of hostility, against the personally-identified aggravator.[108] With this in mind, one notes that Tiglath-Pileser's personal name is included at the beginning of both Ahaz's response to the Aramean-Israelite attack and his movements towards alterations of the Jerusalemite cultus (vv. 7, 10). The use of titles and names contributes to the greater overall impact of Ahaz's character and the sense of "otherness" and subtle hostility engendered in the portrayal of emperor Tiglath-Pileser III.

In vv. 10–18, the more official and political nature of Ahaz's dealings with Assyria may be suggested by the addition of the title "king" to Ahaz's name and the consistent reference to "Uriah the priest."[109] Hence, the hierarchical imbalance between Tiglath-Pileser and the other characters is slightly less in vv. 10–18, but the content, as we shall see in more detail, clearly indicates that Tiglath-Pileser wielded a greater influence on Ahaz than vice-versa.

For the narrator, the relevant consequences of Assyria's defeat of Aram—and of evidently most of Israel, though the narrator does not explicitly state that in v. 9— concern not the military-political sphere, but the cultic-political arena. Post-battle, King Ahaz goes to Damascus to meet Tiglath-Pileser. This may well have been to confirm the covenantal relationship initiated through word and action in vv. 7–9. Whatever the precise reason for the personal meeting between Ahaz and his new overlord, Tiglath-Pileser, the event leads to cultic alterations. The influential role of Assyria in Ahaz's changes to the temple furnishings is indicated by verses that state the Assyrian influence on Ahaz and that also form something of a narratival inclusio around the report of the temple modifications. In v. 10a, Tiglath-Pileser is the reason for Ahaz going to Damascus, where the Judean

---

107. Isaac Kalimi, *The Reshaping of Ancient Israelite History in Chronicles* (Winona Lake, IN: Eisenbrauns, 2005), 166–68, 173–74, 176–79.

108. Ibid., 166–68, 173–76.

109. As observed by Cohn, *2 Kings*, 113.

king sees the altar he chooses to copy.¹¹⁰ Meanwhile, in v. 18b, the king of Assyria is stated as the reason for some, if not all, of the previously described changes to the temple furnishings, though it is unclear precisely how much prior description is implied in the phrase "because of the king of Assyria," מפני מלך אשור.¹¹¹

It is perhaps helpful at this point to discuss briefly where the Assyrians do *not* feature in vv. 10–18. Several generations followed Östreicher in believing that the Damascene altar was Assyrian and that Ahaz's adoption of it was an indication that, as a new vassal of the Assyrian empire, Judah would now take on the imperial state religion.¹¹² More recent Assyriological studies have brought us to understand, however, that the Assyrians did not use altars for burnt animal sacrifices, nor did they necessarily impose the "official" state religion on subordinate peoples—much less, on vassal territories.¹¹³ That said, the account of Ahaz's cultic alterations remains, overall, negative. McKay points out that

---

110. The use of לקראת as "to meet" in v. 10 is unexceptional. This particular "frozen" infinitival form occurs 121 times in the OT. "It can mean to meet on friendly terms, for political benefit, to assist, or, most often, to engage the enemy in warfare"—Michael A. Grisanti, "קרא [II]," in *NIDOTTE* 3:974–75. In the case of v. 10, the context clearly does not indicate the last two possibilities and almost indisputably suggests a political meeting, as the relation between Ahaz and Tiglath-Pileser is posited as a highly political one with inherently overlapping spiritual-religious significance and consequences.

111. The subsequently oft-cited interpretation of A. T. Olmstead, *History of Assyria* (New York: Scribner, 1923), 198–99, that מפני מלך אשור refers to "the face of the statue of the Assyrian king" is usually rejected on the grounds that it suffers from lack of corroborating historical evidence "that the Assyrian kings erected statues or stelae in sanctuaries other than Assyrian ones" (Jones, *1 and 2 Kings*, 2:541). Cogan, *Imperialism and Religion*, 74n43, points out that the erection of a royal stele (or statue, for that matter) should be expected to be given clearer notice. The establishment of royal statues outside the Assyrian heartland is not wholly absent, though it is rare. Hence Holloway, *Aššur is King!*, 193, concludes:

> To attempt to canvass three hundred years of Neo-Assyrian religious imperialism outside of Mesopotamia based on five disparate citations is simply hubris, and signals scholarly self-deception in progress. In light of current evidence, we do not and cannot know the extent of Neo-Assyrian ruler worship outside Mesopotamia, and that is where we must part company with Olmstead and his successors.

For further discussion, see Holloway, *Aššur is King!*, 151–59, 180–93.

112. Theodor Östreicher, *Das Deuteronomische Grundgesetz*, Beiträge zur Förderung christlicher Theologie 4/27 (Gütersloh: Bertelsmann, 1923), 38.

113. For further discussion of Assyrian religious impositions, see Cogan, *Imperialism and Religion*, 73–77; and Holloway, *Aššur is King!* Hobbs, *2 Kings*, 215 goes so far as to state plainly: "The critical notion that the altar seen by Ahaz was of Assyrian design and that it was adopted by the king 'as an expression of subservience to Assyria' . . . must be put to rest. It is strongly disputed, and on good grounds."

None the less, the altar cannot have been introduced simply for aesthetic reasons. There must have been something non-Yahwistic about this new altar, otherwise it is difficult to understand why the Deuteronomist related its introduction at length. It has been noted that there is no criticism of Ahaz's action in 2 Kings 16:10–16, but it may also be noted that there is no praise for him either. Since it is the Deuteronomist's intention to portray Ahaz as an apostate . . . , the incident must have been included in the history as an example of the evils of his reign. . . . [114]

Na'aman adds to McKay's argument

the fact that no changes in the temple of Jerusalem are ever ascribed to reformer kings. Rather, the kings who carried out extensive reforms in the temple are Ahaz and Manasseh, the two major apostate kings of Judah; and it is the righteous king Josiah who purged the temple and restored everything to its original purity. Within the books of Kings, this 'original purity' pertains to the time of Solomon, when the temple was built and al the sacred objects and vessels were fixed therein. . . .

It is clear that the historian judged Ahaz's altar reform negatively. The sending of the priest to the former enemy's capital city (Damascus), the stress on the imitation of the Aramean altar in all details (i.e. the import of a foreign plan and design for the new altar), the emphasis on the king's personal participation in the sacrifice, the removal of the Solomonic bronze altar (see 1 Ki 8:64) and its appropriation by the king for his own private worship—all these are elements in the historian's indirect criticism of the deed. Also, the narrative continuity between Ahaz's voluntary surrender to Assyria (vv. 7–9) and the episode of the building of the new altar (vv. 10–16) were intended to link the

---

Often it is pointed out that Uriah is referred to as one of two "trustworthy witnesses" in Isa 8:2, hence his involvement with the Damascene altar indicates that the altar-making project was in agreement with the Yahwistic orientation of the narrator. See Jones, *1 and 2 Kings*, 2:538–39; John W. McKay, *Religion in Judah Under the Assyrians, 732–609 BC*, SBT2 26 (London: SCM, 1973), 7; Cogan and Tadmor, *2 Kings*, 192–93; and Hobbs, *2 Kings*, 215. However, while Uriah may have fulfilled that role in the circumstances of Isa 8:2, that does not necessarily mean that he was consistently of trustworthy character. King Asa, e.g., earlier demonstrates stark changes in character in 1 Kgs 15.

For further discussion of the debate concerning the exact cultural and/or religious provenance of Ahaz's new altar, see discussions in Jones, *1 and 2 Kings*, 2:537–38; Thompson, *Situation and Theology*, 83–84; Cogan, *Imperialism and Religion*, 73–77; McKay, *Religion in Judah*, 7–10; Cogan and Tadmor, *2 Kings*, 192–93; and Cohn, *2 Kings*, 114.

114. McKay, *Religion in Judah*, 7.

two episodes by suggesting that the second is the direct result of the first.[115]

The adaptation of the Damascene altar—with attention to its religious and cultural distinctiveness—was a voluntary welcome on the part of Ahaz for the infiltration of deeply significant symbols (and likely also, practices) from outside the boundaries of Judah. As such, it was a brazen and ominous step in compromising the holiness and distinctiveness of the people of God in that milieu; further, it opened the way for increased acceptance and integration of foreign customs and beliefs, which was soon to be the case in neighboring Israel (cf. 2 Kgs 17:24–41). Second Kings 16:10–18 does indeed appear to anticipate, if not signal, this shift for both kingdoms.

As in vv. 7–9, Ahaz is culpable, for his alacrity in creating substitutes for the Solomonic, "authentic" Yahwistic cultus incriminates him,[116] as does his deference to the king of Assyria at the expense of the temple's integrity. Tiglath-Pileser is not entirely absolved, however; as observed above, specific mentions of the Assyrian influence form an inclusio to the account of Ahaz's temple alterations. As in vv. 7–8, the king of Assyria functions as an ominous substitute for YHWH with regard to Ahaz's loyalty and dependency.

---

115. Na'aman, "Deuteronomist and Voluntary Servitude," 46–47. Also see Klaas A. D. Smelik, "The New Altar of King Ahaz (2 Kings 16): Deuteronomistic Re-Interpretation of a Cult Reform," in *Deuteronomy and Deuteronomic Literature: Festschrift C. H. W. Brekelmans*, BETL, eds. M. Vervenne and J. Lust (Leuven: Leuven University Press, 1997), 263–78 (277–78). Similarly, idem, "Representation of King Ahaz," 142–85 (157–59), who perceives a similarity between Jeroboam's new altar and Ahaz's new altar (Ahaz thus being likened to Jeroboam not only in cultic alterations, but consequently more broadly in politics and apostasy.

Ackroyd, "Biblical Interpretation," 253–57, suggests that the actual historical circumstances of vv. 10–18 may have been more "acceptable" than the authors depict, albeit Ackroyd does affirm that the biblical authors portray Ahaz negatively. Richard D. Nelson, "The Altar of Ahaz: A Revisionist View," *Hebrew Annual Review* 10 (1986) [*Biblical and Other Studies Tenth Anniversary Volume*, ed. Reuben Ahroni, 267–76], goes a step further and argues that "Kings presents what Ahaz did as a liturgically proper and praiseworthy act" (271). However, Nelson makes light of Ahaz's accommodating tendencies and is unique in his interpretation of texts such as 1 Kgs 15:16–21 and 2 Kgs 15:29 as indicating uncondemned action and "a happy ending," respectively.

116. See Thompson, *Situation and Theology*, 85; Wiseman, *1 and 2 Kings*, 262: "In any event it [i.e., Ahaz's new altar] implied drastic change in the ritual rather than emphasizing Judah's subordination to a higher political power." Cohn, *2 Kings*, 113–15, appreciates especially well the literary depiction of Ahaz's voluntary demotions of the Solomonic cultus. Cogan and Provan have similar, but more reserved interpretations in that Cogan posits that the text depicts Ahaz's voluntary adoptions as "part of a general pattern of cultural accommodation" (Cogan, *Religion and Imperialism*, 77) and Provan interprets that the passage is indicative of Ahaz "as a king who is open to foreign *influence* in his religious policy (as in 16:2–4). He is not presented as one who is under foreign *control*" (Provan, *1 and 2 Kings*, 246).

While in vv. 7–9 Tiglath-Pileser's lordship is both passively and actively enacted, in vv. 10a and 18b the influence of his lordship is conveyed as passive. The absence of Tiglath-Pileser's personal name in v. 18b—this being after a relatively long silence regarding the Assyrian king in vv. 10b–17— increases the sense of distance between the reader and Tiglath-Pileser and renders him less significant at that point. The implication in v. 18, if not in the whole of vv. 10–18, is that the integrity of the Jerusalemite cultus is compromised by Assyria's "preferences," but not its explicit demands. Thus, the characterization of the Assyrian king in this second half of chapter 16 continues that of the first half: Tiglath-Pileser is depicted in such a way that the Assyrian portrayal does not detract from that of the primary focus of the passage, King Ahaz.

It is also instructive to look at the presentation of the Assyrians in chapter 16 in relation to that of Judah's long-term arch-enemy, Aram. In v. 9, the two nations come into direct conflict and the king of Assyria puts a final end to the Aramean kingdom by conquering its capital, Damascus. Biblical mention of a foreign nation's fall is generally exceptional, and it has been pointed out that while this occurs for Aram, "this is not the case with the rest of Israel's neighbours."[117] This noteworthy fall happens not by the hands of Judah nor Israel, despite their long-standing conflicts,[118] but by the power of Assyria.

Although at the level of the characters and events, Assyria overpowered and defeated Aram in v. 9, at the level of the narration, Aram's portrayal overshadows that of Assyria in vv. 10–16. Ahaz has the Aramean political power destroyed in v. 9, but ironically, he prolongs the Aramean influence by way of its religion. As discussed earlier, the Damascene altar copied by Ahaz was likely *not* Assyrian. Further, the wording of v. 10b and the density of occurrences for "Damascus" (6x) in vv. 9–12 suggest that a local provenance is the most plausible option.[119] The almost tedious details of Ahaz's sacrificial practices on the new altar reflect their importance. The question then arises for the modern reader, What or Whom was Ahaz worshiping at his new altar? The usual worship of YHWH would not likely have drawn the Kings author's attention, involving here about half the account of Ahaz's

---

117. Carl-Johann van Axskjöld, *Aram as the Enemy-Friend: The Ideological Role of Aram in the Composition of Genesis–2 Kings*, CBOT 45 (Stockholm: Almqvist & Wiksell, 1998), 152; similarly, 8, 158.

118. See, e.g., discussion summarized in ibid., 151–52.

119. In agreement with Long, *2 Kings*, 178; and Na'aman, "Deuteronomist and Voluntary Servitude," 47. Ackroyd, "Biblical Interpretation," 252, also defends the view that the altar that Ahaz saw "was in fact Aramaean and belonged to the Damascus temple."

cultic movements,[120] nor would the usual worship of YHWH be consistent with its surrounding context of cultic alterations.[121] Syncretistic worship (worship of Aramean/Damascene gods and YHWH) is more likely; however, given the provenance of the new altar and Ahaz's clear disregard for YHWH everywhere else in the chapter, worship of foreign gods (Aramean/Damascene; Assyrian gods would not likely have been imposed) is most likely.[122] At any rate, it appears that Ahaz submits himself to the power of more than one foreign entity. While Assyria's political power is daunting and Ahaz appeals to it and submits himself to it (vv. 7-8, 10, 18), Aram's influence on Ahaz outlasts its national existence, reflecting perhaps the significant role Aram had in the history of Israel. The protracted closure of age-old relations between Aram and Judah-Israel even overshadows momentarily (vv. 10b-16) the ominous new relation between Assyria and Judah, which does not re-appear in the narrative until v. 18b.

It is possible that Tiglath-Pileser, himself perhaps influenced by Aramaic culture and religion,[123] encouraged or required Ahaz to adopt the Damascene altar.[124] An Assyrian adoption of an Aramean sacrificial cult would be greatly limited, however, as it is well-known now that the Mesopotamian cultus did not require blood sacrifice.[125] Still, even if this was the case, the Kings narrative is not concerned with that aspect of the altar. Rather, the emphasis is clearly on the Damascene origin of Ahaz's new altar,

120. E.g., Nelson, "Altar of Ahaz," 270-72, 274; Jones, *1 and 2 Kings*, 538-39.
    I am in agreement with McKay, *Religion in Judah*, 7: "There must have been something non-Yahwistic about this new altar, otherwise it is difficult to understand why the Deuteronomist related its introduction at length."
    Little is known of Aramean religion, but the similarity of cultic practices in vv. 13 and 15 to those of Yahwistic worship does not at all mean that the practices in vv. 13 and 15 are Yahwistic, for "the rites listed are typical of most sacrificial systems," including probably those of Aram. For further discussion, see A. R. Millard, 'Arameans', *ABD* 1:345-50 (350); Benjamin Mazar, "The Aramean Empire and its Relations with Israel," *BA* 25 (1962) 98-120 (109-110); quote from Greenfield, "Aspects of Aramean," 67-78 (70).

121. Cogan and Tadmor, *2 Kings*, 193; and Provan, *1 and 2 Kings*, 246, perceive a general, stylistic assimilation occurring in Ahaz's adoption of the Damascene altar. Thus, in their view, the negative aspect of Ahaz's assimilating activity cannot be in anti-Yahwistic worship practices, but in the compromising of the Solomonic Temple. Similarly, Thompson, *Situation and Theology*, 84.

122. Second Chronicles 28:32 harmonizes well with this view, though our recourse to that text is limited here in that the Kings presentation is the focus.

123. See, e.g., A. Kirk Grayson, "8. The Arameans," in "Mesopotamia, History of (History and Culture of Assyria)," *ABD* 4:732-55 (740-41); A. R. Millard, "Assyrians and Arameans," *Iraq* 45 (1983) 101-8 (106-7).

124. E.g., McKay, *Religion in Judah*, 8.

125. E.g., Cogan, *Imperialism and Religion*, 75-76, though cf. 83.

and Assyria disappears into the background until the completion of the report about this new altar—a last vestige of Aram's influence on Judah. The old arch-enemy now eliminated, Assyria soon re-enters the picture (v. 18b) and proves to be the next dominant foreign power with which Judah-Israel engages.

THEOLOGICAL REFLECTION ON THE INSTRUMENTAL ROLE OF ASSYRIA IN THE FALL OF ISRAEL (2 KINGS 17)

Second Kings 17 concerns the fall of Israel. The narrative eases into the subject by reporting, as expected, the chronologically appropriate Israelite king's reign—in this case, that of Hoshea. That event is recounted with noticeable brevity (vv. 3–6); the author's greater concern is what follows: an extensive theological reflection and explanation for Israel's exile (vv. 7–23) and, in the light of that theologizing, a further illustration of and commentary on the new inhabitants of the land (vv. 24–41).

Second Kings 17:1–6 presents the reign of Hoshea, the chief feature of which was the fall of Samaria. Though Hoshea merits recognition as having done less evil than the Israelite kings before him (v. 2), the faint praise is not enough to further delay the inevitable destruction of the Northern Kingdom. Divine retribution is immediately suggested by the unusual word order that follows: "*Against him* [עָלָיו] came Shalmaneser king of Assyria ..." (v. 3). Assyria is a familiar figure to the reader of Kings by now—the empire has been depicted as both an awesome and undefeatable force, yet also as a distant "other" often used in the narrator's wider purview of history as a test or punishment upon a YHWH-displeasing king. Thus, the appearance of an Assyrian king, now in the form of Shalmaneser, is not entirely surprising to the reader and anticipates difficulties soon ahead. The common translations often render ... וישב ... הושע ויהי־לו (v. 3b) with the simple past ("Hoshea became ... and paid ... ," JPS, NASB, NRSV; similarly, NEB and TEV/GNB), though NIV translates with a pluperfect sense: "who had been ... and had paid." The latter translation appears supported by Hoshea's apparent alliance with Shalmaneser's immediate predecessor Tiglath-Pileser III (in 15:30) and the witness of Tiglath-Pileser III's records,[126] though it is equally possible that Hoshea changed and/or renewed his alliances more than once in ways consonant with the former rendering. Either way, Hoshea's later relations with So king of Egypt and his withholding of

---

126. See *COS* 2:288, 291//*ANET*, 282.

the usual annual tribute are eventually found out by Assyria and identified as "rebellious conspiracy" (קשר), bringing Hoshea into imprisonment and his kingdom under attack by the king of Assyria.

The perspective in v. 4 seems to be as if the narrator is looking alongside Shalmaneser as he "discovered ... in Hoshea conspiracy" and registered the Israelite king's failure to deliver tribute "as [he had] year by year."[127] At this point, the Assyrian king proceeds to take over Israel. Presentation follows content as Hoshea's name no longer figures in the narrative (apart from a fairly incidental chronological reference in v. 6a, see below), and the king of Assyria features as the sole subject in the remainder of the passage. Forceful verbs of conquest describe Shalmaneser. After Hoshea's last active appearance in v. 4a, the king of Assyria follows with eight verbs reflective of an insuperable imperial power: "arrested/restrained," "imprisoned," "went up" (i.e., invaded; 2x), "besieged," "captured,"[128] "took into exile," and "made settle." By contrast, Hoshea's actions in vv. 1–4a are relatively passive and "small": "he became king," "he did evil ... but not like the kings of Israel before him," "he was (a servant/vassal)," "he paid," "he sent (messengers)," "he did not bring." Shalmaneser's imprisonment of Hoshea is depicted as happening easily enough. In one verse, without word of protest or resistance, the Israelite king is restrained by the Assyrian king (v. 4). The fortress of Samaria proves a greater challenge by holding out for three years (v. 5), but the Assyrian forces persist and the king of Assyria reciprocates the resistance with the predictable next step for dealing with difficult territories: exile (v. 6). The northern kingdom now disappears into the land of Assyria and Media. The last explicit mention of Assyria (אשור) is not in the construct form with "king," as it has been for all previous occurrences in these verses. The reference is instead to the land itself (marked with a *he locale*), the new settlements of which are then detailed, bringing a sense of immediate tangibility to the account.[129]

Throughout vv. 1–6, Hoshea is title-less, like Ahaz in the preceding narrative. Moreover, Hoshea is named four times, while "the king of Assyria" appears six times in these verses, the literary appearance of the relatively powerless Israelite puppet king being outnumbered and effectively

---

127. The narrator's sympathy with Shalmaneser's perspective is pointed out by Cohn, *2 Kings*, 117.

128. Lest one miss the intensity of this verb, other translations for לכד would be "seized, caught." Probably originally used to describe the capture of wild animals, "it is not surprising that at an early stage the original meaning of *lkd* was transferred to the capture of human beings in war, the common elements being the use of force and the deprivation of freedom" (H. Gross, "לכד," in *TDOT* 8:1–4, see 1–2).

129. Cohn, *2 Kings*, 117, reaches a similar conclusion.

overwhelmed by the imperial might of "the king of Assyria."[130] Also to note, the Egyptian king's one passive appearance is still identified with his title. As Cohn puts it, "Both Assyrian and Egyptian kings are called by name and title, while title-less Hoshea appears as an object tossed about between the two greater monarchs."[131] The heavy concentration on Shalmaneser's title in place of his name in this short passage concerning the fall of Samaria and effective end of the Northern Kingdom works to associate this negative development with the Assyrian king, even more than with Hoshea. Further, the absence of the personal name for the Assyrian king may reflect an attempt to avoid identifying two separate Assyrian kings associated with the event (i.e., Shalmaneser and Sargon II) and thus the author builds one simpler, "composite" character in the abstract persona of "the king of Assyria."[132] This may not be immediately evident in the NIV and GNB/TEV because those translations interpretively "supply" proper names in places where the Hebrew text does not. The NIV adds "Shalmaneser" to vv. 3b, 4c; the GNB/TEV adds the same to vv. 3b, 4b, 5; NRSV, NEB, JPS, NASB, NKJV, and NJB do not supply additional instances of "Shalmaneser." Thus, in the MT, the author not only telescopes events, but telescopes characters as well in this subunit. Whatever distinguishes Shalmaneser and Sargon II is ignored in the Kings characterization, which fuses the two under "the king of Assyria."

Perhaps contributing to the sense of distance in chapter 17's use of "the king of Assyria" is the same phrase's de-personified use in the latter part of chapter 16. A single occurrence of "the king of Assyria" appears in the second part of the Ahaz narrative (16:18), where it is fairly distant—especially due to the intervening narrative concerning the altar and other cultic alterations—from the earlier content associating the title "the king of Assyria" with Tiglath-Pileser III and his specific actions and circumstances. One may apply to 16:18; 17:4 [2x], 5, 6, 24, 26, 27 the interpretation of Revell regarding 19:4: "The designation 'the king of Assyria' is used to represent a threat (as in 19:4). It distances the individual."[133] At the same time, the

---

130. A similar technique may be seen in earlier passages, such as the Ahaz story (e.g., 16:7–8; possibly also 16:5, though the titles of the Aramean and Israelite kings may have been included simply to distinguish their political roles in a verse discussing three kings).

131. Cohn, 2 *Kings*, 117.

132. For further discussion of the historical circumstances regarding the fall of Samaria, see K. Lawson Younger, "The Fall of Samaria in Light of Recent Research," *CBQ* 61 (1999) 461–82; John H. Hayes and Jeffrey K. Kuan, "The Final Years of Samaria (730–720 BC)," *Bib* 72 (1991) 153–81; Nadav Na'aman, "Historical Background," 76–93. Most scholars agree that both Shalmaneser and Sargon II were involved with the event at least to a minimal degree (with Sargon II crediting Shalmaneser's victory to himself).

133. E. J. Revell, *The Designation of the Individual: Expressive Usage in Biblical*

overall depiction of "the king of Assyria" in chapter 16 affords a striking contrast with that of 17:3–6. In 2 Kings 16, "the king of Assyria" is generally depicted as an idolatrous (albeit passively), influential power, substituting for YHWH as Ahaz's overlord. By contrast, "the king of Assyria" in 17:3–6 is less a passive, spiritual-religious threat,[134] and more an active, political one. This is probably due in part to Hoshea's attitude towards the Assyrian king. The Israelite king does not yield to the temptation to make Assyria its lord as Ahaz had done. Yet still, Assyria proves to be a merciless power in other ways, as its emperor seizes Hoshea and sacks the Israelite capital. "The king of Assyria" initiates the relationship between himself and Hoshea (be it peaceful or hostile), and his actions are confident, aggressive, and sweeping (as one may expect of a colonizing superpower). As a result, the Assyrian king takes on a greater share of the responsibility for events in 17:3–6 than was done in chapter 16. The issue of responsibility is still to be settled and explained in the remainder of chapter 17, but for the moment, the role of Assyria is noticeably more prominent here than in chapter 16.

Before moving on to the next subunit, a remark on the rather unexpected mention of Hoshea in v. 6 is apropos. The dismal end of Hoshea's reign does not receive a concluding formula, and this chronological reference marks the closure, albeit anomalous and tragic, of his reign. That said, possibly this mention of Hoshea and the placement of the Assyrian king's actions in relation to the reign of Hoshea (and not vice-versa) are the author's way of affirming greater significance to Israelite history, as compared with Assyrian history. Despite the failure of the Israelite kings and the kingdom's downfall, the history of the people of God is still the main concern of the narrative.

Verses 7–23 elaborate on the ideological reason behind the final fall and exile of the northern kingdom. Basically a theological reflection, this passage telescopes time and circumstances to include Judah in its condemnation of apostate behavior (explicitly in v. 13; implicitly in vv. 9–10, 17, in that such combinations and references have thus far only appeared in regard to Judah; cf. 1 Kgs 14:23; 2 Kgs 16:4, possibly 16:15).[135] After detailing the sins of Israel and Judah in vv. 7–17, the narrative continues with YHWH's response in vv. 18–23.[136] It is here, in the punitive response of YHWH, that

---

Narrative, CBET (Kampen: Kok Pharos, 1996), 151.

134. To Judah, that is; Assyria was a political threat to Judah's enemies, of course.

135. See Provan, *1 and 2 Kings*, 248–49, for further discussion of the significance of these links between 2 Kgs 17 and the accounts of the beginning of the divided monarchy and Ahaz's reign.

136. In addition to content, these verses concerning YHWH's response to Israel's (and Judah's) apostasy are demarcated by the shared occurrences of the combination

the Assyrians make a minor appearance. With respect to the fate of both kingdoms—though the key phrase is ambiguous (בכל־זרע ישראל), the context seems to imply north and south (see v. 20) —the narrative mentions "plunderers" (שסים), which is probably a general reference to all the nations that attacked and benefited from Israel's resources. Assyria would certainly be understood as included among the "plunderers," who function instrumentally under the purposes of YHWH to discipline his people through affliction. The narrative focus returns to the northern kingdom alone in vv. 21–23. The final statement on YHWH's response to the northern kingdom is that "Israel went into exile from their land to Assyria, [as it is] to this day" (v. 23b). Assyria's appearance here is merely incidental to the greater and decisive action of YHWH in determining to remove Israel from his presence (v. 23a), and thus in this expanded theological explanation for Israel's demise (vv. 7–23), Assyria's role is minimized. Assyria is characterized primarily by what it is not—it is a vast and other land that distinctly does *not* include Israel's territory/homeland. It is the land of Israel's exile, and, in having such a role in Israel's history, Assyria—in all its otherness apart from Israel—provides a tangible and enduring reflection of YHWH's judgment upon Israel.[137] Assyria is not credited with any action in this passage; it is simply a locale to which Israel is exiled. As Cohn observes, "the agent of destruction is not the king of Assyria, but YHWH."[138] That said, it is often observed that the phraseology and basic content of v. 23b seem to refer back to v. 6.[139] I hesitate to identify the resemblance as a repetition on

---

יהוה as subject + ישראל as object + root סור + מעל פניו in the beginning and ending verses of the unit (vv. 18, 23).

137. Consider Brevard S. Childs, "A Study of the Formula, 'Until This Day,'" *JBL* 82 (1963) 279–92 (292; cf. 287).

138. Cohn, *2 Kings*, 120.

139. E.g., ibid., 120; Jones, *1 and 2 Kings*, 2:552; Cogan and Tadmor, *2 Kings*, 207; Long, *2 Kings*, 184–85.

This is, of course, in contrast to the Assyrian emperors' usual claims through written and visual representation of powerful and merciless conquests, plundering, and subjugation of other nations and peoples—including the Israelites, in this particular case. Occasionally in these texts Aššur is credited, and arguably usually Aššur is implied to be the empowering agent of conquest for the emperor in a simplistically-depicted relationship between the head Assyrian god and the Assyrian emperor. That said, the majority of these texts credit the conquest and oppressive aftermath of Israel explicitly and predominantly to Sargon II (quite possibly to defend or raise his status towards divinity). See the Royal Inscriptions of Sargon II, *COS* 2:293–94; the Great "Summary" Inscription, *COS* 2:296–97; the Small "Summary" Inscription, *COS* 2:297; Pavement Inscription 4, *COS* 2:298; the Cylinder Inscription, *COS* 2:298; and especially Nimrud Prisms D and E, *COS* 2: 295–96 (in which Sargon II credits himself with glorifying Aššur by his own actions). For visual examples, see the Black Obelisk and the Lachish Reliefs.

the level of *Wiederaufnahme* (resumptive repetition), because the phrases are not exactly the same, though neither are they distinctive in vocabulary. Still, a connection may be perceived that functions both to signal the end of the expanded explanation for the northern kingdom's fall and to indicate a relation between vv. 3–6 and vv. 7–23. Regarding the latter, it is as if the immediate, on-the-ground reality of the Assyrian king's victory over Samaria is shown to co-exist with the larger, less-apparent reality of YHWH's punishment of Israel for a long history of apostasy. In the former, Assyria figures prominently; in the latter, hardly at all.

If Goldstein's attractive theory is correct that vv. 7–9 include linguistic and phrasal Assyrianisms, resulting in a source that "appear[s] to reflect a theological response to an official Assyrian explanation of the kingdom's downfall,"[140] then this could support that at least part of vv. 7–23 was indeed initially composed to indirectly counter and minimize the imperial presence and impact. To add another layer to Goldstein's attractive theory that the early stratum in 2 Kgs 17 was to counter an Assyrian presumption that the Israelite fall was due to the disloyalty of its king to the Assyrian emperor,[141] it is equally, if not more plausible that vv. 7–9 were initially composed as an ideological response intentionally undermining a typically hyperbolic, braggadocian Assyrian explanation for the fall of Samaria. And then, returning to Goldstein's hypothesis, a later redactor during the Persian era recognizing the significance of the passage for that generation may have reworked the passage to reflect the event's application to their time.[142]

The narrative continues with an account of the new settlers in the land of Samaria (vv. 24–33) and ideological reflection upon this development (vv. 34–41). As Long points out, vv. 24–41 are "a structural and functional twin" of vv. 3–23.[143] Instead of concerning the Israelites, however, the passage is about the immigrants transferred by the Assyrians into the Israelites' former land. The passage illustrates that the land, now depleted of the Israelites, still belongs to YHWH in a special way and that the covenant YHWH made concerning its inhabitants is still operative and binding, apparently regardless of the origins of the new residents. The Assyrian presence is dominant in the first section, which is about the new immigrants brought by Assyria, and is relegated to the background of the second section, which focuses on YHWH's standards for the new people in his land.

---

140. See Ronnie Goldstein, "A Suggestion Regarding the Meaning of 2 Kings 17:9 and the Composition of 2 Kings 17:7–23," *VT* 63 (2013) 393–407, esp. 405; the Royal Inscriptions of Sargon II, 293a; and the Nimrud Prisms D and E, 295b.

141. Cf. ibid., 405.

142. Ibid., 406–7.

143. Long, *2 Kings*, 186.

The opening verses of the subunit depict the perspective of the king of Assyria. Though YHWH's power is recognized in v. 25, and vv. 24–33 are to be read in the light of vv. 7–23 (which, as we saw above, emphasize YHWH's control over historical agents), the king of Assyria is the primary actor in vv. 24–28. It is the king of Assyria who initiates the major events of settling people from throughout the Assyrian empire in the land of Samaria (v. 24), who is informed of the religious ignorance of his settlers and the resultant lion killings by "the god(s) of the land" (v. 26), and who responds by commanding that an Israelite priest be returned to Samaria to teach the people (vv. 27–28). Apart from YHWH, who is the primary character to whom the Assyrian king responds, and the lions, who are clearly depicted as the especial agents of YHWH's judgment in v. 25,[144] everyone else in vv. 24–28 carries out the intents of the king of Assyria. The king of Assyria relocates diverse and foreign peoples, and they settle. He orders for a priest to return, and his officers evidently obey, as does the priest. Hence, the narrative shows that the king of Assyria wields a tremendous degree of power in typical imperial colonialist fashion over his jurisdiction of people, conquered nations, and officers—this much comports with the literary and visual image that the Assyrian empire has forwarded of itself in its own literature and monumental and building ornamentation. However, in the Kings account, when the issue concerns the land, the lions, and the unidentified god(s) who was acknowledged to rule these things, the powerful Assyrian concedes without resistance. For whatever reasons, the Assyrian king shows a respect for YHWH and his law that, ironically, the Israelites themselves did not demonstrate.[145] The overall depiction of the king of Assyria is that of a very competent and effective imperial leader in command of his people throughout the expanse of his empire. At the same time, note that proper Assyrian land does not necessarily include the land of Israel in the eyes of the narrator (cf. v. 23). The Assyrian king evidences adequate humility to recognize

---

144. Cohn, *2 Kings*, 120, and Cogan and Tadmor, *2 Kings*, 210–11, point out that lions in Kings involve the northern kingdom and for the purpose of "mak[ing] his presence known" (Cohn); see 1 Kgs 13:24–32; 20:35–36. Incidentally, both these instances (but *not* here in 2 Kgs 17:25) involve Israelite prophets who did not obey the command of YHWH and who received lethal punishment foretold by another prophet.

145. For an Assyrian analogue to v. 27, see Shalom M. Paul, "Sargon's Administrative Diction in 2 Kings 17:27," *JBL* 88 (1969) 73–74.

Naturally, the propagandistic, hyperbolic rhetoric of Sargon II's imperial reign does not reflect a respect for or even recognition of YHWH, let alone a humble concession to Him. (Note that Nimrud Prisms D and E, 295, may or may not include YHWH—cf. 2 Kgs 17:7–8.) It is difficult to know beyond the Assyrian propaganda whether or not an Assyrian king or governor would have in actuality made such concessions, but one may say that at least in their visual and literary representations of themselves, the Assyrians did not yield or concede to any peoplegroup or foreign gods.

this and to attempt to diplomatically assuage the supernatural power that he acknowledges as over the Israelite land. An explicit moral-theological evaluation of the king of Assyria is not given in this passage, but the implicit depiction of him seems mildly positive in that he responds to the warning from YHWH—in contrast to the Israelites, who did not, according to v. 14. Though the displacement of Israelites from their homeland would normally be considered a negative act, the preceding context (vv. 18–23) places the act of removal in a positive light insofar as it follows the will of YHWH. That said, the Assyrian king's limitations may also be shown in that he apparently does not recognize YHWH's name, nor does he seem to understand that the God of Israel is more than an indigenous phenomenon. At the same time, the Assyrian king may be slightly credited in this characterization in vv. 24–28 in that he respected YHWH even though he did not know YHWH's name, and thus chose to respect a god who was mysterious and uncontrollable to him.

The king of Assyria remains unnamed throughout the entire narrative, and thus is denied the strength of characterization that would have resulted from identification with a personal name. Historically-speaking, the Assyrian king referred to in vv. 24–27 was Sargon II, yet the author evades this fact. Possibly, he wanted to limit the memorability of this most-positively-depicted Assyrian king (of those depicted in the Book of Kings). Another possibility is that he did not want the historical details of the actual and popularly-known Sargon II to interfere with his portraiture of "the king of Assyria" in vv. 24–27. This latter characterization technique was similarly used by the author in vv. 3–6 in blurring the historical details of Shalmaneser and Sargon II to subsume their major actions under the persona of only "Shalmaneser"/"the king of Assyria." This leads to yet another possibility, that "the king of Assyria" in chapter 17 equates only with Sargon II, who is never named in the historical books.[146] This is not likely, however, since "the king of Assyria" is used elsewhere in Kings to refer to Assyrian kings other than Sargon II.

The Assyrian characterization includes not only the king of Assyria (i.e., the empire's chief representative) but also the new settlers deported from other areas of the empire and the "they" who report to the Assyrian king in v. 26 and who are given orders by the king in v. 27. The immigrants are given general descriptions that are no more particularized than their hometown and no more detailed than their usual religious activities. The only specific events concerning the people are their immigration to the

---

146. Montgomery, *Books of Kings*, 466, might be hinting in this direction. Montgomery also observes Sargon is named only once in the entire biblical record: Isa 20:1.

land, the punitive killings by the lions, and the sending of and teaching by the priest at Bethel. Thus, their characterization is done with broad brushstrokes telescoping a wide range of ethnic backgrounds and a considerable span of time. This is not so much in the interest of a colonial minimization, but rather a narratological one at the service of emphasis on the theological explanation for the new circumstances in Samaria.

The new settlers come from peripheral and important (but not core) areas of the empire. Those from Cuthah and Babylon may be expected to be more distinctly "Assyrian" (but still not as Assyrian as if from Assyria proper) than those from Hamath, which was in Syria. Avva and Sepharvaim are more difficult to locate.[147] All these cities were apparently conquered areas that became part of the empire, none of which were in Assyria proper. Hence, the new settlers are presented as Assyrian citizens, but Assyrian citizens ranking fairly low on the range of imperial social strata since they are conquered peoples forced by the government to uproot and resettle as ordered. This gives the new settlers a sort-of hybridity, though the religion and culture that they adopt and adapt are not that of the metropolitan, but of another conquered people group—we could perhaps term this as a two-way hybridity (since classic hybridity is one-way). That said, the text is not concerned with exploring the phenomenon of types of hybridity so much as it is focused on the new settlers' relationship with God, and in that approach the narrative notes that their first action independent of Assyrian command is to *not* worship YHWH. The reader is not given a chance to question the moral-religious quality of this action, for the narrator immediately follows the Assyrians' action with God's punitive response of lions killing among the settlers. The severity of the punishment suggests the severity of the crime. A priest is sent to the new inhabitants and settles in Bethel. Coggins and Cohn indicate that the choice of home suggests a lack of integrity towards the Yahwistic cultus on the part of the priest (cf. 1 Kgs 12:28–13:32).[148]

---

147. Jones, *1 and 2 Kings*, vol. 2, 553, lists as proposals for Avva: Ivvah in Syria (cf. 18:34), Imm, Amnia, Tell Kefr 'Aya, and 'Ama (Cogan and Tadmor, *2 Kings*, 212, support this latter possibility, which is Elamite). Sepharvaim is usually associated with 1) the two quarters of the Babylonian city on the Euphrates, Sippar, 2) Sibraim (Syria; Ezek 47:16), or 3) Sabara'im (Syria) of Shalmaneser's Babylonian Chronicle. For further discussion, see Hobbs, *2 Kings*, 237; Jones, *1 and 2 Kings*, 553; Cogan and Tadmor, *2 Kings*, 212; and Robert William Rogers, *Cuneiform Parallels to the Old Testament*, 2nd ed. (New York: Abingdon, 1926), 210.

148. R. J. Coggins, "The Old Testament and Samaritan Origins," *Annual of the Swedish Theological Institute* 6, eds. Gillis Gerleman, Gösta Lindeskog, H. S. Nyberg, and Hans Kosmala (Leiden: Brill, 1968), 35–48 (38–39, 41), perceives a stronger anti-Bethel–cultus polemic: "whatever its historical worth, the implication of the passage is surely that the form of cultus associated with Bethel is a very debased one" (38); "the very deep-rooted tradition in Judah . . . entertained a peculiar suspicion of Bethel" (41).

Indeed, if the sole teacher of the people prefers a hometown with such a sullied and condemned religious history, the teaching the people receive may be expected to be lacking in vital areas. That said, relative to the rest of the northern kingdom, Bethel is the natural choice, so perhaps the choice of Bethel (as opposed to other Israelite options) is not significant. It seems more likely, however, that the explicit mention of Bethel in the narrative is indeed to evoke through the name of that representative city the condemnable acts of the northern kingdom.

Thus, it is not entirely surprising that the first thing the people are reported doing after receiving the priest's instruction on how to worship YHWH is yet again to not worship YHWH, but instead to make their own gods. Though YHWH already dwells in the land, the people work to make foreign gods (vv. 29–30), the frequent use of עשה and the simple, repetitive phraseology "[god] עשו את־ [place] ואנשי" emphasizing the human construction of the people's "gods." This mix of peoples incorporated into the Assyrian empire brings and creates a mixed, syncretistic religion to the land of Samaria. Though they fulfill the key theme of "worshipping/fearing YHWH" (vv. 32, 33, 41; cf. vv. 25, 28, 34, 35, 36, 37, 38, 39), they counter that action every time: " . . . and appointed [עשים] for themselves from among all sorts of people priests of the high places, and they [i.e., the priests] were officiating for them at the shrines of the high places" (v. 32); " . . . but their gods they were serving" (v. 33); " . . . but their idols they served" (v. 41). The peoples' syncretism persists through generations to the narratival present (v. 41), despite the clear and repeated command of YHWH (vv. 34–39).

Verses 34–41 telescope all generations from the early Assyrian settlers to their Palestine-inhabiting, present-day (in relation to the narrator) descendants. They are characterized together by little more than their syncretism, which is condemned by the narrator for its failure to fulfill the Yahwistic command for exclusivity. Even the immigrants' mixed backgrounds and the "re-portation" of the priest serve in the narrative to explain the syncretism. While foreign hometowns and gods help identify the empire's mixed people groups (vv. 24, 30–31), vv. 34–41 present a new perspective on these inhabitants: they are evaluated by the same standards as the Israelites they displaced, as subject to the standards of YHWH's covenant.[149] In this

---

See also Cohn, 2 Kings, 121.

149. Agreeing with Cohn, 2 Kings, 122; Long, 2 Kings, 187; and Walter Brueggemann, 1 and 2 Kings, Smyth and Helwys (Macon, GA: Smyth & Helwys, 2000), 485. Also, Gray, 1 and 2 Kings, 655, and Montgomery, Books of Kings, 477, interpret vv. 34–40 as referring to the settlers (Montgomery and Gehman nuance that the subunit originally concerned "the imported heathen," but later was understood to mean the "Samaritans"). Cogan and Tadmor, 2 Kings, 213–14, however, insist that the phrase in

way, the inhabitants' "otherness" and foreign identities begin to fade. Hobbs suggests that vv. 29–32 (and, apparently, v. 34) reflect a temporal process, which may be the case, just as vv. 7–21 were primarily summarizing, while also broadly chronological.[150] Either way, by v. 40, it is no longer the inhabitants' foreign background or compromised education that accounts for their syncretism, but a deeper characteristic that recalls the apostasy of the Israelites (vv. 14–17): "they would not listen" (ולא שמעו).[151] The use of this phrase at the beginning of vv. 14 and 40, in addition to the similarity in religious practices described in vv. 14–17 and vv. 29–34, suggests a correspondence.[152] In this way, the Assyrian settlers are shown to be no better in authentic and exclusive worship of YHWH than were the former Israelite inhabitants they replaced. As Provan concludes, "What is clear by the end of the chapter . . . is that the exile of Israel has not led to any improvement in the religion of the people who dwell in the land. . . . Nothing has changed."[153]

The depiction of the Assyrian settlers in chapter 17 therefore does not function as a foil for the displaced Israelites, as one might have expected, but rather as something of a confirmation of the universal failure of human societies to be devoted and faithful to YHWH. The constant focus in vv. 24–41 on the inhabitants' religious practices basically follows and explains the origins of the Samaritans and of their current (at least, from the perspective of the narrator) syncretism. Though the identity of the new settlers began with a relatively strong association with Assyria, as the narrator proceeds to describe their religious observances, the new inhabitants of Samaria are evaluated not by the standard or ways of anything Assyrian, Babylonian, Cuthite, or Avvite, but by the standard of YHWH's people, Israel. Thus, the new inhabitants undergo a curious shift in association from belonging to Assyria and "pagan," foreign lands to effectively being invited to share in belonging to YHWH and his "indigenous" covenant. This subplot ends

---

v. 34 is a *Wiederaufnahme* of the same phrase in v. 23. Thus, Cogan and Tadmor argue, the subunit of vv. 34–40 refers to the Israelites, *not* the new settlers nor the Samarians; furthermore, vv. 24–40 are pre-exilic, Josianic polemic. Long, *2 Kings*, 181, identifies Cogan and Tadmor's argument as unique.

150. Hobbs, *2 Kings*, 239.

151. Focusing more on source critical issues, Gray, *1 and 2 Kings*, 656, similarly understands that: "Unlike the first Deuteronomist, the compiler, the author of this section does not animadvert on the defection to the sins of Jeroboam or to any particular sin except worshipping other gods in defiance of the law of God."

152. Brueggemann, *1 and 2 Kings*, 485, makes a like observation regarding vv. 14 and 40, and Long, *2 Kings*, 188–89, perceives the connection between vv. 13 and 15 and vv. 34b–40.

153. Provan, *1 and 2 Kings*, 251.

negatively, however, in that the new settlers basically repeat the faithlessness of the Israelites they supplanted (vv. 14, 40).

The third party to comprise the Assyrian characterization is the "they" of v. 26 who are, implicitly, the indirect object of the king's command in v. 27. The 'they' are not attributed specific characteristics, and thus they remain agents, functioning instrumentally between the more dominant and actualized characters of the Assyrian settlers, the Assyrian king, and the priest. Most likely, the "they" are people who would have been in a position to act between the king and his people, intermediaries who serve the empire and extend its interests at an intimate level to the far reaches of its conquered lands. Hence, I agree with Cohn that "the informers are meant to be Assyrian officials."[154] These apparent Assyrian officials express a paradigm that does not acknowledge YHWH as the only God, but that does identify him as a national god who holds power over the land of Samaria. Their paradigm evidences an understanding that "the god of the land" has standards that he requires to be kept. Just as the Assyrian officials do not know what distinguishes YHWH from all other gods, so they do not know his requirements. They display a wisdom consonant with the general perspective of the aNE. Such wisdom is a step towards knowing the true God: in this case, it results in the sending back of the priest to teach the ways of YHWH. However, the Assyrian officials' syncretistic attitude is shared by the rest of the Assyrians in the chapter, and as a result of such an attitude, the new inhabitants' understanding and worship of YHWH are compromised. It is in this prevalent attitude of syncretism and limited respect for "the god of the land" that the three parties comprising the Assyrian characterization are most related.

In considering the overall treatment of the Assyrian exile in Kings, one may observe a contrast between the inclusion of a lengthy, theological-parenetic explanation for the Assyrian exile and the absence of such regarding the Babylonian exile.[155] This contrast may be instructive. As Cross remarks:

> When we examine the Exilic editor's account of the fall of Jerusalem and the captivity of Judah, we find that the story is told laconically. There is no peroration on the fall of Jerusalem, much less an elaborate one like that upon the destruction of Samaria. The events are recorded without comment, without theological reflection. This is remarkable, given the Deuteronomist's penchant for composing final addresses, edifying prayers,

---

154. Cohn, *2 Kings*, 121.

155. On the parenetic nature of 2 Kgs 17, see Pauline A. Viviano, "2 Kings 17: A Rhetorical and Form-Critical Analysis," *CBQ* 49 (1987) 548–59, esp. 557–59. We should note that Viviano understands the whole of chapter 17 to be parenetic, but this author would further qualify vv. 7–23, 29–41 as especially sermonic.

and theological exhortations on significant events.... It must be said that the Deuteronomistic historian never tires of repetition of his themes and clichés and is fond of bracketing events and periods with an explicit theological framework.[156]

The difference has been observed by several other scholars, who usually follow Cross in asserting that the primary edition of the Deuteronomistic history was by a Josianic editor (Dtr[1]), followed by a reworked edition by a later Exilic Deuteronomist (Dtr[2]). The first was responsible for the majority of the work and a generally optimistic tone highlighting the promise of the Davidic line; the second revised the work through, perhaps, a more jaded vision reflecting the pessimism of his times. The relatively minor extent of Dtr[2]'s editorial activity, his general reticence, and his pessimistic perspective have all been forwarded as possible explanations for the unusual lack of theological explanation for the Babylonian exile.[157] Burney takes notice of Stade's suggestion that vv. 7–17 were an exilic addition, partly on the basis of v. 16 referring to Assyrian astral worship, an activity of the Southern Kingdom under Manasseh (i.e., 21:3). For redaction-critical reasons, Burney rejects this hypothesis; one may further disregard its applicability due to more recent understandings of Assyrian religion—astral worship is more characteristic of Canaanite religion than Mesopotamian.[158]

Viviano concludes at the end of her rhetorical and form-critical analysis that the deuteronomistic historian, by means of 2 Kgs 17, "speaks *of* Israel *to* Judah. Israel's experience, couched in terms applicable to Judah, serves the Deuteronomist in his concern for Judah's future" [emphasis

---

156. Cross, *Canaanite Myth*, 288.

157. See Cogan and Tadmor, *2 Kings*, 324; and Gray, *1 and 2 Kings*, 39–41. Wiseman, *1 and 2 Kings*, 312, seems to imply that an extensive theological comment regarding the Babylonian exile was simply unnecessary for the Kings author's emphases:

> The absence of theological comment (as in the other accounts) may be explained in part by the selection of items to lead to the conclusion that "Judah went into exile away from the land" (25:21), thus fulfilling the prophecy last reiterated in Josiah's reign (23:27) that the evil done since the time of Manasseh would result in exile.

See also Martin Noth, *The Deuteronomistic History*, JSOTSup 15 (Sheffield: JSOT Press, 1981), 97–99; Richard Elliott Friedman, *The Exile and Biblical Narrative: The Formation of the Deuteronomistic and Priestly Works*, HSM 22 (Chico, CA: Scholars, 1981), 32–34; and Jon D. Levenson, "The Last Four Verses in Kings," *JBL* 103 (1984) 353–61 (353–56, 361). Provan, *1 and 2 Kings*, 280–81, begins his concluding comments to 25:27–30 by stating: "Yet it is difficult to believe that this is all there is to it," but then he elucidates further significance implied in the final verses. Still, Provan's reading does not compare to the substantiveness in chapter 17.

158. See, e.g., Cogan and Tadmor, *2 Kings*, 266. Burney, *Notes on the Hebrew Text*, 331.

hers].[159] If we adopt Cross' theory, then Viviano's conclusion makes perfect sense. Judah still had a future, in the eyes of the Josianic Dtr[1]. Assyrian activity in the land was not the "final straw" for God's people in the same way that Babylonian activity came to be by the end of the monarchy. The Exilic Deuteronomist, respectful of Dtr[1]'s work, did not significantly alter Dtr[1]'s parenesis to the Josianic audience. However, the Babylonian exile did not afford the same hope of avoiding an exile as the earlier Assyrian exile had. Hence, the Assyrian exile and related subsequent activity in the land provided a more timely object lesson during the composition of the work.

The theological-parenetic nature of chapter 17, in contrast to chapter 25, perhaps explains the unusual frequency of גלה in the former. גלה is used in the OT with two distinct meanings: 1) "to uncover, reveal," and 2) "to be/go away (into exile)." The second definition is operative in Kings and, specifically, chapter 17. It occurs 15 times in 2 Kings and (hardly surprisingly) not at all in 1 Kings.[160] Seven of the Kings occurrences occur in chapter 17 (vv. 6, 11, 23, 26, 27, 28, 33), and the occurrence in 18:11 refers back to the events of the final exile of the northern kingdom. Two more instances refer to previous exiles conducted by Assyria. The remaining five concern the Babylonian exile (24:14 [2x], 15; 25:11, 21). At first blush one may expect this dominant term for exile to occur more in relation to the Babylonian exile,[161] which was more recent and probably had a more immediate impression on the final biblical redactor. Perhaps the vocabulary of exile is emphasized in chapter 17 and other Kings passages regarding the Assyrians' exiling activities because those exiles proved to be permanent, whereas at least a partial return of the Babylonian exiles was expected (Jer 29:10). Most defendable, given the above discussion of the difference between Kings' treatment of the Assyrian and Babylonian exiles, is that גלה occurs more often with regard to Assyrian activity because the Assyrian exile was further exposited upon by the Kings contributors and better served as a warning to then-un-exiled Judah. Thus, the repeated occurrences of גלה express an emphatic warning—גלה is the key event and activity the Josianic reader should take care to avoid.

---

159. Viviano, "2 Kings 17," 559.

160. The greatest number of occurrences of the verb גלה with the meaning "to be/go away into exile" are in Kings (12x) and Jeremiah (13x). David M. Howard, Jr., "גלה," in *NIDOTTE* 1:861–64 (862).

161. גלה in the sense of "to be/go away into exile" appears to be the dominant term for exile in "Deuteronomistic diction," but not in Deuteronomy itself. See C. Westermann and R. Albertz, "גלה," in *TLOT* 1:314–20 (316), and Bruce K. Waltke, "גלה," in *TWOT* 1:160–61 (161). Also, on the primacy of גלה as a term for exile, see Howard, "גלה," 862.

On a different note, not-so-frequent vocabulary for chapter 17 is the *hapax legomenon* חפא, a verb of uncertain etymology and rendering. Until recently, the main explanations in scholarship appealed to (in some cases, supposed) Akkadian cognates. If חפא is indeed directly related to Akkadian, we might have an example of an ethnoflect,[162] evoking a sense of foreignness and, by association, what is non-Israelite and forbidden. Driver, relying on Scheil, defends the meaning, "to say, utter," for חפא, and numerous scholars have adopted this conclusion ever since.[163] As Cogan and Tadmor, followed by Dray, point out, however, Scheil's supposed *hapu* was later corrected to *hawu*, which means "growling" and thus fits neither the etymology nor context of 17:9.[164] Haupt suggests a relation to Akkadian *xepu*; thus, "to act abominably,"[165] which Dray evaluates as "seem[ing] to be an attempt to produce a rendering that fits the context and [that] appears to be unique to him."[166] Hobbs concedes that "the popular rendering of 'to utter' for the root is attractive," but "this is no guarantee of its accuracy. It must be established that there was a conscious (i.e., consistent) borrowing of such a word and meaning from the Akkadian. Evidence is lacking."[167] Moreover, Becking surveys the Semitic use of *hp'* and its probable parallel root, *hb'*, and concludes that 1) חפא, like חבא, probably has the meaning "to hide, conceal," and 2) regarding the [difficult] combination חפא + דברים, "Misschien, dat de MT het beste vertaald kan worden met: 'de Israëlieten verborgen zich in/achter dingen' of 'zij deden verborgen (nl. heimelijke) dingen.'" [Prob-

---

162. The terminology of Kaufman and Rendsburg would be "style-switching" or "addressee-switching" (*à la* broader sociolinguistic "code-switching"), respectively. For further discussion, see Benjamin Bailey, "Switching," in *Key Terms in Language and Culture*, ed. Alessandro Duranti (Malden, MA: Blackwell, 2001), 238–40; Gary A. Rendsburg, "Morphological Evidence for Regional Dialects in Ancient Hebrew," in *Linguistics and Biblical Hebrew*, ed. Walter R. Bodine (Winona Lake, IN: Eisenbrauns, 1992), 65–88 (69); idem, "Linguistic Variation and the 'Foreign' Factor in the Hebrew Bible," in *Israel Oriental Studies 15: Language and Culture in the Near East*, eds. Shlomo Izre'el and Rina Drory (Leiden: Brill, 1995), 177–90 (179, 184). Though Kaufman and Rendsburg appear to have most recently studied such linguistic variations in-depth, the general phenomenon was suggested earlier for biblical literature; e.g., N. H. Tur-Sinai, *The Book of Job: A New Commentary* (Jerusalem: Kiryath Sepher, 1967), xxxi, and Eduard Yechezkel Kutscher, *A History of the Hebrew Language* (Leiden: Brill, 1982), 72–73.

163. See discussion in Carol A. Dray, *Translation and Interpretation in the Targum to the Books of Kings*, SAIS (Leiden: Brill, 2006), 182–86. Also, G. R. Driver, "The Modern Study of the Hebrew Language," in *The People and the Book: Essays on the Old Testament*, ed. Arthur S. Peake (Oxford: Clarendon, 1925), 73–120 (89).

164. Cogan and Tadmor, *2 Kings*, 205, and Dray, *Translation and Interpretation*, 184.

165. Paul Haupt's editorial comment in Stade and Schwally, *Books of Kings*, 262.

166. Dray, *Translation and Interpretation*, 184.

167. Hobbs, *2 Kings*, 232.

ably the MT could best be translated with "the Israelites hid themselves in/behind things" or "they did hidden (in particular, secret/private) things."]¹⁶⁸ Thus, while popular interpretations suggest that חפא in v. 9 is an "Assyrianism," which is an attractive hypothesis, the current state of evidence has not been able to support this explanation.

CONCLUSION

Thus, we have considered in this chapter both detailed and broader, merely hypothetical and demonstrably-provable, aspects of the characterization of the Assyrians in 2 Kgs 15–17.

Even before the Assyrians' explicit arrival in the world of the text, their brutality and violence is foreshadowed by their influencee and apparent vassal, Menahem, king of Israel. When Tiglath-Pileser III/Pul does arrive on the scene, he is immediately confrontative and oppressive. Meanwhile, in the account of Pekah's reign, Tiglath-Pileser III conducts even further-reaching conquests and oppression of Israel, but the narrative noticeably minimizes the report of this act, relegating Assyria to a position of instrument instead of supreme ruler. These accounts are succinct, but the selective use of dramatic vocabulary, the particular narratological perspective (POV) applied towards characters and events, the historical, social, cultural, and economic details reflected in circumstances described, and the levity of the events themselves deliver impact, profundity, and sometimes implicit moral-ideological evaluation to the narrative and the characters it features.

Narrative time suddenly slows down for 2 Kings 16 as the focus turns to Judahite king Ahaz, his international relations with Aram, Israel, and Assyria, and the political-religious outcome of Ahaz's decisions in the so-called Syro-Ephraimite War. In a manner similar to that of the account of Pekah's reign, Assyria's historically consequential acts are presented in such ways as to convey the nuances of its instrumental functions. On the one hand, Tiglath-Pileser III is depicted as an "alternative choice" (vs. YHWH) for Ahaz's loyalty, submission, and unjustly-intended "gift" (16:8). At the same time, the Assyrian presence in the narrative provides a contrast that elevates: 1) the initiative and responsibility of Ahaz in the displacement of Israelites and altering of YHWH's temple; and, with less dramatic intensity, but still with significant space devoted to it, 2) the longevity of Aram's influence on Israel and Judah. Notably in this chapter, the consistent use of

---

168. Bernhard Engelbert Jan Hendrik [Bob] Becking, *De ondergang van Samaria: Historische, exegetische en theologische opmerkingen bij II Koningen 17* (Meppel: Krips, 1985; ThD diss., Utrecht), 170–71, see also 169.

title—and not simply personal name, as is the case with Ahaz in 16:1–8—create narratological distance between the Assyrian king and the audience throughout the account. Additional narratological techniques, such as the Assyrian-influence-on-Ahaz motifs creating an inclusio framing the Damascene altar description, contribute nuances to the depiction of Assyria (in this specific case, the inclusio reminds the audience that Assyria is not entirely absolved of responsibility as YHWH's temple is compromised).

Second Kings 17 returns momentarily to its brief narrational style for the account of Hoshea's reign and the fall of the northern kingdom at the hands of Assyria. Then, the narrative not only slows down, but pauses for a considerable length to ideologically reflect on the Assyrian exile and to make clear to the audience that the fall of Israel was not so much at the hands of instrumental Assyria, but very much a direct consequence of the Israelites' decisions and their broken relationship with YHWH. Yet again, the details are telling, such as in the use of forceful verbs of conquest used to describe Shalmaneser and the careful use of titles and/or personal names in reference to various kings. As well, perspective is everything as the Assyrians are drastically minimized and even "exposed" as humbly conceding to and encouraging the worship of YHWH despite both YHWH's mysteriousness to the Assyrians and the new settlers' disobedience to YHWH. Second Kings 17 features three sub-groups composing the Assyrians as a whole, including the Assyrian settlers in Israel, who gradually weaken in their association with Assyria and develop into a living example of the universal failure of human societies to be devoted and faithful to YHWH. Key vocabulary such as גלה is explored for its predominant usage with Assyrian exiles, while it is demonstrated that the hypothesis tha *hapax legomenon* חפא is an "Assyrianism" remains in need of support.

3

Sennacherib and YHWH at War
Assyrian Attack, Prophetic Oracles, and YHWH's Deliverance of Jerusalem and Hezekiah (2 Kings 18–20)

THE REIGN OF HEZEKIAH AND ASSYRIA ON THE RISE (2 KGS 18:1-12)

THE 2 KINGS ACCOUNT concerning the reign of Hezekiah predictably begins with introductory formulae (18:1–2) leading up to a moral-theological evaluation of the Judean king (v. 3), an account of his cultic reform (v. 4), and a further moral-theological summary statement underlining the foundational and commendable trust (בטח) in YHWH that Hezekiah possessed (vv. 5–6).[1] This latter statement that Hezekiah "trusted" in YHWH is especially significant in 1) its rare use of the indicative verbal form paired with YHWH as the object, and 2) the generally rare use of the verbal and nominal forms found in the Hezekiah narrative in comparison to that of the remainder of Genesis–Kings.[2] As Moberly points out, 2 Kgs 18–19 is "that

---

1. A similar observation is made by Bostock, *Portrayal of Trust*, 13. For a good, brief discussion on the incomparability formula in v. 5, see Bostock, *Portrayal of Trust*, 32–34.

2. See Alfred Jepsen, "בטח," in *TDOT* 2:88–94 (93); E. Gerstenberger, "בטח," in *TLOT* 1:226–30 (229); John W. Olley, " 'Trust in the LORD': Hezekiah, Kings and Isaiah," *TynBul* 50 (1999) 59–77 (62–63); and Bostock, *Portrayal of Trust*, 2, 5, 13.

section of the OT in which the language of trust occurs more frequently than anywhere else."[3] These matters will be discussed in more detail later in this chapter, but in the meantime, it will suffice to observe that v. 5 is a key statement within the introductory verses of the Hezekiah Narrative.

It is within this context of commending Hezekiah's faithfulness to YHWH that the story of Sennacherib's attack and YHWH's victory is introduced. With the first mention of Assyria in Hezekiah's reign (v. 7), the context already implies the positive outcome ahead for Hezekiah. This suggestion, given the unusually long narrative ahead, probably functions less as the "spoiler" modern eyes would perceive and more as a helpful means of sustaining reader interest with many turns, anticipations and climaxes, and even a couple of "false dawns." The reader knows from the beginning to expect success for Hezekiah and defeat for Assyria, the resistance of the oppressed to triumph over the insistence of the would-be colonizer, and—importantly for the ideological perspective of the text—the sustenance of YHWH's covenant servant (David, through his progeny, Hezekiah) and city over the presumptuous threat of the failed, non-covenant servant (Assyria). Yet precisely how and when that will actualize in the story remains the task for the rest of the narrative to present. It has been suggested that particular military encounters may be alluded to in vv. 7–8—creating the possibility that the statement does not necessarily refer to events narrated ahead.[4] This is unlikely because the statement's placement and content read as a summary. That said, it could still be consistent with the statement's summary form that vv. 7–8 summarize several military encounters of a particular period—e.g., Hezekiah's encounters with Assyria before the events of vv. 13ff and/or 17ff. Further precision on these verses, with regard to which exact military successes are referred, is not possible. Still, the verses convey an example of Hezekiah's faithfulness being rewarded by YHWH through success over foreign powers, the mighty and domineering Assyrian empire included.

INTRODUCTION TO THE ATTACK OF SENNACHERIB ON JERUSALEM (2 KGS 18:13–16)

The narrative concerning Sennacherib's attack on Jerusalem may be identified as properly beginning in v. 13,[5] preceded by vv. 9–12, which is a reca-

---

3. R. W. L. Moberly, "בטח," in *NIDOTTE* 1:644–49 (646).

4. Bostock, *Portrayal of Trust*, 37.

5. In addition to the fact that the substance of the story begins in 18:13, the "annalistic" chronological note sets the story within Hezekiah's reign and indicates the

pitulation of the Assyrians' activity in ch. 17. This brief review functions in two ways: 1) to remind the reader of the grave danger Assyria could pose; and 2) to suggest that Hezekiah's trust in YHWH will protect him from the Assyrian threat.[6] The imperial threat is a very real one, having recently destroyed the northern kingdom (vv. 9–10), and, in the process, effectively brought the Assyrian conquering machine next-door to Judah (v. 11).[7] But, the narrator has planted a subtle seed of hope for the reader by way of contrast. All that has been said thus far concerning Hezekiah is opposite that of the disobedient northern kingdom, and hence one may anticipate that the outcome will also be opposite for Hezekiah and his city in what is about to occur.

The narrative's perspective then quickly shifts from the historically, geographically, and conceptually broader view of history (specifically, over three years, numerous lands, and the visible and invisible events concerning YHWH and his people) in vv. 9–12 to the slower pace and "ground-level" view in 18:13—19:36.

After a brief, annalistic introduction chronologically setting the story within the reign of Hezekiah, a new Assyrian king enters the picture.[8] Like most of his predecessors in Kings (2 Kgs 15:19, 29; 17:3; 18:9), Sennacherib is immediately characterized by his actions (ויתפשם . . . עלה, v. 13), which are aggressive and highly threatening for Jerusalem as the Assyrian king campaigns against Judah and seizes all its fortified cities—except, presumably, Jerusalem (v. 13). The gravity of the Assyrian threat is reflected in what may be seen as Hezekiah's singular lapse of faith in YHWH, expressed in his humiliating appeal to emperor Sennacherib to withdraw—using penitent language normally directed towards YHWH,[9] but here directed to the

---

narration of a significant event. For further discussion on the annalistic nature of this phrase, see Hobbs, *2 Kings*, 247; and Jones, *1 and 2 Kings*, vol. 2, 564.

6. Also observing the contrastive function of vv. 9–12 are Long, *2 Kings*, 198; Hobbs, *2 Kings*, 247; Wiseman, *1 and 2 Kings*, 273; Bostock, *Portrayal of Trust*, 17; and intimated in Provan, *1 and 2 Kings*, 253.

7. Bostock, *Portrayal of Trust*, 40–41. John H. Hull, *Hezekiah—Saint and Sinner: A Conceptual and Contextual Narrative Analysis of 2 Kings 18-20* (unpublished PhD thesis; The Claremont Graduate School, 1994), 251–53, basically agrees.

8. This begins what has been popularly called "Account A," 18:(13)14–16. See Brevard S. Childs, *Isaiah and the Assyrian Crisis*, SBT 3 (London: SCM, 1967), 69, 69–70n1; and Christopher R. Seitz, "Account A and the Annals of Sennacherib: A Reassessment," *JSOT* 58 (1993) 47–57 (47–48n2) for further discussion regarding the extent of the unit as beginning from v. 13 or v. 14 (the difference in assessment basically depends on whether one prioritizes the Kings version or the Isaiah version of the Assyrians' attack). It is the present view of this author that the unit begins at v. 13.

9. BDB, 306–7.

king of Assyria instead—and the Judean king's subsequent delivery of tribute at the expense of the royal treasury and especially of YHWH's temple (vv. 14–16). An alternative interpretation of vv. 14–16 has been espoused by several scholars.[10] These verses may be understood to emphasize the characterization of Sennacherib more than that of Hezekiah, reducing the impact of a "contradiction" in Hezekiah's behaviour (cf. vv. 5–6).[11] "Thus, Sennacherib is revealed to be thoroughly dishonourable and arrogant, accepting tribute and yet still seeking to overthrow Hezekiah, and to take the city of Jerusalem."[12] Bearing in mind v. 7, the following interpretation may be accepted as a valid possibility, though perhaps the aNE mind would not perceive a "contradiction" between v. 7 and vv. 14–16 regardless of how one interprets vv. 14–16:

> 2 Ki 18:7 states that Hezekiah rebelled against the King of Assyria and would not serve him. 2 Ki 18:14–16 makes it clear that when he considered even a one-time payment to the Assyrian king, in order to avoid a military assault, the result was negative. The emphasis is not on the disobedience of Hezekiah specifically, but on the fruitlessness of foreign rapprochement generally.[13]

Relatedly, Bostock and van den Berg perceive that 20:12–19 is a counterpart to 18:13–16. In both passages, "treasures sooner or later disappear to Assyria and Babylonia."[14] Van den Berg infers that the message is: "earthly possessions are not things you can rely upon,"[15] while Bostock suggests more generally—and in a way that resonates with Seitz's interpretation above—that "paying tribute to Assyria fails to prevent the Assyrian siege, and treasure will, in the future, not avert the deportation of Hezekiah's descendants."[16]

---

10. See sources in Seitz, "Account A," 47–57.

11. Seitz, "Account A," 56. Bostock, *Portrayal of Trust*, 50. Scholars such as Marvin A. Sweeney, *1 and 2 Kings: A Commentary*, OTL (Louisville: Westminster, 2007), 414, observe that Hezekiah's apparent "early capitulation heightens narrative tension, particularly with regard to Sennacherib's arrogance and blasphemy . . ."

12. Bostock, *Portrayal of Trust*, 49. Contra Aarnoud van der Deijl, *Protest or Propaganda: War in the Old Testament Book of Kings and in Contemporaneous Ancient Near Eastern Texts*, SSN 51 (Leiden: Brill, 2008), 247, who interprets that "the act of paying with treasuries in 18:15–16 entails the eventual ending of the story."

13. Seitz, "Account A," 56.

14. Evert van den Berg, "Fact and Imagination in the History of Hezekiah in 2 Kings 18–20," in *Unless Someone Guide Me . . . Festschrift for Karen A. Deurloo*, eds. J. W. Dyk, J. Midden, K. Spronk, et al. (Maastricht: Shaker, 2000), 129–36 (130).

15. Ibid., 130.

16. Bostock, *Portrayal of Trust*, 161.

The "fruitlessness of foreign rapprochement" exhibited in Sennacherib's deceptive maneuver concerning Hezekiah's tribute extends at the end of the Hezekiah narrative to Babylon and its future king (20:16–18). The implicit typological postcolonial message is that the merely secular empire cannot be trusted, regardless of which exact empire it is.

Evans proposes an innovative interpretation regarding 18:13–16 worth considering.[17] Observing that 1) the word זהב is not actually stated in the description of the overlaid temple doorposts in v. 16; and 2) the Assyrian account records a tribute payment from Hezekiah of 30 talents of gold and 800 talents of silver—which is 500 talents more than what Hezekiah gave Sennacherib in v. 14, yet also is reckoned after Sennacherib's departure to Nineveh[18]—Evans suggests that Hezekiah only gave a partial tribute in vv. 15–16, intentionally withholding gold from the temple treasures. This may serve to "lionize Hezekiah as a faithful king who does not give away the true treasures of the temple,"[19] and thus also to perhaps explain why Sennacherib still sends a delegation after the tribute payment.[20] While this interpretation is attractive, one wonders why the narrative was not more clear that the doorposts were not overlaid with gold or enough gold or that Hezekiah withheld the golden temple treasures from the king of Assyria. But if this interpretation is the case for vv. 13–16, then Hezekiah's characterization remains somewhat heroic, the Assyrians at this point in the narrative are only given a compromise of what they demand, and narrative tension therefore heightens considerably as the reader is poised to expect an

---

17. See Evans, *Invasion of Sennacherib*, 143–51.

18. See "Sennacherib's Siege of Jerusalem," COS 2:119B on 303d. Other scholars suggest that the differences between the amounts in the accounts reflect differences in weights used or Assyrian exaggeration or scribal error. L. M. W. Beal, *1 and 2 Kings*, Apollos Old Testament Commentary 9 (Nottingham, UK: Apollos, 2014), 466, acknowledges that it could be either a difference in calculating weights or that the Assyrian account includes additional payments (albeit annual ones). Gabriel A. Sivan, "The Siege of Jerusalem: Part I: Assyria the World Power," *JBQ* 42/3 (2015) 83–92 (88), attributes the difference to exaggeration or scribal error in the Assyrian account since not only is there the difference in the amount of silver enumerated, but a curious silence in the biblical account of the remaining items that the Assyrians claimed to have been given as tribute—including supposedly Hezekiah's daughters and "palace women"—and a further notable lack in the Assyrian account of any reference to actually capturing or looting Hezekiah's royal city. Sivan thus articulates an intelligent and common conclusion that this was "a sure indication that the victory Sennacherib claimed was by no means decisive" (88).

19. Evans, *Invasion of Sennacherib*, 151.

20. Agreeing with Evans that usually the payment of tribute signals the end of an invasion narrative. See ibid., 150.

Assyrian response to being disrespectfully resisted not just once, but at least twice (cf. v. 14a).

THE DELEGATION ARRIVES: THE INVADING ASSYRIANS CLOSE-UP IN TEXT AND SETTING (2 KGS 18:17–18)

Thus far the characterization of the Assyrians has been developed at a relative distance from the reader. There are a few explicit statements of the Assyrians' actions, but most of the Assyrians' characterization up through v. 16 is indirect and intuited through the response of Hezekiah. Sennacherib and part of his forces remain physically absent, being at Lachish,[21] and the sense of distance is subtly conveyed through the narrator's notice that Hezekiah "sent (a message)" to Assyria (v. 14). In v. 17, though Sennacherib remains in Lachish, his delegation of high-ranking officers along with the large army—essentially an extension of the imperial presence and agenda—invade the scene. This "invasion" occurs in the world of the story through the Assyrians' sudden arrival at Jerusalem and their violation of the "rules of the game" in accepting Hezekiah's tribute while still advancing;[22] it is likewise expressed in a literary invasion of the Assyrian forces unexpectedly appearing in the narrative.[23] The aggressive nature of the Assyrian forces' arrival is emphasized by the unusual repetition of verbs and phrases, such that various traditions deleted some of them: ירושלם ויעלו ויבאו ירושלם ויעלו ויבאו (v. 17).[24] The verbal accumulation builds up to "and they stood" (ויעמדו), a confrontative verb which is reinforced in its impact in the narrative by immediate details of a local site (the conduit of the Upper Pool that was by

---

21. The Assyrian army would have had relative ease in strategically and effectively dividing their forces during the campaign, since it would have been composed of both the royal standing army (*kiṣir šarri*) and provincial forces supplied by the *ilku* system—at the very least, including those overseen by the Rab-šaqeh, the Tartan, and the Rab-saris (though the Rab-saris normally oversaw the *kiṣir šarri*, apart from that part which composed the personal forces of the king). For further explanation of the Assyrian army, the *kiṣir šarri*, their divisions, and their official leadership, see Mattila, *King's Magnates*, 149–57.

22. See Provan, *1 and 2 Kings*, 255: "The rules of the game, as they have been followed thus far, are that kings who accept silver and gold should keep their side of the bargain. For the first time these rules are broken."

23. This marked change in literary pace, focus, style, and length between 2 Kgs 18:(13)14–16 and 2 Kgs 18:17—19:37 has classically led source critics to render this latter passage as "Account B."

24. See critical apparatus in BHS.

the highway of the Washer's Field, v. 17) that would have presumably been familiar to the narrative's original audience.

The importance of the delegation is reflected in its members and in the Judean delegation that responds to them (vv. 17, 18). All three of the Assyrian officials are among the seven highest-ranking officials in the Neo-Assyrian empire and were seasoned commanders over significant military forces in the overall Assyrian army.[25] The Hebrew technical term "Tartan" (תרתן) is derived from the Akkadian *ta/turtānu, ta/turtannu*, designating "one of the highest officials of the king," overseeing a province and often the military second-in-command to the king[26] from the time of Shalmaneser III through that of Tiglath-Pileser III.[27] The Tartan/*turtānu* may be best translated as "commander-in-chief,"[28] and is described by Mattila as

> the most widely and frequently attested high official and his role as the commander of a strong standing army in the West and as the supreme commander of the Assyrian army is well documented....
>
> The commander-in-chief led the provincial governors and other magnates on campaigns, especially in the absence of the king. Thus he represented the military aspects of royal power.[29]

Note, however, that the power and status of the Tartan declined slightly during the reign of Sargon II as the role was divided into two and as the Rab-saris / *rab ša-rēši* rose in power, overseeing more of the *kiṣir šarri*, the imperial central army.[30] Rab-saris (רב־סריס) is a loanword from Akkadian *rab ša-rēši*, "chief eunuch," and likely the eunuch's inability to establish a "hereditary elite group to oppose the monarchy" contributed, among other factors, to the increased rise of this office.[31] In addition to commanding the

---

25. See Mattila, *King's Magnates*, 3, 153, 155, 161, 163–65.

26. *HALOT*, 4:1789–9; *HA* 3:1332.

27. Mattila, *King's Magnates*, 152–53.

28. Mattila, *King's Magnates*, 153, 161.

29. Ibid., 165.

30. Ibid., 114–16, 152–53, 165. Note that with the establishment of the right and left Tartans, they consequently oversaw two provinces.

31. In agreement with Hayim Tadmor, "Monarchy and the Elite in Assyria and Babylonia: The Question of Royal Accountability," in *The Origins and Diversity of Axial Age Civilizations*, ed. Shmuel N. Eisenstadt (New York: State University of New York Press, 1986), 203–26 (208).

Though Jones, *1 and 2 Kings*, 569, states that "there is no proof that such an officer [as a chief eunuch] was known as a member of staff at the Assyrian court," we know now that many of the most senior Assyrian officials were eunuchs. See Karen Radner, "Royal Decision-making: Kings, Magnates, and Scholars," in *The Oxford Handbook of*

central army of Assyria (especially on punitive expeditions against rebellious vassal states), the Rab-saris had impressive political and personal influence and belonged to the king's close, immediate circle.³² Finally, the Rab-šaqeh (רב־שקה) was a senior official who oversaw a province (literally, "the Land of the *rab šāqê*") that was strategically located on the Urartian border.³³ As such, he commanded his own army unit and hence is considered the "commander of the northern army."³⁴ The Rab-šaqeh was also sent by Sargon II to help conduct military operations outside his own province (to Kar-Aššur in eastern Babylonia) along with the Tartan and provincial governors.³⁵ Thus, it is not surprising that Sargon II's precedent was followed by Sennacherib and Assurbanipal, who also sent the Rab-šaqeh on significant military operations beyond his province with other high-ranking officials.³⁶ Following Sargon's conquest of Urartu, the holder of the office of Rab-šaqeh would have been one who was especially adept at international diplomacy and negotiations as well as military ability in the interest of establishing and reinforcing imperial Assyrian rule in a geographically challenging area—surely, the nature of his role at that time required it.³⁷ Thus, Sargon and Sen-

---

Cuneiform Culture, eds. Karen Radner and Eleanor Robson (Oxford: Oxford University Press, 2011), 358–79 (359–60); and Mattila, *King's Magnates*, 131–32.

32. Mattila, *King's Magnates*, 163. Also, 164:

> The political influence of the chief eunuch at the court is made clear by the grants that king Aššuretel-ilani made to several members of the chief eunuch's military staff:
>
> "Sin-šumu-lešir, the chief eunuch, one who deserved well of my father and begetter, who led me constantly like a father, installed me safely on the throne of my father and begetter and made the people of Assyria, great and small, keep watch over my kingship during my minority, and respected my royalty." (SAA 12 35 and 36)
>
> The chief eunuch's position in the immediate circle of the king is reflected also in the type of sources in which he is attested, for example in the Wine Lists, in the grants, and in the queries. Because the chief eunuch belonged to the close circle of the king, there was no province attached to his office.

33. Ibid., 48–51, 155. See also Karlheinz Kessler, *Untersuchungen zur historischen Topographie Nordmesopotamiens nach keilschriftlichen Quellen des 1. Jahrtausends v. Chr.*, Beihefte zum Tübinger Atlas des Vorderen Orients 19 (Wiesbaden: Reichert, 1980), 150–82.

34. Mattila, *King's Magnates*, 161.

35. Ibid., 155, 163.

36. See chart on ibid., 152.

37. Karen Rader, "Urartu, Assyria's northern archenemy," *Assyrian empire builders*, University College London, 2013 [http://www.ucl.ac.uk/sargon/essentials/countries/urartu], states that the "appoint[ment of] the highest military commanders over Assyria's border regions in areas where major conflict was to be expected and major troop availability was necessary" stretches back to Shalmaneser III, though it was not

nacherib drew on the Rab-šaqeh's abilities occasionally when conquering distant foreign lands (note especially the similar circumstances and tactics used in Sargon's conquest of Urartu— which included the help of the Rab-šaqeh, whose province bordered that land—and in Sennacherib's attempted conquest of Jerusalem).[38] Possibly the shift in power balance between the Tartan and the Rabsaris during that time also contributed to the presence, and even dominance, of the Rab-šaqeh on Sennacherib's third campaign.

Contrary to popular belief of a generation ago and even for some in the present-day, clearly during the Neo-Assyrian empire the Rab-šaqeh was not an actual butler or "a high official whose duties were usually restricted to the court and the king's person[, and he] never took part in military campaigns."[39] Rather, "chief cupbearer" was a traditional, eponymous title to denote what was actually one of the most senior Assyrian officials who oversaw his own province in a strategic and challenging border region, commanded the Assyrian northern army, and—as a member of the elite magnates of the king—generally assisted the king in ruling the empire.[40] Serving additionally as an actual cupbearer to the king seems logistically impossible for the Rab-šaqeh, who would have been well-occupied with ruling his own

---

consistently put into practice until the Sargonids.

38. Ibid., 152; John Marriott and Karen Radner, "Sustaining the Assyrian Army Among Friends and Enemies in 714 BCE," *JCS* 67 (2015) 127–43 (138):

> the army which Sargon took on campaign in 714 emerges not as an unstoppable fighting machine formed of war-hungry warriors, but a far more heterogeneous group of specialists, whose skills allowed the army to function smoothly for months, far away from the empire. They relied on intimidation, not brute force, to seize enemy settlements, and the troops relatively rarely engaged in combat....
> ... This army had to be able to move at speed over difficult terrain, to intimidate and plunder, and to fight if unavoidable. But crucially, this organism had to be capable of offering protection to each of its members and allowing the king and his troops a good chance to return safely to their Assyrian homeland.

Observe also the Assyrians' heightened degree of strategic information-gathering and maintenance of relations in that region during the reigns of Tiglath-Pileser III and Sargon II. Peter Dubovsky, *Hezekiah and the Assyrian Spies: Reconstruction of the Neo-Assyrian Intelligence Services and its Significance for 2 Kings 18–19*, Biblica et Orientalia 49 (Rome: Editrice Pontificio Istituto Biblico, 2006), 32–72, 134–53.

39. Cogan and Tadmor, *2 Kings*, 230; Ronald T. Hyman, "The Rabshakeh's Speech (2 Ki 18–25): A Study of Rhetorical Intimidation," *JBQ* 23 (1995) 213–20 (see, e.g., 213, 215n4).

40. E.g., Radner, "Royal Decision-making," 359; Mattila, *King's Magnates*, 3, 155, 163. The precise history behind this title remains to be discovered, but the evidence supports these roles for the Rab-šaqeh during the Neo-Assyrian period, while Assyriologists currently view the title as eponymous, which is the most sensible explanation.

province, managing a key, relatively recently-conquered border region, and overseeing his own army at a location far from the king's palace. Moreover, "[t]here is no Neo-Assyrian reference to the chief cupbearer functioning as the cupbearer to the king, as his title implies."[41] Though Mattila allows the possibility that the function of cupbearing was included for the Rab-šaqeh (he cites the usual example of Neh 2:1, to which one should add Neh 12:26; 13:6–7), given the Rab-šaqeh's enormous responsibilities and established distant location, as well as the absence of Neo-Assyrian evidence that such a function was operative for his role at that time, I currently conclude that it is highly unlikely.

The Rab-šaqeh's familiarity with Hebrew and some aspects of Judean religious beliefs and practices has led scholars to intelligently propose that the Rab-šaqeh was an Israelite exile, if not Israelite defector.[42] However, that the Assyrian king would have elevated an Israelite or Judean (or any foreigner) to such a high, militarily and politically powerful rank would be highly surprising. Even if one allows that such a premise is not impossible, it is also not necessary to explain the Assyrian delegation's familiarity with "Judean" and Israelite religious matters, especially in light of the fact that Assyria had already conquered the northern kingdom and "all the fortified cities of Judea" (v. 13) and would thus have had ready access to Israelite and Judean resources.[43] Since, as discussed above, the Rab-šaqeh during

---

41. Mattila, *King's Magnates*, 163.

42. Hayim Tadmor, *Enc Miqr* 7, 323–25; b. *Sanh.* 60a; and Peter Machinist, "The Rab Šāqēh at the Wall of Jerusalem: Israelite Identity in the Face of the Assyrian 'Other,'" *Hebrew Studies* 41 (2000) 151–68 (159 and n23); similarly, Hayim Tadmor, "On the Role of Aramaic in the Assyrian Empire," in *Near Eastern Studies: Dedicated to H. I. H. Prince Takahito Mikasa on the Occasion of His Seventy-Fifth Birthday*, eds. Masao Mori, Hideo Ogawa, and Mamoru Yoshikawa (Wiesbaden: Harrassowitz, 1991), 419–26 (423).

43. Along similar but more speculative lines, Sivan and Gevaryahu's suggest that the Rab-šaqeh was an officer in the king's personal guard who served alongside the descendants of Israelite exiles, from whom he learned Hebrew and a rather patchwork knowledge of religious life in Judah. While this is possible, given that we know now that the position of the Rab-šaqeh was a much higher office than that of being just part of the king's personal guard, this scenario would need to have occurred before one held the post. And again, the Rab-šaqeh could just as well have gained his knowledge of Judah from previously gathered resources and Israelite exiles (and, further, Judahite exiles; whether or not Sennacherib's claim to have been sent Hezekiah's *urbi* and elite troops is factual, the previously conquered regions of Judah would have provided ample resources and personnel regarding the language, culture, and religion of the nation). See Haim Gevaryahu, "Isaiah and Hezekiah: Prophet and King," *Dor le-Dor* 14/2 (1987–1988) 78–85 (80–81); Gabriel A. Sivan, "The Siege of Jerusalem: Part II: The Enigmatic Rabshakeh," *JBQ* 43/3 (2015) 78–85 (80–81); and Jacob L. Wright, "Surviving in an Imperial Context: Foreign Military Service and Judean Identity," in *Judah and the Judeans in the Achaemenid Period: Negotiating Identity in an International Context*,

the time of Sargon and Sennacherib would have been especially adept at international diplomacy and conflict, he already would have the experience to know how to confront a foreign state and likely the abilities to prepare for that (such as with language and salient cultural knowledge).

In contrast to the Judean delegation, which includes Judah's own high-ranking officials, the Assyrian delegation's members 1) are described with mostly, if not entirely, Akkadian-derived terminology, 2) are each preceded by the direct object marker (אֶת־), emphasizing their high status, 3) are identified by title only, 4) are radically more militarily experienced and powerful than the Judean delegation, and 5) are accompanied by a large force. All these factors create a measure of empathetic distance between these Assyrian characters and the reader.[44] Bostock voices the suggestion that the sending of the Judean delegation instead of Hezekiah to confront the Rab-šaqeh may be "usual practice or a way of signifying that Hezekiah is not to be seen submitting himself in any way to the Assyrians."[45] Bostock's first proposal (that the sending of the delegation is "usual practice") is most consistent with the delegation's function throughout the Sennacherib narrative. We may fairly confidently affirm the first proposal, while allowing that the second could possibly function as another motive on behalf of the sender. This may be seen to apply to 18:18, though not to the similar situation of 19:2.

The battle is psychological, using the vehicle of rhetoric.[46] What is said and heard (i.e., implicitly spoken) among the characters in the Hezekiah narrative is key, as reflected in the high percentage of vocabulary and references to speaking and hearing. As Fewell points out, there are thirteen speech formulas (discounting when ויאמר indicates quotations) in 18:13—19:37, sixteen references to speaking in 18:20—19:23, and fifteen references to hearing in 18:26—19:28.[47] As well, there are various psychological-rhetorical techniques used, whether they were intuitively employed and/or consciously utilized.[48]

---

eds. Oded Lipschits, Gary N. Knoppers, and Manfred Oeming (Winona Lake, IN: Eisenbrauns, 2011), 505–28 (507).

44. Agreeing with Cohn, *2 Kings*, 128–29.

45. Bostock, *Portrayal of Trust*, 51.

46. For social psychologists, this is not a surprise. See, e.g., Michael Billig, *Arguing and thinking: A rhetorical approach to social psychology*, 2nd ed. (Cambridge: Cambridge University Press, 1996), 82: " . . . the pragmatic side of rhetoric has always been closely connected with psychological issues."

47. Fewell, "Sennacherib's Defeat," 79–90.

48. Billig, *Arguing and Thinking*, 82–83:

> The pragmatic side of rhetoric was inevitably based upon psychological assumptions, whether or not these were just shrewd intuitions held by practising

PSYCHOLOGICAL RHETORIC I: THE RAB-ŠAQEH'S FIRST SPEECH (2 KGS 18:19–25)

The Rab-šaqeh opens with a command that immediately denigrates Hezekiah, whom the Assyrians will persistently refer to by personal name without title, and elevates Sennacherib, whom the Rab-šaqeh describes here by titles only—thus emphasizing the Assyrian king's position but not person—and in language reminiscent of that used for YHWH. Revell comments that

> Disregard of a king's status can also signal disrespect, as where the Rab-shakeh ... refers only to "Hezekiah" in speaking to his subjects (2 Ki 18:19, 22, 29, 30, 31, 32). His disregard of Hezekiah's status as king adds a significant psychological element to his argument on the weakness of Hezekiah, and the futility of opposing the king of Assyria.[49]

Regarding the use of Sennacherib's title without his personal name, Revell says: "The designation 'the king of Assyria' is used to represent a threat ... It distances the individual."[50] The precise expression המלך הגדול occurs in the Bible only here, in the mouth of an Assyrian (2 Kgs 18:19 [Isa 36:4], 28 [Isa 36:13–14]), and the unique form was probably chosen by the biblical author so as to avoid a strong correlation between Sennacherib and YHWH, the latter being referred to as מלך גדול in Psa 47:3; 95:3; and Mal 1:14.[51] Though there may be a reflection of the common Assyrianism *šarru rabû* in המלך הגדול,[52] the biblical author's selection of גדול instead of רב still seems to stress the confidently loud, denigrating voice of the Rab-šaqeh (18:28; cf. 19:22).

The first sentence of Sennacherib's message attacks the characteristic for which Hezekiah is most celebrated by the narrator (v. 5): his trust (בטח). Thus, the reader is made aware of both the critical nature of the psychological

---

orators, or were fashioned by the theorists into an academic system. The ancient teachers of rhetoric recognized that, to be successful as a persuader, the orator must possess psychological insight. The experts might have disagreed amongst themselves about the other skills required of an orator, but they all stressed the need to study the thoughts and feelings of audiences.

49. Revell, *Designation of the Individual*, 131.

50. Ibid., 151.

51. Agreeing with Ehud Ben Zvi, "Who Wrote the Speech of Rabshakeh and When?," *JBL* 109 (1990) 79–92 (82).

52. For related discussion, see Abraham Malamat, "A Political Look at the Kingdom of David and Solomon and Its Relations with Egypt," in *Studies in the Period of David and Solomon and Other Essays: Papers Read at the International Symposium for Biblical Studies, Tokyo, 5–7 December, 1979*, ed. Tomoo Ishida (Winona Lake, IN: Eisenbrauns, 1982), 189–204 (197).

battle the Assyrians provoke, and also the likelihood that somehow Hezekiah will triumph in maintaining his trust in YHWH in the end. The theme of trust proves to be the dominant one in the Rab-šaqeh's first speech. The root בטח occurs twice in the Rab-šaqeh's first sentence, and seven times in all in the six verses of the first speech. Perhaps even more instructive is the distribution of בטח in the Hezekiah narrative: the first instance is voiced by the narrator in v. 5; the remaining nine are in Assyrian speech.[53] It is as if the fact of Hezekiah's trust in YHWH is established, and then the Assyrians present relentless challenges to it. Perhaps it is no surprise that Bostock concludes: "Sennacherib is the personification of the opposite of trust in YHWH."[54] Possibly the frequent inclusion of בטח in the Rab-šaqeh's speech also "represent[s] a reflex of Neo-Assyrian annalistic style."[55] Cohen observes that "the concise stereotypic phraseology describing the behaviour of Assyria's enemies and rebellious vassals almost invariably involves the usage of the verb *takālu*, 'to trust.'"[56] Linebarger and Dubovsky observe that undermining trust, particularly of leaders' motives and competencies, is a powerful propaganda weapon in psychological warfare.[57] And indeed, the issue of trust is the key battle here.

After directly questioning Hezekiah's trust, the Rab-šaqeh challenges the integrity of Hezekiah's words—and thus, implicitly elevates the Assyrian rhetoric. Shifting between speaking in the first and third person, the Rab-šaqeh's speech blurs the distinctions between the sender (Sennacherib) and the messenger (the Rab-šaqeh),[58] and thus "minimizes the effect of intermediation,"[59] which is remarkable in that Sennacherib effectively has a presence and voice when the Rab-šaqeh speaks, though Sennacherib himself is actually not present and is miles away from the scene.[60]

53. As observed by Olley, " 'Trust in the LORD,'" 62–63.

54. Bostock, *Portrayal of Trust*, 210.

55. Chaim Cohen, "Neo-Assyrian Elements in the First Speech of the Biblical Rab-šāqê," in *Israel Oriental Studies 9* (Tel Aviv: Tel Aviv University, 1979), 32–48 (41).

56. Cohen, "Neo-Assyrian Elements," 39; see also 40–41. Also, Cogan and Tadmor, *2 Kings*, 231. For a contrasting perspective on these matters, see Ben Zvi, "Who Wrote the Speech," 79–92.

57. Paul M. A. Linebarger, *Psychological Warfare* (Washington, DC: Combat Forces Press, 1954), 155–57; Dubovsky, *Hezekiah and the Assyrian Spies*, 19–20.

58. Agreeing with Long, *2 Kings*, 210. The portrayal of the Rab-šaqeh's speeches in Kings evidence unusually sophisticated and complex psychology and rhetoric such that the implications of Vater's thesis regarding this passage are of limited use here. See Ann M. Vater, "Narrative Patterns for the Story of Commissioned Communication in the Old Testament," *JBL* 99 (1988) 365–82 (376, 381; cf. 373).

59. Cohn, *2 Kings*, 129.

60. Of the use of intermediaries in this respect, Hull, *Hezekiah—Saint and Sinner*,

With an unusual density of emphatic adverbs (עַתָּה[וְ] occurs four times in this speech [vv. 20, 21, 23, 25] and וְכִי occurs in v. 22),[61] the Assyrian speech alternates between undermining Egypt (upon whom Judah has apparently relied at least for resources) and undermining the integrity of Hezekiah's relationship with YHWH. The speech's tone is peppered with negativity, sarcasm, and claims that confuse, all of which are intended to contribute to deflating the recipient's confidence. Through such clever rhetorical smoke and mirrors, the crucial relationship to discern here is that of Hezekiah and YHWH, though the Rab-šaqeh's focus is scattered. Likely, his initial focus on the relationship between Judah and Egypt reflects the Assyrians' own concerns that Judah is apparently an ally of a powerful Assyrian enemy (cf. 19:9). Note that the reference to "this splintered reed...," a metaphor used elsewhere in the OT (Ezek 29:67; see also 1 Kgs 14:15; Isa 9:13, 14 [MT]; 42:3; 58:5), is also attested in Neo-Assyrian literature for defeated enemies of Assyria (*kīma qanê ḫuṣṣuṣu*, "to break [the enemy] like a reed").[62] Possibly the biblical author included the metaphor as a realistic touch or reflection of the "Assyrian-ness" of the Rab-šaqeh's rhetoric.[63]

Especially insidious are the Assyrian attempts to undermine the special relationship between Hezekiah and YHWH. Verse 22 mixes truth and falsity, manipulating the truth of Hezekiah's destruction of the high places—for which the narrator earlier commemorated him (v. 4)—with an untrue

---

304, makes the following general observation:

> The skilful use of intermediaries by the narrator slowly brings the true nature of the conflict into view. But the tension builds as the real powers are kept apart. They never do come in direct contact. But as they draw closer, the tension mounts.

61. Bruce K. Waltke and M. O'Connor, *An Introduction to Biblical Hebrew Syntax* (Winona Lake, IN: Eisenbrauns, 1990), 667, states concerning עַתָּה[וְ]: "The logical force of עתה is usually confined to the combination ועתה, introducing a shift in argumentative tack with a continuity in subject and reference."

62. Cohen, "Neo-Assyrian Elements," 41–43. Cohen, 43, asserts regarding the phrase "a broken reed":

> There would hardly be a more appropriate way for a Neo-Assyrian official to denounce the worthlessness of trusting in an ally whom Assyria had defeated many times in the past. The "broken reed" is clearly a reflex of Neo-Assyrian annalistic style.

63. Similarly, Mikhal Oren, "Interference in Ancient Languages as Evidenced by Governed Prepositions," *Journal of Semitic Studies* 58 (2013), 1–11, see 8–10. suggests that the relative frequency of בטח על and בטח אל in the Rab-šaqeh's speech reflects a pseudo-Aramaism "meant to highlight the manner in which Rab-saqe, a foreigner and an enemy, used Hebrew in dramatic circumstances," "to reflect the Neo-Assyrian locutions as faithfully as possible," and to "[add] flavour to the speech of a foreign character." As Oren acknowledges, however, more evidence would be required to confidently assert this.

attribution of those high places as genuinely belonging to YHWH. It is unclear whether the Assyrian rhetoric in v. 22 is intended by the biblical author to be comically short-sighted in that the Assyrians make claims regarding Hezekiah's religious policy that are clearly not correct to the reader, or that the Rab-šaqeh's speech is deliberately trying to twist the truth and confuse the Judean populace overhearing the conversation (cf. vv. 26–27).[64] If the case is not both, fabrication seems more likely for v. 22, since the continuation of Sennacherib's challenge of the relationship between Hezekiah and YHWH in v. 25 involves a fabrication. Yet, even the fabrication that YHWH has sent Sennacherib to destroy Jerusalem and Judah is not entirely evident to the reader nor perhaps to the Judeans in the world of the story, since Sennacherib's predecessors were recently enabled by YHWH to conquer Israel (17:18–23; 18:10–12). Moberly defends Assyrian short-sightedness contributing to

> a high degree of irony in the envoy's appeal ... He is portrayed as a pagan, as one who thinks that a multiplicity of shrines must be pleasing to the deity, not realizing that exclusive worship in Jerusalem is precisely what the Lord in fact requires ... This means that the theologically discerning reader can realize that the apparently threatening Assyrian theological argument in fact rebounds.[65]

Bostock perceives this to a stronger degree: " ... the reader of the canonical book of Kings is clearly aware of the true situation. The reforms betray a Deuteronomistic outlook that would make the Assyrian's argument seem very stupid."[66] That said, while the Assyrians may be exposed as short-sighted or even "stupid," they are also depicted as being clever. The Assyrians anticipate likely Jerusalemite arguments and "[reject] their defense even before they can raise it."[67] That cleverness, however, is used in a worldly way and proves to be futile in trying to overcome YHWH. (Similar "cleverness" and strategy in anticipating the enemy's rhetorical-psychological tactics may be seen on the Judeans' side in v. 36, in which the people have been primed for the Assyrian rhetorical onslaught.)

Both sides, in fact, use the rhetorical-psychological tactic of knowing the audience's values and circumstances, and anticipating their audience's

---

64. Relatedly, possibly the Rab-šaqeh was trying to exploit a popular rumour or misconception.

65. Moberly, "בטח," 647.

66. Bostock, *Portrayal of Trust*, 55.

67. Hyman, "Rabshakeh's Speech," 216.

arguments.⁶⁸ The Rab-šaqeh attempts to evince an impressive degree of knowledge concerning the Jerusalemites, and in the world of the story that may impress and intimidate;⁶⁹ for the reader, however, cracks in the Assyrian armor are already exposed and growing.

Having considered the actions and dominant motives exhibited by the Assyrians through Rab-šaqeh's first speech, let us now look at the explicit and implicit claims the Rab-šaqeh and Sennacherib make concerning themselves. Sennacherib's initial rhetorical question (v. 19b) and the one that follows ("Now upon whom do you trust, that you rebel against me?," v. 20b) imply that Assyria and its king should be trusted and that rebellion against Assyria is futile. Verse 21, in which Sennacherib undermines Egypt's ability, indicates that Assyria is far superior to her arch-superpower enemy. The Rab-šaqeh/Sennacherib indicates that the Assyrian empire has "omniscient" eyes, being aware (however erroneously) of internal religious matters.⁷⁰ Assyria implicitly boasts of its abundant military resources in v. 23 with the offer of a thousand horses. This claim is heightened by the Rab-šaqeh's high-low polarization of Hezekiah (low, in that he should not even "turn away from the presence of . . .") and the bottom ranks of Sennacherib's officers (high) in v. 24, illustrating the supposed superiority of Assyria's military. It may also be seen that the Rab-šaqeh's rhetorically powerful use of a wager skillfully demonstrates his psychological and rhetorical acumen.⁷¹ Most startling of all is Sennacherib's concluding statement: "Now, without YHWH have I come up against this place to destroy it? YHWH said to me, 'Go up against this land and destroy it!'" (v. 25), indicating—in combination with v. 22—that YHWH is not with Hezekiah, but *is* with Sennacherib. The Assyrian king implicitly claims to be a faithful servant of YHWH.⁷²

---

68. Billig, *Arguing and thinking*, 224: "All the classical textbooks emphasize that the successful orator should understand how an audience thinks, and, before addressing an audience, the orator shoud be well aware of its opinions."

69. Dubovsky, *Hezekiah and the Assyrian Spies*, 13, 20–21. Dubovsky calls it "shocking knowledge" and identifies that "creating the impression of the attacker's omniscience" is a psychological warfare technique here. I am currently not convinced that omniscence is either claimed or attributed to the Assyrians in 2 Kgs 18–19, but Dubovsky's point is to be taken in that the Assyrians are at least trying to establish their superiority over the Jerusalemites in the realm of knowledge and information.

70. Dubovsky, *Hezekiah and the Assyrian Spies*, 253, suggests that the impression of Assyrian omniscience is a reflection of the intents of the superior Assyrian intelligence system, which the biblical authors demythologize by exposing its errors in the attack on Jerusalem and by recounting the triumph of YHWH over the Assyrian forces, intelligent and military.

71. Dubovsky, *Hezekiah and the Assyrian Spies*, 23.

72. This is not only a significant claim within the context of the Bible, but probably also reflects the common aNE belief that local deities were on the side of the (would-be)

Cohn and Machinist suggest that the Rab-šaqeh's argument reflects the views of Judeans opposing Hezekiah's reforms and the theology behind them for various possible religious, economic, and/or political reasons.[73] If this is the case, the biblical author went to unusual lengths to rectify particular policies and theology—the relevance of which were fairly past and moot—by the time of his writing. Given Kings' general exaltation of Josiah,[74] it seems more likely that—*if* internal critics are being represented through the Assyrians—the Rab-šaqeh's argumentation represents not so much the critics of Hezekiah's day, but those closer to the time of the biblical redactor, perhaps opponents of persistent Josianic theology and reform, or of current policies that were similar to past Hezekian and Josianic policies. Following the trajectory that the Assyrian argumentation is part of an internal Judean debate, Machinist reasons that

> the ease with which Judaeans become Assyrians in the letter-address [assuming that the Rab-šaqeh is an apostate Israelite], and the Assyrians threaten to become Judaeans, testifies to the writers' ambivalence. Coming to terms with Assyria, therefore,

---

victor. See discussion and sources in Jones, *1 and 2 Kings*, 2:571; Hobbs, *2 Kings*, 258; and esp. Cogan and Tadmor, *2 Kings*, 232.

Note also the intelligent suggestion of Jonathan Stökl, "Divination as Warfare: The Use of Divination across Borders," in *Divination, Politics, and Ancient Near Eastern Empires*, eds. Alan Lenzi and Jonathan Stökl, ANEM 7 (Atlanta: SBL, 2014), 49–63 (60–61), that

> [i]f Judah had some form of contractual understanding with Assyria, it is likely that the treaty included treaty curses. In such a circumstance, both Judean and Assyrian ideologues and theologians would have understood the Assyrian's action as the carrying out of the curses, which would have been udnerstood to have been enforced by at least Assur and YHWH.

My only slight reservations with this are that 1) most certainly, Assyria and Judah would have had a legally binding agreement in their empire-vassal relation regarding the annual giving of tribute to the emperor (see Karen Radner, "Abgaben an den König von Assyrien aus dem In- und Ausland," *Geschenke und Steuern, Zölle und Tribute; Antike Abgabenformen in Anspruch und Wirklichkeit*, CHANE 29, eds. H. Klinkott, S. Kubisch, and R. Müller-Wollermann [Leiden: Brill, 2007], 213–30 [219–220]), but the degree to which religious-spiritual aspects were invoked or seriously relied upon beyond perfunctory participation and tributes in cultic festivals remains further to be seen; and 2) neither the biblical or Assyrian accounts of Sennacherib's attack on Jerusalem make clear that this was a motivation for the Assyrians' attack, whereas numerous other motivations underlying the Rab-šaqeh's statements are evident in the accounts. Still, the possibility warrants serious consideration.

73. See Cohn, *2 Kings*, 130; and Machinist, "Rab Šāqēh at the Wall," 163–65.

74. E.g., consider Knoppers, *Two Nations under God*, 238, 246.

is an essential part of the self-definition of our writers and, we must suppose, of other Judaeans around them.⁷⁵

Such a conclusion should be held tenuously, however, in that it relies heavily in both its first and second parts on assumptions that require further support before certainty.

At least in the world of the story, the overall intent of the Rab-šaqeh's speech represents Sennacherib and the Rab-šaqeh's views and purposes. We may further deduce from the Rab-šaqeh's attempts to appeal to the values and language of the audience in vv. 22, 25, 28, 31–32 that he is attempting the ancient rhetorical technique of identification with his audience,⁷⁶ the Jerusalemites. The would-be colonizer's misunderstandings of his colonial target, however, significantly compromise the efficacy of his attempts to persuade the colonial target that boundaries are minimal and that an embrace of imperial rule would be fitting and harmonious.

The psychological effect of the verbal onslaught in vv. 19–25 proves to be enough to prompt the Judean delegation to plead for negotiations to continue in a non-vernacular language (v. 26). Their vulnerable human frailty is conveyed implicitly through the use of their personal names (in contrast to the Rab-šaqeh's identification with only his title) and the more mundane and "intellectual" nature of the Judean delegates' offices (in contrast to the ancient titles and military-political nature of the Assyrian delegates' posts); explicitly, through their language (נא; עבדיך) and appeal, which immediately

75. Machinist, "Rab Šāqēh at the Wall," 166.

76. Kenneth Burke, *A Rhetoric of Motives* (Berkeley: University of California Press, 1969), 55–56:

> You persuade a man only insofar as you can talk his language by speech, gesture, tonality, order, image, attitude, idea, *identifying* your ways with his. Persuasion by flattery is but a special case of persuasion in general. But flattery can safely serve as our paradigm if we systematically widen its meaning, to see behind it the conditions of identification or consubstantiality in general. And you give the "signs" of such consubstantiality by deference to an audience's "opinions." For the orator, following Aristotle and Cicero, will seek to display the appropriate 'signs' of character needed to earn the audience's good will. True, the rhetorician may have to change an audience's opinion in one respect; but he can succeed only insofar as he yields to that audience's opinions in other respects. Some of their opinions are needed to support the fulcrum by which he would move other opinions.

See also Billig, *Arguing and Thinking*, 224–25.

The Neo-Assyrians' intentional employment of identification with conquered peoplegroups may be seen in a variety of examples. One stark example evidenced in both text and archaeology is that of Esarhaddon assumption of key elements of Babylonian kingship. See Barbara Nevling Porter, *Images, Power, Politics: Figurative Aspects of Esarhaddon's Babylonian Policy* (Philadelphia: American Philosophical Society, 1993), 78–82, 87.

places them in a vulnerable and submissive position to the imperial Assyrian delegation.

PSYCHOLOGICAL RHETORIC II: THE RAB-ŠAQEH'S SECOND SPEECH (2 KGS 18:27–35)

The Rab-šaqeh's response is harsh and his language borders on, if not reaches, the level of expletives.[77] Thus, by means of his manner, the Rab-šaqeh's response in v. 27 communicates threat, intensity, and attack—the rhetorical technique is pure negativity, psychological aggression, and intimidation, and is obviously a strong effort to evoke fear, to silence and marginalize the voice of Hezekiah and his officers, and to promote cooperative subjugation on the part of the people.[78] Xella adds that the expression "to eat their own dung and to drink their own urine" refers to the after-life fate of the condemned.[79] In other words, the Rab-šaqeh uses an expression 1) to convey that the besieged Jerusalemites will effectively die if they do not surrender to Assyria, and 2) to imply that the Jerusalemites, in resisting Assyria, engage in a self-condemning act. Thus, surrendering to Assyria will mean both life and a reversal of condemnation. One should hold this interpretation lightly, however. Xella's hypothesis finds support in Egyptian literature,[80] but not in Mesopotamian literature.[81] One should also recall here that, at the same time by way of his upcoming speech's content and language, the Rab-šaqeh is making an attempt to expand his audience beyond the Judean emissaries

---

77. Both שִׁין and חראים are rare terms in the OT. The verbal form שִׁין occurs 6 times in the OT and only idiomatically. The nominal form occurs only here and in the Isaianic parallel, Isa 36:12. חראים occurs only here, in Isa 36:12, and in 2 Kgs 6:25, which has recensional complications (see BHS textual apparatus). See Roy E. Hayden, "שִׁין," in *NIDOTTE* 4:98–99; and idem, "חראים," in *NIDOTTE* 2:256–57. Given the traditions' penchant for euphemizing terms and the marked rarity of the terms in the OT, it seems probable that such explicit references were used in unsavoury contexts.

78. As social psychologists Marie-Claude Gervais, Nicola Morant, and Gemma Penn observe in "Making Sense of 'Absence': Towards a Typology of Absence in Social Representations Theory and Research," *Journal for the Theory of Social Behaviour* 29 (1999) 419–44 (429), "The mark of power is to marginalise, silence or subjugate others, and this results in the imposition of certain representations on others." This is exactly what the Rab-Šaqeh attempts towards Hezekiah and his officers.

79. Paolo Xella, "Sur la nourriture des morts: Un aspect de l'eschatologie mésopotamienne," in *Death in Mesopotamia: XXVIe Rencontre assyriologique internationale*, ed. Bendt Alster, Mesopotamia 8 (Copenhagen: Akademisk Forlag, 1980), 151–60 (154–55, 157).

80. Xella, "Sur la nourriture," 157.

81. I agree with Dubovsky, *Hezekiah and the Assyrian Spies*, 17n40, that Xella's arguments are insufficient on this point.

and to connect with the common people,[82] identifying with their values and dreams, and thus their circumstances. A not-so-subtle attempt to divide and conquer is at play.

On the heels of his dramatically vulgar response in v. 27, the Rab-šaqeh reasserts himself (ויעמד, literally, "he stood (up), took a stand")[83] and increases the intensity of his attack even more with a second speech delivered in a loud (גדול, "great") voice in Judean—blatantly countering the Judean leadership's request by Eliakim (cf. v. 26). Again, the Rab-šaqeh does not refer to the one he represents by personal name, but by epithet and title (v. 28, cf. v. 19), this time emphasized by the repetition of גדול in vv. 27–28. The reference to Sennacherib simply as "the king" in v. 29 "psychologically . . . [may suggest] that there is now only one king that matters, and he is the one in charge of the situation."[84] The Rab-šaqeh's persistent elevation of his king is paired with his persistent degradation of Hezekiah,[85] whom he continues to refer to by personal name only.

Before continuing further in the narrative, an alternative reading of vv. 26–28 is worth considering. Bostock suggests that the Judean delegation intentionally led the Rab-šaqeh into raising his voice, so that the people would hear for themselves the Rab-šaqeh's ludicrous misunderstandings:

> . . . that the Rabshakeh speaks in a loud voice (18:28), presumably louder than before, may have been the intention of the Jerusalem officials. Their urging of the Rabshaekh [sic] not to speak in the Judean dialect may have been a subterfuge on the part of the Judeans. Because they have confidence in the reforms of Hezekiah and in the people's acceptance of them, they encourage the Assyrian to speak in a louder voice to enable the people on the wall to hear what he is saying. The thinking of the courtiers

---

82. Billig, *Arguing and thinking*, 237: "In debate, the orator will urge the audience to consider the matter in terms of one sort of vocabulary, while the opponent will be urging the categorization of the issue under an opposing set of terms." We can see here in 18:26–27 that the Rab-šaqeh deftly makes a move to win the support of the common people through his choice of the vernacular language.

83. I agree with Long, *2 Kings*, 210–11, that Würthwein, "makes the repetition of a single verb carry too much weight" in regard to that ויעמד in v. 28 is a resumptive repetition from v. 17. Ernst Würthwein, *Die Bücher der Könige: 1. Kön. 17—2. Kön. 25: Übersetzt und erklärt* (Göttingen: Vandenhoeck & Ruprecht, 1984), 418: " . . . die Wiederaufnahme des „und er stellte sich auf" von 18, 17 in 18, 28 weist darauf hin, daß V. 18–25 vor V. 28 gestellt und V. 26f. zur Überleitung geschaffen wurden."

84. Bostock, *Portrayal of Trust*, 57.

85. This may well reflect standard Neo-Assyrian psychological warfare practices. Dubovsky, *Hezekiah and the Assyrian Spies*, 180, identifies the "discrediting of enemy leadership" as one of "the primary non-violent tools used by Neo-Assyrian propaganda."

> may be that, if the people hear the Rabshakeh for themselves, they will be convinced of the foolishness of his words and pay no attention to them.... that the Rabshakeh responds by shouting in a loud voice in the Judean dialect indicates the success of the ploy. Human nature being what it is, the Assyrian does the opposite of what he thinks the Judeans want. If this interpretation is correct, it portrays a sophistication on the part of Hezekiah's representatives in contrast to the Rabshakeh, who is thus portrayed as a gullible buffoon.[86]

Bostock's interpretation might be further supported by the apparent anticipation by Hezekiah and the Jerusalemites of a need to give the Rab-šaqeh a non-response (v. 36). Thus, it may be seen that Bostock's interpretation leads to a characterization of the Rab-šaqeh—and, consequently, the Assyrians he represents—as gullibly led, in their arrogance and ignorance, to expose their own foolishness. Nevertheless, Bostock's reading overlooks the play on גדול in v. 28, and it does not account for Hezekiah and the delegation's response to the Rab-šaqeh's words (18:37; 19:1)—a response that indicates that the Rab-šaqeh's speech was received as more harmful than encouraging for the Judeans.

The Rab-šaqeh continues with a second speech, beginning with three negative imperatives denying the reliability of Hezekiah and then YHWH. The Assyrian king then is implicitly presented as the trustworthy one, offering an antithetical alternative to what the Rab-šaqeh has just predicted for those who do not surrender to Assyria. At the level of the narrator and reader, the speech continues the biblical author's ironic means of depicting the Assyrians' short-sighted perspective. As Moberly points out, near the beginning of the speech,

> When the envoy later says to the Israelites, "Do not let Hezekiah persuade you to trust in the LORD when he says, 'The LORD will surely deliver us; this city will not be given into the hand of the king of Assyria'" (18:30), the discerning reader should appreciate the irony and see that Hezekiah's policy is in fact entirely right and his expectation entirely justified (even though not to be taken for granted).[87]

Instead of "eat[ing] their dung and drink[ing] their urine" (v. 27), the Assyrian king invites the Jerusalemites to eat and drink in a manner evoking the ideal Solomonic age (1 Kgs 4:20–25). As well, there is a possible double

---

86. Bostock, *Portrayal of Trust*, 56–57.
87. Moberly, "בטח," 647.

entendre promising safety and security for the Judeans' wives.[88] These claims may not have been unfounded,[89] though their impact in the context of the Hezekiah story and the OT is more in their stereotyped language and irony. After all, as evident throughout the Rab-šaqeh's speeches, factual truth is not so much his concern as persuasive rhetoric. Ironically, the Assyrian leadership offers the Judeans "a land like your own land," but not their land. Hobbs finds such irony indicating that "in the writer's mind the comments of Rab-shakeh are a parody of Deut 8:7–9."[90] Still, in the world of the story, the Rab-šaqeh's use of biblical language to promote the temptation of emigration to Assyria is an insidious and serious—if not also, to the reader, comical—attempt to win the trust of the Jerusalemite populace. The Rab-šaqeh then states clearly and succinctly the bottom line: "Live and do not die!" (v. 32b) The first section of the speech is reinforced with a repetition of his imperative "Pay no attention to Hezekiah . . . " (v. 32c, cf. v. 31a), and is concluded with a negation of the claim that "YHWH will deliver us."

In the Assyrians' claim to offer benefits that are attributed in the OT only to YHWH, their implicit claim is that Sennacherib assumes the sovereignly autonomous role of YHWH. As Fewell comments:

> From the beginning the Assyrian has intimated that he has control over life and death. Only he can offer such a choice to the oppressed city. . . . Thus, in his claiming control over life and death, Sennacherib has not simply ridiculed Yahweh's power, but he has attempted to usurp the role of Yahweh.[91]

Moreover, I would add that Sennacherib's proposed metanarrative to the Judeans here is crafted so as to appear similar enough to the historic Judean metanarrative such that they may be persuaded that the shift of identification between the two is neither large nor difficult, and that Sennacherib's metanarrative simply differs in being more effective and under the Assyrian king's—instead of Hezekiah's—allegiance.

This latter argument of the Assyrians is developed in the second section—the remaining three verses—of the speech, in which the Rab-šaqeh delivers a series of rhetorical questions upholding the examples of previously

---

88. See Hobbs, *2 Kings*, 259, who adds that such an "appeal is clever, if typical propaganda."

89. See, e.g., Cogan and Tadmor, *2 Kings*, 233; and Hobbs, *2 Kings*, 259.

90. Hobbs, *2 Kings*, 259. Hobbs also makes the likely suggestion that "the threefold repetition in the description of the land . . . might reflect a popular form of speech."

91. Fewell, "Sennacherib's Defeat," 86. Similarly, Hull, *Hezekiah—Saint and Sinner*, 297: "The contest is not simply about which king will achieve his goals regarding entering and exiting the city. The *real* opposition is about control of the world."

conquered peoples and the relatively recent (and geographically close) demise of Samaria. I agree with Provan and Wiseman that the Rab-šaqeh's list of cities in v. 34a is not the same as the "they" used in relation to Samaria in v. 34b; "they" in v. 34b are the gods of Samaria,[92] though this is not to deny the possibility that the gods of some of the cities in v. 34a became the gods of Samaria.[93] As attractive as the latter view is, the import of foreign gods into Samaria is probably not an emphasis for the Rab-šaqeh in v. 34b (though there could be a subtle allusion, as discussed below), since parallel phrasing in 19:12-13 places emphasis on the home location of the entity (in the case of 19:12-13, that would be the kings) of the cities.[94]

Bostock expresses bemusement that YHWH is recognized as the God of Jerusalem but not Samaria in vv. 34-35. He suggests that

> perhaps the narrator is not wanting to give more ammunition to the Assyrian. If YHWH was perceived to be the god of Samaria, then he had conspicuously failed to protect that land. The Assyrian's arguments would have seemed conclusive if that were acknowledged.[95]

---

92. See Wiseman, *1 and 2 Kings*, 278; and Provan, *2 Kings*, 261:

> Arpad and Hena are new to us. This fact alone makes it unlikely that the Assyrian is asking whether the gods of these cities had rescued Samaria from his hand, for there is no mention of the people of Arpad and Hena being resettled in Israel in 17:24ff. The emphasis is in any case upon what has happened to the *home* cities of the gods, as it is in 19:12-13, where the kings of these cities are mentioned. We should understand by they, then ('have they rescued Samaria?'), the original gods of Samaria in general, not the particular ones mentioned just beforehand.

93. Helpfully observed by Ingrid Hjelm, *Jerusalem's Rise to Sovereignty: Zion and Gerizim in Competition*, JSOTSup 404 (London: T. & T. Clark, 2004), 36; Evans, *Invasion of Sennacherib*, 82-83, esp. n136; Michael D. Press, " 'Where Are the Gods of Hamath?' (2 Kings 18.34 // Isaiah 36.19): The Use of Foreign Deities in the Rabshakeh's Speech," *JSOT* 40/2 (2015) 201-23 (212-13).

94. Provan, *2 Kings*, 261. Alternatively, Evans, *Invasion of Sennacherib*, 83, reasons that

> the letter-threat mentions the same regions, but in contradistinction highlights the fate of the *kings* of those defeated regions (2 Kgs 19:13). This is understandable given the different addressee of the letter-threat. Each threat is tailored to its audience.

This is a thoughtful counter-argument and worth considering. However, the difficulty is that the subjects in 19:13 (kings) are still presented in the same literary forms as the subjects of 18:34 (gods). If there is to be a tailoring of communication, it would usually be indicated more at the broader level (i.e., that of form) than at the more particularized level.

95. Bostock, *Portrayal of Trust*, 59.

However, Bostock's conclusion above is not necessarily so. Perhaps the narrator wanted *not* to confuse Jerusalem's situation (especially in that the city was led by Hezekiah, a king with outstanding faith) with that of Samaria. Indeed, the present syncretistic religious practices of Samaria were likely recognized by the Assyrians and were evidently acknowledged by the narrator (cf. 2 Kgs 17:34–41). At the very least, it may suffice to note that it is Jerusalem—not Samaria—that is threatened in v. 35, and thus the reference to Jerusalem alone is perfectly natural.

At the same time, there is still enough similarity between vv. 33–34a and 17:24, 30–31 to evoke the memory of the Samarian conquest and to reinforce its explicit mention in v. 34b, helping to keep the northern kingdom's defeat and exile in the background of the Hezekiah story,[96] as 18:9–12 does similarly. And so, as alluded to above, *if* there is an allusion to the movement of foreign gods into Samaria in v. 34b, it is with respect to the wider tragedy of the northern kingdom. In addition to these subtle stings, Sennacherib's argument uses blatant exaggeration, for, in fact, he did not conquer all the listed cities himself, as he claims.[97] Sennacherib/The Rab-šaqeh confidently concludes with typical aNE logic, that YHWH is just like the supposed local gods of other lands, and that therefore YHWH will not be able to deliver Jerusalem. Though expressing a pervasive aNE concept, the Rab-šaqeh's conclusion will prove to be his fatal mistake, as will be discussed later with regard to chapter 19.

While the Rab-šaqeh's previous speech emphasized trust (בטח), this speech features a high percentage of instances of the root נצל, "to deliver." נצל occurs eleven times in the Hezekiah story—all of which are in the mouth of the Assyrians, and nine of which are in this second speech (18:29, 30 [2x, with the infinitive absolute], 32, 33 [2x, with the infinitive absolute], 34, 35 [2x]; 19:11, 12). Again, ironically, the Assyrians appear to understand that there is a close connection between trust and deliverance, as the OT authors recognize elsewhere.[98] Having argued in the first speech that Hezekiah and Egypt cannot be trusted, and that Hezekiah and the Jerusalemites lack proper standing before YHWH to expect YHWH's aid, the Assyrians try in the second speech to attack from a different angle by attempting to undermine trust in YHWH by denying his ability to deliver.[99] The issue of deliverance

---

96. Agreeing on this point with Long, *2 Kings*, 216; cf. 215; and Hobbs, *2 Kings*, 260.

97. Hamath was taken by Sargon II; Arpad, by Tiglath-Pileser III; Samaria, probably by Shalmaneser V and his son, Sargon II. Agreeing for the most part with Cogan and Tadmor, *2 Kings*, 233.

98. E.g., Psa 22:4 [5]–5 [6]; 25:1–2; 28:7; 31:14–15 [15–16]; 86:2; Jer 39:18. See Moberly, "בטח," 646–49, for further discussion.

99. I am in agreement with Hobbs, *2 Kings*, 259, in that the change of Assyrian

is almost always explicitly linked in this speech with getting away from the power of the Assyrian king (מִיָּד). יָד occurs twelve times overall in the Hezekiah story (in addition to those noted below, 19:10, 14, 18, 19, 23, 26), and eight times in reference to the king of Assyria (six of which are in this speech: 18:29, 30, 33, 34, 35 [2x]). In the immediate context, the Assyrians' use of נצל and יד attempts to inculcate "the idea that Sennacherib's power over Jerusalem is already a present reality from which there is no escape."[100] As strongly as the Rab-šaqeh makes his argument for the triumph of Assyria over Jerusalem here, so strongly will be the Assyrian defeat, in which Hezekiah and Isaiah's rhetoric proves true.

In contrast to the Rab-šaqeh's first speech, the second speech reads more clearly as a message delivered on behalf of Sennacherib. Though the speech begins with a brief indication that the words to follow are a message that has been sent (in contradistinction to being the Rab-šaqeh's own immediate communication), Vater's thesis that 2 Kgs 18:28–37 is a scene focusing on the messenger does not well apply here.[101] The speech itself is long enough for its commissioned nature to remain easily in the background. Apart from the subtle reminder "until I come and I take you . . . " (v. 32a), which perhaps abruptly reminds the reader that the Assyrian king is not on-site but still at Lachish, the density of large and confident claims that could only be from the overlord of a powerful nation combined with the first-person references to "my hand" give a much stronger impression in vv. 28–35 of Sennacherib's presence (however "virtual" it is).[102]

Meanwhile, Sennacherib's argumentation more directly challenges and attacks YHWH in this second speech. Thus, the polarization of Sennacherib and YHWH becomes more pronounced. In both speeches, Rudman perceives the Rab-šaqeh to be functioning effectively as a false prophet—the

---

argument is not a self-contradiction within the Assyrian rhetorical attack:

> The argument of the Rab-shakeh now shifts ground, presumably against what he considers the intransigence of the Judeans. He depicts Yahweh's role now not as participant or as initiator of the invasion, but a helpless bystander who can do nothing against the Assyrian designs. Again, to impose upon this the standards of western logic is quite unfair and those commentators who see this section as a secondary insertion on those grounds are to be disregarded.

100. Fewell, "Sennacherib's Defeat," 85.
101. Vater, "Narrative Patterns," 366, 376, 381.
102. Long, *2 Kings*, 212, appears generally to agree:

> The Rabshakeh and Isaiah at times fade behind the words they carry and both project in their speech the force and personality of their respective masters (cf. A. Vater, "Narrative Patterns . . . ") Moreover, the narrator-writer emphasizes the substance of speech rather than descriptive prose or the formalities of emissarial protocol.

Assyrian counterpart to Judah's Isaiah.[103] Bostock supports Rudman's interpretation of the Rab-šaqeh's characterization as "prophet-like," resulting in an "effect . . . heighten[ing] the audacity of the Assyrian."[104] Rudman bases his argument on the presence of "prophetic" themes in the Rab-šaqeh's rhetoric. However, these themes—such as "trust," introductory calls to "hear the word of [someone]," various eschatological blessings expressed in agricultural terms, and covenantal language—while represented in biblical prophetic literature, are also present in other aNE genres. Though there is a limitation in that the Rab-šaqeh's role and speech target military-psychological circumstances and not divine representation, Rudman's hypothesis does draw attention to the godlike claims spoken on behalf of Sennacherib. As well, it may be seen to be operative to the extent that the words of the Rab-šaqeh and those of Isaiah are counterpoised and representational of authoritative powers. Ellul contemplates at length the polarization between Sennacherib and YHWH, drawing attention to the rational, empirical nature of the Rab-šaqeh's argumentation:

> "God does not exist. Do not let yourselves be deluded into living by faith. God will not save. God will not console. God will not revive. Those who make these fair promises are merely speaking empty words. It is in their own interests and for their own advantage that they speak about God . . . The aim is to keep you in bondage and exploitation (we note in passing that this is the serpent's charge against God himself). Stop looking forward to a future fashioned by God. Make your own future, or rather, trust Sennacherib to make it for you. Stop looking to heaven for deliverance and the establishment of justice. It is within your reach. Simply surrender and bow before the might of the world. Stop believing in this useless God and make reasonable decisions which can be calculated on the human level." This is how Rabshakeh continues in forceful and realistic terms.[105]

---

103. See Dominic Rudman, "Is the Rabshakeh also among the Prophets? A Rhetorical Study of 2 Kings 18: 17–35," *VT* 50 (2000) 100–110 (105, 106, 108, 110).

104. Bostock, *Portrayal of Trust*, 51.

105. Jacques Ellul, *The Politics of God and the Politics of Man*, trans. and ed. Geoffrey W. Bromiley (Grand Rapids: Eerdmans, 1972), 158.

In effect, in this second speech the Rab-šaqeh challenges the sacred, defining elements of the Judahite collective identity,[106] and offers the Jerusalemites an alternative collective metanarrative.[107] As Alasdair MacIntyre puts it,

> Is there any way in which one of these rivals might prevail over the others? One possible answer was supplied by Dante: that narrative prevails over its rivals which is able to include its rivals within it, not only to retell their stories as episodes within its story, but to tell the story of the telling of their stories as such episodes.[108]

In all these respects, we can see that the Rab-šaqeh's alternative collective metanarrative is positioned to prevail. Yet it remains to be seen whether the psychological-rhetorical tactics have succeeded, whether the Jerusalemites will accept the new, proposed collective metanarrative.[109]

THE JERUSALEMITE RESPONSE (2 KGS 18:36—19:5)

The seriousness of the Assyrian threat is reflected in the Jerusalemite response. The people obey Hezekiah and resist voicing a reaction (v. 36).[110] Hobbs seems to imply differently for v. 36, as if the Rab-šaqeh's speech ef-

106. Christian Smith, *Moral, Believing Animals: Human Personhood and Culture* (Oxford: Oxford University Press, 2003), 76–77:

> Durkheim's reductionistic suggestion that all religions are ultimately nothing but the worship of sacred social ideals is highly debatable. The connection of the sacred and the social, however, when viewed through the other end of the telescope, may hit closer to the mark: that all social orders are in a sense ultimately religious, in having sacreds at heart, in the form of sacrosancts set apart from the ordinary and profane through and by which the social orders live, move and have their being.

107. Ibid., 77:

> But we should note that the sacred ideals that define social orders do not float freely in the sky of ideas, like arbitrary clumps of ideas and beliefs that somehow happen to get invested with religious qualities. Rather, the sacred at the heart of any social order is always embedded in and arising from its collective narratives.

108. Alasdair MacIntyre, *Three Rival Versions of Moral Enquiry: Encyclopaedia, Genealogy, and Tradition; Being Gifford Lectures Delivered in the University of Edinburgh in 1988* (London: Duckworth, 1990), 80–81.

109. Hull makes the rather unique suggestion that the "demand call" of Sennacherib in v. 31 is eventually fulfilled in the surrender of Jehoiachin to Nebuchadnezzar (24:12). This theory may be attractive to some, but it requires reading emphases in the text which are difficult to support. See Hull, *Hezekiah—Saint and Sinner*, 269.

110. In agreement with Jones, *1 and 2 Kings*, 2:573; Cohn, *2 Kings*, 132–33; Wiseman, *1 and 2 Kings*, 278.

fectively silenced the people: "In the face of this powerful, if erratic, speech of the Rab-shakeh no answer is forthcoming."[111] However, the narrative supplies the reason for the people's silence as being Hezekiah's command. To overlook this aspect of the text, one must propose an emendation, as Cogan and Tadmor do.[112] An emendation is unnecessary to resolve the narrative; Hezekiah could easily have anticipated that the Assyrians would deliver a message designed to provoke a reaction and forewarned his people not to engage with it. Dubovsky supplies military insight on this matter:

> In difficult moments, the simplest and most efficient way to keep troops under control has always been to order them to keep silent and thus prevent discussions which could undermine their morale.... If Rab-shaqeh's speech was indeed anticipated and the people of Jerusalem had been prepared for it, then its delivery would cause just the opposite effect: instead of becoming frightened, the people became even more convinced that they were fighting against a blasphemer of their God.[113]

Indeed, silence is rarely a non-action or non-response,[114] and v. 36 is clear that the Jerusalemites' silence is intentional on both their part and their king's part. A number of social-psychological dynamics are operative in this respect. For one, in obeying Hezekiah through their silent response, the people continue to operate in a relationship with Hezekiah in which they are respectful and subservient to him as their king (as v. 36 notably identifies him) and leader. This suggests that, secondly, the community of Jerusalem continues to embrace their own collective identity and narrative. Thirdly, the Jerusalemite collective response rejects engagement in the interaction and paradigm offered by the Assyrian delegation; the Jerusalemites will, instead, respond on their own terms.[115] This is not to deny that a

---

111. Hobbs, *2 Kings*, 260.
112. Cogan and Tadmor, *2 Kings*, 233.
113. Dubovsky, *Hezekiah and the Assyrian Spies*, 254–55.
114. Crediting F. De Singly, "La gestion sociale du silence," *Consommation* 4 (1982), for introducing the concept, Gervais, "Making Sense of 'Absence,' " 428, recognizes "the concept of the 'social management of silences' to account for the subject's active manipulation of disclosures in social encounters. Here, absence expresses a degree of agency."
115. In a sense, this could be using passive-aggressiveness in a warfare context.
Note the observation of Billig, *Arguing and thinking*, 225–26, that "if orators can control crowds, it is only because crowds control orators.... In fact, some orators' successes are only possible because the audience colludes with the orator in sustaining the myth." However, in the case of 18:36, the people chose not to promote the Assyrian "myth."

response of fear on the part of the people may also have been present (cf. v. 37); but still, the response that they give the Assyrian leaders takes ownership of and communicates a choice to reject the Assyrian agenda despite their possible fears.

The gravity of the situation has been conveyed, and the Jerusalemite community's response has heightened the conflict in the world of the story, and thus the narrative tension. Verse 37 depicts this in actions, as Hezekiah's delegates return to him with torn clothes. As Cohn observes, v. 37 gives the perspective of Hezekiah in that the delegates "came"—not "went." Thus, the reader may feel Hezekiah's surprise as his representatives appear with a visual sign of remorse and grief. "Before they can even speak their apparel signals a peril!"[116] Possibly, a sobering discouragement on the part of the Judean delegation is conveyed through the titleless use of "Hezekiah" in v. 37. As Revell remarks, "The use of the name suggests that they regard him as if already dethroned by the Assyrians; their tearing of their clothes reflects similar despair."[117] Revell's suggestion may be a stretch, especially in that kings are mentioned by personal names sometimes in Kings without apparent added significance to the absence of titles or epithets. At any rate, this possible understanding of the titleless use of "Hezekiah," as well as Sennacherib's and the Rab-šaqeh's clear disrespect for Hezekiah through their titleless references to him, are soon contrasted by the narrator's inclusion of Hezekiah's proper title in 19:1, "where 'King Hezekiah' takes effective action."[118] At the same time, this reference to Hezekiah's position elevates him more than before, attributing greater strength to his character. The Judean king's own response reinforces the severity of the situation. He not only tears his clothes, but wears sackcloth and has his delegates wear sackcloth as well. Without Joah (perhaps a recorder was unnecessary for a visit to a prophet; cf. 18:37), but with the addition of the leading priests— "impl[ying] a concerted effort on the part of the Jerusalem establishment to seek a way out of their dilemma,"[119] the representatives are now sent to the prophet Isaiah. Although no direct response to the Assyrian speeches is immediately given, Hezekiah's actions in 19:1–5 are his indirect response to the Assyrians. His summation of the situation indicates the gravity of the Assyrian threat and the fear the Assyrian speeches have induced in Jerusalem—not least, in King Hezekiah (19:3).[120] But, instead of entering their

---

116. Cohn, *2 Kings*, 133.
117. Revell, *Designation of the Individual*, 124.
118. Ibid., 124n2; see also Cohn, *2 Kings*, 133.
119. Hobbs, *2 Kings*, 274.
120. As Fewell, "Sennacherib's Defeat," 81, puts it: "This figurative expression not

parley, Hezekiah directs his efforts in an appeal to YHWH and YHWH's mouthpiece, Isaiah (19:1–5).

שמע—THE ISSUE OF RESPONSE AS THE CONFLICT INTENSIFIES (2 KGS 19:1-21)

The battle is acknowledged by Hezekiah as one of words (19:4 [2x], cf. 19:6). Also, as Fewell observes, there is a high density of שמע vocabulary in the Hezekiah story—and, we may also note, in 19:1–16. Thus, the issue in these verses is "not so much the receiving and comprehension of sound, but the *response* that results from the hearing of certain words" [emphasis mine].[121] Thus, the issue of response—how Hezekiah responds to the Assyrian rhetorical attack (v. 1), how YHWH might respond to Assyria (vv. 4, 6, 7), how YHWH will make Sennacherib respond to a report (v. 7), how the field commander responds to a report and increased pressure (vv. 8–9), and how Hezekiah will respond to the immediate reality of Assyria's previous victories (v. 11)—is key in 19:1–16. If one follows just these occurrences of שמע, an outline of the unfolding conflict emerges. Hezekiah's "hearing" (i.e., response) to Assyria's words is that of distress and desperation, reflecting the gravity of the Assyrian threat and the efficacy of its rhetoric, as discussed above (v. 1). Hezekiah hopes that YHWH will "hear" (i.e., recognize) the words of the Rab-šaqeh as directed against YHWH himself and that, in turn, YHWH will defend his reputation and his people by taking appropriate action against Assyria (v. 4). Through Isaiah, YHWH acknowledges Hezekiah's fear ("do not be afraid before words that you have heard . . . ") of Assyria's threat, then minimizes that threat—the Assyrians' words are not worth fearing, and though they are an attack against YHWH, they issue from people who, relative to YHWH, are merely "minions" (JPS), "underlings" (v. 6c), נער being used sarcastically here to refer not simply to the Assyrian king's "attendants,"[122] but their inferiority as well.[123] YHWH promises victory in that he will cause Sennacherib to respond ("when he hears . . .") to "a report" (שמועה) that will relieve Jerusalem (v. 7). The Rab-šaqeh

---

only confesses responsibility for the crisis at hand, but also exhaustion and impotence." Similarly, Wiseman, *1 and 2 Kings*, 279.

121. Fewell, "Sennacherib's Defeat," 84.

122. It may be expected that if the biblical author intended simply to convey the idea of "attendants, servants," the more common term עבדים (in Kings, עבד occurs 135x; נער occurs 35x) would have been used.

123. Generally agreeing here with Cogan and Tadmor, *2 Kings*, 234, though Hobbs, *2 Kings*, 275, disagrees.

hears that his master, the king of Assyria, has relocated and that Tirhakah threatens the Assyrian forces (vv. 8–9), so he retreats while at the same time he attempts to increase pressure on Hezekiah (vv. 10–13). The Assyrian rhetorical argument raises the heard (i.e., commonly known) example of the past—previous Assyrian victories, in particular—to argue for the likelihood of their continued victory in the present (v. 11–13). The peoples listed in the Rab-šaqeh's message, which is later indicated to be communicated by letter, were not actually "utterly destroyed" (להחרימם, literally, "to destroy them utterly/completely, devote them to the ban"), nor does our knowledge of Assyrian religio-political policy reflect such aims. Hobbs suggests that the Rab-šaqeh's language here is hyperbolic, hence the Assyrian self-depiction is exaggerated to make the empire's power and ruthlessness seem unmerciful to those who resist. "Putting the destruction of so many cities in this light would certainly make good propaganda for the Assyrians. It is an effective use of hyperbole."[124] Dubovsky points out that the word "gods" in the rhetorical questions of 18:34 is replaced by the word "king" in 19:13.[125] It is a small but important change in the verbal onslaught of the Assyrians.[126] The focus of the attack shifts from the gods to Hezekiah; the Assyrians have adjusted with the change in audience and personalize matters—the implication in v. 13 is that Hezekiah is effete and that his own future is doomed. In v. 16, Hezekiah begs YHWH to respond ("hear," 2x) to the Assyrian threat, and the use of words as a means of attack is once again explicitly acknowledged—"Hear the words of Sennacherib that he sent to defy the living God" (v. 16c).

The overall flow of events suggests at first blush that the king of Assyria will immediately meet his defeat. Isaiah delivers the promise of YHWH, that Sennacherib's hearing of a report—the double use of the root שמע reinforcing the sign—will lead to his retreat (שב) home, which will eventually lead to his death by sword (v. 7). The narrator's description of the Rab-šaqeh's actions in the next verses—especially the double use of the root שמע and double application of וישב in vv. 8–9—suggests to the reader that defeat is near for Assyria. Moreover, the aspect of delivery emphasized by the narrative regarding the third Assyrian rhetorical attack is its long-distance nature. The Rab-šaqeh's words are sent in the midst of retreat and no longer have the impact of live, personal delivery (v. 9). They are in a form that Hezekiah can manipulate and physically bring before YHWH (v. 14). As well,

124. Hobbs, *2 Kings*, 277.
125. Dubovsky, *Hezekiah and the Assyrian Spies*, 27.
126. Again, this probably reflects standard Neo-Assyrian psychological warfare tactics. Ibid., 235, observes Neo-Assyrian examples of propaganda that included repetitions or slight changes.

the narrator depicts Hezekiah in a more active role, while Sennacherib's role has become more passive (e.g., vv. 1–2, 14–19; and discussion regarding the inclusion of King Hezekiah's proper title, above).[127] From the perspective of Hezekiah and the Jerusalemites, however, the Assyrian pressure was evidently unabated, as reflected in Hezekiah's response to the letters (vv. 14–19). Thus, in vv. 6–13, the narrative anticipates the eventual fulfilment of YHWH's promise and the retreat and defeat of Sennacherib. This is held in tension, however, with the present situation and the characters' perspectives, whose shorter purview—whether Assyrian or Jerusalemite here—results in greater difficulty seeing beyond the realistic likelihood of Assyrian victory. In this respect I agree with both Fewell and Cohn, who perceive the increasing shift of power and sense of control in the narrative in the direction of Hezekiah and YHWH and away from Sennacherib and the Rab-šaqeh.[128] Hull makes a similar conclusion, based on his summation of "Messenger Sending Language," which includes incidences of שלח, מלאך/מלאכים, and commissioned messenger patterns and formulae.[129] I also agree with Long and Provan, who appear to emphasize the narrative's linear presentation of perspectives—the narrator hints at on-coming relief for Jerusalem in vv. 8–9, but the characters' actions and thoughts suggest otherwise.[130]

127. Agreeing with Fewell, "Sennacherib's Defeat," 82–83:

> Hezekiah ... personifies the shift of dominance and power that takes place between Sennacherib and Yahweh. As Hezekiah moves from total impotence to total effectiveness, Sennacherib moves from being totally autonomous to being totally manipulated by the will of Yahweh.

128. Ibid., 82–83, and Cohn, 2 Kings, 134.

129. See Hull, Hezekiah—Saint and Sinner, 280–86. "The pivotal point in the narrative comes when Hezekiah decides to send to Isaiah (the YHWH prophet) rather than Rabshakeh (the Sennacherib 'prophet')."

130. Long, 2 Kings, 225:

> Normal sequentiality resumes in v. 9b ... But now a reader knows that the threat to Jerusalem remains pretty much as it has been, except that Sennacherib will press his demands from Libnah while engaging there the Ethiopian forces ... In other words, the threat to Jerusalem is not at all diminished.

Provan, 1 and 2 Kings, 257–58:

> The prophecy is reassuring, but somewhat vague about the circumstances of its fulfilment.... There is a suggestion of reprieve for the city as early as verse 8, as the field commander "hears" that Sennacherib has left Lachish and "returns" to find him, now fighting against Libnah. Nothing comes of this, however. Sennacherib stays firmly rooted in the land, and the "great army" evidently remains outside Jerusalem, under the supreme commander (18:17). A second false dawn follows close behind. The Assyrian king "hears" about the advance of Tirhakah, king of Cush (v. 9). This time he himself "returns," but only to his verbal assault on Hezekiah ... It seems that the prophecy is not to be fulfilled immediately. Far from being sent to his death in Assyria,

While in chapter 18 the depiction of the Assyrians was mostly through the perspectives of the narrator and the Assyrian leadership, in chapter 19 the portrayal is more mixed as the conflict intensifies. In vv. 1–4, the Assyrian threat is a reason for severe distress at the national level. Hezekiah recognizes the Assyrian leadership as opposed to YHWH himself, and the Judean king defers to YHWH in responding to the Assyrians; as Cohn observes, "the challenge needed to be handled on the proper plane."[131] As seen above, from YHWH's perspective, the high-ranking officials of Sennacherib are "boys," "minions," "underlings" (v. 6). It is no longer the Assyrians who determine the situation, but YHWH (v. 7). Retrospectively, YHWH's perspective in v. 7 will prove to be far larger than the immediate, day-to-day purview of the human characters, for his words apply to events spanning, in fact, twenty years (i.e., Sennacherib's eventual death by sword in 681 BC). In vv. 8–9, the narrator depicts Assyria in more difficult straits as the Rab-šaqeh receives what might have been delayed notice of Sennacherib's change of battle plan. As well, a new enemy enters the scene—Tirhakah, king of Cush—with a dramatic הנה from the narrator to mark his impact. For the first time in the narrative, the Rab-šaqeh retreats, the repetitive use of שוב and twisting of its meanings highlighting its third occurrence here (v. 9). Still, the Rab-šaqeh attempts to maintain an unconquerable and intimidating front. This third Assyrian rhetorical attack is directed to the Judean king and attempts to undermine his confidence, forcing him into surrender, but it is the presumptions regarding YHWH in the Assyrian rhetoric that cross the boundary into the insulting of God. The Assyrian leadership increases the effect of its blasphemy (cf. 18:30, 32–35) by again equating YHWH with mere, ineffective gods that Assyria has conquered. In making this assertion, the Assyrians exalt the kings of Assyria over YHWH, in addition to over "all the lands" and, implicitly, all gods. And so, in its rhetoric, Assyria presumes godlike abilities and status, and thus attempts to supersede YHWH.

Hezekiah is evidently affected by the threat (v. 14–15a), but not to the degree that he accepts the Assyrian perspective of its supposedly almighty status.[132] Hezekiah does perceive Assyria to be sufficiently powerful such

---

Sennacherib remains to compound his sin of blasphemy by committing it a second time (vv. 10–13) . . .

Jones, *1 and 2 Kings*, vol. 2, 575, neglects the literary aspect of the text and states that, in regard to vv. 7–9, the biblical author "has confused the sequence of events."

131. Cohn, *2 Kings*, 134.

132. Adam E. Miglio, "The Literary Connotations of Letter-Writing in Syro-Mesopotamia and in Samuel and Kings," *BN* 162 (2014) 33–46 (38–39), makes the attractive suggestion that Hezekiah's actions in 19:14–16 was a subversion of a normative Neo-Assyrian kingly practice of writing letters to Aššur regarding military victories. The

that he does not even attempt to respond directly to Sennacherib, but begs YHWH to intercede. Moreover, Hezekiah recognizes that Assyria's most serious crime in its attack is not against Hezekiah's confidence, but against YHWH's reputation (vv. 16b, 19). He affirms the reality of Assyria's proven ability to destroy nations (v. 17), but he also recognizes that the Assyrian perspective of "the gods" is hugely exaggerated and erroneous in associating YHWH as one of them (v. 18). Deliverance from Assyria is not Hezekiah's only stated motive for seeking YHWH's intervention; rather, the exalted reputation of YHWH demonstrated through his delivering Jerusalem from Assyria is the final reason (v. 19). Hence, in Hezekiah's prayer, Assyria itself is removed from centre stage to fulfil a more instrumental role as offering the challenge that provokes YHWH into demonstrating his sovereign superiority. As well, it is stressed that YHWH alone is able to bring deliverance to this particular situation of the Assyrian threat.[133]

Possibly some word play on Sennacherib's name presents itself in vv. 16–17, as well as—to a lesser degree—in vv. 4, 22–24, 36–37. The connection between root חרב and סנחריב is especially pronounced in vv. 16–17 with the use of החריבו (cf. v. 11, in which the verb of destruction used is החרים). Hull states:

> Using Sennacherib's name in close proximity with the charge of blasphemy (חרף) solidifies the word play on this name that Garsiel has noted. This word play continues in the next verse when Hezekiah switches to the evils of Assyrian deeds. This language is very similar to the rhetorical arguments that Rabshakeh and Sennacherib used in their speeches (19:11–12; 18:33, 35) though it is not an exact quotation. One subtle change is Sennacherib's

---

difficulty with this view is that Sennacherib's letter in vv. 10–13 was not written to Aššur, nor was it commemorating any military victory (let alone over Jerusalem, since none had been had). Indeed, as Beate Pongratz-Leisten, "All the King's Men: Authority, Kingship, and the Rise of the Elites in Assyria," in *Experiencing Power, Generating Authority: Cosmos, Politics, and the Ideology of Kingship in Ancient Egypt and Mesopotamia*, eds. Jane A. Hill, Philip Jones, and Antonio J. Morales, PMIRC 6 (Philadelphia: University of Pennsylvania Museum of Archaeology and Anthropology, 2013), 285–309 (295), points out,

> Royal reports and divine letters do not seem to have been the rule in a military campaign. Rather they were written in the case of severe violations of tacit and explicit international agreements and fratricide, i.e., in cases when the action of a king was in need of an overruling divine command that sanctioned the royal deed.

133. Samuel E. Balentine, *Prayer in the Hebrew Bible: The Drama of Divine-Human Dialogue* (Minneapolis: Fortress, 1993), 92: "In both its form and its rhetoric this prayer is carefully designed to affirm that the Lord, and the Lord alone, can be trusted to deliver the people"; Bostock, *Portrayal of Trust*, 68, follows Balentine on this point.

boast that the kings of Assyria put all the lands to the ban (החרים) becomes החריב in Hezekiah's prayer. The more distant sound parallels to סנחריב (חרם, חרף) have not only shifted to חרב, but the H-stem form brings the חריב part of the name into close proximity. This shift prepares the way for YHWH to charge Sennacherib with חרף and then quote Sennacherib's own boast of "drying up the Nile" חרבוא (with defective writing) beginning the shift back to the sword חרב of the מלאך יהוה.[134]

While a progression from חרף <-- חרם <-- חרב may be an unlikely string of connections for the Kings author to be concerned about, the semblance between "Sennacherib" and חרב does appear remarkable. It should be kept in mind, however, that while the root חרב has distinctive uses in vv. 17 and 24, its use in v. 37 appears to be demanded by the context. Had a word play between סנחריב and בחרב been an emphasis of the Kings author, one may expect stronger indications of such.

Eschewing details of how and when exactly Isaiah conveyed a response to Hezekiah's prayer, the narrative thus concentrates more fully on the response itself. Finally, after repeated occurrences of שמע and of the motif of response, YHWH explicitly states that he has a response concerning Sennacherib. For good or ill, the Assyrians now have the direct attention of YHWH.

THE ORACLES: YHWH'S SOVEREIGNTY, JERUSALEM'S TRIUMPHANT RESCUE, AND ASSYRIA'S DOWNFALL (2 KGS 19:21–34)

Often described by scholars as a taunt-song more or less in *qinah* metre,[135] the first oracle (vv. 21–28) of the set begins with a rhythmic and word-initial assonantal colon, בזה לך לעגה לך (*bazah leka loʿăgah leka*). "The virgin daughter Zion," i.e., Jerusalem, is depicted as defiant of Assyria. The general sentiment of derision and mockery is often perceived by scholars.[136] Moreover, the implication is clear that Assyria is effectively defeated.[137] Cogan

---

134. Hull, *Hezekiah—Saint and Sinner*, 380–81.

135. E.g., Karl Budde, "The Poem in 2 Kings 19:21–28 (Isaiah 37: 22–29)," *JTS* 35 (1934) 307–13; Cogan and Tadmor, *2 Kings*, 236; Jones, *1 and 2 Kings*, 2:578; Hobbs, *2 Kings*, 271; Wiseman, *1 and 2 Kings*, 282; see also Long, *2 Kings*, 227.

136. Wiseman, *1 and 2 Kings*, 282; Hobbs, *2 Kings*, 279; Jones, *1 and 2 Kings*, 2:578.

137. Long, *2 Kings*, 228: "V. 21b . . . invokes an image of a morally and physically vanquished foe . . ."

and Tadmor suggest that "the gesture is one of sorrow and commiseration."[138] This may be the case, though it is to be asked why the phrase in v. 21 does not precisely match the idiom with which Cogan and Tadmor equate it. Either way, there is irony present in v. 21 in that the attacked is now in an elevated position in relation to the attacker, the colonial target over the would-be colonizer. More recently, Chapman has contributed to part of this matter of interpretation by drawing attention to possible gender-based implications in the imagery. Sennacherib is "no longer the unrivalled king and military commander; he is a hopeful young suitor aiming to impress a young girl with boastful talk,"[139] "a king who had come presenting himself as a military victor, divinely legitimate, and an abundant provider [who] is turned away first by the derisive laughter of a young girl."[140] The new imagery of v. 21 brings a new level of meaning to the conflict "by heightening the perception of a masculine contest between a young male suitor and a divine father."[141] Later in the oracle, among the last few occurrences of בוא ("enter") in a passage with an unusually high occurrence of the root,[142] is a reinforced inclusio that "he will not enter this city//this city he will not enter" (vv. 32a, 33a). The implication is that the "virgin daughter Zion" remains "unentered,"[143] and thus YHWH's fatherly protection of her—and rejection of the would-be suitor, Sennacherib—proves effective:

> As an oracle [i.e., vv. 33–34] that follows the Daughter Zion poem, however, this statement strengthens the divine response to Sennacherib and adds to it sexual innuendo. On a literal level, Yahweh is promising that Sennacherib will not even begin to succeed militarily against Jerusalem, but on the figurative level introduced by the story of a suitor approaching the virgin Daughter Zion, this second oracle of Yahweh becomes the words of a father protecting the chastity of his daughter against a grossly unworthy suitor. The repeated refrain that frames this divine oracle is "He shall not enter this city . . . Into this city, he shall not enter." The personification of the city as a woman

---

138. The difference is that of *ro's heni'a* and *henid bero's* (e.g., Jer 18:16; Job 2:11; Psa 69:21). Cogan and Tadmor, *2 Kings*, 237. Cohn, *2 Kings*, 137, allows for both interpretations.

139. Cynthia R. Chapman, *The Gendered Language of Warfare in the Israelite-Assyrian Encounter*, HSM 62 (Winona Lake, IN: Eisenbrauns, 2004), 87.

140. Ibid., 86.

141. Ibid.

142. בוא occurs 7x in 19:21–34.

143. Chapman, *Gendered Language of Warfare*, 95; see also 87–88, as quoted in this paper.

spurning the advanced of a male suitor allows for a sexual reading of the verb "enter" on one level, and the interpretation of the verse as Yahweh's protecting his masculine honour as head of household by controlling the sexual access to his daughter.[144]

While Chapman's suggested interpretations may indeed be present, these "sexual" readings should be qualified as *not* the exclusive meanings of the imagery,[145] but rather as an additional layer of meaning to that of military and cosmic victories. One may also ask, if the gender/sexual imagery is so strong at the beginning and end of the oracle set, why it apparently occurs—according to Chapman—only in those places.

Verses 22–23a continue the oracle, the three bicola cohering by way of shared content, voice/perspective, direction (i.e., Sennacherib), and poetic repetition and chiastic aspect—as distinct from chiasmus proper.[146] Chiastic aspect is demonstrated here (parallel elements are in italics; chiastic elements are underlined):

ועל־מי הרימות קול		את־מי חרפת וגדפת	
<u>קול</u>/'voice' *רום* 'against whom'		<u>חרף</u> 'Against whom'	
על־קדוש ישראל		ותשא מרום עיניך	
'the Holy One of Israel'		*רום*	
אדני		ביד מלאכיך חרפת	
'my lord'		<u>חרף</u>	

The repetitions and chiastic arrangement underline the themes of Assyria's insulting and scoffing (חרף) of YHWH ("Against whom?" [2x]; "the Holy One of Israel," "my lord") and Assyria's arrogance (רום). Bostock comments: "By his disparagement of God [depicted through the fourfold use of חרף in chapter 18], Sennacherib is trying to boost his own standing and emphasize his own greatness."[147] קול is distinguished both by its end-colon placement and chiastically central position. This contributes to the impact of קול's echo

---

144. Ibid., 87–88.

145. Ibid., 89, suggests an unnecessary narrowing of focus here, in my opinion: "Daughter Zion's presence in this narrative enhances the element of a masculine contest by reducing a hostile military approach to a romantic courtship attempted by a suitor who aims to impress but is rejected out of hand."

146. For further definition and discussion, see Mary Katherine Y. H. Hom, "Chiasmus in Chronicles: Investigating the Structures of 2 Chronicles 28:16–21; 33:1–20; and 31:20—32:33," *AUSS* 47/2 (2009) 163–79, and related chapters in this book regarding those same textual passages.

147. Bostock, *Portrayal of Trust*, 67. E. Kutsch, "חרף II," in *TDOT* 5:209–15 (211–12), approaches a similar conclusion.

of 18:28 and the self-glorifying words that followed (18:29–35), which are mimicked by YHWH in 19:23–24. As Fewell explains,

> The use of the word "voice" (קוֹל) not only recalls the instance when the Rabshakeh stands and calls in a "loud voice" to the people in order to tempt them to insurrection, but it specifies the nature of the offense. The Assyrian has boastfully asked, "Has *any* of the gods of the nations *ever* delivered his land out of *the hand of the king of Assyria*?" The Assyrian offense is verbal and Yahweh mimics this offense with an attributed quotation: "For *you said*: 'With *my* many chariots, *I myself* ascended the heights of the mountains . . . *I* cut down the tallest of its cedars . . . *I* came to its remote shelter . . . *I myself* dug a well and *I* drank foreign waters. *I* dried up, with the sole of *my* foot, all the streams of Egypt.'" [emphasis hers]

Nine times in the six cola of vv. 23b–24 Sennacherib is depicted as referring to himself: "*my* many chariots," "*I* have ascended,"[148] "*I* have cut down," "*I* have entered," "*I* dug,"[149] "*I* drank," "*I* dried up," "*my* feet." Further, the poem's Sennacherib gushes the superlative: "highest mountains," "remotest parts of Lebanon," "tallest cedars," "choicest firs," "remotest lodge," "most fertile forest," "all the streams of Egypt."[150] The poem's Sennacherib speaks mostly in v. 23 three abc//b'c' couplets—"limping synonymous parallelism"[151]—which reinforces the somewhat "stand-alone" quality of the 'a' elements, themselves repeatedly self-glorifying Sennacherib's achievements. Long interprets the abc//b'c' structure as directing attention especially to the b' and c' elements "to build an edifice of thematic specificity and intensification."[152] While Watson acknowledges that "the significance of the abc//b'c'-patterned couplet is not clear,"[153] it may at least be agreed that the pattern renders its content more memorable and aesthetically-pleasing.

Verse 24 rounds off the poem's "self-description" of Sennacherib with a repetition of the first-person pronoun "I" (אֲנִי) and a balanced parallelism, the latter perhaps bringing a sense of closure to the literary Sennacherib's

---

148. This phrase involves two indications of the first-person: אֲנִי עָלִיתִי.

149. This phrase also involves two indications of the first-person: אֲנִי קַרְתִּי.

150. Agreeing with Cohn, *2 Kings*, 137. Regarding מָצוֹר, I am currently in agreement with most major translations (NIV, JPS, ESV, ASV, and NRSV) and scholars who consider it a poetic equivalent of מִצְרַיִם, though the LXX "misunderstands everywhere"—see BDB, 596—and KJV translates as "fortified cities," "fortresses," etc.

151. Long, *2 Kings*, 228.

152. Ibid., 229.

153. Wilfred G. E. Watson, *Classical Hebrew Poetry: A Guide to its Techniques*, JSOTSup 26 (Sheffield: JSOT Press, 1984), 176.

words.¹⁵⁴ Possibly there is mild sexual innuendo heightening the sense of the Assyrian's victory over maiden nations in the references to "most fertile forest" and the acquisition and drinking of wells, but even without continued imagery of masculine conquest, the point comes through of Sennacherib's "exaggerated view of his own accomplishments . . . He thinks of himself as a god."¹⁵⁵ The historical fact that Assyria did not invade Egypt until Esarhaddon (671) is beside the literary depiction of Assyria's hyperbolic rhetoric.¹⁵⁶ The mimicking of Assyria in vv. 23-24 may well reflect Assyria's own boasting, as one may observe in the Assyrian royal inscriptions,¹⁵⁷ though the biblical portrayal is not necessarily dependent on such a correspondence in order to convey its own portraiture of the Assyrian monarch.

Bostock suggests that Sennacherib is characterized in vv. 24-25 by the term נבל, "fool." While Bostock makes some thoughtful correlations between the biblical concept of נבל and the Assyrian king, the point should not be pressed, for the term is not actually found in the Hezekiah narrative, as Bostock himself acknowledges.¹⁵⁸

YHWH's direct perspective and voice break in to respond to Sennacherib—and, indirectly, to Hezekiah and the Jerusalemites—for the remainder of the oracle set. This response of YHWH makes ample use of first- and second-person references, the occurrences of each nearly matching, and perhaps reflecting, the conflictual tension. First-person pronominal forms—all referring to YHWH—occur 11 times in vv. 25-28, and second-person pronominal forms—all referring to Sennacherib—occur 12 times. The relative numbers of instances underline that the conflict is really between

---

154. Long, *2 Kings*, 230, finds that this structure for v. 24 actually "loosens the form" and that its content involves "an even more wondrous achievement" [i.e., "I dried up with the sole of my foot all the streams of Egypt," Long's translation].

155. Provan, *1 and 2 Kings*, 262.

156. The exaggerated representation by the poetic Sennacherib in vv. 23-24 puts the issue of interpretation of מצור into perspective, as Provan, *1 and 2 Kings*, 262, points out:

> Much ink has been wasted debating whether Hb. *masor* can really be Egypt (as in Isa 19:6) when Sennacherib never literally conquered Egypt. The absurdity of the discussion becomes evident as soon as we ask whether we are meant to think that he "literally" ascended the heights of the mountains and cut down Lebanon's tallest trees (v. 23), or "literally," once in Egypt, dried up all her streams with the soles of his feet (v. 24). . . . The passage is not meant to be taken literally. . . .

Jones, *1 and 2 Kings*, vol. 2, 579, shares a similar perspective.

157. *ARAB* 2: §§118, 236, 823; *ARI* 2: §§19, 30, 468; regarding the difficulty of using chariotry in mountainous regions, see, e.g., *ARI* 2: §§16, 216, 468.

158. Bostock, *Portrayal of Trust*, 68.

YHWH and Sennacherib. YHWH's first words are הלא־שמעת ("Have you not heard?"). הלא + שמע occurs only six times in the OT (1 Kgs 1:11; 2 Kgs 19:25// Isa 37:26; 40:21; Psa 94:9; Ruth 2:8).[159] Its form as a rhetorical question in this context (and, actually, all others listed above) naturally contributes emphasis and implies that a strong affirmation is expected on the part of the party to whom it is directed.[160] Also adding to the phrase's emphasis are its placement at the beginning of YHWH's "interruption" of Sennacherib and its inclusion of the final occurrence of שמע in the main Assyria pericope (chapters 18–19, though chapter 20 does have four more occurrences of the root). After ten occurrences of שמע, all of which concern the understanding or response of the Jerusalemites, Hezekiah, or YHWH—often because of the rhetorical and/or physical challenge of the Assyrian forces and leadership—YHWH finally speaks and, in doing so, he does not simply request a response from Assyria, but makes it happen (19:7-9).[161] In the case of YHWH's "direct," imagined retort to Sennacherib in v. 25, the deity expects a response to have already been given by the Assyrian king. The matter of which the Assyrian king is expected to be aware is the fact of the sovereign intent of YHWH—triply emphasized by the three brief statements of cola 25b-d before any specifics concerning Sennacherib's actions are addressed. Only after establishing this context of YHWH's sovereign purposes and control is the devastating power of Assyria given attention. While in the previous, Assyrian speeches the Assyrian kings' victories were evidence of the empire's supremacy, Isaiah's oracle re-contextualizes those Assyrian victories and makes them examples of the efficacy of YHWH's sovereignty. It is as if the message of vv. 25b-26 is that YHWH intended that you, Assyria, be a destroyer of powerful peoples, and indeed, YHWH's intention has been fully realized in your success. Hence, the description of fortified cities' inhabitants cowering, weak in spirit and strength, before the Assyrians does convey on its own a picture of Assyria as intimidatingly mighty and destructive. In the context of the oracle, however, this description gains another layer of meaning in that the grass-like weakness of normally strong cities before the Assyrians demonstrates the power of YHWH's will, and As-

159. Results are from an Accordance 6.1.2 search of "שמע <WITHIN 1 Words> לא <WITHIN 1 Words> ה."

160. See, e.g., GKC § 150e; Godfrey Rolles Driver, "Affirmation by Exclamatory Negation," *JANES* 5 (1973) 107-14 (107-8); GKC and Driver appear to be followed in this understanding by Robert L. Hubbard, *The Book of Ruth* (Grand Rapids: Eerdmans, 1988), 154; Frederic W. Bush, *Ruth, Esther*, WBC (Dallas: Word, 1996), 119; and Edward F. Campbell, *Ruth: A New Translation with Introduction, Notes and Commentary*, AB 7 (Garden City, NY: Doubleday, 1975), 96.

161. Fewell, "Sennacherib's Defeat," 85, makes a similar observation regarding the correspondence and contrast between vv. 11 and 25-28.

syria's great destructiveness is just a fine example of that. YHWH does not respond directly to Sennacherib's exploits in the poem or even to his specific conquests in 18:34; 19:12–13;[162] there is no denial of Assyrian achievements. Rather, Assyrian success is relativized in the perspective of YHWH/Isaiah's oracle. Building on Fewell's observation, these verses are also an ironic affirmation and play on Sennacherib's earlier claim in 18:25 (NIV: "... have I come to attack and destroy this place without word from the LORD? The LORD himself told me to march against this country and destroy it").[163] Bostock proposes that there is a contrast between the poem's Sennacherib in vv. 23–24—verses that have to do with nature—and YHWH's own description of Sennacherib's effect in v. 26. According to his reading, it is implied that Sennacherib thinks too highly of himself, describing himself as a conqueror of creation in vv. 23–24, while YHWH lowers Sennacherib's conquests to humbler images of the overpowering of mere grass.

> Some of Sennacherib's boasts are clearly fanciful, but, significantly, all are to do with the domination of nature.... God, on the other hand, makes a more realistic statement when he describes the devastation of fortified cities and the dismay and confusion of their inhabitants.... Compared with felling the great trees of Lebanon, the Assyrian is only good at bringing down feeble wild plants and scrawny grass.... Sennacherib is concerned with claiming wonders of nature. God is characterized as showing concern for his highest creation, humankind, which in comparison to the trees mentioned by Sennacherib, seems as ephemeral and vulnerable as grass.[164]

Bostock is unique and thoughtful in this interpretation, but his reading here seems to require a forced reduction of the power of the grass metaphor in v. 26. The point of the imagery in v. 26 seems to be not so much in making a contrast between the metaphorical imagery of vv. 23–24 and 26, but to convey the weakness engendered in the peoples Assyria attacked, thus illustrating the efficacy of YHWH's sovereign intents.

YHWH continues to put Assyrian dominance in its place in v. 27. Every action of Assyria is stated as known by YHWH. Put another way, there is no escape for the Assyrians from the sight of YHWH and, as the next few lines will indicate, from the judgment of YHWH as well. Repetition of the root רגז (in Hithpael) + אלי provides a transition between vv. 27

---

162. Cohn, *2 Kings*, 137, makes a similar observation, but considers the "earlier boasts about the nations [Assyria] destroyed" as confronted in vv. 25–28.

163. Fewell, "Sennacherib's Defeat," 85.

164. Bostock, *Portrayal of Trust*, 74.

and 28, between YHWH's omniscience in relation to Assyria and YHWH's subsequent judgment of Assyria. Again, Fewell makes a keen observation in that these occurrences of רגז, in addition to חרף and גדף (vv. 22, 23; see also 4, 6, 16), "compose the semantic category of blasphemy,"[165] the application of which re-interprets the Assyrian rhetorical argumentation as anti-YHWHistic and, implicitly, false and unreliable. Hence, it is implied that the Assyrian rhetoric's converse is true—Hezekiah is right to trust in YHWH, YHWH can be trusted to deliver Jerusalem, Sennacherib's strength is limited.[166] As Brueggemann contemplates for the poem as a whole,

> Most likely the purpose of the poem is to permit and authorize Israel to be "at the wall" with a different perception of reality and therefore with a different voice. It is important that Assyria be deabsolutized so that someone else may speak. It is even more important that Judah experience and perceive Assyria to be deabsolutized.... Without this oracle, Assyria seemed inordinantly powerful, even as it claimed to be.[167]

Sennacherib's strength and accomplishments are not the reasons for YHWH's judgment upon the Assyrian king. Rather, it is Sennacherib's attitude towards YHWH—"your raging"—and himself—"your arrogance"—that condemn him (v. 28a). In both of these attitudes Sennacherib exhibits too high a view of himself—we may recall also v. 22—such that he attempts to elevate himself above YHWH. YHWH expresses his punishment of Sennacherib in the language of aNE victory and humiliation over an enemy foreign ruler, humbling the captive to the level of beasts. Verse 28 indicates that in Sennacherib's return to Assyria the total control and dominance of YHWH over Sennacherib will be demonstrated. Irony adds to the impact of the prophecy in that YHWH likens his imminent victory over Assyria to that of perhaps typical Assyrian practices, as seen, for example, on the Zinjirli stele on which Esarhaddon leads Baal of Tyre and Tirhakah of Egypt by rope and lip-rings, and in the records of Assurbanipal in which that Assyrian king passed a rope through the jaw of Uate', king over Arabia.[168] The use of the root שוב, last seen in vv. 7–9 which featured the "false dawn" of the Rab-šaqeh's retreat, renews anticipation that the prophecy of v. 7 will at last be fulfilled.

165. Ibid., 74.

166. Similarly, ibid., 85–86.

167. Walter Brueggemann, "Isaiah 37:21–29: The Transformative Potential of a Public Metaphor," *HBT* 10 (1988) 1–32 (15–16).

168. *ANEP*, plate 447; *ANET*, 300//*ARAB* 2: §319; see also *ARAB* 2: §212; 2 Chr 33:11; Ezek 19:4, 9; 38:4; Amos 4:2.

YHWH then addresses Hezekiah in a tightly structured oracle.[169] On first appearance, vv. 29–31 do not involve Assyria. However, the conflict with Assyria and the Assyrian rhetoric are both addressed in these verses. To begin, the agricultural phenomenon is described as האות, "the sign," a word that denotes "not necessarily a miraculous occurrence, but . . . a natural process that can be vested with symbolic meaning."[170] Moreover, Helfmeyer observes the incidental nature of "signs":

> A sign in itself must not motivate the people to believe; crucial instead is the word that accompanies the sign. This word declares in what or whom the sign is intended to motivate a person to believe. Therefore, there is no sign revelation without a corresponding word revelation interpreting the sign.[171]

The "sign" described and commented upon in vv. 29–31 indeed qualifies for this definition in that it appears to include a natural phenomenon, perhaps occurring at an unusually fast rate, which is subsequently interpreted. Regarding v. 29, the "natural" restoration of crops in the land likely reflects prior Assyrian destruction of the countryside, whether incidental from invasion and warfare or intentional.[172] Ehrlich surmised that deficiencies in agriculture would continue for a time because of a lingering fear of the Assyrians,[173] but such a situation is unattested, while Assyrian destruction of enemies' land is both attested and seems more likely. Jones and Wiseman observe the possibility that the Assyrians' presence in the land from about March or April to about October would have prevented both a harvest and a ploughing and sowing, resulting in a need to depend on "what is self-grown."[174] Nevertheless, Jones finds that the probable late provenance of the

---

169. Verse 29 has an attractive a//a'//a"bc structure. Verses 30–31 link not only through content, but through chiastically linked key vocabulary, the word פליטה and the root שאר. Verse 31's own chiastic structure followed by the closing formula קנאת יהוה [צבאות] תעשה־זאת gives a sense of cohesion and finality to this particular oracle.

170. Jones, *1 and 2 Kings*, 2:580. See also Hobbs, *2 Kings*, 281; Paul A. Kruger, "מופת," in *NIDOTTE* 2:879–81 (881); Robert L. Alden, "אוה," in *TWOT* 1:18–19 (18); Alden, "אפת," in *TWOT* 1:67; and F. Stolz, "אות," in *TLOT* 1:67–70 (70); compare BDB, 16d–17a and 68d–69a. F. J. Helfmeyer, "אות," in *TDOT* 1:167–88.

171. Helfmeyer, "אות," in *TDOT* 1:177.

172. Cogan and Tadmor, *2 Kings*, 238, support the likelihood of intentionality on the part of Assyria in devastating the countryside, as "amply attested in Assyrian literature." See, e.g., *ARAB* 1, §§ 776, 792.

173. Ehrlich is noted in Cogan and Tadmor, *2 Kings*, 238.

174. Wiseman, *1 and 2 Kings*, 283; Jones, *1 and 2 Kings*, 2:580–81.

verse makes it "doubtful if an exact description of events was intended."[175] Late provenance of the final form of a text does not necessitate a lack of detail in the account, however.

The basic connection between the sign (v. 29) and its meaning (vv. 30–31) is rejuvenation.[176] Like the state of the crops in the land, so will be the people in the land. Recovery may seem slow, but the fact of its occurrence and the eventual flourishing constitutes the intentional work of YHWH and a miracle—the latter is especially so in view of the ability of Assyria to reduce its enemies to fearful and shrinking victims comparable to frail grass easily destroyed before the Assyrian presence.[177] Unlike Assyria's previous objects of attack, Judah receives YHWH's protection and sustaining, implicitly because of the deity's covenant promises to Israel and the house of David (v. 34). Furthermore, within the greater context of the Hezekiah story, YHWH's promise and the vocabulary of abundant crops and life are an apt rejoinder to the Assyrian leadership's insistence that 1) the Jerusalemites, if they would not surrender to Assyria and continued in their trusting allegiance to YHWH to deliver them, would "have to eat their own excrement and drink their own urine" (NIV, 18:27), and 2) Sennacherib was actually the master who is able to provide life and eschatological blessings (18:31–32).[178]

The oracle set closes with a final prophecy in direct response to Hezekiah's prayer of 19:15–19. This direct response at the end of the set—instead of after v. 21, as Jones suggests was its original placement[179]—contributes through its specificity of events and authenticity (נאם־יהוה, "which always authenticate[s] a prophecy")[180] a strong sense of both closure to the oracle set and connection to Hezekiah's prayer and the rest of the narrative. As

---

175. Jones, *1 and 2 Kings*, 2:581.
176. Long, *2 Kings*, 231: "It will be a sign in nature of a people's rejuvenation."
177. As Provan, *1 and 2 Kings*, 259, puts it:

> The sign that this human recovery will take place in the long term is to be found in the way the remnant will be provided for in the short term. In the aftermath of the Assyrian assault, life will be bleak. But the people will be able to survive because of the crops that spring up from what is already in the ground, and in the third year it will be possible to resume normal agricultural practice. The initial fragility of both human and economic conditions, in other words, should not be a reason for despair. This is not a people under god's judgment, like those in verse 26—grass sprouting on the roof, withering in the sun for lack of deep roots. This is a people under God's providential care, guaranteed to bear fruit.

178. See Fewell, "Sennacherib's Defeat," 86.
179. Jones, *1 and 2 Kings*, 2:581.
180. Wiseman, *1 and 2 Kings*, 284.

well, the phrasal repetition within the oracle—"he will not enter this city// this city he will not enter," vv. 32–33—and within the oracle set (vv. 28c, 33) brings coherence to both the oracle and the set as a whole. This final oracle is tightly constructed, the fourfold parallel לא clauses emphasizing the expected failure of the Assyrian attack on Jerusalem. As in the rest of the oracle set, Sennacherib is neither named nor titled; and, in these verses, the Assyrian king is simply an element of the verbal forms—"he will not . . ." Two key motifs are emphasized through the phraseological repetitions (vv. 28c, 32, 33): that Sennacherib will return/retreat (שוב), and, relatedly, that the only way he will "come" (בוא) now is coming back to his home, not into Jerusalem. As discussed earlier regarding v. 21, the use of בוא may be euphemistically employed here to suggest the Assyrian "suitor's" rejection by YHWH, who protects his daughter's chastity and honour.[181] In v. 34, which is identified by Cohn as an addendum,[182] YHWH's stated motivation for delivering Jerusalem—"I will protect this city to save it for my sake" (v. 34a)—could be understood to imply that upholding his reputation in the face of the Assyrian blasphemy is a dominant reason, in addition to his covenant promises to David.[183] For reasons both external and internal to the Israelite nation of that time, YHWH preserves Jerusalem. The metanarrative of YHWH conceptually triumphs over the metanarrative of the Assyrian empire; in the section to follow, this triumph actualizes in space and time (albeit from a prophetic, teleological view).

FULFILLMENT OF THE ORACLES (2 KGS 19:35–37)

The narrative proceeds to demonstrate the fulfillment of YHWH's words in two loosely-connected parts—through the use of ויהי at the beginnings of vv. 35 and 37[184]—that evidently telescope time, since it was well-known that Sennacherib was killed approximately twenty years after this attempt to conquer Jerusalem. Also, as Hobbs observes, "the term וישב 'and he lived' implies in fact that he was there over a period of time before his death."[185] Still, the narration of consequences begins with a sense of immediacy: it was "during that night" that a "messenger" (מלאך) of YHWH strikes the As-

---

181. See Chapman, *Gendered Language*, 88; and earlier discussion.

182. Cohn, *2 Kings*, 138.

183. For further discussion regarding the ultimately minor role of Hezekiah in Jerusalem's deliverance and the significance of YHWH's grace through his promise to David, see Hobbs, *2 Kings*, 282; and Provan, *1 and 2 Kings*, 259–60.

184. See, e.g., GKC §111f.

185. Hobbs, *2 Kings*, 282.

syrian camp. This מלאך of YHWH is a direct and definitive response to Assyria's previous מלאכים (vv. 9, 14, 23), who had blasphemed YHWH (v. 23). Even van den Berg acknowledges that the narrative claims this, though he denies its historicity: "In 2 Kings we get the impression that the appearance of the angel of YHWH definitively puts an end to Assyria's power. However, we know that Hezekiah's son, Manasseh, was its vassal. . . ."[186] Not only does "the appearance of the angel . . . rather than YHWH himself [look] like a purposeful device of the storyteller" in this way,[187] but there seems to be a further nuanced play on the word מלאך, which can mean both "angel" and "messenger":

> Sennacherib's messengers speak many words against the LORD (vv. 9, 14, 23), but neither Sennacherib nor his messengers have any power to act. The LORD has power of both speech and action and a messenger who is terribly effective.[188]

Brueggemann affirms that:

> There surely is irony in the work of a "messenger" to counter the Assyrian "messengers" who earlier were so arrogant but now are completely impotent and irrelevant. Yahweh's messenger is decisive because Yahweh has sent him. Conversely the Assyrian messengers do not matter now because—it turns out!—they were dispatched by impotent kings and feeble gods.[189]

YHWH's great victory over Sennacherib is expressed in the impressively high numbers given to the slain Assyrian camp. The figure of 185,000 need not be an exact quantity, nor emended to be consistent with the message of the text; the rhetorical use of numbers is well-attested in biblical and aNE literature.[190]

The visual image of countless numbers of dead Assyrian soldiers suddenly strewn over the landscape is dramatically appreciated from the perspective of the Jerusalemites.[191] There could not be a more definitive victory for YHWH, nor a more conclusive defeat for the invading Assyrians. The

---

186. Van den Berg, "Fact and Imagination," 135.

187. Cogan and Tadmor, *2 Kings*, 239.

188. Provan, *1 and 2 Kings*, 262.

189. See Brueggemann, *1 and 2 Kings*, 514–15.

190. See, e.g., M. H. Pope, *IBD* 3:561–67 (563–67); and Marco De Odorico, *The Use of Numbers and Quantifications in the Assyrian Royal Inscriptions*, State Archives of Assyria Studies 3 (Helsinki: University of Helsinki Press, Neo-Assyrian Text Corpus Project, 1995), esp. 133–79. Cogan and Tadmor, *2 Kings*, 239, agree and include good brief discussion on this point.

191. Agreeing with Cohn, *2 Kings*, 139.

Assyrian army is not just overcome, but killed; moreover, the Assyrians are killed not over a period of months or weeks, but simply overnight; further still, the Assyrians are suddenly killed without damage or military effort on the part of Jerusalem; and on top of all this, the Assyrians are suddenly "effortlessly" killed in accordance with the prophecy of Isaiah, which has already established that any victory is the work of YHWH, and against the "realistic odds" favouring victory by the Assyrian empire—circumstances which themselves establish that any victory over Assyria could indeed only be the work of a god above all the other "gods" and powers of the world. The Assyrians could not have experienced a more humiliating defeat, and it is a defeat that, within the context of the Hezekiah narrative, demonstrates decisively the power and honour of YHWH. Hull suggests that the "invisibility" and outcome for the Assyrian army in 19:35 retrospectively indicate that Assyrian power was overrated:

> As a sign that Assyrian power may be overrated, the silence of both the Tartan and the invisibility of *the army* are instructive. The army appears again (not by name but as the "camp" מחנה of Assyria) only with the victory of YHWH's messenger in the "dead of night." Their appearance there is as 185,000 dead bodies which are discovered at dawn the next morning (19:35). Thus, the Assyrian army frames the conflict at Jerusalem, from the first arrival of Assyria in the capital to the end of Assyrian presence in Judah. [emphasis his][192]

Hull's proposal should be qualified in that, in the context of the Sennacherib Narrative as a whole, such overrating could only be in the light of YHWH's able defeat of Assyria.

Sennacherib is given no room in the narrative for a verbal response—the last word literally and figuratively belongs to YHWH.[193] Instead, the Assyrian king's response is non-verbal, presented by the narrator with a sense of alacrity as the next sentence begins with three verbs describing his actions: "He broke camp, he went, and he withdrew/returned," the last of those verbs featuring the final occurrence of the key root שוב, which had been anticipated earlier through seven uses (18:14, 24; 19:7, 8, 9, 28, 33) and—as van der Kooij observes below—three distinct episodes in chapters 18-19.

---

192. Hull, *Hezekiah—Saint and Sinner*, 268.
193. Hobbs, *2 Kings*, 284: "The response of Sennacherib to this claim is never made. He is a silent actor in the rest of the drama, retreating to his homeland, where he eventually dies in simple fulfilment of the word of Yahweh." Similarly, Hull, *Hezekiah—Saint and Sinner*, 303: "Thus, Sennacherib's entire communicative effort receives no direct reply from anyone. . . . Even when Rabshakeh returns (19:8–9), no narration of a report about Jerusalem is mentioned."

The tension created in the Hezekiah-Sennacherib story leading to this final resolution of the hoped-for Assyrian "return" emphasizes narratologically that only YHWH could effect the defeat and departure of the seemingly insuperable Sennacherib and his empire. As van der Kooij remarks:

> The fact that Sennacherib does not return the first time, nor the second, but only at the third occasion, creates a great deal of suspense: as a reader, one becomes curious to know if and when the king of Assyria will actually withdraw and return to his country.
>
> Presented in this way, the motif also has a dramatizing effect. The king of Assyria did not depart after Hezekiah had paid the large amount of silver and gold, nor did he leave when he heard of Tirhaka, king of Egypt. He only withdrew and departed because of the destruction which the angel of the Lord inflicted upon the Assyrian army. Thus, it is ultimately God who made him return . . .[194]

Van der Kooij's conclusion is consistent with that of Balentine regarding 19:15-19, "that the LORD, and the LORD alone, can be trusted to deliver the people."[195] Cohn suggests that the triple sequence of verbs in 19:36 parallels the triple sequence of verbs in 18:17 ("they went up and they came and they stood").[196] Thus, the Assyrian delegation's initial arrival at Jerusalem and Sennacherib's withdrawal from the Judean land may be seen to form an inclusio around the primary narrative concerning the 701 invasion. That such a significant structuring device spanning a sizable amount of text would be this subtly indicated is questionable, though Cohn's observation is not without merit in that Sennacherib's retreat may have been depicted in such a way through the triple verb sequence so as to reverse the triple verb confrontation of his representatives. Šanda also observes the unusual density of verbs in v. 36, but he does not perceive a literary function in the verbs, and hence decides that an emendation is necessary.[197]

---

194. Arie van der Kooij, "The Story of Hezekiah and Sennacherib (2 Kings 18–19): A Sample of Ancient Historiography," in *Past, Present, Future: The Deuteronomistic History and the Prophets*, eds. Johannes C. de Moor and Harry F. van Rooy (Leiden: Brill, 2000), 107–19 (110–11, see also 109).

195. Balentine, *Prayer in the Hebrew Bible*, 92, as discussed earlier in this chapter, 31, n. 87. Hull, *Hezekiah—Saint and Sinner*, 279–80, agrees.

196. Cohn, *2 Kings*, 139.

197. Šanda, *Die Bücher der Könige*, 285:

> Der Text ist wahrscheinlich überladen. וילך וישב sieht wie eine spätere Zutat aus. Denn die Stellung des Subjekts nach dem 3. Verb ist ungewöhnlich. . . . Vielleicht ist für וישב mit Änderung der Punktation וישב zu lesen und das folgende ב auszulassen.

About twenty years may be compressed in the simple phrase וישב בנינוה, "and he dwelt in Nineveh" (v. 36b). The narrative is not concerned with the events of Sennacherib's intervening twenty years, but fast-forwards narrative time to his death. Again, Assyrian powers do not experience an ambiguous demise, but a definitive end. Sennacherib's death is a definite taking of his life—a murder, not a natural death. It is presented by the narrator such that the irony cannot be missed. The one who mocked the true God and all other "gods" is not safe even in the house of his own god, nor is he safe from his own flesh and blood.[198]

The final sentence in the Sennacherib story is striking, for it is the same concluding formula used in Kings for Judean and Israelite kings. In the greater scheme of Kings' chronology and in view of the sovereignty of YHWH implied through the rise and demise of kings, Cohn's suggestion that the use of the concluding formula in v. 37 "[implies] finally that this succession [i.e., from Sennacherib to Esarhaddon] is also sponsored by YHWH" is apropos.[199] The kings of Assyria may (or may not) be mighty; they may be anti-YHWH in their intents; they may be "other" than the house of Judah; they may be the most threatening imperial colonizers the aNE has heretofore known—but even their greatest positions and personages are under the control of YHWH, expressed in both the exceptional events of history, such as those of vv. 35–36, and the "ordinary" events that flow with the passage of time, as in v. 37.[200]

---

198. Agreeing with Provan, *1 and 2 Kings*, 260. Cohn, *2 Kings*, 139, also observes the irony. The very real danger that was often encountered by neo-Assyrian sovereigns was acknowledged by the Assyrians themselves—see Villard, "La notion de famille royale," 520–21.

199. Cohn, *2 Kings*, 139.

200. While it is not the purpose of this study to engage in comparative analysis between the Hebrew and Assyrian accounts of the invasion of Sennacherib but rather to explore and elucidate the Hebrew account itself, I will note that Sennacherib's famous phrase concerning Hezekiah—"He himself, I locked up within Jerusalem, his royal city, like a bird in a cage"—is understood in the light of Assyrian propaganda to be hyperbole for a compromised and botched invasion attempt. Tadmor, *Inscriptions of Tiglath-Pileser*, 79n11, sheds insight on the phrase *kima issur quppi esirsu*, which is in both the Annals of Tiglath-Pileser III and the Annals of Sennacherib:

> This simile, with *esirsu*, first attested here [i.e., in Tiglath-Pileser III's Annal 23, ln. 11], is also used by Sennacherib in describing the siege of Jerusalem during his campaign against Hezekiah in 701.... In neither case is this a description of an actual assault (employing siege-engines, etc.). The true sense of these passages is that of a total blockade, and the hyperbole is employed as a face-saving device to cover for a failure to take the enemy's capital and punish the rebellious king. In the case of Rezin, this was accomplished in the following year (732); in the case of Hezekiah, Sennacherib was forced to make do with heavy tribute delivered to Nineveh after his retreat.

REGARDING HULL'S THEORY THAT THE SENNACHERIB NARRATIVE IS DRAWN FROM ASSYRIAN IDEOLOGY

The ideology of Kings—and of the Sennacherib Narrative in particular—may draw from and implicitly respond to Assyrian ideology. As Hull suggests:

> In many ways the conceptual underpinning of Kings might be described as the clash of Deuteronomic and Assyrian ideologies. The Deuteronomic ideology both draws from and reacts to the concepts presupposed in Assyrian texts.[201]

He further remarks that the Deuteronomistic ideology reflected in Deut 17:16–17, the prohibition against the king's excessive accumulation of horses or of wealth,

> is unusual in the context of kingship in the ancient Near East.... If Kings is read from the perspective of Assyrian ideology, many of the deeds of the kings are positive accomplishments. It is only when Deuteronomic ideology is consistently regarded as the measuring stick for Kings that some of the 'praise' may be viewed as ironic condemnation. In many ways Deuteronomic ideology turns Assyrian ideology upside down. Good is bad and bad is good![202]

Hull proceeds to elaborate on two areas in particular, weapons and wealth/building projects. Though it may be questioned whether wealth and building projects belong in the same category—indeed, it seems that Hull forcibly extends the category of "building projects" to include "wealth" so that he can fit his two categories neatly under the rubric of forbidden-acquisitions-according-to-Deuteronomy 17:16–17—his ideological comparisons are worth considering.

Hull perceives a connection made in Assyrian literature between the theme of trust and military battles. Primary examples he gives are the account of Sennacherib's third campaign (against Hezekiah and the Egyptian and Ethiopian armies) and the story of Esarhaddon's battle to maintain his

---

201. Hull, *Hezekiah—Saint and Sinner*, 565. It should be observed that Hull qualifies the term 'Deuteronomic' "for the ideology of the implied author of Kings because of the close connections between Kings and Deuteronomy.... Whether this ideology is Deuteronomic (Dtn) or Deuteronomistic (Dtr) is a relative question."

202. Ibid., 567, 568.

throne, during which he relied on his gods and persisted towards battle without many horses nor provisions.[203] As he continues:

> While this [latter] narrative does not depict the gods fighting without him, as in 2 Ki 18:35, it certainly demonstrates the trajectory of divine aid in defeating an enemy without advanced weapons or even an army. The fact that this text refers to Esarhaddon's victory in taking the throne is suggestive for Kings in view of the portrayal of Sennacherib's overthrow and Esarhaddon's succession as ultimately caused by YHWH (19:7, 36–37). The Assyrian literary tradition itself thus contains possible seeds of a divine victory without the aid of armies.
>
> However, it does not go nearly as far as the ideology implied in Kings which holds that horse and chariot warfare was totally unacceptable for Judean kings. It is one thing to see weapons as expendable in exceptional cases where the gods fight alongside the king. It is another to see advanced weapons as anathema and evidence of a failure to trust in the deity. Furthermore, the idea of fighting without weapons is certainly not the dominant image in Assyrian texts. Assyrian kings boast in their own weapons and the capture of such weapons from opponents. Dtn/Dtr ideology thus takes an important positive symbol of power and accomplishment in Assyrian ideology and turns it into a symbol of evil and a lack of trust in YHWH.[204]

I would add that, if there is implicit ideological commentary on Assyrian literary ideology in the biblical Sennacherib Narrative, the comparison is reflected not only in 2 Kgs 18:35; 19:7, 36–37, but also in 18:17, 23–24; 19:23.

Regarding wealth and building projects, Hull refers to biblical passages concerning Manasseh, Ahab, Ahaz (e.g., 2 Kgs 16:14–18), Solomon (specifically, 1 Kgs 11:7), and Hezekiah (specifically, 2 Kgs 20:20). Hull implies that, in these passages, the Kings author uses the "symbols of Assyrian greatness" to indicate instead "the symbols of abuse of power by the Israelite and Judean kings."[205] That said, 2 Kgs 20:20 does not necessarily convey that Hezekiah's construction of water works were "evil" deeds.[206] Hull's interpretation seems partly to emphasize the biblical author's depiction of Assyrian

---

203. See *ANET*, 289–90; *ANET*, 287//*ARAB* 2, §§ 240; cf. *ARAB* §§ 153, 253–54, 785.
204. Hull, *Hezekiah—Saint and Sinner*, 568–69.
205. Ibid., 572, see also 573.
206. See ibid, 572.

ideology in the Sennacherib Narrative—especially 18:23-24; 19:23—which he thus relates it to the wider, general ideology of Kings:

> It is true that Sennacherib's texts present these construction projects as evidence of his greatness. But that is precisely the point of Dtn/Dtr ideology. The symbols of Assyrian greatness—horse and chariot, the forests of Lebanon, canals, palaces and silver and gold stored in the palace treasure house—become the symbols of the abuse of power by the Israelite and Judean kings. Reliance on these symbols instead of complete trust in and devotion to YHWH and the house of YHWH lead to the fall of the kings and the punishment of the nation. And as in Assyrian texts which regularly depict the tearing down of the neglected temple before a new one may be built, and in one case the destruction of the first temple by fire . . . , the Jerusalem temple is destroyed in Kings as an act of "cult reform."[207]

The further suggestion is made that "the biblical narratives are not an independent witness, but rather a product of literary reflection *based on* the Assyrian texts."[208] While this may be possible, the burden of proof remains with Hull, who proposes a few correlations between the biblical account and the Assyrian account without substantial support. Further, why emphasis should be given to the resemblances between the biblical account and the Assyrian one—in contrast to the historical situation—is not made clear; the correlation may lie more in the historical circumstances than in literary parallels.

THE REMAINDER OF THE HEZEKIAH NARRATIVE IN ITS RELATION TO THE PORTRAYAL OF THE ASSYRIANS (2 KGS 20:1-19)

Though the Sennacherib narrative closes with 19:37, the greater story of which it is a part—the Hezekiah narrative—continues through chapter 20. An explicit link is made between chapters 18–19 and 20 in 20:6—the verse situates the events of 20:1–11 in the time of the 701 invasion. In addition to the situational link, the themes and phraseology shared between 19:34 and 20:6b link the two accounts and emphasize the themes of YHWH's defence of Jerusalem, YHWH's upholding of his honour, and YHWH's faithfulness to the Davidic covenant. A third connection made in v. 6 is that of the

---

207. Ibid., 572.
208. Ibid., 582; see also 579–81.

private Hezekiah with the public Hezekiah. "The fate of Hezekiah, the ideal king, is bound up with that of Jerusalem, the ideal 'city of God.'"[209] Hobbs and Cohn also observe a possible symbolic, cultural connection between the king, the physical body, and society such that "the act of healing has social meaning for the king."[210] While this connection could indicate that vv. 1–11 "[reflect] the author's concern for the effects of Assyrian domination on the [social] body politic,"[211] the emphasis in this passage appears to be more on Hezekiah himself and the miraculous healing of his body. Still, a correlation between Hezekiah and the people he rules may be seen, and that Hezekiah's healing not only corresponds to the deliverance of Jerusalem from the Assyrians, but also that the healing's finite nature indicates the "limited immunity of the city to foreign invasion … the threat of Assyria will be replaced by the threat of the Babylonians foreshadowed by the visit of Merodach-Baladan."[212] As far as the narratological emphases of the Scripture passage are concerned, what 20:1–11 contributes to the Hezekiah story is essentially an extended account on the faithfulness and integrity of Hezekiah towards YHWH. Clements suggests that, in this way, the passage implies that such deliverance as that from the Assyrians in 19:35–37 is exceptional and dependent upon a Davidic king fulfilling the covenantal call to faithfulness and obedience to YHWH.[213]

Along the same lines, the story about the Babylonian delegation from Merodach-Baladan may be seen to illustrate "the dangers of complacency" in relation to the influence of the empire (whether Assyrian or Babylonian) and "that Yahweh had already determined not to give such unqualified protection to Jerusalem from the Babylonian threat as he had against the Assyrians."[214] According to this interpretation, then, the Assyrians function in the first half of chapter 20 as providing an occasion—along with Hezekiah's illness—for YHWH to demonstrate his faithfulness to himself and to David, the latter in part shown because of the righteousness of Hezekiah,

---

209. Long, *2 Kings*, 238.

210. Hobbs, *2 Kings*, 292, see also 291; Cohn, *2 Kings*, 143.

211. Cohn, *2 Kings*, 43.

212. Bostock, *Portrayal of Trust*, 113, see also 120; Bostock follows Hobbs, *2 Kings*, 113.

213. R. E. Clements, *Isaiah and the Deliverance of Jerusalem: A Study of the Interpretation of Prophecy in the Old Testament*, JSOT 13 (Sheffield: JSOT Press, 1980), 65.

214. Ibid., 63, 67. In a similar vein, Bostock, *Portrayal of Trust*, 119, comments that

> The narrator seems to suggest that YHWH's ultimate aim is to spare Hezekiah, possibly to increase his faith in view of the siege of the Assyrians, or so that the people of Jerusalem may see what YHWH has done for their leader and learn to trust in YHWH.

made explicit in this passage. Thus, the twin threats of Sennacherib and Hezekiah's illness also provide an opportunity for the excellence of Hezekiah's character to be upheld. In the second half of chapter 20, the previous passages concerning Sennacherib remain in the background but significantly so in that they provide a contrast between the outcome of Hezekiah's faithfulness to the Davidic covenant—namely, Jerusalem's deliverance from Assyria—and the consequences of Hezekiah's complacency towards the covenantal relationship with YHWH—resulting in assured defeat at the hands of Babylon. Closing the entire Hezekiah narrative in this way "disturbs the feelings of relief that the stormy fury of Assyrian conquest and Hezekiah's illness have passed."[215]

Bostock contributes thought-provoking observations and reading in regard to 20:12–19. In comparing the two world superpowers in the Hezekiah narratives, Bostock perceives a heightened difference in the two empires' intentions and approaches towards Hezekiah:

> Threats, invective and propaganda pour forth from the Rabshakeh's mouth, but not a word spoken by the Babylonians is recorded. The difference between the two may lie in their different intentions; the Assyrians come to conquer, the Babylonians come ostensibly to honour Hezekiah. On the other hand, perhaps there is the suggestion from the narrator that whereas Assyria is openly aggressive towards Judah, the Babylonian embassy is to be seen as furtive and guileful.[216]

These observations are helpful in appreciating the characterization of the Assyrians both in the Sennacherib narrative and indirectly in 20:12–19.

In relation to the pericope of 20:12–20 as a whole, Bostock finds that

> comparison of the Assyrians with the Babylonians suggests that the agenda is different in this narrative from the earlier one. That difference would appear not to lie in the characterization of Hezekiah, but in the purpose of the narrative.[217]

He also notes that the emphasis moves from what is heard (שמע) to what is seen (ראה).[218] While this difference may exist, it does not seem that hearing, seeing, and the contrast between them are "clearly given emphasis" (as

---

215. Long, *2 Kings*, 246.

216. Bostock, *Portrayal of Trust*, 129.

217. Ibid., 146. See also 125, where Bostock lists more comparisons between the Assyrians and Babylonians in the Hezekiah narrative, but all simply to conclude as he has done (and articulated better, in this author's opinion) on 146.

218. Ibid., 147:

Bostock puts it) to the degree that they best indicate the purpose of the narratives. This is not to deny that "what is seen" is an issue in vv. 12-19, but it is to say that other issues, themes, and topics may well operate in the narrative as well. Hezekiah's relations with foreign nations, for example, seem to be a more significant *topos* in both narratives.

Bostock perceives a contrast between the Assyrians' evaluation of YHWH's words in chapters 18-19 and Hezekiah's evaluation of the same in 20:19—namely, that the Assyrians consider YHWH's words as untrustworthy ("if the evaluation of the Assyrians is accepted at face value"), while Hezekiah upholds and trusts YHWH's word and expresses gratitude for the delaying of inevitable judgment on Judah.[219] This interpretation, which is basically shared by Ackroyd,[220] denies a moral action-consequence relation between vv. 13-15 and 16-18. The events prophesied in vv. 16-18 are not understood as judgment on Hezekiah, but simply as an irreversible decision of fate, hence Hezekiah—in willing acceptance of YHWH's decision—is not even recorded as having prayed for a reversal or change of the divine will. Again, positing a contrast seems to strengthen Bostock's reading, but the theological presuppositions involved in this reading seem inconsistent with that of the OT biblical authors.[221] It may also be questioned whether or not a contrast between the Assyrians' perspective on YHWH's words and Hezekiah's perspective on YHWH's words in 20:19 is a contrast consistent with the intention of the biblical author. What in the narrative dictates a contrast between Assyria's opinion on this matter and Hezekiah's? If such a comparison is to be made, it is not evident. A better comparison would be one between Assyria and Babylon (as seen above), two world empires threatening Israel/Judah with exile. A stronger argument also could be con-

---

What the Babylonians said is never revealed in contrast to the lengthy records of the speeches of the Assyrians, but the completeness of what was seen by the Babylonians and their coming from a distant land are clearly given emphasis.

P. R. Ackroyd, "An Interpretation of the Babylonian Exile: A Study of 2 Kings 20, Isaiah 38-39," *SJT* 27 (1974) 329-52 (339), also perceives that weight is given to ראה in 20:12-19.

219. Bostock, *Portrayal of Trust*, 143-45, 147.

220. Ackroyd, "Interpretation of the Babylonian," 335-37. Bostock, *Portrayal of Trust*, 140, states: "*Several* scholars reject an interpretation of Hezekiah's words that implies cynicism or smugness" [emphasis mine]. However, the scholars he notes are only Ackroyd and Nelson (see Richard D. Nelson, *First and Second Kings*, Interpretation [Louisville: John Knox, 1987], 246).

221. Such fatalistic theological presuppositions—which include a willingness for even one's forebears to suffer without attempting intercession—are out of line with the biblical authors' perspectives, but, of course, not necessarily out of line with those of particular characters who may exhibit negative and/or contrasting perspectives.

structed for contrasting 20:19 with a number of different individual verses, especially considering that 20:19 is a specific verse while "the evaluation of the Assyrians" is fairly general. Perhaps a contrast between Hezekiah's earlier and later expressions of trust is more apropos. Perhaps Bostock's earlier correlation between 20:3 and 19, which both use אמת, טוב, and שלם is more supportably emphasized.²²² Moreover, the word בטח is not present in 20:19, nor in the rest of the chapter. Perhaps more fundamentally, before contrasting 20:19 with any other verse, one should ask, Does Bostock's and Ackroyd's "positive" interpretation reflect faithfully what is narratologically being communicated in the text? The fact that Hezekiah says one thing, while withholding public expression of his inner thoughts regarding the matter, suggests that his internal response would not be acceptable to Isaiah if known. Thus, while the comparison of the Assyrians' and Hezekiah's evaluations of YHWH's words may be attractive to some, the positing of such a contrast requires a highly selective reading of the text that disregards other key elements in the narrative's interpretation. In sum, Bostock's comparison and consequent conclusion cannot be sustained in this case.

A few subtler suggestions of Assyrian influence in 20:12–19 should be considered. Firstly, Hull suggests that the presence of the Rab-saris in 18:17 is an anticipation of the prophecy that some of Hezekiah's sons will become eunuchs in Babylon (20:18):

> *The Rabsaris*, whose title means "chief of the eunuchs," may be even more symbolic. Since Isaiah conveys the announcement that some of Hezekiah's sons will be eunuchs in the palace of the Babylonian king (20:18), the reference to this silent chief eunuch (18:17) may be anticipatory.²²³

While the presence of the Rab-saris in 18:17 is justified on historical grounds, at the narratological level, Hull makes a promising observation. However, it is not so much that 18:17 is anticipatory as it is the case that 20:18 alludes back to the Assyrian delegation and, in particular, the member of that delegation who was the most relationally-committed to the emperor and who held the greatest military might in the empire apart from the king. In other words, the inner-narrative allusion functions to suggest not simply that some of Hezekiah's descendants will become servants of the enemy emperor and will be rendered unable to carry on Hezekiah's lineage, but—in the manner of the Rabsaris and other royal eunuch officials of that time

---

222. Bostock, *Portrayal of Trust*, 81–82.
223. Hull, *Hezekiah—Saint and Sinner*, 268–69.

and region[224]—that they will change their effective father from Hezekiah to the king of Babylon, and their allegiance from Judah to Babylon, from the kingdom of the covenant people of God to the future imperial oppressor.

Secondly, on a smaller note, possibly the apparent Akkadian loanword בית נכת, from *bit nakkamtu*, in v. 13 subtly adds to the reminder of Akkadian influence in both the previous narrative and Hezekiah's reign.[225]

And finally, it is often suggested that the Babylonian delegation was proposing an anti-Assyrian alliance.[226] While this may have been the case, it is worth observing that the issue of the Babylonian delegation's—and Hezekiah's—true intention is evaded by both Hezekiah and the narrator.[227] Assyria may indeed still be in the background and serve to provide a contrast with Hezekiah's apparent unfaithfulness to YHWH in his relations with Babylon. With the threat of Assyria past and literally in the background, Babylon gradually rises to supersede Assyria's place as the new world power and imperial enemy of Judah. The story indicates, however, that the reason for this is not simply the vicissitudes of history, nor the waning strength of Assyria and the growing dominance of Babylon, but YHWH's decision in response to Hezekiah's heart and behaviour. In chapter 20, world powers such as Assyria and Babylon merely serve to demonstrate the power of YHWH, both in upholding faithfulness to the Davidic covenant and responding to disregard of it.

CONCLUSION

In this chapter, we have taken a slow, exegetically-focussed look at the characterization of the Assyrians through the unfolding plot of the account of Sennacherib's attack on Jerusalem in 2 Kgs 18–20. While this specific narrative is within the wider context of the account of Hezekiah's reign, the narrator shifts perspective and focus between characters—Sennacherib and Hezekiah, the representative officers of each, YHWH, YHWH's representative Isaiah, and the Jerusalemite people—and rates of narrative time.

The portrayal of the Assyrians is primarily indirect and intuited in the beginning section of the narrative (2 Kgs 18:1–16) until the story pace slows

---

224. See Radner, "Royal Decision-making," 359–60.

225. See *CAD* 11/N1: s.v. *nakkamtu*, 183–84. For further discussion on בית נכת as an Akkadian loanword, see Harold R. (Chaim) Cohen, *Biblical Hapax Legomena in the Light of Akkadian and Ugaritic*, SBLDS 37 (Missoula, MT: Scholars, 1978), 40, 67.

226. E.g., Roger S. Nam, *Portrayals of Economic Exchange in the Book of Kings*, Biblical Interpretation Series 112 (Leiden: Brill, 2012), 87. See also secondary literature listed in Long, *2 Kings*, 243.

227. Agreeing esp. with Cohn, *2 Kings*, 144; see also Wiseman, *1 and 2 Kings*, 288.

(2 Kgs 18:17—19:36), at which point it proceeds to convey direct and indirect elements of the Assyrians' characterization, such as their emotive and physical distance (through the use of titles in contrast to personal names alone, and the geographical distance between Sennacherib and Jerusalem, which is repeatedly noted in the text), their aggressiveness (through the unusual use and repetition of confrontative verbs), their very high ranking in the empire (which is explored from Assyrian sources), their psychology and related skills and abilities (through direct content in the narrative), possibly their foreign-ness or "Assyrian-ness" (through the use of phrases that are likely derived from an Assyrian provenance), the Assyrians' own claims about themselves (in their speeches and message, including comparisons to the Solomonic age and their conquests over other nations), the extreme to which they will forward negativity (in the Assyrians' intimdating and crass language and threats), and that they will retreat that that retreat will lead to Sennacherib's deserved defeat (through clearly-stated content and the use of שמע and שוב). In addition to all this, the Assyrians' cunning folds on itself several times in the narrative—for example, in Sennacherib's attack on Hezekiah's trust in YHWH, he unwittingly gives that trust the opportunity to be demonstrated and strengthened.

Isaiah's oracle characterizes the Assyrians through further content and poetic structures. Examples of this are the repeated use of the first-person pronoun to emphasize Sennacherib's arrogant self-sufficiency, the explicit descriptions and moral-theological evaluations of the Assyrians as being (temporarily) powerful, blasphemous, raging, and stubbornly proud, and the use of chiastic aspect and parallelism to emphasize Assyria's arrogance and insulting of YHWH.

Following the immediate death of the Assyrian forces threatening Jerusalem, narrative time speeds up again, telescoping the remainder of the fulfilment of Isaiah's oracle and presenting the ironic implication that the one who challenged and mocked YHWH is not even safe in the house of his own god nor from his own flesh and blood. In this effectively two-part fulfilment of Isaiah's prophecy, the narrative illustrates through the Assyrian outcome that YHWH is sovereign through both his intervention in historical circumstances but also the normal flow of events through time. Possibly the remainder of the Hezekiah Narrative in 2 Kgs 20:1–19 continues this theme through allusion to the Assyrians and their encounter in the previous chapters and the movement of Babylon into the typological place of imperial enemy that was once held by Assyria.

The intriguing hypothesis by Hull that the Sennacherib Narrative in 2 Kgs 18–19 is influenced by and responds to Assyrian ideology is discussed and considered. It is a worthwhile suggestion, though unfortunately one that needs more support to be considered conclusive.

4

Ancestors and Aggressors
The Portrayal of the Assyrians in 1 Chronicles
(1 Chronicles 1:17; 5:6, 22b-26)

AN EMPIRE IS BORN (1 CHRONICLES 1:17)

THE GENEALOGIES OF 1 Chronicles include the eponymous ancestor אשור among the early progeny of the human race, many of whom are founders of nations (1 Chr 1:17). If one considers 1 Chr 1:1-23 to be evocative of Genesis 10, then the appearance of אשור/Asshur in the genealogy has further associations. In Gen 10:22 (as in 1 Chr 1:17), אשור is a son of Shem, who is previously characterized as a righteous, YHWH-fearing man deserving of blessing (Gen 9:23-27). Hence, the reader may expect by this association that אשור will be predisposed to fearing and obeying YHWH. That a foreign entity may be portrayed as sharing the ideals of the narrator is not as unexpected as one may initially assume, at least for Chronicles.[1] The association of major Assyrian cities with the Hamites, Nimrod, and Cush, however (Gen 10:8-12), adds ambiguity to the characterization of Assyria. Nimrod stands out in the genealogy as one of only two individuals given

---

1. For example, conscious alignment of foreign monarchs with the desire of YHWH is attested in several places in 2 Chronicles (2:10-15; 9:8; 35:21-22; 36:22-23). See Ehud Ben Zvi, "When the Foreign Monarch Speaks," in *The Chronicler as Author: Studies in Text and Texture*, eds. M. Patrick Graham and Steven L. McKenzie, JSOTSup 263 (Sheffield: Sheffield Academic, 1999), 209-28, esp. 224-28.

narratival description. He is a "mighty man" in relation to both the world and hunting (and even YHWH, as the idiom suggests).² The first mention of a 'kingdom' in the OT is that of Nimrod. With all this, Nimrod seems to be an apt precursor to the known kingdoms that later developed in his land, particularly Assyria and Babylonia. As the metanarrative of the OT unfolds, אשור's mixed heritage leaves the reader in suspense. Will Assyria prove to be a true son of Shem, following in Shem's God-fearing ways, or will Assyria take after the manner of Nimrod and the Hamites?³ Or, might the Assyrians evidence distinctive qualities of both? For the reader mindful of Genesis 10, the ambiguity in the Assyrian subplot and sub-characterization sustains interest while laying the incipient suggestion of an inherent tension in the character of Assyria, especially in its relation to the world at large and YHWH.

While אשור is included in Chronicles' universal genealogy, it is clearly כל־ישראל (particularly the tribes of Judah, Levi, and Benjamin)—not אשור—that is the overall focus of the genealogies.⁴ Hence, Assyria is included as part of the "human family," but within that context its place is secondary and defined in relation to that of all-Israel and its constituent tribes.⁵ As far as the genealogy at the beginning of Chronicles is concerned, the originary narrative of the future empire is defined by the "metanarrative" of this Judean originary account.

ENTER ISRAELITE מעל, TIGLATH-PILESER III, AND ASSYRIAN EXILE (1 CHRONICLES 5:6, 22b–26)

First Chronicles 5 concerns the Transjordanian tribes. The chapter begins by explaining the shift in firstborn rights. Though Reuben retains firstborn status (בכור), the sons of Joseph receive firstborn privileges (בכרה). The narrative's early presentation of Reuben's moral lapse prepares the reader

---

2. See Mary Katherine Y. H. Hom, "'... A Mighty Hunter before YHWH': Genesis 10:9 and the Moral-Theological Evaluation of Nimrod," *VT* 60 (2010) 63–68.

3. Though it is beyond the bounds of this study, an interesting investigation may be made by comparing the Judahite accounts of Assyria's genealogy (esp. in Gen 10:8–12, 22) and the Assyrians' own depictions of their genealogy (particularly that of Sennacherib, in which legendary and human figures are mixed—see Villard, "La notion de famille royale," 519 and n32).

4. E.g., 1 Chr 9:1; cf. 2:1.

5. Agreeing with Gary N. Knoppers, *1 Chronicles 1–9: A New Translation with Introduction and Commentary*, AB 12 (New York: Doubleday, 2003), 473: "[The Chronicler] puts the various tribes of Israel in their place, much as he put the nations in their place within his universal genealogy (1:1—2:2)."

to expect, in line with the retributive theology of Chronicles, a retributive punishment upon Reuben. Thus, the sudden introduction of the aNE superpower Assyria under the highly effective leadership of Tiglath-Pileser III coupled with mention of the catastrophic event of exile is perhaps not entirely shocking to the post-exilic reader.

The actual form of the Assyrian ruler's name used in 1 Chr 5, "Tilgath-Pilneʾeser/Pilneser," is unproblematic in that variants of Tiglath-Pileser III are common in Kings and Chronicles. Braun observes that "no less than 4 variations are extant in 6 OT occurrences" and notes 2 Kgs 15:29; 16:7, 10; 1 Chr 5:6, 26; 2 Chr 28:20.[6] It therefore seems overly cautious for Braun to continue: "It is open to conjecture whether one or more of these forms might be the result of intentional malformation or whether all represent imperfect attempts to transliterate the Assyrian '*Tukulti-apil-Esarra*' . . ."[7] Tiglath-Pileser III is presented in 1 Chr 5:6 by both his proper name and his kingly epithet: "Tilgath-Pilneʾeser King of Assyria." Hence, Tiglath-Pileser III is both specified as an individual and associated with his role as Assyrian sovereign (and representative, to a degree). Further, Tiglath-Pileser III performs one important action for which a single word suffices and serves in part to characterize its subject: הגלה, "he took into exile." Tiglath-Pileser King of Assyria has the power simply to dislodge the Reubenites, via the exile of Beerah, from their land. The strength of Tiglath-Pileser III's action is underlined by the additional comment that Beerah was a leader of the Reubenites (v. 6c).

Consonant and vowel assonances may be seen to highlight Tiglath-Pileser III as exiler in v. 6. As well, segment 6b appears to "interrupt" the description of Beerah and his descent, perhaps reflective of the interrupting effect of the Assyrian exile on the Reubenites' continuation in the land. The first and last phrases both concern Beerah and his status within the lineage of Reuben. As well, both phrases end with בנו/בני. The middle clause is enveloped by the consonants אשר at both ends, demarcating the description of Tiglath-Pileser III. Within the middle clause repeated consonants (ח, ת, ל, ג) and double *segols*[8] facilitate aesthetic flow and thus a sense of coherence to the clause.

Verse 6:

הוא נשיא לראובני	אשר הגלה תלגת פלנאסר מֶלֶךְ אשר	בארה בנו
בְּנִי	אֲשֶׁר	בְּנוֹ
He (Beerah), leader of the Reubenites	TP, King of Assyria	Beerah, son of Reuben

---

6. Roddy Braun, *1 Chronicles*, WBC 14 (Waco: Word, 1986), 70.

7. Ibid., 70.

8. Note that this applies to the vocalization at the time of the Masoretes; we cannot necessarily assume the same vocalization before then.

It should be kept in mind that, in the context of 1 Chr 5:1-6, Tiglath-Pileser III's action is recognized as significant but also, it is implied, sovereignly predetermined in the ancient history of Israel as a retributive consequence of the eponymous Reuben's moral laxity. Assyria's exiling of the Reubenites is emphasized and portrayed more as a function of predetermined "fate" (i.e., the sovereign ways and will of YHWH) than as a development of Tiglath-Pileser III's own volition.

The account of the Reubenites continues in 1 Chr 5, listing more genealogical heads, contrasting the loss of territory in v. 6 with earlier days of prosperity in vv. 8-10,[9] then proceeding to the account of their Transjordanian neighbours, the Gadites. In addition to geography, the Transjordanian tribes are united by common warfare, which is undertaken in 5:19-22b in heartfelt dependence upon, and trust in, God. Note especially in v. 20 vocabulary characteristic of those faithful to God in Chronicles: עזר (Niphal stem, which is passive, hence the people are helped by God), זעק (indicating acutely-felt need),[10] and בטח.

The faithfulness of the Transjordanian tribes and their God-granted success (vv. 20, 22b) will be seen to act retroactively as a foil for the situation to come, as intimated in v. 22b: "until the exile," the significance of this contrasting event perhaps enhanced by its conclusive position (v. 22c) and brevity (עד־הגלה). As well, the Assyrian exile has gained something of a nonpareil status; it is 'the exile' in v. 22c.[11] The consonantal form of הגלה also links the reference to v. 6 (הגלה) and its brief account of the disaster wrought

---

9. William Johnstone, *1 and 2 Chronicles*, vol. 1, *1 Chronicles 1–2 Chronicles 9: Israel's Place among the Nations*, JSOTSup 253 (Sheffield: Sheffield Academic, 1997), 29 suggests that there are intimations in v. 8 of the Reubenites' eventual moral downfall.

> It may be by deliberate design that C[hr] lists climatically in v. 8 a place name associated with Baal (cf. Num 32:38; Josh 13:17) as a reminder of the temptations to worship other gods that constantly assailed the Israelites on settlement and to which they finally succumbed (cf. v. 25-26).

Johnstone's proposal is attractive, and similar observations (e.g., J. A. Thompson, *1, 2 Chronicles*, NAC [Nashville: Broadman & Holman, 1994], 79: "The name Baal points to a northern link where the name Baal was well known, especially in names which had more than one element") may be construed to argue likewise. A closer look at the biblical tradition makes this position difficult to maintain, however, on at least three counts: 1) the use of "Baal" as an element in PNs is not unusual in the OT; relatedly, 2) as Knoppers, *1 Chronicles 1–9*, 385, points out, Chronicles contains "the only attestations of Baal as a PN in the HB . . . (1 Chr 5:5; 8:30; 9:36)"; and perhaps most importantly, 3) "Baal-meon" is the place name used elsewhere (as Johnstone himself points out) in the biblical tradition concerning the land of Reuben.

10. For further discussion, see analysis of 2 Chr 32:30 later in this book.

11. As pointed out by Magnar Kartveit, *Motive und Schichten der Landtheologie in I Chronik 1–9*, ConBOT 28 (Stockholm: Almqvist & Wiksell, 1989), 137.

by Tiglath-Pileser III on the Reubenites—a disaster now explicated in vv. 22c and 26 as extending to all two-and-a-half tribes of the Transjordan.[12]

Verses 23–24 proceed to describe the geographic area and leaders of the eastern half of the tribe of Manasseh. Williamson finds the placement of these verses problematic in several respects, two of which concern this study. First, Williamson asserts that "a reference to the half-tribe of Manasseh *after* the more general editorial treatment of the two and a half tribes in the previous paragraph is awkward."[13] However, if the Manassites were primarily responsible for leading the Transjordanian peoples to behaviour unfaithful to YHWH, then the MT reads consistently within the world of Chronicles and also with the historical situation. As well, it is not uncommon for biblical narrative to move between general and specific perspectives. Williamson's second assertion is that "the material in vv. 23–24 . . . would be more at home in 7:14–19."[14] The MT remains preferable, however; the aptness of vv. 23–24 in its immediate context may be better appreciated when one considers the similar description of the other Transjordanian tribes in 1 Chr 5 (which include, specifically, the area inhabited and a handful of family heads, vv. 3–16, 22c). Also, in vv. 23–26 the Chronicler is evidently focusing on East Manasseh and the conditions concerning that half-tribe that led to the consequence of Assyrian exile, while in 7:14–19 the Chronicler's purpose appears to be more general, concerning both halves of Manasseh, and is interested in Manasseh not in terms of its East Bank elements, but as a tribe of Israel and Joseph.

It is perhaps worth noting Johnstone's suggestion that the use of the place name "Baal Hermon" in v. 23 is a deliberate choice by the Chronicler to indicate the prevalence of Baal worship in the land in which the East Manassites settled (and thus to anticipate the punishment of exile by the Assyrians): ". . . here Half-Manasseh is crowded around Hermon, a famous seat of Baal: C[hronicler] is using geography ideologically."[15] Oddly enough, Johnstone's support of this assertion is that "the association of Hermon with Baal is indicated by Ps 42:6 [MT 42:7]; 89:12; and 133:3,"[16] which begs the

---

12. Matthias Ederer, "Der Erstgeborene ohne Erstgeburtsrecht 1 Chr 5, 1–2 als Schlüsseltext für die Lektüre von 1 Chr 5,1–26," *Bib* 9 (2013) 481–508 (504) makes a similar observation of this "Steigerung" of the exile theme through these verses.

13. H. G. M. Williamson, *1 and 2 Chronicles*, NCBC (London: Marshall, Morgan & Scott, 1982), 66.

14. Ibid., 66–67. Thompson, *1, 2 Chronicles*, 82, evidences hesitations similar to Williamson in that he apparently assumes that the combination of 5:23ff and 7:14–19 as one account is more original and/or preferable to the received text's separate accounts.

15. Johnstone, *1 Chronicles–2 Chronicles 9*, 79.

16. Ibid, 79.

question, for none of these references has anything to do with Baal (instead, they all support the worship of Israel's God!). If anything, Johnstone's citations may be used to defend, by way of contrast, that "Baal-Hermon" is an unusual place name in the OT.

Though one should bear in mind my observations under note 9, exceptional circumstances regarding "Baal-Hermon" and v. 23 lead me to conclude independently of Johnstone's argument that "Baal-Hermon" is indeed an intentional choice by the Chronicler to suggest the Manassites' religious-moral depravity to the extent of impending judgment and destruction by YHWH: 1) Judges 3:3 is the *only* other occurrence of "Baal Hermon" in the OT, and it is part of a dense unit of verses (Judg 3:1–6, note also 3:7) concerning the anti–YHWH nations that were left in the land "to test the Israelites to know whether they would obey the commands that YHWH had given their fathers . . . " (Judg 3:4); and 2) the accompanying use of the Amorite designation "Senir" is distinctive,[17] indicating a precarious state (usually towards judgment and destruction).[18]

The reader is reminded of the Manassites' strength and prosperity in 1 Chr 5:24b (cf. vv. 18–22a, 23a), which immediately functions to heighten contrast with what follows. 1 Chronicles 5:25 begins with the verb that is most often used in Chronicles to describe behavior antithetical to the Davidic-Solomonic ideal, וימעלו ("But they were unfaithful").[19] The object of their unfaithfulness is "the God of their fathers," an especially Chronistic

---

17. Whether or not one regards "Baal Hermon," "Senir," and "Mount Hermon" to be in sequential or epexegetical relation (both interpretations may be reasonably defended), the use of distinctive place names is of significant interest here (especially when one considers the fluid use of place names and boundaries—see, e.g., discussion on vv. 11, 16, 23 in Braun, *1 Chronicles*, 76–78).

18. "Senir" (שניר) occurs only four times in the OT: Deut 3:9; Ezek 27:5; 1 Chr 5:23; Song 4:8. As acknowledged Amorite vocabulary (Deut 3:9), the term surely had associations with a nation on the brink of judgment and danger because of its sinfulness before YHWH (cf. Gen 15:16). In the first three instances of שניר, the context clearly involves conflict between YHWH and powerful peoples rejecting him and for whom defeat is imminent, if not already accomplished. Possibly, the appearance of שניר in Song 4:8 is to evoke this sense of danger and thus excitement in the lovers' escapades. This could explain the mention of lions and leopards/panthers—which "commentators have been sore vexed to explain" (Marvin H. Pope, *Song of Songs: A New Translation with Introduction and Commentary*, AB [Garden City, NY: Doubleday, 1977], 475)—immediately following in the same verse.

19. See Kartveit, *Motive und Schichten*, 143:

> Als Grund für die Deportation wird Sünde gegen das erste Gebot angegeben, V. 25. *m'l*, <<treulos sein>>, ist, wie schon erwähnt, ein chronistischer Terminus, findet sich aber auch in P, Ez und Dtn. Die Vokabel führt in ethischer Sprache den Bruch des Gottesverhältnisses vor, der umso abscheulicher ist, als er gegen den treuen und rettenden <<Gott ihrer Väter>> gerichtet ist—in

epithet.[20] The phrase appeals to a traditional spirituality and develops an indirect but inherent theme throughout Chronicles that "each generation has a responsibility to appropriate the faith handed down by its predecessors."[21] The possible allusion of v. 23b to Judg 3:1-6 (note esp. vv. 4, 6b) regarding testing and the ideal of faithfulness from generation to generation supports this use in v. 25.[22] The deplorable extent of the Manassites' מעל is conveyed by the verb in the parallel, explanatory phrase that follows, "and they went like prostitutes (זנה) after the gods of the peoples of the land . . ." (v. 25b). "The gods of the peoples of the land" contrasts with "the God of their fathers," delineating the challenge to the people for commitment to YHWH. The same language (and attendant challenge) will appear again in the rhetoric of the Assyrians in 2 Chr 32, the inner-Chronicles usage reinforcing the irreverence in Assyria's depreciation of YHWH as like other gods. We should note especially that אלהי עמי־הארץ occurs in the OT in

---

schroffem Gegensatz zu den Vätern selbst, die auf ihn vertraut *batehû bô*, V. 20.

See also Mary Katherine Y. H. Hom, "Significant Vocabulary Pertaining to the Davidic-Solomonic Ideal in Chronicles," *EJ* 35/1 (2017) 10–17, esp. 16–17.

20. Sara Japhet, *The Ideology of the Book of Chronicles and Its Place in Biblical Thought*, tr. Anna Barber (Frankfurt: Lang, 1989), 14, reports 19 extra-Chronicles occurrences and 27 Chronicles occurrences of "God of the fathers" and its variants, while Leslie C. Allen, "Aspects of Generational Commitment and Challenge in Chronicles," in *The Chronicler as Theologian: Essays in Honor of Ralph W. Klein*, eds. M. Patrick Graham, Steven L. McKenzie, and Gary N. Knoppers (London: T. & T. Clark, 2003), 123–32 (123, 128–29) counts 32 Chronicles occurrences and 20 instances of specifically "God of their/his Fathers" in Chronicles.

21. Allen, "Aspects of Generational Commitment," 123. Also, 131: "The Chronicler employed older literary traditions, direct intertextuality with earlier material, and current liturgical and cultic usage in order to disseminate the overall formula throughout his work as a rhetorical device for spiritual challenge and commitment." Japhet, *Ideology*, 17–19, interprets the epithet to express the temporal continuity of the relationship between YHWH and the generations of his people. Japhet's view evidently does not include the imperatival instruction perceived by Allen. Somewhere between Allen and Japhet's views is that of Steven S. Tuell in *First and Second Chronicles*, IBC (Louisville: Westminster John Knox, 2001), 33–34. Tuell's brief excursus from v. 25 on "The God of the Ancestors" focuses on the Pentateuch's use of the name and tradition-covenant continuity with an disproportionate amount of exposition developed from his one Pentateuchal reference to curse (seemingly in an effort to explain the name's use with the very un-traditional Manassites in Chronicles). Given Allen's case-by-case treatment of the epithet's occurrences in Chronicles, along with the overall rhetorical thrust of Chronicles and its heightened use of addresses (commonly recognized by scholars nowadays), Allen's view seems best supported and preferable to that of Japhet and Tuell, though the contribution of both is appreciated.

22. Interestingly, Allen, "Aspects of Generational Commitment," 128, perceives a similar intertextual link via the epithet of 2 Chr 28:6 with Judg 2:12.

only two places, 1 Chr 5:25b and 2 Chr 32:19b. The use of the phrase in 2 Chr 32:19b indicates foreign (or at least, non–ideal-Israelite) gods, the presence of which is in direct opposition to YHWH. This understanding of אלהי עמי־הארץ in 2 Chr 32:19b could suggest that the phrase's usage in 1 Chr 5:25b also indicates foreign gods and a foreignness about the Transjordan. Hence, the Chronicler may be seen to make a subtle condemnation of the land east of the original promised land and the two and a half tribes' preference for "foreign" territory. Regardless of whether one is convinced of this intertextual connection or not, אלהי עמי־הארץ in 5:25b denotes by itself negative circumstances.

The final clause of v. 25, "whom God had destroyed before them," alludes most immediately to vv. 10, 18–22, though perhaps most famously to the Conquest. The overall effect is to remind the reader for the third time (cf. vv. 23a, 24b) of the provision and faithfulness of God to the Transjordanites as especially elaborated in vv. 18–22. As with the previous reminders of God's blessings on the Manassites, v. 25c serves as a contrast emphasizing what follows. Though formerly God had fought for his people to give them the land (v. 25c, cf. 18–22), he now incites battle against them to remove them from that same land (v. 26).

God is described as having "roused . . . the spirit of Pul, king of Assyria" (i.e., Tilgath-Pilneser, king of Assyria). The action of YHWH through the agency of Tiglath-Pileser III—a phenomenon previously induced by the reader in 5:6—is now confirmed by the narrator's statement in v. 26. The combination עור in the Hiphil + רוח as object especially conveys the idea of causing someone or something to become and remain engaged in an activity, usually through inward prompting and by YHWH.[23] Most often when God is the subject of this phrase, the roused object is non-Israelite and functions instrumentally towards God's people, who are thus the recipients of the judgment or deliverance.[24] Johnstone further observes that the expression "is always used in C[hronicles] of the initiative of God in inspiring the action of foreigners against . . . or for . . . Israel."[25] The use of עור in the context of 1 Chr 5 agrees with this generalization. As well, Selman's suggestion for the post-exilic use of this phrase is worth considering. He highlights the seminal aspect of עור: " 'the God of Israel stirred up the spirit' (NIV, NRSV) is a typical post-exilic expression for *a new divine initiative in human affairs*

---

23. Schreiner, "עור," in *TDOT* 10:568–74 (570).

24. Only two occurrences feature Israelites as those in whom YHWH "stirred up the spirit" (Hag 1:14; Ezra 1:5). See Victor P. Hamilton, "עור," in *NIDOTTE* 3:357–60 and Knoppers, *1 Chronicles 1–9*, 391, for further discussion.

25. Cf. 2 Chr 21:16; 36:22. Johnstone, *1 Chronicles–2 Chronicles 9*, 80.

(cf. 2 Chr 21:16; Ezr 1:1; Hag 1:14)" [emphasis mine].²⁶ That the Assyrian exile was consequential would have been an obvious given to the post-exilic reader. Rather, the contribution of this idiom lies in its recognition of the governing movement of God in human history. Relatedly, Hamilton notes that in the OT the use of עור with God as subject is part of the language of faith:

> When God is the subject of the verb, the emphasis is on the affirmation of faith in the power and authority of God. No nation, whatever its superpower status, operates autonomously. And no nation, however dominant militarily, is immune to his hand of judgment. . . . Thus, the aroused nations of the earth are Yahweh's servants for weal or woe.²⁷

As in vv. 20 and 22, the Chronicler provides in vv. 25–26 an explicitly theological perspective on events that affirms the sovereign work of God in the military and political outcomes of the Transjordanian tribes and the nations with which they engage. In former incidents God gave the eastern tribes victory; later, the tribes merited defeat. In all these events, however, God determined the outcome, and the reader is encouraged to view Tiglath-Pileser III's exile of the Transjordanian tribes as a deserved punishment and no less a reason to recognize God as sovereign or that he is "the God of Israel" (v. 26a). Tiglath-Pileser III and the Assyrian empire may conquer and rule the world—or rather, parts of the world, for 1 Chr 5:26 is very clear regarding the limitations within which the Assyrian king moved and conquered—but YHWH exercises his sovereignty over all, notably in this case, the king of Assyria. Thus, in the exiling of the Transjordanian tribes by Assyria, it continues to be demonstrated that God rules over all the nations (whether or not they acknowledge him), while at the same time he remains particularly the God of Israel (whether or not the Israelites acknowledge him; moreover, for the post-exilic audience, whether or not the Israelites politically succeed or remain in the land).

In את־רוח פול מלך־אשור ואת־רוח תלגת פלנסר מלך אשור, the ו is best interpreted epexegetically or explicatively,²⁸ since both names historically

---

26. Also, 2 Chr 36:22. Martin J. Selman, *1 Chronicles: An Introduction and Commentary*, TOTC (Leicester: Inter-Varsity, 1994), 107.

27. Hamilton, "עור," 357–58.

28. For general discussion on the explicative *waw* and the epexegetical *waw* (this clause rather illustrating the point!), Waltke and O'Connor, *Introduction*, §39.2.1, 39.2.4. GKC² § 154a, note 1 (b); David W. Baker, "Further Examples of the *Waw Explicativum*," VT 30 (1980) 129–35. On the use of the explicative *waw* specifically in 1 Chr 5:26, see Seth Erlandsson, "Några exempel på Waw Explicativum," *Svensk exegetisk årsbok* 41–42 (1977) 69–76.

were held by one potentate and the nouns govern singular verbs (ויגלם and ויביאם). While the fluidity of Hebrew syntax allows the possibility that "the author was here misled by the separate references to Pul and Tiglath-pileser ... into thinking of them as different people,"[29] such a conspicuous error on the part of the well-read Chronicler regarding a notorious enemy seems unlikely. The use of both names for Tiglath-Pileser III may be better explained in a number of ways (not necessarily exclusive to each other). 1) Inclusion of Tiglath-Pileser III's neo-Babylonian name "Pul" may remind the reader of Tiglath-Pileser III's exceptional establishment of the Assyrian throne over both northern and southern Mesopotamia.[30] 2) פול מלך־אשור may be an allusion to the only other occurrence of the form in the OT, 2 Kgs 15:19, in which "Pul the king of Assyria" invaded the northern kingdom and exacted tribute from Menahem.[31] This interpretation focuses on Tiglath-Pileser III's Palestinian conquests, whereas the former emphasizes Tiglath-Pileser III's influence in Mesopotamia. Finally, 3) as touched upon above, the two nominal clauses are simply in apposition. The *waw* itself suffices to explain this. Further, it may also be worth considering that epexegetical/explicative *waw* + a repeated construct word + PN was an acceptable convention in post-exilic literature for specifying multiple appellations of an individual (consider Dan 6:29 MT and Wiseman's related proposal).[32] This is only a working hypothesis, of course, and would require further research beyond the purposes of this study to argue more confidently for or against it. Interpretations 1) and 2) remain possible and attractive in that they draw on particular associations of "Pul" that enrich meaning (namely, they increase the power attributed to Tiglath-Pileser III beyond that evoked by his usual epithet). If 3) is correct, however, we might expect the Chronicler to communicate more evidently these "enrichments."

It has been frequently asserted elsewhere that the account of the Transjordanian tribes' exile appears to be a conflation of two distinct stages of

29. Williamson, *1 and 2 Chronicles*, 67. Similarly, Kartveit, *Motive und Schichten*, 137n1; Simon J. De Vries, *1 and 2 Chronicles*, FOTL (Grand Rapids: Eerdmans, 1989), 62.

30. Simply put by A. Kirk Grayson, "History and Culture of Assyria," in "Mesopotamia, History of (Assyria)," *ABD* 4:732–55 (744): "Once he had suppressed the rebellion, Tiglath-pileser, angry about the time he had wasted on this problem, ascended the Babylonian throne himself. Thus we have for the first time in Neo-Assyrian history a unified state of Assyria and Babylonia under one king."

31. See Sara Japhet, *1 and 2 Chronicles: A Commentary*, OTL (Louisville: Westminster John Knox, 1993), 142.

32. D. J. Wiseman, "Some Historical Problems in the Book of Daniel," in *Notes on Some Problems in the Book of Daniel*, D. J. Wiseman and others (London: Tyndale, 1965), 9–18 (9–16, esp. 12–16).

the northern kingdom's exile as given in 2 Kgs 15:29 (Williamson and Selman include 15:19) and 17:6, 18:11.[33] Since there is no explicit reference in Chronicles to an Assyrian exile of the entire northern kingdom (contra the Kings account), and since vv. 25-26 contain the only apparent "reproductions" of the Kings account of the northern kingdom's exile, it is understood by most that vv. 25-26 involve a more or less direct relation to the exile of the northern kingdom, whether it is that of describing an initial stage,[34] functioning as representative,[35] or functioning as substitute.[36] Among those who seem to advocate the most extreme alterations between the Kings and Chronicles accounts (i.e., a hypothesis of substitution), Wright allows that a partial exile of the (presumably non-Transjordanian) northern kingdom is assumed elsewhere in Chronicles (2 Chr 30:6-9).[37] Japhet also recognizes the allusion of 30:6-9 to a partial exile of the northern kingdom, but emphasizes Chronicles' use of the Kings account to describe in vv. 25-26 a complete and permanent exile of the Transjordanian tribes only—"the Chronicler draws together all the principal data referring to the subordination of the northern kingdom, but limits it exclusively to that kingdom's eastern component";[38] "as the two episodes become one, the principal exile to 'Halah, Habor, Hara, and the river Gozan' . . . only involves tribes living east of the Jordan."[39]

I find it difficult to accept on the present evidence that Chronicles' relative silence on the general Assyrian exile necessitates such an extreme redefinition of that event on the Chronicler's part. While it does appear that the Chronicler alludes to 2 Kgs 15:19-20 ("Pul king of Assyria," v. 26a) and borrows the list of exile destinations from 2 Kgs 17:6, 18:11, these subtle intertextual relations do not seem enough to indicate an implicit wholesale

---

33. E.g., Japhet, *Ideology*, 372-73; idem, *1 and 2 Chronicles*, 141; Williamson, *1 and 2 Chronicles*, 67; Selman, *1 Chronicles*, 107; Braun, *1 Chronicles*, 75; Knoppers, *1 Chronicles 1-9*, 392-93.

34. De Vries, *1 and 2 Chronicles*, 358; and Knoppers, *1 Chronicles 1-9*, 391-92, who indicates that 1 Chr 5 is an earlier exile by identifying the phrase "exiled them" (v. 26) as "referring to TP's campaigns of 733-732 BC" (391). Knoppers also later contrasts "the early deportations [of 2 Kgs 15:29]" with those of 722 BC. Williamson, *1 and 2 Chronicles*, 67, 344, seems implicitly to hold this view, too.

35. Cf. Selman, *1 Chronicles*, 107.

36. Cf. John W. Wright, "The Fight for Peace: Narrative and History in the Battle Accounts in Chronicles," in *The Chronicler as Historian*, JSOTSup 238, eds. M. Patrick Graham, Kenneth G. Hoglund and Steven L. McKenzie (Sheffield: Sheffield Academic, 1997), 155.

37. Wright, "Fight for Peace," 155n18.

38. Japhet, *1 and 2 Chronicles*, 142.

39. Japhet, *Ideology*, 373; see also 372.

transference of the Kings account of the northern kingdom's general exile to the Transjordanian tribes' circumstances. Adoption, maybe; minimization, probably; but transference or denial of the northern kingdom's exile, not convincingly. As seen above, it is generally recognized that Chronicles itself acknowledges at least a partial exile of the northern kingdom in 2 Chr 30:6. Second Chronicles 28:12 may also reflect the reduction of the northern kingdom to the rump state of Ephraim through exile by Assyria[40]—the verse mentions Ephraimite leaders where one might expect instead a reference to a northern "king of Israel" (cf. 28:19 and Williamson's explanation).[41] Further, the Chronicler could confidently assume that his audience was knowledgeable about the fact of the general exile of the northern kingdom. Though the author-redactor may evidence a penchant for drastic minimization or even silence concerning events presented at length in his *Vorlage* of Samuel-Kings (e.g., the civil war, 2 Sam 2:8—4:2; Bathsheba and conflict within David's family, 2 Sam 11–19; 1 Kgs 1–2), selectivity—not denial—appears to be what is generally operative in the shaping of the Books of Chronicles.

I suggest that the Chronicler maintains a focus on the Transjordanian tribes throughout 1 Chr 5 and that the events involving Assyria are mentioned insofar as they impinge on those tribes and broader themes of his concern (such as exile and restoration). As he does throughout Chronicles, the author-redactor minimizes and localizes the power of the Assyrians,[42] but at the same time does not deny the basic fact, and the serious effects, of their acts.[43] The Chronicler gives the Transjordanian tribes' exile more attention than the exile of the northern kingdom generally because the Transjordanians' exile apparently held greater significance for his post-exilic audience with respect to his historical-theological concerns. Possibly the reason for the significance of the Transjordanian tribes' exile is that it signaled the beginning of the Assyrian exile (which might be termed better as "the Assyrian exiles," since the overall exile comprised several smaller exiles). Another possibility is that the Chronicler perceived the Assyrian exile

40. Williamson, *1 and 2 Chronicles*, 347; Dillard, *2 Chronicles*, 222; Aharoni, *Land of the Bible*, 371–74; 2 Kgs 15:29.

41. H. G. M. Williamson, *Israel in the Books of Chronicles* (Cambridge: Cambridge University Press, 1977), 118; idem, *1 and 2 Chronicles*, 348. Note that if 2 Chr 28:12 does reflect the Assyrian exile, then a stage of the Assyrian exile would need to be assumed to occur between the events of 28:5b–8 and 28:12–15. The implicit stage of Assyrian exile would need to be either the final stage (cf. 2 Kgs 17:6; 18:9–12) or a stage prior, which reduced Israel to the Ephraimite hill country and its ineffective vassal king (cf. 2 Kgs 15:29).

42. Japhet agrees in her discussion of exile. See Japhet, *Ideology*, 373.

43. E.g., see Knoppers, *1 Chronicles 1–9*, 399.

to be more severe for the eastern tribes than for the western ones. Japhet, for example, contends that the Transjordanians' exile is permanent—to the extent that these tribes are excluded from Chronistic descriptions of the land in later chapters—but that the other Israelite tribes' exile is "only temporary."[44] A third viable option is that the Transjordanian tribes, by virtue of their more equivocal and sometimes negative reputation in contrast to the rest of Israel,[45] were simply the best candidates through which the Chronicler could present the Assyrian exile with the least amount of shock and attention. In this way, the Assyrian exile would be minimized, but not denied, in the Chronicler's account, and the full impact of Israelite מעל and tragic deportation would remain reserved for the climactic end with the Babylonian exile (2 Chr 36:11–21).

Indeed, the two-verse account of the Transjordanian tribes' exile by Assyria contributes, by way of contrast and similarity, to the longer and more vivid account of Judah's defeat and exile by Babylonia (2 Chr 36:13b–20). Similar vocabulary, phrases, and themes link the two exile episodes. As

---

44. Japhet, *Ideology*, 372; 2 Chr 30:5–11, esp. v. 6. Japhet also asserts that "because these tribes were exiled, they do not appear in Chronistic descriptions of the land during the reigns of Hezekiah (2 Chr 30:5) and Josiah (2 Chr 34:6)." For the sake of clarity, it should be qualified that the sense of "complete" exile conveyed by Chronicles operates, as usual, in the realm of hyperbole to impress the tragic extent of the exile-punishment on the Transjordanian tribes (one may perhaps better speak of a "relative" completeness/permanence). I am in agreement with B. Oded, "Observations on Methods of Assyrian Rule in Transjordania after the Palestinian Campaign of Tiglath-Pileser III," *JNES* 29 (1970) 177–86 (183) (though his cited support for a Transjordanian remnant seems mostly conjectural [see his n46], and his argument otherwise is based on assumed historical analogy to the situation described in 2 Chr 30:6, 10) and especially K. Lawson Younger, Jr., "The Deportations of the Israelites," *JBL* 117 (1998) 201–27 (206–14, esp. 213–14) that it is more likely than not that there was some degree of an Israelite population remaining in the Transjordan after the Assyrian exile. This Transjordanian "remnant," however, was apparently not significant enough to be further recognized.

45. E.g., Josh 22, as interpreted by Rudolf Mosis, *Untersuchungen zur Theologie des chronistischen Geschichtswerkes*, FTS (Freiburg: Herder, 1973), 30n39. For a brief and relevant overview, see sources in discussion in Knoppers, *1 Chronicles 1–9*, 395–400. Knoppers asserts a more nuanced approach on the part of the Chronicler to the Transjordanian tribes: Chronicles presents a more positive (even idealized) view of the Transjordanian tribes than do earlier biblical authors, but still distances those tribes in terms of exile.

> The authors of Chronicles do not share the sentiment of earlier biblical writers, who distance the Transjordanian tribes from the rest of the Israelite tribes by reference to dialect, polity, and religious practice. Quite the contrary, the two and a half tribes exhibit polities similar to those described for other tribes. Nevertheless, the text distances these tribes through another means—exile. (400)

Selman observes, 1 Chr 5:25–26 "follows almost exactly the structure of the explanation of Judah's exile in 2 Chr 36:14–20."[46] It should be added that the circumstances concerning the Babylonian exile are depicted as more extreme than those of the Assyrian exile of the East Bank. The Transjordanian tribes committed מעל (1 Chr 5:25), but Israel committed למעול־מעל (2 Chr 36:14). The eastern tribes "prostituted themselves to the gods of the peoples of the land" (1 Chr 5:25), while the Israelites followed "all the loathsome [things/ways] of the nations" (2 Chr 36:14). In 1 Chr 5:26, God simply motivates foreign monarch Tiglath-Pileser III to exile the people to Assyria; in 2 Chr 36:15–20, God's reaction of immitigable wrath is first presented, followed by his rousing of foreign monarch Nebuchadnezzar to kill the people, followed by the plundering and deportation of the temple and palace treasures, destruction of the temple, wall, and palaces, and finally, exile of the remnant to servitude in Babylon.[47] Chronicles' more detailed and intense description of Nebuchadnezzar and the Babylonian exile renders that king and event as far more egregiously and memorably ruthless than Tiglath-Pileser III and the Assyrian exile. This is not to deny the severity of Tiglath-Pileser III's actions in 1 Chr 5:6, 22, 25–26, but it is to understand that the Assyrian exile of the Transjordanian tribes functions on one level as a precursor of the Babylonian onslaught and exile of Judah.

As well, the MT structure, which continues 1 Chr 5 up to 5:41 (6:15 in LXX and most English translations) closes the subunit of 5:27–41 in a parallel way to the subunits of vv. 6, 22, and 26—with a reference to exile. Notably, only this last mention of exile in MT 1 Chr 5 is that of Babylonia. If one adheres to the MT structure, the Assyrian and Babylonian exiles are more noticeably linked, and a general pattern of prosperity-unfaithfulness-exile becomes more pronounced.[48] (That said, the narrative substance of MT 1 Chr 5 remains concentrated in that of the LXX version—i.e., in 5:1–26 and the outcomes of the Transjordanian tribes.)

---

46. Selman, *1 Chronicles*, 107.

47. Ibid., 107, has a similar and briefer version of the relationships between the two exiles; Knoppers, *1 Chronicles 1–9*, 398, makes a couple general statements along the same line. Selman and Knoppers emphasize, however, the similarity of the exiles, while I find it instructive to observe further the difference, which highlights a general movement from Assyrian exile to Babylonian exile of bad-->worse.

48. My thoughts on this are developed from those of Kartveit, who helpfully observes, in the organization of the MT, this connection indicated between the two exiles. He further suggests that the motif of exile is repeated in such a way that it functions in 1 Chr 5 as a kind of 'refrain' developing a theme of earlier grandeur coming to tragic end. As Kartveit will discuss later, the decisive factor in such change, according to the Chronicler, is *m'l*. See Kartveit, *Motive und Schichten*, 137, 143–44.

CONCLUSION

Having considered the characterization of the Assyrians in 1 Chr 1 and 5, it may be appreciated that, though explicit references to Assyria are few, they are significant and well-integrated in a complex history presented in Chronicles' beginning genealogies and beyond. The mixed heritage of אשור presented in 1 Chr 1:17 introduces the Assyrians with a narrative situation ripe for suspense, conflict, and possibilities as Assyria could follow its ancestry in either the ways of Shem, Nimrod and the Hamites, or all. At the same time, the context makes clear that, while Assyria is part of the "human family," its place within that family is defined by its relation to Israel. In 1 Chr 5, the particularities of the Transjordanian tribes' situation, along with the intentional and selective use of vocabulary and epithets, especially shape the portrayal of the Tiglath-Pileser III and the Assyrians.[49] The undeniably great strength and impact of the Assyrian emperor towards the Transjordanian tribes is acknowledged, but Tiglath-Pileser III is also tempered in the eyes of the narrator as being an agent of YHWH and his punitive purposes. Though the point is clear in 1 Chr 5, the nuances by which this is communicated have been explored in this chapter to appreciate the richness and detail of the portrayal. And finally, while 1 Chr 1:17 looks to the past to explain the powerful and occasionally moral-theologically liminal role of Assyria in Chronicles, on a wider level 1 Chr 5 looks to the future to anticipate the Babylonian Exile and its egregiousness, which will surpass even that of the Assyrian exiles in begun and intimated in 1 Chr 5.

---

49. Williamson, *Israel in the Books of Chronicles*, 82, perceives that "the interests [of vv. 23–26] are international rather than inter-tribal" (and therefore partial reason for scepticism that these verses are part of the Chronicler's original work). However, his dichotomization of international/inter-tribal along the lines of vv. 23–26 versus the rest of 1 Chr 5 is not supported by the biblical record. A more biblically-resonant reading is that the outcomes of the Transjordanian tribes is the major focus of chapter 5 and that vv. 23–26 involve international matters because they concern inter-tribal circumstances.

5

The Failure of Assyria as an "Alternative" to YHWH (2 Chronicles 28)

A MUTED PORTRAYAL OF THE EMPIRE

IT IS REPORTED BY the Chronicler's *Vorlage* of 2 Kings that most of the northern kingdom was exiled by Assyria during the reign of Ahaz (2 Kgs 15:29; see also 15:30; 16:5–9; 17:3–6; 18:9–11). The Assyrian exile is not explicitly mentioned in 2 Chronicles 28 ('the Ahaz chapter'), however. Given the thoroughly dark description of Ahaz's reign and the focus of the chapter on the stubborn unfaithfulness of Ahaz and the contrastive penitence of the Israelites,[1] it is perhaps not surprising that the injury imposed by Assyria is not emphasized. One "villain" (Ahaz) and one foil to that villain (the penitent Israelites) occupy the spotlight of chapter 28. All other troublemakers and apostates—Assyria included—feature in ways that support these leading roles and the themes the Chronicler conveys through these leading characters.

Verse 12 may provide the first hint of an Assyrian deportation in chapter 28. Where one might expect a "king of Israel" to feature (as in vv. 5–6), Ephraimite leaders assume authority instead. The striking absence of a

---

1. Japhet, *1 and 2 Chronicles*, 897, comments on the dark characterization of Ahaz' reign in 2 Chr 28: "Unlike the kings who precede him, Ahaz enjoys no change of fortunes; the script is uniformly black, moving toward a climax of evil. The severe gloom of the history of Ahaz is matched only by that of Jehoram before him and Zedekiah after him." The foci of 2 Chr 28 may be seen not only through the content and amount of space given to each, but the structure also, as will be discussed later in this chapter.

northern "king of Israel" beyond v. 6 and the apparent change in leadership may suggest that an exile of the northern kingdom by Assyria had already occurred.² We should note as well the reference to Ahaz's jurisdiction as "Israel" in vv. 19, 23, and 27 (unremarkably, also v. 26); with a further disintegration of the northern kingdom, the term "Israel" now may be applied to Judah with less confusion as to whether the north or south is intended.³ If, by way of telescoping events in 2 Chr 28, the effective end of the northern monarchy is the case, one would need to assume the occurrence of the exile of Samaria (cf. 2 Kgs 17:6; cf. 18:9–12) and/or a prior exilic stage which reduced Israel to the Ephraimite hill country and its ineffective vassal king (cf. 2 Kgs 15:29; 17:3b) between the events of 2 Chr 28:5–8 and vv. 12–15. The occurrence of an Assyrian invasion during the events of vv. 8b–15 actually may be assumed by בעת ההיא (v. 16), which links vv. 8b–15 with vv. 16–21. Though vv. 16–21 do not explicitly state the occurrence of an Assyrian exile, the strong indication in those verses of an Assyrian arrival in Palestine, with consequent exiles, would not be lost on the reader familiar with the prior account in 2 Kings. All that said, it should be allowed that the Chronicler may have intended in v. 12 simply to distinguish the righteousness of the Ephraimites apart from any consideration of the Assyrians.

My current position on the matter is that v. 12 does reflect circumstances of *an* (not *the*) exile and a *temporary* change in effective northern leadership, given the highlighting of northern leaders in place of a king, the apparent transfer within the chapter of the title "king of Israel" from

---

2. Similarly suggested by Raymond B. Dillard, *2 Chronicles*, WBC (Waco: Word, 1987), 222; and Williamson, *1 and 2 Chronicles*, 344, 347. See also Ehud Ben Zvi, "A Gateway to the Chronicler's Teaching: The Account of the Reign of Ahaz in 2 Chr 28,1–27," *SJOT* 7 (1993), 216–49//chap. 11 in *History, Literature and Theology in the Book of Chronicles* (London: Equinox, 2006), 210–42 (224–25), perceives that the northerners are "kingless" from v. 8 and onwards.

3. Williamson, *1 and 2 Chronicles*, 343–44; and idem, *Israel in the Books of Chronicles* (Cambridge: Cambridge University Press, 1977), 118, perceives in relation to these uses of "Israel" a Chronistic emphasis on the ideal of a unified Israel. As Ben Zvi notes, however, this notion of a reunited Israel on the part of Chronicles is limited, both because of "the corpus of facts about Israel's history that were accepted by the community for which Chronicles was written" and what is communicated in the narrative itself. Reunification is nowhere explicitly stated or explicitly demonstrated, and significant passages still identify Jerusalemite kings as kings of Judah. Moreover, sometimes in these same passages identifying a "king of Judah," a monarchic king—David or Solomon—is distinctively identified as a "king of Israel." Still, there were ways (mostly in the area of worship) in which Israelites proper were invited or perceived as part of the "true Israel" represented by the South. See Ehud Ben Zvi, "The Secession of the Northern Kingdom in Chronicles: Accepted 'Facts' and New Meanings," in *The Chronicler as Theologian: Essays in Honor of Ralph W. Klein*, eds. M. Patrick Graham, Steven L. McKenzie, and Gary N. Knoppers (London: T. & T. Clark, 2003) 61–88 (83–86; quote from 84).

Pekah to Ahaz (vv. 6, 19), and the historical fact that a significant part of the Assyrian exiles occurred either during or close to the time of the events in 28:8b-15. Though Williamson suggests that "the northern monarchy had fallen,"[4] and Dillard affirms such an interpretation,[5] I cannot agree that the text reflects an actual termination of the northern monarchy. "Tillegath-Pilneʾeser" is recognized in v. 20 as the Assyrian king, and though it was known that Tiglath-Pileser III was responsible for sizable deportations of Israelites (e.g., 1 Chr 5:26; 2 Kgs 15:29), there is no tradition crediting the conquests of Samaria to Tiglath-Pileser III.[6] It is thus unlikely (and unnecessary for an internally consistent reading) that the Chronicler understood or telescoped conquests of Samaria by Shalmaneser V and/or Sargon II as occurring before 28:12-21.

Though still a secondary player in the narrative, Assyria most clearly features in vv. 16-21. To begin, some observations of literary structure are apropos. Within the overall chiastic structure of 2 Chr 28, verses 16-21 form a unit that parallels vv. 5b-8 and immediately follows the central unit of vv. 8b-15. By means of the parallelism, vv. 16-21 and vv. 5b-8 reinforce YHWH's judgment against Judah through the instrumentality of other nations. While this motif contributes to the condemnation of Ahaz in the overall structure, it seems secondary to the motif of judgment wrought by YHWH through Aram (vv. 5a and 22-23). Proceeding through the chapter straightforwardly, in their immediate location after the central unit concerning the penitence of the Israelites (vv. 8b-15), vv. 16-21 resume in striking contrast with the direct characterization of apostate Ahaz.[7] The chiastic structure of 2 Chr 28 is as follows:[8]

---

4. Williamson, *1 and 2 Chronicles*, 347, cf. 344; idem, *Israel in the Books of Chronicles*, 118.

5. Dillard, *2 Chronicles*, 222.

6. Younger, "Fall of Samaria," 461-82 (482), asserts that the city of Samaria fell in 722 to Shalmaneser V and was recaptured in 720 by Sargon II. For further background on the exiles of the northern kingdom by Assyria, see idem, "Deportations of the Israelites," 201-27.

7. This counters De Vries, *1 and 2 Chronicles*, 364, who asserts that "the section vv. 16-21 has neither structural nor thematic connection to the anecdote of the Judahite captives."

8. Strangely enough, the chiastic structure of chapter 28 has been discussed by few. Japhet, *1 and 2 Chronicles*, 896, observes a basic chiastic structure for the Ahaz chapter:

a) v. 1 Introduction
  b) vv. 2-4 Ahaz's transgressions
    c) vv. 5-21 Political and military afflictions
  d) vv. 22-25 Ahaz's further transgressions
e) vv. 26-27 Conclusion

28:1: Introductory formula

   a   28:2–4: Ahaz promotes idolatrous practices, neglects YHWHism.

      b   28:5a: YHWH's judgment through defeat by other nations: Judah struck (נכה) by king of Aram; captives to Damascus.

         c   28:5b–8: YHWH's judgment against Judah through Israel.

            d   28:8b–15: Israelite reversal of Judahite captives in Samaria; key vocabulary: השביה ('the captives'), אשמת יהוה ('guilt before YHWH').

         c'   28:16–21: YHWH's judgment against Judah through Assyria.

      b'   28:22–23: YHWH's judgment implied through futility of Ahaz's actions; allusion to Judah's defeat (נכה) by 'the kings of Aram'; Ahaz sacrifices to the gods of Damascus.

   a'   28: 22–25: Ahaz promotes idolatrous practices, attempts to terminate YHWHism.

28:26–27: Concluding formula

Thus it should be seen that vv. 16–21 contribute both contrast and reinforcement to motifs and characterizations elsewhere in chapter 28. Let us now proceed to particulars within the unit.

The structure of 2 Chr 28:16–21 itself is a chiasmus.[9] As made clear in the diagram, Assyria functions within the literary structure as the object by which Ahaz' faithless appeals for help apart from YHWH are proven futile (vv. 16, 21). As well, Assyria is a foreign enemy—like the Edomites and Philistines—posing a threat to Israel (vv. 16, 20). Though Assyria has a significant role in vv. 16–21, the central point of the pericope does not directly involve Assyria. As seen in the pivot, v. 19, the key communication of the pericope is that King Ahaz's extreme מעל retributively results in YHWH's humbling of the nation. Assyria and Tiglath-Pileser III function second-

---

William Johnstone, *1 and 2 Chronicles*, vol. 2, *2 Chronicles 10–36: Guilt and Atonement*, JSOTSup 254 (Sheffield: Sheffield Academic, 1997), 174, posits a very simple chiasmus: "MT thus divides the chapter into two main sections: vv. 1–15 and vv. 16–27. These sections are chiastically arranged: apostasy precipitates foreign invasion (vv. 1–15); the experience of foreign invasion leads to still greater apostasy (vv. 16–27)." Williamson, *Israel in the Books*, 114, finds that "only the introduction to and conclusion of the reign are parallel from a literary point of view, and even then there are some significant alterations."

9. A version of this discussion was published in Hom, "Chiasmus in Chronicles," 165–66. I wish to thank *Andrews University Seminary Studies* for allowing me to republish parts of that article in the present book.

arily, the narratorial implication being that they enact YHWH's retributive humiliation of Judah. The empire is present, but only within the place that this Judean narrative gives it. Yet again, the oppressed resist and triumph over the oppressor by way of the subtleties of the text and its structure.

The structure of 2 Chr 28:16–21:

- a   28:16: King Ahaz sends to Assyria for help (עזר).
    - b   28:17–18: Invasion by foreign enemies (Edomites and Philistines).
        - c   28:19: The reason for Judah's troubles: YHWH humbles (כנע) Judah as judgment on Ahaz's infidelity to Him (יהוה—ומעול מעל—ביהוה).
    - b'   28:20: Enmity from foreign enemy (Assyria).
- a'   28:21: Ahaz gives tribute to Assyria, but receives no help (עזר).

One may legitimately describe Assyria's role in this pericope as instrumental, noting that Assyria serves the desires of YHWH, but presumably unconsciously. Still one may press further regarding the nature and characterization of Assyria within this secondary, instrumental role.

The first explicit appearance of Assyria in the pericope (and chapter) is in the title מלכי אשור ("the kings of Assyria"; v. 16)—the plural form most likely functioning as a typologization for the Assyrian empire and its demonstrated power through history.[10] Possibly "the kings of Assyria" is hyperbole along the lines of Isa 10:8, in which the Assyrian ruler is poetically paraphrased as boasting "Are not my commanders all kings?" It is, however, better to interpret the pluralization in 2 Chr 28:16 primarily in the context of Chronicles (cf. 2 Chr 30:6; 32:4) than necessarily in relation to Isaiah. The use of the phrase in 2 Chr 30:6 clearly serves for an historical retrospect, common in Chronicles speeches.[11] Apart from the phrase in question, the language in 30:6–9 is clearly broad and as wide-encompassing as possible. Thus, a generalized sense for 30:6 is consistent with its context. 2 Chr 32:4 is admittedly less clear on its own (though Japhet perceives that this usage, as well as that of 28:16, "is more emphasized" than that of 30:6 with regard to being "a plural of abstraction" presenting " 'the kings of Assyria' as a historical phenomenon"[12]).[13] As I will discuss in my treatment of 2 Chr 32,

---

10. Agreeing with Dillard, *2 Chronicles*, 219.

11. See, e.g., Mark A. Throntveit, *When Kings Speak: Royal Speech and Royal Prayer in Chronicles*, SBLDS 93 (Atlanta: Scholars, 1987), 20, 32, 41, 75.

12. Japhet, *1 and 2 Chronicles*, 945.

13. Thomas Willi, *Die Chronik als Auslegung: Untersuchungen zur literarischen Gestaltung der historischen Überlieferung Israels* (Göttingen: Vandenhoeck & Ruprecht,

within the context of Hezekiah's reign, the pluralized form in 32:4 may be understood on one level there as representative of the people's affirmation and adoption of Hezekiah's ideology and homiletic address in 30:6–9. Thus, of the three appearances in Chronicles of "the kings of Assyria," only 30:6–9 clearly seems a typologization for the might-that-is-Assyria, though 32:4 may be understood as based upon 30:6–9. Second Chronicles 28:16 is the most obscure of the three and on its own could be understood as either typology or hyperbole. The verse's proximity to the other two occurrences and the probability that the other two occurrences are typological tilts the balance towards a typological understanding, and this is the position assumed for the remainder of this chapter. In the end, whether one understands the pluralized form as denoting typologically general imperial Assyrian might or hyperbolically the unusually strong military forces of Assyria, still "kings of Assyria" indicates the superlative strength of Assyria.

Though it is the narrator's voice that states the typologized form in v. 16, I think this typologization reflects more an articulation of Ahaz's point of view than the narrator's own perspective. There is no reason why this particular typologization must be necessarily exclusive, however,[14] and I am inclined at present to adhere to a nuanced interpretation in that the function of the typologization in its immediate context of 28:16 is primarily to convey Ahaz's appeal to the might-that-is-Assyria, and that this primary function contributes to a secondary development of broader themes, such as that of the Assyrians' imperial power, exilic threat, and function as unwitting instrument of YHWH's testing and judgment.

As noted above, Ahaz appeals to Assyria in vv. 16 and 21. Ahaz's resort to Assyria is an outer expression (vv. 16 and 21) of his inner מעל against YHWH (v. 19). The chiastic structure of vv. 16–21 perhaps highlights this outward-inward situation. Assyria thus functions as an option competing with YHWH for the Judahite king's dependency. The futility of Ahaz's choice

---

1972), 164, n. 214 agrees. He also observes Rudolph's position that the pluralization is with a view towards future sieges, but I think that is to press the point too far. Hezekiah and his city seem wholly concerned with the crisis at hand.

14. Regarding the history of approaches to typology, see discussion in Friedbert Ninow, "Approaches to Typology," chap. 1 in *Indicators of Typology within the Old Testament: The Exodus Motif* (Frankfurt: Lang, 2001), 22–97; consider also Michael Fishbane, *Biblical Interpretation in Ancient Israel* (Oxford: Clarendon, 1985), 350–51. Relatedly, on the use of typology for biblical historiography, see Willi, "d) Typology," in *Die Chronik als Auslegung*, 160–69. For a similar discussion regarding hyperbole and history (specifically in the examples of poetic passages Judg 5 and Ps 48), see Robert P. Gordon, *Holy Land, Holy City: Sacred Geography and the Interpretation of the Bible* (Carlisle, UK: Paternoster, 2004), 39–45.

is demonstrated by the empire's subsequent failure to help,[15] emphasized by way of the repeated עזר and the conspicuous appearance of ולא in v. 21c:

End of v. 16: לעזר לו	אשור
End of v. 21: ולא לעזרה לו	אשור

On one level in the narrative, the appearance in v. 20 of Tiglath-Pileser III as "the king of Assyria" renders him a representative of the imperial might embodied in the phenomenon of "the kings of Assyria." Tiglath-Pileser's response to Ahaz's request begins, "He came against him, Tiglath-Pileser . . . "[16] The next verb makes clear Tiglath-Pileser III's duplicity: "he oppressed him," the Hiphil of צרר referring almost always in the OT to "the distress prompted by an enemy" (Deut 28:52 [2x]; 1 Kgs 8:37; 2 Chr 6:28; Jer 10:18; Zeph 1:17; consider also 2 Chr 28:22; 33:12).[17] The third action of Tiglath-Pileser III (ולא חזקו) is problematic in that the MT has חֲזָקוֹ, which is in the Qal. All other Qal forms of חזק are intransitive, fitting in the general semantic range of "be(come) firm, strong."[18] The BHS critical apparatus reads the Piel instead, חִזְּקוֹ ("strengthened him"), which is the sense that most translations support.[19] This immediately renders v. 20c consistent with v. 21c. It should be allowed that this consistency is of a somewhat woodenly logical nature, however, and one may perceive the double mention of Ahaz's futile results to be an awkward repetition. Japhet supports the MT by drawing attention to the explanatory function of v. 21a: "*For* Ahaz took from the house of the Lord . . . and gave tribute to the king of Assyria."[20] She

---

15. Beyond the deficiency in material returns from Assyria, vv. 16, 19–21 indicate that "Ahaz' real failure, however, was to seek human rather than divine help" (Martin J. Selman, *2 Chronicles: A Commentary* [Leicester: Inter-Varsity, 1994], 481–82). Again, the foundational problem remains Ahaz's מעל.

16. על should be translated in v. 20 as "against" and not "to." Similarly, יבא is best understood here as having a sense of hostility. For further discussion, see Mary Katherine Y. H. Hom, " 'To' or 'Against': The Interpretation of יבא על in 2 Chr 28:20," *VT* 60 (2010) 560-64.

17. Citation from H.-J. Fabry, "צר [I]," in *TDOT* 12:455-64, 458; see also I. Swart and Robin Wakely, "צרר I," in *NIDOTTE* 3:853-59, 855.

18. BDB, "חזק," 304; *HALOT*, "חזק," 302-3.

19. E.g., NIV, NRSV, NASB, JPS. See also BDB, 304c; and *HALOT*, "חזק," 303c. Jacob M. Myers, *2 Chronicles* (Garden City, NY: Doubleday, 1965), 163; Williamson, *1 and 2 Chronicles*, 349; and De Vries, *1 and 2 Chronicles*, 365. Other commentators (apart from Japhet) conveniently do not comment on this specific clause—Selman, *2 Chronicles*, 481-82; Thompson, *1,2 Chronicles*, 339; Peter R. Ackroyd, *1 and 2 Chronicles, Ezra, Nehemiah* (London: SCM, 1973), 178.

20. Japhet, *1 and 2 Chronicles*, 907. As far as I can tell, Japhet appears to be unique

continues that חֲזָקוֹ should therefore "be understood as the common usage, 'overcome,' 'overpower' ... [hence, v. 20c reads as] 'he did not overcome him.' " Japhet then concludes, "The statement is then fully coherent: the king of Assyria marched against Ahaz but did not conquer him, because Ahaz 'gave tribute.' "[21] The defense of the MT and the ready consistency of this interpretation with 2 Kgs 16:7-9 make this an attractive reading. Japhet does not resolve, however, how her interpretation harmonizes with the clear indication of v. 21b that Ahaz's tribute-giving to the Assyrian king was not helpful for the Israelite king. Further, כי may be understood not only causatively/explicatively ("For"), but also intensively ("Indeed," "Surely"). For both interpretations regarding v. 20, the third clause (v. 20c) is taken as elaborating on the second and first (v. 20a and b): in the case of Japhet's reading, Tiglath-Pileser III's oppression is limited; in the case of the overwhelming majority's reading, the disappointing, counterproductive nature of Tigalth-Pileser III's response is underlined. Taking all these matters into account, both interpretations present difficulties, but it seems that the majority understanding presents the least difficulties, and for this reason it is accepted here.

The precise ways in which the Assyrian king failed to strengthen Ahaz are not specified, though the context suggests military-political expectations and disappointments.[22] We know immediately from v. 21 that Ahaz depleted national resources, with no apparent return from Assyria. We also know from other sources that Assyria received tribute from Ahaz (*Ia-ú-ha-zi* is Ahaz's full name)[23] and did not hand over the involved enemy states to Ahaz (the Philistine territories, Aram-Damascus, Israel, Edom; cf. 28:5, 17-18; 2 Kgs 16:5-9; 17:1-41), but eventually incorporated them into the empire.[24]

---

in forwarding this interpretation. *DCH*, 185, 186, lists both Qal and Piel possibilities for חזקו.

21. Japhet, *1 and 2 Chronicles*, 907.

22. Williamson, *1 and 2 Chronicles*, 348-49, perceives that in v. 20c "the Chronicler's point is theological," though the remainder of Williamson's comment wholly concerns Ahaz's material-political disadvantage at the hands of Assyria. See also Luis Robert Siddall, "Tiglath-pileser III's Aid to Ahaz: A New Look at the Problems of the Biblical Accounts in Light of the Assyrian Sources," *ANES* 46 (2009): 93-106, which articulates well a resolution of the supposed discrepancy between the accounts in 2 Kgs 16:5-9 and 2 Chr 28:5-21 (esp. v. 20) with regard to the efficacy of Tiglath-Pileser III's aid to Ahaz. Cudworth, *War in Chronicles*, 108, observes that ועוד in 28:17 as reflecting that "his plea to Assyria still did not help him."

23. *COS* 2:289, n. 10; also Myers, *2 Chronicles*, 163; Selman, *2 Chronicles*, 481, n. 3.

24. John H. Hayes and J. Maxwell Miller, eds. *Israelite and Judaean History* (Philadelphia: Westminster, 1977), 432, 436; Yohanan Aharoni and Michael Avi-Yonah, *The Macmillan Bible Atlas* (New York: Macmillan, 1968), 95; *ANET*, 282; *COS* 2:289.

THE FAILURE OF ASSYRIA   147

As well, Judah itself was soon to be restricted further by the empire (cf. Isa 7:17), at the very least by means of its continued vassalage under Assyria and the advance of Assyrian influence towards Judah's borders.²⁵ These situations and events may have been assumed by the Chronicler to be known and understood through the phrase 'and did not strengthen him' (functioning euphemistically) by his post-exilic audience.

Thus v. 20 reflects the hostile nature of Tiglath-Pileser III's approach (ויבא עליו, "... came to/against him"), the demonstration of the Assyrian king's unfriendly actions towards Ahaz (ויצר לו, "and oppressed him"), followed by an emphasis on the counterproductive nature of the Assyrian king's response to Ahaz's request (ולא חֲזָקוֹ [read חִזְּקוֹ], "but did not strengthen him"). While the main focus of the pericope is on Ahaz's character, Assyria is secondarily characterized as a mighty, fearsome entity that, in relation to Ahaz, functions as a temptation away from faithfulness to YHWH (vv. 16, 19) and also as a means by which YHWH retributively punishes Ahaz (vv. 20–21). Assyria's duplicitous, oppressive, opportunistic, intimidating character in vv. 16–21 makes that superpower fittingly able to impair Judah through the dual role of tempter and oppressor.

Finally, it is instructive to consider that Ahaz's beseeching of Assyria is evoked three times in vv. 16–21. The first occurrence is at the beginning of the unit (v. 16), without mention of Assyria's response. At this point, the two kings appear as equals, one requesting the help of another. The narrative continues, explaining the urgency of Judah's situation (vv. 17–18) and the reason why Judah was experiencing such urgent difficulties (v. 19). Tiglath-Pileser's response "belatedly" appears in v. 20, reminding the reader of Ahaz's request, especially as Assyria's response is contrary to Ahaz's narratively long-awaited expectation. This opportunistic response of Tiglath-Pileser III and the trouble he inflicts on Judah begin to alter the power dynamic between the two kings. The third reference to Ahaz's appeal to the Assyrians follows in v. 21. The events of v. 21 may or may not occur simultaneously in real time with those of v. 20, but still the repetition of general content (assuming it is a repetition—see discussion above regarding חזקו) achieves a literary effect akin to parallelism's "x and what's more, x+1." This third reference elaborates upon Ahaz's subordination of himself to the King of Assyria (the exploitation by Ahaz of the Judahite treasuries for Assyria demonstrating his religio-moral weakness primarily and Assyria's imperialist opportunism secondarily) and reiterates Assyria's cold refusal to help (with doubled emphasis from the sonancy of לא and לו in both vv. 20 and

25. For further discussion on Judah's vassalage under Assyria, see Cogan, *Imperialism and Religion*, 65–72, 113; regarding the increased proximity of Assyrian influence and policy, consider Hayes and Miller, *Israelite and Judaean History*, 436–37.

21).[26] The narratological impact of Ahaz's desperate but futilely-directed appeals to Assyria is even more pronounced at the end of the unit by the chiastic contrast of v. 21 with v. 16 (see above).

CONCLUSION

Thus, the overall narrational characterization of Assyria in 28:16–21 develops as Assyria functions as an alluring—but anti-YHWH and futile—source of help for Ahaz. At the primary narratival level, the Assyrian presence is used to demonstrate the religio-moral degeneration of Ahaz and the inevitable failure of such dependencies. While supporting this characterization of Ahaz, the characterization of Assyria moves from that of a fairly neutral recipient of Ahaz's request to that of an opportunistic and unreliable oppressor.

---

26. Gary N. Knoppers, "Treasures Won and Lost: Royal (Mis)appropriations in Kings and Chronicles," in *The Chronicler as Author: Studies in Text and Texture*, eds. M. Patrick Graham and Steven L. McKenzie, JSOTSup 263 (Sheffield: Sheffield Academic, 1999), 181–208 (201) identifies the "exploitation of the treasuries [as] a sign of abject weakness and moral turpitude, rather than a defensive strategy in the context of international diplomacy."

6

Covenant Broken and Restored through the Intermediaries of the Assyrians

Two Brief References to the Assyrians in the Early Chapters of Chronicles' Hezekiah Account (2 Chronicles 29:9; 30:6–9)

A BROKEN COVENANT CAUSES THE ASSYRIANS TO BE (IMPLIED) INTERMEDIARIES OF YHWH (2 CHR 29:9)

THIS VERSE OCCURS WITHIN the context of Hezekiah's speech of commission and encouragement to the Levites for the consecration of themselves, the purification of the temple, and the general reestablishment of the temple and its service (2 Chr 29:5–11). Second Chronicles 29:9 is part of the historical retrospect (vv. 6–9) given in explanation of Hezekiah's resolution in vv. 10–11. In vv. 6–7, Hezekiah identifies the root problem with vocabulary (מעל; doing evil // not doing what is "right in the eyes of YHWH"; cf. 28:1, 19, 22) and specific examples (v. 7; cf. 28:24) that most immediately point to Ahaz and the events of chapter 28. Though the speech keeps a wide reference and applicability with "our fathers" and the use of the plural, the leaderly responsibility of Ahaz in these matters is evoked, both among Hezekiah's contemporaries and within the Chronicler's history of Judahite kings. In this way, King Hezekiah humbly recognizes the egregious unfaithfulness of his own father, while also calling the people to accountability and to enact change.

Next, Hezekiah articulates a direct link between "our fathers' " unfaithfulness and the punishment that soon followed (vv. 8–9). It is commonly observed in discussions of these verses that the language of v. 8 is echoed in Jer 29:18—specifically, being made (נתן) an object of terror (זועה), horror (שמה), and hissing/scorn (שרקה). It is generally because of this and the Persian-era provenance of the final form of Chronicles that scholars often affirm the assertion of Ackroyd: "The terms are so explicit as to make it clear that the Chronicler is here commenting on the exilic situation . . . "[1] At this point, some critical remarks are apropos. To begin, the distinctive language of Jer 29:18 may most closely echo 2 Chr 29:8, but it should be kept in mind that this language begins in Deuteronomy 28 (where the curses for disobedience are initially presented) and features more immediately and programmatically in 1 Kgs 8//2 Chr 6, Solomon's dedicatory prayer for the temple. Hence, I agree with Mason that "it may be safer to say that it is the more general Deuteronomistic/prophetic language of judgement which is being employed,"[2] while at the same time recognizing that a connection with Jer 29:18 is perhaps being evoked on one level for the Chronicler's immediate audience. Secondly, the allusions to Ahaz and chapter 28 cannot be taken for granted in interpreting this passage. The question that follows is in what ways 2 Chr 28 bears on 29:9. Japhet and Williamson perceive that at least on one level 29:8–9 refers back to the days of Ahaz in 2 Chr 28. The specific passages and events they identify, however, involve the northern kingdom's capture of Judahites[3]—a situation that is importantly *reversed* in significant part in 28:14–15. The Israelite/Samarian captivity of Judahites is an illogical and narratologically contradictory explanation for the punishment that Hezekiah's audience is now "seeing with your own eyes" and for why "our sons and our daughters and our wives are in captivity" (vv. 8, 9), though v. 9a may refer to the Israelite/Samarian killing of Judahite soldiers in 28:6. Selman forwards a similar proposal to that of Williamson in this regard, but makes the simple addition of 28:5 and 17 in his list of references

---

1. Ackroyd, *1 and 2 Chronicles*, 181. See also Thompson, *1, 2 Chronicles*, 345; Rex Mason, *Preaching the Tradition: Homily and Hermeneutics after the Exile* (Cambridge: Cambridge University Press, 1990), 101; Selman, *2 Chronicles*, 487; Williamson, *1 and 2 Chronicles*, 351.

2. Mason, *Preaching the Tradition*, 101.

3. Japhet, *1 & 2 Chronicles*, 919; Japhet, "Female Names and Gender Perspectives in Chronicles," in *The Writings and Later Wisdom Books*, eds. Christl M. Maier and Nuria Calduch-Benages, The Bible and Women (Atlanta: SBL, 2014), 33–53, esp. 41; Williamson, *1 and 2 Chronicles*, 351.

to captivity in chapter 28. Selman makes no further comment on 28:5, 17, but the almost-incidental observation draws attention to the possibility that 29:8–9 also reflects the attacks by the Arameans and Edomites; and, the Philistines in 28:18 may also be added to the list. Ben Zvi's general comments that Ahaz's final acts contrastively anticipate Hezekiah's reformations and reign also seem to support these latter two possibilities. Ben Zvi points out that Hezekiah's cultic reforms result in an avoidance of threat from Philistia and Edom—only Assyria remains a menace,[4] but ultimately that presence serves to exalt YHWH's victory in chapter 32. Finally, given the literary role of the Assyrian menace (which seems to underlie the main narrative from chapter 28 up to its appearance in chapter 32), the oppressive presence of Tiglath-Pileser III in Palestine in vv. 16–21, the probability that significant deportations of Israelites were understood to have occurred by 28:12, if not by 28:21, and the connection made in 30:6, 9 between a remnant escaping the hand of Assyria and that remnant's brethren and children being held in captivity (on one level, by the logic of the references to Hezekiah's audience, those in captivity in Assyria; perhaps more broadly to the Chronicler's audience, the Diaspora), the Assyrians must be considered a very likely candidate for the means behind the devastation and captivity that Hezekiah witnesses, learns a bitter lesson from, and resolves to change. I myself will expose one complication to this proposal, however: Hezekiah locates "the wrath of YHWH" (29:8a) as upon Judah and Jerusalem. While Tiglath-Pileser III presumably wrought havoc on Judah and Jerusalem (28:20–21), evidence is lacking for a significant deportation of Judahites by Tiglath-Pileser III. True, given the wide parameters of Hezekiah's language in this speech, the dissolution of the northern kingdom, and the Chronicler's ideal of Israel as one entity,[5] the referents seem fluid enough to encompass Assyria as a means behind the people's oppression. And even if Assyria were not considered a means of destruction in vv. 8–9, its great and imminent threat of becoming so certainly would have been evoked through Hezekiah's warning.

It would have been accepted fact by the Chronicler's initial audience that Israelites,[6] Arameans, Edomites, and perhaps the Philistines contributed in varying degrees to the devastation described in 29:8–9. As well,

---

4. Ben Zvi, "Gateway to the Chronicler's," 216–49// chap. 11 in *History, Literature and Theology in the Book of Chronicles* (London: Equinox, 2006), 210–42 (221–22).

5. Note that the list of Levites that immediately follows the speech is reminiscent of the list accompanying David's speech to the Levitical heads during the assemblage of "all Israel" (1 Chr 15).

6. For further discussion of facts accepted by the Chronicler's first audience and that the narrative contextualization of those facts imparts new meanings to them, see Ben Zvi, "Secession of the Northern," 61–82.

the massive deportations of Israelites by the Assyrians would not have been denied (cf. 30:6, possibly 30:9). The narrative's circumspect evasion of specifying who exactly contributed to the curse-punishments that the people experienced noticeably avoids attention being directed towards the impressive, worldly instruments of judgment (Assyria being the key threat then) and, moreover, an empire that normally draws attention. Instead, Hezekiah's speech maintains a strong, streamlined focus on the breach of relationship and covenant committed by the people and the divine and inevitable consequences suffered by all Israel because of such violations.[7] This narrative evasion of specification also facilitates broadened application of Hezekiah's speech to the circumstances and events in the recent memory of the Chronicler's audience (i.e., the Babylonian exile, colonial powers in general). In vv. 5–11 the primary issue remains, however, the breach of covenant relationship by God's people and God's response to that breach; the importance of this matter relegates intermediaries—however powerful and consequential they may seem—to the background.

A RETURN TO RESTORED COVENANT BECAUSE OF THE ASSYRIANS AS INTERMEDIARIES OF YHWH (2 CHR 30:6–9)

Second Chronicles 30 narrates a crucial and strategic event, within which Hezekiah's speech is placed at a particularly crucial juncture. Hezekiah's proclamation to all Israel and Judah functions within the narrative of 30:1—31:1 as the motivating articulation of why the Israelites and Judahites should assemble together in Jerusalem for the re-institution and celebration of the Passover. Two aspects of that call are emphasized in the narrative. 1) Most dominantly, assemblage of Israelites and Judahites *together*. The greatest move in this regard is required of the Israelites, who have generally constituted the renegade northern kingdom (though signs of exemplary Israelite piety become evident in 2 Chr 28). As well, the extension of the invitation to Israel—indeed, the appeal to Israel—was a bold move on the part of Hezekiah to attempt the beginning of a ground-breaking reunification of north and south. 2) The re-institution and celebration of the Passover. Again, Hezekiah initiates a history-making event, though the re-institution of the Passover celebration is relatively less epochal in both Hezekiah's

---

7. Japhet, "Female Names and Gender," 41, 52, observes the notably inclusive perspective of the Chronicler in passages such as 2 Chr 29:9 (and, in Japhet's view, by way of supposed direct relation also 28:8) regarding the essential role of women as part of basic Israelite social structure in contrast to that which is depicted in the book of Kings.

time and the narrative than the actively-pursued inclusion of Israelites in the assembly. The two aspects converge to varying degrees throughout the narrative, of course, multiplying at times the significance of various other elements of the dual-purpose event. For example, it is explicitly stated in v. 26 that Hezekiah's Passover was unsurpassed since the days of "Solomon son of David king of Israel." The situation is thus stated not only because the Passover assembly occurred (it presumably occurred not long before, prior to Ahaz' reign) but implicitly because it was the first time since the golden era of the united monarchy that the Passover was celebrated by representatives of the north and south alike.

As several scholars have observed, the narrative involves a number of unorthodoxies (e.g., the landmark inclusion of representatives from the northern kingdom; the delayed observance of the Passover by one month; the apparently historically early conflation of the Feast of Unleavened Bread with the Passover; the unclean state of the people and priests resulting in the Levites' sacrificing for them, Hezekiah interceding with a special prayer, and many priests being consecrated at that time [vv. 17–19, 24]; the voluntary extension of the festival by seven days [v. 23]) such that the narrative flows with a sense of realism. Eccentricities in praxis that could have been easily elided by the Chronicler are maintained, apparently in faithfulness to a tradition that the Chronicler did not consider himself to have the authority to overwrite. For some scholars, the upholding of the "uneven" contributions of that tradition attest to its verifiable historicity—why else would the Chronicler feel compelled to include the apparent irregularities? Since our concern is with the final form of the text, it will suffice to note that unusual and seminal cultic circumstances in chapter 30 distinguish the Chronicler's presentation of events and suggest the importance and innovation of the occasion.[8]

The speech in vv. 6–9 functions in a number of ways. On one level, we see that Hezekiah's purpose was to motivate and appeal to all the people "to come to Jerusalem and celebrate the Passover to the LORD, the God of Israel" (v. 5). Apparently, this purpose was to be carried out through the fulfilment of a second and even more important purpose, for the speech itself does not even mention celebration of the Passover or the particular site of Jerusalem—the theme of Hezekiah's speech is the necessity of a *return* by the people to their covenant relationship with YHWH. Thirdly, the speech functions as a message to the Chronicler's own immediate audience, who, in their post-exilic circumstances, would have easily applied the broad

---

8. Readers interested in further discussion on this issue of historicity are encouraged to consult Williamson's summary of the scholarly debate in his commentary. See Williamson, *1 and 2 Chronicles*, 361–65.

language of vv. 6–9 to themselves. Each of these concerns of the Chronicler shapes his presentation of Hezekiah's speech, as we shall see below.

At the story level, there are four basic parties presented in Hezekiah's speech: the people residing in Israel–Judah, YHWH, "kings of Assyria"/"captors" (i.e., enemy foreign nations, oppressive colonizers), and "fathers"/"brothers"/"sons" (i.e., familial relations). The main relationship with which Hezekiah is concerned is that of the people and YHWH. Though scholars usually recognize that the narrative describes the people—the addressees—as both Israelites and Judahites (vv. 1, 6a), there is a tendency to emphasize the certainty of an address to the Israelites while more hesitantly acknowledging the inclusion of Judah in the addressees.[9] While scholars may be quick to emphasize the relation of vv. 6–9 to the northern kingdom, the explicit statements of vv. 1, 6a and the language affinities of vv. 6–9 with the Chronicler's recent accounts of the south—i.e., Ahaz's מעל and deconstructive actions on the temple and its service, 2 Chr 28, 29:5–11—are undervalued, in my opinion. It seems that the sole, overwhelming internal evidence for why commentators understand vv. 6–9 as primarily addressing the Israelites is their interpretation of "the escaped remnant . . . from the hand of the kings of Assyria" (v. 6b). Because the Assyrians had wreaked havoc on the north, it is concluded that the speech addresses the north. However, despite the claim of Japhet that "the Assyrian threat has become a devastating reality" for the north "alone,"[10] the reality of the text is that the Chronicler explicitly acknowledges the troublesome effect of Assyria on the south (28:16, 20–21) while he remains silent regarding the actions of

---

9. E.g., Williamson, *1 and 2 Chronicles*, 366–68; Japhet, *1 and 2 Chronicles*, 942; and Thompson, *1, 2 Chronicles*, 352, 353; see also Dillard, *2 Chronicles*, 244, who simply reads that the audience was only northern.

Interestingly, Williamson, *1 and 2 Chronicles*, 366–37, concludes regarding the address of vv. 6–9: "Thus in the Chronicler's presentation there is nothing here that cannot apply to Judah as much as Israel." However, he then comments for v. 6: "of all OT writers, only the Chronicler applies this expression ['the remnant of you who have escaped'] either to those left in the north or to the whole population remaining in the land after the fall of Samaria." Affirming Williamson's first view, see idem, *Israel in the Books*, 127 (cf. 117).

Japhet, *1 and 2 Chronicles*, 942, articulates well the extent to which she perceives the fluidity of the addressees:

> In presenting the addressees of the letter the text returns to the terminology of v. 1, in which a clear distinction is drawn between "Israel" and "Judah," the two parts together qualified by "all." Although much of the content may apply also to Judah after the days of Ahaz . . . , the primary addressees are nevertheless the people of the North, for whom alone the Assyrian threat has become a devastating reality.

10. Japhet, *1 and 2 Chronicles*, 942.

COVENANT BROKEN AND RESTORED 155

Assyria on the north. To emphasize the point, it could be argued that the allusion to Assyria relates literally to the south and more historically to the north. However, this would be to the neglect of the broad scope of the speech. Both north and south are intended by the literary speech, as may be further seen in that the reference to Assyria is clearly phrased to be as broad as possible with the plural of abstraction ("the kings of Assyria"). Hence, Assyrian power is conceived as a generalized entity rather than in relation to any particular monarch (for further discussion, see below).[11] The explicit, but generalized mention of Assyria in v. 6b applies Hezekiah's words easily and aptly—though perhaps in different ways—to both Judah and Israel.[12]

The onus is on the people (Israel *and* Judah), and thus Hezekiah addresses them to restore their side of their relationship with YHWH. Hezekiah knows and assures the people that YHWH will respond with a restoration of their covenant relationship from his side. This dynamic is epitomized in the root שוב ("return"), which evidences itself as high-frequency vocabulary in this brief speech by occurring six times in a mere four verses. Its use is further reinforced by a use of the near-homonymic root שבה (שוביהם, "their captors")—and a use of the semantically-close סור through the word יסיר ("he will turn"). The selection of סור instead of שוב is striking, and the Chronicler apparently chose a word other than his usual שוב to avoid confusing his idiomatic, transitive sense of "turn" with the more direct and heavily spiritualized sense of covenantal relationship with which he imbues שוב. The Chronicler capitalizes on several nuances of שוב that operate within the covenantal context: repent (on the part of the people; one could interpret this sense as "relational," which seems too broad a use here, but it connects this nuance more clearly with the next), return to a particular way in a relationship (on the part of YHWH), physical turning, and geographical return. This rich complex of meaning for שוב has affinities with that of Zech 1:2-6 and the Book of Jeremiah (esp. 3:12, 14, 22; 8:4-5; 15:19), reinforcing the likelihood that the Chronicler had a theology of return strongly influenced by, if not reflective of and applicable to, the postexilic situation. W. L. Holladay demonstrates in his well-known monograph,

---

11. As ibid., 945, puts it, " 'the kings of Assyria' is a historical phenomenon rather than any particular royal figure." While I agree with Japhet's addition of "historical," it should be noted that the pluralization generalizes imperial Assyria into a phenomenon at the literary level without reliance on precise historicity. See also Dillard, *2 Chronicles*, 244.

12. To complete the overall picture concerning which of the former twelve tribes are and are not included in Hezekiah's address, observe that the Transjordan tribes are excluded. This is evident in both the speech's descriptions and the narrative's account (30:1, 5, 10–12, 18, 31:1; cf. 1 Chr 5:6, 25–26).

The Root Šûbh in the Old Testament,[13] that the prophet Jeremiah was the first to develop the rich semantic possibilities of the word,[14] which were then appropriated by later writers such as the Chronicler. For "further post-exilic Prophets and the Hagiographa," "there are no new patterns to emerge in the subsequent period; the field had been laid out by Jeremiah, and subsequent writings followed his usages as their particular outlook bade them."[15] The base meaning for שוב in Jeremiah and subsequent writings involving the motif of a "return" to YHWH remains a matter of debate. Holladay asserts that שוב means, in the Qal:

> having moved in a particular direction, to move thereupon in the opposite direction, the implication being (unless there is evidence to the contrary) that one will arrive again at the initial point of departure.[16]

Similarly, the "covenantal" usage of שוב

> means "return to God," "turn back to God" (to whom one has a prior obligation), not merely "change one's loyalty by turning to God." It is the re-establishment of something old, not the establishment of something altogether new.[17]

Graupner recognizes, however, "a whole series of witnesses" positing exceptions to the exclusivity of this statement. Hence, Graupner qualifies Holladay's definition by proposing a more neutral directive sense:

> [The normal case assumes that the goal of the movement is the original point of departure. Because the latter condition is clearly not fulfilled in a whole series of witnesses,] perhaps the basic meaning is rather "turn around, turn" (cf. Prov 20:26)

---

13. Note William L. Holladay, *The Root Šûbh in the Old Testament: With Particular Reference to its Usages in Covenantal Contexts* (Leiden: Brill, 1958), 54, 156.

14. Graupner adds Dtr History as an initiator of "the reinterpretation of the prophets into proclaimers of the law" using the summons to "return" as a demonstration of guilt (504), but I remain unconvinced that the few instances of this use of שוב in the Dtr History support a significantly influential innovative role by the Dtr History in the development of the meaning of שוב—esp. when compared with the abundant use and play on שוב by Jeremiah. M. Graupner and H.-J. Fabry, "שוב," in *TDOT* 14:461–522 (501; cf. 498), begins his very brief treatment of שוב by stating that "the root *šwb* plays a less significant role in the Dtr History than statistical information might initially suggest. Of the 284 occurrences, only 18 are used in theological contexts."

15. Holladay, *Root Šûbh*, 154; see also 116–20; 152–55; Mason, *Preaching the Tradition*, 105.

16. Holladay, *Root Šûbh*, 53. *HALOT* 4:1428d–29b.

17. Holladay, *Root Šûbh*, 120.

without any explication of direction. The consequence of this view is that (contra Holladay and Soggin) even the theological use of *swb* in the sense of "turn around to God" does not automatically imply a return to the point of departure (cf. Dietrich). This understanding also makes it possible to understand *swb* in its pretheological stage as a liturgical turning to the god/idol, and in its theological stage to understand the turning around also as an initial turning toward.[18]

Either way, both scholars acknowledge that שוב developed in later biblical stages related yet contradictory senses of turning to evil and (re)turning to God, which is most dominantly evidenced in Jeremiah and is apparently adopted by the Chronicler.[19]

Interestingly, all instances of שוב with the people as the subject in 30:6–9 have the sense of "return" (spiritually-relationally and to YHWH, in vv. 6b, 9a, 9c; geographically in v. 9b). The two instances of שוב for which YHWH is the subject use the sense of "return" (spiritually-relationally, v. 6b) and "turn" (v. 8b). A change and restoration of relationship is called for on the part of both parties in the human-divine relationship between Israel-Judah and YHWH—and more so on the part of the people than of YHWH.

The motivation for change is chiefly provided by the other two parties in the speech, foreign enemy nations and familial relations. The familial relations of "your fathers and your brothers" (v. 7) and "your brothers and your sons" (v. 9) serve as negative examples for Hezekiah's audience. Their behaviour is not to be emulated—מעלו (v. 7) being the same root describing the wickedness of Ahaz (28:19, 22) and his generation that Hezekiah earlier had related directly to their devastation (29:6–9)—and their awful fate is asserted to be a direct and observable result of such unfaithfulness. Hence Hezekiah warns the people present, "Do not be like your fathers and brothers . . . " "Do not 'stiffen your neck' like your fathers . . . ," " . . . and he may turn from you his burning anger" (vv. 7–8) builds on these warnings by implying a potential for YHWH's anger to be expressed again as it was for their familial predecessors).[20] At the same time, other, more ancient (and relatedly, more traditional) familial relations are evoked. One must

---

18. M. Graupner and H.-J. Fabry, "שוב," 464. See also 497.

19. Ibid., 492–96; 504 (though cf. 503); Holladay, *Root Šûbh*, 118–19; 152–54, 157.

20. The "stiffening of the neck" is an idiom for obstinacy and stubbornness. BDB, "ערף," 791b–c; Neil O. Skjoldal, "צואר," in *NIDOTTE* 3:772–75 (points 1 and 5); M. Zipor, "ערף," in *TDOT* 11:336–71 (368). Note that the OT links the neck with strength and that in particular צואר "describes the neck and, more broadly, the back" (Skjoldal, "צואר," 773)—hence, the similarity of idioms in Hezekiah's first two speeches of re-establishment is unsurprising (cf. 29:6).

avoid the temptation to over-dichotomize and posit these more traditional generations as necessarily being just a positive example. They are *more positive* examples than the immediate condemned generations, but the story of Abraham, Isaac, and Jacob was not without its recognition of human failure, sin, and unfaithfulness. What is connoted by the references to these older generations ("their fathers"), and reinforced by the Chronicler's distinctively confessional epithets at the beginning and end of the speech (using "Israel" for "Jacob" [v. 6] and the ancient confessional epithet "gracious and compassionate" [v. 9]),[21] is a long-standing covenant relationship which the people are called to return. The studies of Japhet and Allen concerning wider usage of the descriptor "God of [the/your/his/our/their] Fathers" in Chronicles support the idea that the epithet "emphasizes the continuity of the relationship between the LORD and His people"[22] and that "the overall formula [was] . . . a rhetorical device for spiritual challenge and commitment. The purpose of his creative borrowing was that his own and later generations might firmly grasp the baton of traditional faith, while they each ran their laps as living representatives of the faith community."[23]

The relation between the condemned immediate familial relations (i.e., those who are a negative example) and YHWH involves another party, the enemy foreign nations ("the kings of Assyria," "their captors," vv. 6b, 9a).

---

21. "The God of Abraham, Isaac and Israel" appears only three times in the OT—1 Kgs 18:36, 1 Chr 29:18, and here. The first two instances are part of prayers (Elijah and David) for whole-hearted devotion and worship on the part of the people towards YHWH. As well, both instances occur during seminal events of biblical history. Second Chronicles 30:6 appears to comport with these similarities. Mason, *Preaching the Tradition*, 104, suggests that the epithet in 30:6 indicates the fulfilment of David's charge to Solomon regarding the Temple as being fulfilled by Hezekiah and, relatedly, that "the David/Solomon golden age . . . is finding its expression and fulfilment in the life of a purified temple again functioning at the centre of a unified Israel." Japhet, *1 and 2 Chronicles*, 944, thinks that both 1 Chr 29:18 and 1 Kgs 18:36 are evoked in 2 Chr 30:6 to connote more broadly through "this rare and solemn epithet . . . the unity of the northern and southern tribes, their common faith stemming from one revelation and one tradition." Japhet's suggestion is attractive, but difficult to support since Israel-Judah unity does not appear to be a significant factor in the passage concerning Elijah at Mount Carmel. Mason's proposal remains possible, though one should bear in mind that it could also be the case that no strong inner-biblical allusion is intended apart from the overt ones of Abraham, Isaac, and Jacob/Israel. See also Allen, "Aspects of Generational," 128, who adds to the recall of patriarchs the twelve tribes, whose genealogies compose 1 Chr 2–9. As Japhet, *1 and 2 Chronicles*, 944, observes, the Chronicler typically prefers the name "Israel" to "Jacob." This does not wholly negate Allen's proposal, but helps us to recognize that the evocation of the twelve tribes is probably not just a particularized evocation, but part of a wider theological-stylistic phenomenon applied throughout Chronicles. Regarding the closing epithet, see Exo 34:6–9.

22. Japhet, *Ideology of the Book*, 14–19 (esp. 19, cf. 17).

23. Allen, "Aspects of Generational," 131.

While the Assyrian force is the most likely candidate for the identity of "their captors," the Arameans, Edomites, and Philistines at the story level (28:5, 17–18; at the level of the Chronicler to his post-exilic audience, that would be the Babylonians) may also be suggested by the broad term. The Chronicler does not deny the strength of the inimic, colonial-type nations—they are, after all, "captors" (שוביהם, a word whose assonance with the thematic root שוב might distinguish it, as similarly observed earlier) and Assyrian power is pluralized into the abstract ("the kings of Assyria")—this pluralization elevates the Assyrian threat from being associated with any particular Assyrian monarch to being a typologized entity. Its occurrence in v. 6 links with, and builds upon, its previous appearance in 28:16, in which the narrator's voice taps into the perspective of Ahaz and perceives a worldly, powerful force that is imperial Assyria.[24] In 30:6 that typologization is further reinforced through its second occurrence and issuance from Hezekiah.[25] As is commonly recognized by Chronicles scholars today,[26] the Chronicler uses speeches especially to convey his views and theology. It further appears that the Chronicler uses the voice of exemplary characters to add authoritative and emotional weight to his views. As Duke explains:

> The quotation of direct speech also created the ambiance of reliability and played an important role in Chr.'s rhetorical strategy. Direct speech has the character of external proof, because it purports to be not the words of Chr. but the "testimony" of other persons. It is *their* ethos that gives weight to the contents of the speeches, even if it is Chr. who controls the content of those speeches. Such material allowed Chr. to avoid a blatant dependence on his own authority and yet speak through authoritative characters.
>
> ... the use of speech material creates not only an ethical appeal, but also an emotional one. When speeches are quoted directly, they have the impact of addressing not just the audience within the narrative, but also the narrator's external audience, Chr.'s audience.[27]

---

24. See chapter 5 regarding the characterization of the Assyrians in 2 Chr 28.
25. This typologization will be reinforced a third time in 32:4.
26. E.g., see scholars and works listed in Japhet, *1 and 2 Chronicles*, 36–37.
27. Rodney K. Duke, "A Rhetorical Approach to Appreciating the Books of Chronicles," in *The Chronicler as Author: Studies in Text and Texture*, eds. M. Patrick Graham and Steven L. McKenzie, JSOTSup 263 (Sheffield: Sheffield Academic, 1999), 100–136 (see esp. 129–34; quotations from 129–30, 134). Similarly, idem, *The Persuasive Appeal of the Chronicler: A Rhetorical Analysis*, Bible and Literature Series 25 (Sheffield: Almond, 1990), 119, 123, 137, 146.

Hence, the Chronicler uses Hezekiah's authoritative voice to establish further the typologization of the mighty Assyrian threat. Assyria is not only an imposing imperial power, but, through the speech of Hezekiah, is now a force that definitively has wreaked witnessable havoc on Israel-Judah while at the same time operating wholly under the will of YHWH. I would also add that the typologization of Assyrian might in 30:6 facilitates the fluidity with which other nations may be associated with this growing type of the foreign enemy oppressor.

In vv. 6–9, the Chronicler is concerned with Assyria and enemy foreign nations only as they function within the relationship between YHWH and his people.[28] Implicitly, Hezekiah's present audience received mercy from YHWH in that they escaped the Assyrian threat (v. 6). Relatedly, "your fathers and your brothers" were conquered and made "a horror" (שמה) because they breached their relationship with YHWH by acting unfaithfully towards him (vv. 6, 7b). Presumably, condemned immediate familial relations have also been exiled by "their captors" because of their unfaithfulness to YHWH. Though the close familial relation of father-son may contribute to the efficacy of the formula in v. 9, it is nonetheless a striking claim that the restoration of the relationship between YHWH and one segment of the population may effect the beginning of restoration between YHWH and another (v. 9). Consistent with the intermediary, instrumental role of enemy foreign nations in bringing to expression YHWH's judgment, the Chronicler indicates that those same enemy foreign nations (implicitly, Assyria included) may serve as agents of YHWH's grace and compassion (v. 9).

It cannot be overemphasized that the enemy foreign nations—and imperial Assyria, in particular—are depicted by the Chronicler as wholly serving the purposes of YHWH. Where the human eye might see a wasteland left by the Assyrians, the Chronicler attributes this destruction to YHWH (v. 7). In this case, what matters are the central relationships and dynamics. Peripheral parties and relationships (i.e., those involving the enemy foreign nations and superpowers) fall into line with the primary ones, those of YHWH and his people. Moreover, the peripheral parties are depicted in vv. 6–9 as being totally passive, completely acting under the will of YHWH.

There is also an implicit influence of Assyria present in Hezekiah's ability to issue his proclamation to the north, which was still under official Assyrian hegemony as a wholly conquered province.[29] Hezekiah's summons to the former northern kingdom surely would have been viewed by the As-

---

28. See Appendix 2 for a simplified diagram of this relational complex.

29. See Bustenay Oded, "Judah and the Exile," in *Israelite and Judaean History*, eds. John H. Hayes and J. Maxwell Miller (London: SCM, 1977), 436–37.

syrian empire as an affront, if not as insurgence, on his part. A lapse in the Assyrian political-military grip in Palestine, however, would have provided an opportune time for Hezekiah to enact the initiative, which at other times would have been simply impossible under Assyrian suppression.[30]

The wider narrative of chapter 30 may include an additional and indirect reflection of the Assyrian influence. In 30:25 the worshipping assembly includes "the immigrants (גרים) who came from the land of Israel." There is no parallel in the narrative with any such גרים from Judah, and it seems that they are distinctive to Israel's situation—quite possibly they are (or, at least, included) peoples deported by Assyria to Israel (2 Kgs 17:24).[31]

CONCLUSION

Finally, I would like to conclude with some remarks concerning the wider literary contribution of 2 Chr 30:6-9 to Chronicles. Others have suggested an important structural role which asserts that 2 Chr 29-31 "must be considered the high point of his narrative of the post-Solomonic kings."[32] Similarly, he continues: "If 2 Chronicles 10 to 36 has a structural center, it is surely the cultic reforms of Hezekiah."[33] Plöger suggests that the speeches of Abijah and Hezekiah in 2 Chr 13:4-12; 30:6-9 are *Umkehrreden* ("return" speeches, calls to return) which thus demarcate *inclusio*-like the period of the divided monarchy:

> So ist das Ereignis der Reichstrennung der tiefe Einschnitt, der die davidisch-salomonische Zeit, die Zeit der Planung und Erbauung des Tempels, von der Konigszeit trennt, und die beiden Umkehrrufe Abias und Hiskias interpretieren die Konigszeit als eine Periode weniger zweier getrennter Reiche als vielmehr zweier getrennter „Kirchen."[34]

30. Agreeing with Japhet, *1 and 2 Chronicles*, 944; Williamson, *1 and 2 Chronicles*, 361; and Thompson, *1, 2 Chronicles*, 352. See also H. W. F. Saggs, "The Assyrians," in *Peoples of Old Testament Times*, ed. D. J. Wiseman (Oxford: Clarendon, 1973), 156–78 (162–63).

31. Selman, *2 Chronicles*, 500; Japhet, *1 and 2 Chronicles*, 956; the GNB rather misleadingly conflates the גרים from Israel with the יושבים of Judah as "the foreigners who had settled permanently in Israel and Judah."

32. Roddy L. Braun, "The Significance of 1 Chronicles 22, 28, 29 for the Structure and Theology of the Work of the Chronicler" (ThD thesis, Concordia Seminary, St. Louis, May 1971), 154.

33. Ibid., 157.

34. See Otto Plöger, "Reden und Gebete im deuteronomistischen und chronistichen Geschichtswerk," in *Aus der Spätzeit des Alten Testaments: Studien zu seinem*

It does appear that the relational triad forged by the thematic use of שוב in 30:6-9 presents a series of interrelated relationships that draw together previous passages concerning the covenantal relationship (especially 2 Chr 6:14-42//1 Kgs 8:23-53; some would add 7:14,[35] though I think there are stronger links with 2 Chr 6//1 Kgs 8 for the themes of captivity situations and YHWH hearing the prayers of the people)[36] and anticipate the remainder of Chronicles. Literary aspect mirrors the process of historical and theological aspects as Hezekiah's purification and restoration of the priesthood in 2 Chr 29 (note the one use of שוב in 2 Chr 29 is in v. 10) prepares the way for the restoration[37] of the relational triad in 2 Chr 30-32. That basic relational triad is: the people are to return to YHWH (vv. 6b, 8, 9b), YHWH is to return to the people (vv. 6b, 9b), and partly indicative of this change by both parties is that the enemy foreign nations will expedite the people's return to the land (v. 9a). Chapters 30-31 see the first part of this "formula" fulfilled: the people return to YHWH. As well, the passages show the second part of the formula enacted: YHWH returns to the people—he hears their prayers (30:20, 27) and responds positively to Hezekiah's request for the healing of the people (30:20). It also appears to be the case that YHWH grants general success to Hezekiah (31:21). The third and rather intermediary part, however—the return of Israelites from their captors—remains unresolved. Chapter 32 will exploit this anticipation in an engaging way. The issue of the enemy-intermediary's relationship between the people and YHWH will be addressed and resolved in part in chapter 32, but not entirely. Instead, the Chronicler sustains the tension of resolving this second part to the very end of his work. In this process, the primary explicit expression of the enemy foreign nation typology moves from Assyria in chapters 30, 32, and 33 to Egypt, Babylon, and finally Persia in the remainder of Chronicles.

---

60. *Geburtstag am 27.11.1970 herausgegeben von Freunden und Schülern* (Göttingen: Vandenhoeck & Ruprecht, 1971), 50-66 (quote from 57-58).

35. E.g., Williamson, *1 and 2 Chronicles*, 368; Selman, *2 Chronicles*, 495; Dillard, *2 Chronicles*, 243; and Thompson, *1, 2 Chronicles*, 355. See, however, Japhet, *1 and 2 Chronicles*, 943, who observes that 1 Kgs 8:50, which is strikingly missing from the Chronicler's parallel of Solomon's prayer (see 2 Chr 6:39-40), is included, in substance, in 30:9.

36. This is not to deny the uniqueness of 7:13-15 for Chronicles and that 7:14 particularly reflects the Chronicler's theology. For further discussion, see Dillard, "Reward and Punishment in Chronicles: The Theology of Immediate Retribution (2 Chron 10-36)," in *Chronicles*, 76-81 (76-77); Williamson, *1 and 2 Chronicles*, 225-26; Selman, *2 Chronicles*, 336-41; Thompson, *1, 2 Chronicles*, 235; Leslie C. Allen, *1, 2 Chronicles*, Communicator's Commentary (Word: Waco, 1987), 238-39.

37. More or less; see discussion to follow.

7

YHWH is Greater than Assyria
The Characterization of the Assyrians in 2 Chronicles 32 through Chiastic and Linear Readings (2 Chronicles 32)

INTRODUCTION

THIS CHAPTER CONSIDERS THE portrayal of the Assyrians in 2 Chronicles 32 from two structural perspectives: its chiastic structure and its linear structure. One may expect a study in 2 Chr 32 to be either dull or repetitive—until recently,[1] Chronicles itself was often slighted as a later and less-skilled adaptation of the Samuel–Kings/Isaiah traditions, and the one well-trodden passage in 2 Chronicles of which articles, monographs, and theses have been copiously written felicitously happens to be the primary text for this chapter as well. It is my contention, however, that 2 Chronicles 32 remains a rich and viable text for fresh study. In its structures, events, and story, 2 Chr 32 continues to evidence engaging complexity and points of interest for the reader concerning the Assyrians.

---

1. See contributions to *The Chronicler as Author: Studies in Text and Texture*, eds. M. Patrick Graham and Steven L. McKenzie, JSOT Sup 263 (Sheffield: Sheffield Academic, 1999).

THE CHARACTERIZATION OF THE ASSYRIANS IN THE CHIASMUS OF 2 CHRONICLES 32[2]

Second Chronicles 32 utilizes a variety of poetic structuring devices—particularly, chiasmus—to organize and contribute meaning to its content.[3] The identification and function of poetic techniques is a necessary step in appreciating the message of a text,[4] and this is no less true regarding chiasmus. Breck's words are apropos:

> Although at first literal translations of these forms might appear strange to modern readers, the advantages in conveying precise meaning and poetic beauty certainly outweigh any temporary inconvenience.
>
> Above all, however, respecting the literary form of biblical passages goes far towards throwing light on the literal sense of the text. Understanding and elucidating that sense remains the exegete's primary task. The beauty of chiasmus lies in the fact that its form expresses its meanings with such directness and clarity. The surest way to discover and proclaim that meaning, then, is to proceed by a thoroughgoing analysis of the form by which that meaning is conveyed.[5]

Although the degree of "precise meaning" and "clarity" conveyed by chiasmus and other devices is debatable, the vital contribution of these techniques towards that intention should be self-evident. Furthermore, with regards to Chronicles in particular, if one affirms the conclusion of Japhet and Mason that the Chronicler's work is strongly rhetorical,[6] then it naturally follows

---

2. A significant part of this section concerning the chiastic structure of 2 Chr 32 appeared in a previous version of Hom, "Chiasmus in Chronicles," 163–79.

3. Studies of 1–2 Chronicles' structuring devices and their functions are relatively recent and few in number. See brief discussion and sources in Rodney K. Duke, "A Rhetorical Approach to Appreciating the Books of Chronicles," in *The Chronicler as Author: Studies in Text and Texture*, eds. M. Patrick Graham and Steven L. McKenzie, JSOT Sup 263 (Sheffield: Sheffield Academic, 1999), 100–135 (118–19 and n58).

4. E.g., Wilfred G. E. Watson, *Traditional Techniques in Classical Hebrew Verse*, JSOT Sup 170 (Sheffield: Sheffield Academic, 1994), 324, 368; Kalimi, *Reshaping of Ancient*, 215–16; John Breck, "Biblical Chiasmus: Exploring Structure for Meaning," *BTB* 17 (1987) 70–74.

5. John Breck, *The Shape of Biblical Language: Chiasmus in the Scriptures and Beyond* (Crestwood, NY: St. Vladimir's Seminary Press, 1994), 61.

6. Japhet, *1 and 2 Chronicles*, 37: " . . . the Chronicler's particular position may be seen in his strong inclination towards 'the rhetorical' in general, as illustrated by the preponderance of rhetorical elements in his work and their great variety"; and Mason, *Preaching the Tradition*, 138–41. As well, von Rad, Noth, Plöger, Throntveit, and others recognize the importance of speeches—rhetorical pieces in themselves—in conveying

that analysis of aesthetic devices and structures is necessary to understanding and appreciating Chronicles.

In broad outline, I will establish the methodology for discerning chiasmus, and then proceed to the chiastic analysis of 2 Chr 32. For the most part, this will be organized according to specific chiastic pairs, concluding with discussion of the characterization of the Assyrians in the pivot and the chiasmus as a whole.

Methodology

To begin, brief definition of a few often variously-defined devices is in order. "Chiasmus" denotes a pattern involving inversion, as in ABBA, ABB'A,' etc. A pivot may be included (ABCBA), but is not necessary to qualify a pattern as chiastic (contra Breck).[7] Secondly, my definition of "sonancy" restricts itself to "consonantal assonance" (in agreement with Kselman),[8] which as a form of word-play in Hebrew poetry may be further identified as "primarily a matter of similarity in *combinations of consonants*" (emphasis Holladay's).[9]

The term "chiastic aspect" is coined here to denote literary counter-positioning, which can vary in degree of strength. For example, all else being equal, a rare word is more likely to have a greater chiastic aspect than a common word, and two verses equi-distant from the pivot will almost always have greater chiastic aspect than two verses not equi-distant from the pivot. "Chiastic aspect" may be contrasted to "chiasmus" in that the latter implies that the *entirety* of a text explicitly exhibits chiastic aspect. It seems safe to say that chiasmus proper in biblical narrative prose is extremely rare, and when it does occur, it borders on—if not crosses over—the grey divide between prose and poetry. Perhaps it would help if we qualify as *narratival* chiasmus a narrative text with overall strong chiastic aspect approaching chiasmus proper.

the distinctive thought of the Chronicler throughout his work. Regarding speeches in particular, see Gerhard von Rad, "The Levitical Sermon 1 and 2 Chronicles," in *The Problem of the Hexateuch and Other Essays*, trans. E. W. Trueman Dicken (Edinburgh: Oliver and Boyd, 1966), 267–80; Martin Noth, "The Nature of the Composition," in *The Chronicler's History*, trans. H. G. M. Williamson, JSOT Sup 50 (Sheffield: Sheffield Academic, 1987), 75–81; Throntveit, *When Kings Speak*, 226–27, 245; and bibliography under Throntveit, "Chronicler's Speeches," 226n8. Note also Plöger, *Aus der Spätzeit*, 50–66, which perceives a structural function as well to the speeches and prayers.

7. Breck, "Biblical Chiasmus," 71.

8. John S. Kselman, "Semantic-Sonant Chiasmus in Biblical Poetry," *Bib* 58 (1977) 219–23 (220). Cf., however, definitions under Watson, *Classical Hebrew Poetry*, 222–29.

9. William L. Holladay, "Form and Word-Play in David's Lament over Saul and Jonathan," *VT* 20 (1970) 153–89 (157).

In line with this, it may be said that I have a somewhat circular perspective of chiasmus. A legitimate narratival chiasmus has a strong enough overall chiastic aspect that it may be recognized as an intentional structure. Elements of the text signify the chiasmus; the chiasmus, in turn, contributes its own meaning to the text. As seen in the relationship between other literary biblical structures and their content, one may expect that the chiastic structure's contribution is consistent with other meanings and emphases clearly conveyed through the text's content.

Chiastic aspect, on the other hand, does not necessarily render a text as a chiasmus. Weak chiastic aspect may help to delineate a pericope, or mildly accentuate its unity, but the text of which it is a part may not be further involved in the chiastic dynamic. Strong chiastic aspect draws more of the text into chiastic relation. The stronger the chiastic aspect, the more a text approaches chiasmus proper and the "circular" effect of structure-informing-content dynamics may be considered.

The most rigorous procedure for discerning chiasmus that I have encountered so far is by Butterworth, of "Isaiah 67" fame.[10] I have summarized his procedure below:

1) Establish the text form and its divisions independently of structural considerations.

2) Examine *all* repetitions, and discard those that seem to be insignificant.

3) Estimate the likely importance of the repeated words that remain. Butterworth gives more priority here to repetitions of whole phrases, rare words, words used in characteristic ways, and clusters of related words, and less priority to technical terms.

4) Consult and compare conclusions with the work of scholars in various branches of OT research.

5) Attempt to explain the purpose(s) of the authors in presenting material in this particular way.

In addition to my focus on "chiastic aspect" instead of "chiasmus," there are two matters on which I diverge from Butterworth's approach that deserve further comment here. The first regards his evaluation of the repetition of common words. While I agree with Butterworth that, in general, "common words are of minimal value in indicating structure" because of the natural

---

10. See Butterworth, *Structure and the Book*, 13–61, esp. 53–61. Butterworth's randomly-created "Isaiah 67" entertainingly demonstrates that repetitions can sometimes be mere coincidences.

frequency of common words in longer passages,[11] I cannot agree that this necessarily calls for complete disregard of common vocabulary. True, more often than not common vocabulary is simply used in a common way. At the same time, common words may indeed be used chiastically; their chiastic aspect may not be strong and one should approach common words with more reserve than not, but still their potential contribution to structure cannot be presumed null.

Secondly, with regard to the more subjective element of a text (i.e., its conceptual content), Butterworth finds it "strange for a writer to avoid using certain words more than once, if he wanted to draw the reader's attention to the correspondence [between one part and another]."[12] This assumes a particularly rigid style on the part of the writer, and that is a presumption I am not led to make concerning the authors of the ancient Hebrew text. Further, Butterworth's wariness of eisegetic misinterpretation of subjective material is such that it results in a complete avoidance of the consideration and evaluation of subjective elements. I readily concur that the evaluation of subjective aspects of a text is difficult. Yet, difficult as these matters are, subjective elements remain a vital part of the text and should not be excluded from evaluating its structure.

For this study, the chiastic structures presented were found incidentally during exegetical translation of the passages. The texts and delineation of units had already been established independently of any consideration of chiasmus or chiastic aspect. Unusual repetition of vocabulary, phrases, and motifs presented themselves, however, and chiastic aspect appeared evident. To evaluate the apparent chiastic features in the passages, I applied Butterworth's procedure, *mutatis mutandis*, and further tested the strength of my own observations by discussing, presenting, and forwarding them to various colleagues for critical feedback. Naturally, for good or ill, I assume full responsibility for the final results regarding the presence of chiastic aspect in 2 Chr 31:20—32:33 (or other chiastically-arranged passages presented elsewhere in this book, for that matter).

The Chiasmus[13]

Second Chronicles 32 evidences a masterfully constructed chiasmus; it demonstrates strong enough chiastic aspect that, for all intents and purposes, we

---

11. Ibid., 55–56.

12. Ibid., 59.

13. Though it is less familiar of a term, "palistrophe" technically also describes the literary structure at work in 2 Chr 32. A palistrophe is basically a chiasmus in a larger

will call it a narratival chiasmus. In the interest of highlighting the chiastic structure, only the most salient details are presented in the diagram, and further relevant points of interest will be included in the discussion that follows. Having said that, note that our focus here shall remain particularly on the portrayal of the Assyrians.

In the diagram below, chiastically-arranged verses and elements exhibiting strong chiastic aspect are described in plain, black print, and elements with weaker chiastic aspect are noted in 50% grayscale.

The chiastic structure of 2 Chr 31:20—32:33:

A. Summary formulae about Hezekiah (31:20-21)

   B. Foreign power (Assyria) tests Hezekiah's faithfulness (32:1-2)

      C. Hezekiah סתם the springs (32:3)

         D. ר–ב occurs twice; abundant resources for Jerusalem in time of war (32:4)

            E. מגנים made; Hezekiah's building projects in time of war (32:5)

               F. לבב; public encouragement by Hezekiah (32:6) (32:7)

                  G. Hezekiah utterly dependent on God for a miracle (military) to survive and overcome the "flesh" (32:8)

                     H. Introductory statement, אחר זה; "to Hezekiah, king of Judah"; content: foreign nation hostile to Jerusalem (32:9)

                        I. cluster: "Sennacherib king of Assyria" and issue of what happens to ישבים . . . בירושלם; Sennacherib's questions . . . (see I', v. 22) (32:10)

                          J. Content: Hezekiah defamed by the king of Assyria; Sennacherib predicts death for Jerusalemites . . . ; Sennacherib challenges the ability of the Jerusalemites' God to save them (32:11)

                            K. Content: Sennacherib looks at the Israelite cultus and begins his challenge of the exclusivity of the one God YHWH and the centralized cultus (32:12)

                               L. cluster: "the lands"; root עשה; "my [Sennacherib's] hand"; implicit comparison of YHWH to other gods (32:13) (32:14)

---

unit of text. A notable example of this term applied to another text is Gordon J. Wenham, "The Coherence of the Flood Narrative," *VT* 28 (1978) 336-48 (see esp. 337-42); and idem, *Genesis 1-15*, WBC 1 (Waco: Word, 1987), 156-57.

M. Content and phraseology: Sennacherib defames Hezekiah; likens YHWH to the gods of other nations; "[the Israelites'] god(s) will not deliver them from my hand" (32:15)

   N. *Pivot*: self-contained chiasmus and assonance (32:16)

M'. Content and phraseology: Sennacherib defames YHWH; likens YHWH to the gods of other nations; "Hezekiah's god will not deliver his people from my hand" (32:17) (32:18)

L'. cluster: "the land"; root עשה//radicals ע-ש-ה; "the hands of humanity"; explicit comparison of YHWH to other gods (32:19)

  K'. Content: Hezekiah and Isaiah appeal exclusively to YHWH in a way not restricted by the formalisms of the cultus, but pray "(to) the heavens" (32:20)

    J'. Content: Hezekiah proven correct by YHWH; Assyrian enemy forces and Sennacherib himself die; Sennacherib not saved in "the house of his own god" (32:21)

I'. cluster: "Sennacherib king of Assyria" and issue of what happens to ישבי ירושלם . . . are well-answered! (see I, v. 10) (32:22)

H'. Concluding statement, מאחרי־כן; "to Hezekiah, king of Judah"; content: foreign nations honor the king in Jerusalem (32:23)

G'. Content: Hezekiah utterly dependent on God for a miracle (bodily) to survive (32:24) and overcome the flesh (32:25)

F'. לב; private act of Hezekiah has public consequences (32:26)

E'. מגנים in treasuries; Hezekiah's building projects in time of rest and prosperity (32:27–28)

D'. ר-ב occurs twice; abundant resources for Hezekiah in time of peace (32:29)

C'. Hezekiah סתם the spring (32:30)

B'. Foreign power (Babylon) tests Hezekiah's faithfulness (32:31)

A'. Concluding formulae about Hezekiah (32:32–33)

The Assyrians feature most evidently in 2 Chr 32:1–23, though as the chiasmus suggests, all of 2 Chr 32:1–32 is to be viewed as a complete unit, with each verse of the chapter (apart from the pivot, v. 16) reinforcing at least its chiastic counterpart. Hence, the association of Hezekiah's illness and subsequent dealings towards the Babylonians (in vv. 24–26, 31) with the Assyrian invasion is structurally prescribed. This is not to deny source-critical arguments creating a necessity on the part of the reader for familiarity with 2 Kgs 20:1–11//Isa 38:1–22, but the given unity and coherence from 2 Chr 32's structure does relativize the importance of that necessity. Inner-biblical allusions (insofar as they may reflect the ideological concerns of the Chronicler) still play a role in connecting events, but not to the negation of the chiasmus that draws the chapter together.[14] Likewise, vv. 27–30 need not be considered "additions," "addenda," or simply "unsuitable in the context," but harmonious components of the chiasmus that reinforce and draw on the otherwise long-forgotten early verses of the chapter.[15] Thus, while traditionally a study of the portrayal of the Assyrians in 2 Chr 32 would focus on 32:1–23, it will be beneficial to draw on vv. 24–33, which now may be appreciated as part of the chiasmus.

One should first observe that the account of the Assyrian threat in 2 Chr 32 is contained within the narrative about the faithfulness of Hezekiah, as the AB/A'B' inclusio (31:20—32:2, 31–33) indicates. Thus, as we may expect and as the content affirms, the story of the Assyrians in 2 Chr 32 serves to illustrate the structurally greater issue of Hezekiah's faithfulness. Another chiastic feature that should immediately draw our attention is the pivot, v. 16. In addition to its central position in the chiasmus, v. 16 features assonance and is a self-contained chiasmus. These three aspects combine to distinguish v. 16 triply and to strongly emphasize 1) the centrality of "YHWH the God" in the midst of the events of chapter 32, and 2) the conflict being waged between the servant of YHWH, Hezekiah, and the servants of Sennacherib, whose name and title are minimized so as to not even appear in this important verse.

We will now continue to the portrayal of the Assyrians through the chiastic pairs.

A/A' (31:20–21; 32:32–33): These verses bookend chapter 32 in an inclusio of formulae about Hezekiah's faithfulness in the face of the impending Assyrian assault. This pairing features standard formulae in predictable places.

---

14. Cf. Japhet, *1 and 2 Chronicles*, 992–93; Williamson, *1 and 2 Chronicles*, 386.
15. Japhet, *1 and 2 Chronicles*, 994; Williamson, *1 and 2 Chronicles*, 387.

The verses share no distinct vocabulary, and chiastic aspect for these verses is low.

B/B' (32:1-2, 31): Verse 2 features the foreign power of Assyria while v. 31 presents Babylon—i.e., the preeminent world empire at present, and the dominant world empire to come. The narrator's mention of God's intentional sovereignty over the Babylonian test suggests his same sovereignty over the Assyrian challenge.

Apart from the chiastic relation between vv. 2 and 31, v. 31's brief retrospect to vv. 24-26 seems both awkward and unnecessary; awareness of the chiasmus, however, both elucidates the verses' meaning and renders v. 31's placement and content structurally necessary.

C/C' (32:3, 30): The correspondence relies on the distinctive occurrences of the fairly rare root סתם, "to shut, stop." This root occurs 13-15 times in the OT,[16] and three times in Chronicles, all of which appear here in 2 Chr 32. Lowering the chiastic aspect is the fact that there is a third occurrence, in v. 4, but strengthening the chiastic aspect is the particular motif of the manipulation of springs leading to Jerusalem. The sharing of this motif was observed by Ackroyd, but without exploration of further literary-structural relevance.[17] Similarly, Otzen noted the shared use of סתם, with both occurrences being in the Qal, and surmised an indirect connection, but to no further discussion.[18] Overall chiastic aspect for this chiastic pair is strong.

These verses feature no direct bearing on the portrayal of the Assyrians other than the indication in v. 3 of the serious extent to which Hezekiah and the people prepare for an invasion by Assyria. Water supplies and water passages into the city are expected to be conduits of which the enemy would take advantage, and their blockage is of primary importance as Hezekiah and the leaders anticipate an Assyrian attack. The pairing of these verses elucidates how Hezekiah prevents the Assyrians from exploiting one water supply while Jerusalem is maintained by another.

D/D' (32:4, 29): The repetition of ר-ב by itself is unexceptional. The combination initial-ר followed by ב occurs 118 times in Chronicles, 68 times in 2 Chronicles, and 8 times in 2 Chr 32. However, its occurrences in vv. 4 and

---

16. See discussion in B. Otzen and H.-J. Fabry, "סתם," *TDOT* 10:359-62, esp. 359-61.

17. Peter R. Ackroyd, "Chronicler as Exegete," 11-12.

18. Otzen, "סתם," 359-60.

29 have an additional distinctive feature, and that is ר-ב's double appearance in each verse.

2 Chr 32:4 ויקבצו עם־רב ויסתמו את־כל־המעינות ואת־הנחל השוטף בתוך־הארץ לאמר למה יבואו מלכי אשור ומצאו מים רבים:

2 Chr 32:29 וערים עשה לו ומקנה־צאן ובקר לרב כי נתן־לו אלהים רכוש רב מאד:

This parallel double use of רב in these verses emphasizes the strength and abundance of Hezekiah and Jerusalem's resources, an implicit sign of God's favor,[19] whether under threat of imperial attack (v. 4) or in time of peace (v. 29). The chiastic highlights suggest that mention of the Israelite concern about Assyrians discovering the abundance of their waters is more a positive comment on Jerusalem's blessing than a negative fear of Assyrian invasion. As well, the immediate narrational impact of v. 4b's particularities is lessened somewhat by the plural use of "kings," which moves the reference to a typological level.[20] Thirdly, v. 4 appears to contribute to a minor theme in Chronicles concerning the involvement of the people.[21] The chiastic use of רב, the typologization of the Assyrian threat, and the evocation of the "people's-involvement" motif work in concert to lessen the negative effect of the Israelite concern about Assyrian invasion and to highlight instead the evidence of blessings in Jerusalem.

The chiastic reading suggests an explanation for Japhet's comment that the rhetorical question of v. 4 articulates "in fact the only case in the Bible where this topic is referred to—the active diversion of a water supply from an invading enemy."[22] The topic may indeed be rare in biblical description, but perhaps that is because the issue of water supply was commonplace and presumable for defensive tactics. This is not to deny the importance of water

---

19. See Dillard, *2 Chronicles*, 78. I also agree with Steven Tuell's general and sensible observation that rivers and their abundance are associated with the divine presence in passages such as Gen 2:10–14 and Ezek 47:1–12, which themselves are connected to Jerusalem imagery. (Tuell's first, fourth, and fifth subsequent cited examples, however, fail to directly support this *topos*.) See Steven Tuell, "The Rivers of Paradise: Ezekiel 47:1–12 and Genesis 2:10–14," in *God Who Creates: Essays in Honor of W. Sibley Towner*, eds. William P. Brown and S. Dean McBride Jr. (Grand Rapids: Eerdmans, 2000), 171–89 (181–86).

20. See Section Two of this chapter regarding the three occurrences of the plural "kings of Assyria" in Chronicles; P. R. Ackroyd, "The Chronicler as Exegete," *JSOT* 2 (1977) 2–32 (11–12), extends this typology to "cosmic," mythological levels, but I share Williamson's (*1 and 2 Chronicles*, 381) hesitation of this.

21. See 1 Chr 29: 14–18 and Braun, "Significance," 86. E.g., in the reign of Hezekiah alone, the people figure significantly (2 Chr 29:36; 30:1–13; 17–20; 25–31:1; 31:4–10; 32: 6, 26, 8, 33).

22. Japhet, *1 and 2 Chronicles*, 982.

supply for military defence in the historical situation;²³ at the same time, for the literary situation in v. 4, the emphasis is not on military defense, but on the wealth of resources for the city and its king, along with the divine blessing associated with it.

E/E' (32:5, 27–28): These verses share the word מגנים, "shields," which occurs 10 times in 2 Chronicles, and twice in this chapter. The placement of מגנים in v. 27 has been considered so unusual that the Greek and Latin interpreters preferred to emend מגנים to the biblically-unattested form מגדנים ("choice, excellent things," cf. 32:23).²⁴ מגנים is maintained in the MT, however. Bearing in mind the unusual use of מגנים (at least, in antique and modern eyes) the chiastic aspect here is significant.²⁵

As with C/C', these verses do not directly portray the Assyrians, though they do reflect the gravity of the threat posed by them towards the Jerusalemites. The Assyrian threat calls for not only the reinforcement of structures, but the production of weapons—notably shields (מגנים). While this latter point may seem obvious, it is a link between vv. 5 and 27–28 that is noteworthy. After YHWH delivers Jerusalem from Assyria, the מגנים go to rest in Hezekiah's treasuries, no longer required for active engagement (reminiscent of the glory and peace of Solomon's kingdom, cf. 2 Chr 9:15–16). Details such as this affirm the completion of Jerusalem's deliverance from Assyria.

F/F' (32:6, 26): These verses share vocabulary (לבב/לב) and possibly content (which would be, Hezekiah's public influence on Jerusalem, whether demonstrated overtly or initially hidden).²⁶

---

23. Also bear in mind the immediately previous verse, 2 Chr 32:3; cf. Gen 26: 14–15, 18; 2 Kgs 3:9, 16–20, 25; and esp. 19:24, in which Isaiah recounts the boastfulness of Sennacherib: "I have dug wells in foreign lands and drunk the water there.//With the soles of my feet I have dried up all the streams of Egypt."

24. [מגדנה] occurs in the OT in only the feminine plural form and in just three clear instances: Gen 24:53; 2 Chr 21:3; 32:23.

25. For modern interpreters questioning the use of מגנים, see *BHS*; *NAB*; *NJB*; Wilhelm Rudolph, *Chronikbücher*, HAT (Tübingen: Mohr/Siebeck, 1955), 312; Ackroyd, *1 and 2 Chronicles*, 195; and Williamson, *1 and 2 Chronicles*, 387. See also discussion in Mark A. Throntveit, "The Relationship of Hezekiah to David and Solomon in the Books of Chronicles," in Graham, McKenzie, and Knoppers, *Chronicler as Theologian*, 105–121, esp 116.

26. The relation and consequences between the public and private aspects of a Judahite king may be seen in the narrative concerning Hezekiah's human, but still fairly paradigmatic predecessor, King David. E.g., see David M. Gunn, *The Story of King David: Genre and Interpretation*, JSOT Sup 6 (Sheffield: JSOT, 1978), 87–111, esp. 88–94; and Kenneth R. R. Gros Louis, "The Difficulty of Ruling Well: King David of Israel,"

Though וידבר על־לבבם (v. 6) is an idiom, the parallelism reinforces the לבב imagery such that one is inclined to consider further the significance of the לבב.²⁷ Both verses refer to the heart as the place of fear and humility, encouragement and pride. The pairing of vv. 6 and 26 clarifies the nuance between a healthy YHWH-based encouragement and unhealthy self-based pride. That Hezekiah attempts to foster the former in the Jerusalemites suggests, as observed previously, that the Assyrian threat induced a degree of fear in the city.

G/G' (32:8, 24): In both these verses Hezekiah evidences faith and dependency on YHWH to overcome "the flesh" (v. 8), whether it is military or bodily. Possibly the mention of deliverance and a miraculous sign in v. 24 intimates a similar outcome ahead for the events of v. 8.

From here to the pivot (vv. 9–23), the chiasmus explicitly involves the Assyrians.

H/H' (32:9, 23): Both verses share similar positions marking the beginning or conclusion of a subunit within the plain prose structure of the text by means of temporal markers incorporating אחר. This also occurs in v. 1, which could be understood as reinforcing an echo of the uses in vv. 9 and 23, or contrarily, may indicate that the correspondence in vv. 9 and 23 is less exceptional. The latter conclusion is supported by the fact that אחר is very common vocabulary. At the same time, the epithet יחזקיהו מלך יהודה ("Hezekiah king of Judah") occurs five times in the whole of Chronicles (1 Chr 4:41; 2 Chr 30:24;²⁸ 32:8, 9, 23), which is surprisingly seldom, relative to the thirty-eight occurrences of יחזקיהו and five occurrences of חזקיהו in Chronicles. What should not be taken into account for the chiastic aspect are the shared occurrences of "to Jerusalem," a phrase that uses different prepositions in the two verses. Moreover, ירושלם occurs 12 times in chapter 32 alone, half those occurrences being preceded by a preposition.

Sennacherib "and all his dominions' " great show of power, which is representationally conveyed to Jerusalem via their contingent in v. 9, is suggestively undermined by its relation to v. 23, in which many instead bring offerings and precious things with reverence to Jerusalem. Assyria intends to oppress Jerusalem and its king, but the eventual outcome is that all the nations exalt Hezekiah. The participatory reader, encountering the might

---

Semeia 8 (1977) 15–33.

27. Perhaps as well, the parallelism explains the difference in forms.
28. Minor variant spelling: חזקיהו.

that is Assyria in v. 9, is not allowed to lose sight of YHWH's Jerusalemite glory ahead. That said, the fact that Assyria is contrasted to "all the nations" may also serve to remind us of the vastness and impressiveness of imperial Assyria. The Assyrian menace is a national imperilment of such proportions that its overcoming by Jerusalem results in international honor and homage.

I/I' (32:10, 22): סנחריב מלך אשור ("Sennacherib king of Assyria") occurs fairly frequently in chapter 32, and it seems that the Chronicler is simply following his Kings *Vorlage* in repeating this epithet. The combination ישב + ירושלם also occurs frequently in 2 Chronicles with at least thirty-eight instances, and in chapter 32 with four instances.[29] The clustering of both these combinations together occurs only in vv. 10 and 22, but that could be coincidental, given the unexceptional nature of both. Chiastic aspect for this possible correspondence is very low.

That said, one may still appreciate the effect of this pairing on the characterization of the Assyrians. Sennacherib is named less frequently in 2 Chr 32 than one may initially expect: סנחריב מלך אשור occurs 4x (vv. 1, 9, 10, 22); סנחריב alone appears only once (v. 2). His title alone (מלך אשור) is used in vv. 7, 11. Thus the relative infrequency of Sennacherib's PN + title in chapter 32 combined with its parallel appearance in these verses draws attention to its use beyond reinforcing the chiastic structure here. Building on the observations of Kalimi, note that the mention of one's personal name in unfavourable circumstances often serves to distance the reader from the character and to attribute responsibility unambiguously to the named personage, while use of a character's general title tends to have the effect of evoking hierarchy, "officialism," and again, distance.[30] All these tactics are used in vv. 10, 22. In v. 10, Sennacherib is to be clearly identified with the blasphemous speech to follow; in v. 22, the rescue effected by YHWH away from the grasp of that same Sennacherib king of Assyria is to be equally—if not more[31]—recognized. At the same time, the appearance of the title of the potentate of Assyria alienates the reader.

Verses 10 and 22 share the issue of the outcome for "those dwelling in Jerusalem" (בירושלם ... ישבים/ישבי ירושלם). In v. 10, the Jerusalemites are

---

29. Accordance search of "ירושלם <WITHIN 3 Words><FOLLOWED BY> ישב."

30. My interpretations of the use and omissions of names and titles agrees generally and in most respects to those of Kalimi, *Reshaping of Israelite*, 166–85, though I do not think the primary and most frequent difference evoked by the use of names, titles, and epithets—as Kalimi presents the situation, see esp. 174–79—is a matter of greater or lesser "significance," but of distance and degree of identification with the reader and, moreover, the ideology of the narrator.

31. The "x and what is more, x + 1" principle may be effected between these verses.

about to dwell, or are remaining,[32] under siege, while in v. 22 the inhabitants have been completely and even excessively (the narrative adds וּמִיַּד־כֹּל) saved. Sennacherib cleverly articulates a realistic fear for the Jerusalemites, but the reality of YHWH in the story calls for trust instead, as the outcome in v. 22 affirms.

Finally, Sennacherib's rhetorical question, . . . עַל־מָה אַתֶּם בֹּטְחִים (v. 10), is well-answered by the events of v. 22: YHWH is the basis of Hezekiah and the people's confidence, and YHWH's reliability as such is abundantly demonstrated in the very situation Sennacherib operated within and for which he predicted unavoidable defeat on the part of YHWH and his people. Sennacherib evidently knows in v. 10 that the people's trust in YHWH is their source of resistance to Assyria, and Sennacherib's arguments thus will focus on challenging that trust in YHWH. In a way, what issues from the Assyrian king's mouth is part of the "hand" (v. 22) from which YHWH delivers Jerusalem. The battle is waged here not only in the military sphere, but on spiritual, psychological, and communicative grounds.

---

32. Japhet, *1 and 2 Chronicles*, 987 questions the "tension" between no apparent siege and the description of "being under siege." Dillard, *2 Chronicles*, 257–58, proposes two resolutions to this [perceived] problem: 1) understanding יֹשְׁבִים as modal (e.g., "in what are you trusting that you are ready/willing to/going to/would stay" or 2) interpreting that "the siege was just beginning with the arrival of a large force." I find the former most convincing, for it involves the least amount of liberties with the text. At any rate, given the major preparations for the Assyrian attack (vv. 2–8), the narrator's description of the city's deliverance as a salvific event (v. 22), the extreme responses during the Assyrian rhetorical attack (e.g., vv. 18, 20), and the Quasi-YHWH-War-Story (slight adjustment of DeVries' terminology; see DeVries, *1 and 2 Chronicles*, 294, 390, 434, language throughout [as esp. seen in vv. 7–8]), the Assyrian threat in chapter 32 is not simply a matter of "a modest delegation [sent] for the purpose of negotiating" (Japhet, *1 and 2 Chronicles*, 987), but is portrayed as an imperiling attack—on the level of a national emergency—against Hezekiah, the people, and YHWH.

In response to the question of why the Chronicler did not portray the Assyrian attack as an unambiguous affront with on-site military forces instead of as an imminent and expected menace (vv. 7, 10), I offer two possible explanations (from a literary perspective): 1) an association intended with Jehoshaphat's fightless battle victory (2 Chr 20:1–30, esp. vv. 17–30), and/or 2) the avoidance of an association between the full stigma of outright invasion and Hezekiah, whom the Chronicler portrays elsewhere (i.e., in chapters 29–31) as one of the most—if not the most—exemplary of kings in the tradition of David and Solomon. I build here on the conclusions of Wright, "Fight for Peace," 169–70, 173–75, that

> [b]attle accounts in 2 Chronicles . . . serve a pedagogical purpose within Chr's narrative: they move the narrative both towards and away from a "historical" norm of peace under a Davidic king, ruling in Jerusalem with the proper temple personnel practicing the proper rites, open to submissive northerners, all seeking faithfulness to Yahweh alone. Battle accounts provide an interpretative scheme for recounting the "history" of the divided monarchy. (174)

J/J' (vv. 11, 21): The verses are related by content—Hezekiah is accused of falsehood by Sennacherib in v. 11; he is proven true by YHWH in v. 21. Also, Sennacherib challenges the ability of Judah's God to save them in v. 11, while the same king was not saved in the house of his own god). Present as well are the motif of one party leading another to death and imagery (palm/face, "insides"). Chiastic aspect for this pair appears weak, but may be functioning.

The motif of one party leading another to death is the strongest structural connection and encourages the other correlations between vv. 11 and 21. Sennacherib accuses Hezekiah of leading Jerusalem on a path to death,[33] but the ironic reality is that the Assyrian military leadership and Sennacherib himself are the ones who die.[34] Thus, two contrasts are made: one regarding who is leading whom to death, and the other regarding the reliability of Hezekiah. Sennacherib attempts to dissuade the people of Hezekiah's trustworthiness in v. 11, but Hezekiah's credibility is upheld by YHWH's actions in v. 21.

Not only does Sennacherib verbally attack Hezekiah's reputation, but YHWH's as well. What Sennacherib claims in v. 11—that YHWH cannot save Jerusalem—is negated in that YHWH does save Jerusalem in v. 21. The defeat that this salvation of Jerusalem means for Assyria is reinforced by the Assyrian leadership's deaths, as noted above. The final nail in the casket is the ironic use of אלהים in both verses. Sennacherib denies the ability of YHWH, Israel's אלהים, to save, but the Assyrian monarch's own אלהים proves unable to save Sennacherib from even ומיציאו מציו ("those coming forth from his [own] insides/loins," i.e., his sons).

Imagery contributes to the ironic contrasts as well. Sennacherib implies the inescapable power of his כף ("palm"), but retreats with בשת פנים ("shame of face") and is killed by his own flesh-and-blood, יציאו.

The combined effect of these verses is first to portray the Assyrian king as confident and boastful of his strength while he also denies the reliability of Hezekiah and YHWH his God. The pairing, then, demonstrates the embarrassingly erroneous and even fatal nature of Sennacherib's claims and confidence.

---

33. The deliberateness of this "death" motif is additionally apparent when one considers that the Assyrian king delivers a prediction of graphic death, not mere defeat, relinquished tribute, etc.

34. Post-exilic readers would still have been close enough to the events to have known that Sennacherib lived for another twenty years before his murder. The accounts in 2 Kgs/Isa and 2 Chronicles telescope this familiar event to draw a close causal relation between YHWH's deliverance of Jerusalem from Sennacherib's threat in 701 BC and Sennacherib's death in 681 BC.

K/K' (32:12, 20): There is a shared motif here regarding Hezekiah's approach to the cultus. Sennacherib challenges Hezekiah's enforcement of centralized cultus, while Hezekiah and Isaiah appeal to YHWH in a way not restricted by the cultus but reaching heaven.

The Assyrian king continues to challenge Hezekiah's reliability, this time by focusing on Hezekiah's enforcement of the centralized cultus and exclusive worship to YHWH. Moreover, Sennacherib gives a false presentation of authentic YHWH worship as originally involving many points of access which Hezekiah has now reduced to one (supposedly, according to Sennacherib, a worldview that belittles the value of the centralized and exclusive cultus). In v. 20, however, Hezekiah and Isaiah evidence steadfast faith and appeal exclusively to YHWH, ironically affirming that aspect of the Assyrian king's accusation. Further, Hezekiah and Isaiah exhibit a more mature understanding of worship and YHWH than the Assyrians present[35]—YHWH is not restricted to the cultus or temple, but resides in השמים.[36]

The unexpected movement from earthly situations in vv. 12 and 20 to the heavenly sphere at the very end of v. 20 distinguishes השמים, which quite appropriately to the issues of vv. 12 and 20, denotes in the OT the exalted and divine sphere where YHWH dwells and from whence he reigns sovereignly (e.g., Ps 103:19). The rare epithet אלהי השמים (9x in the OT) "presents YHWH as a universal deity,"[37] and it seems reasonable to expect that the use of השמים in v. 20 functions similarly (cf. 2 Chr 6:18, 21; 30:27). The pairing draws attention to the theological point that the sovereignty of YHWH is far beyond the limited vision and understanding of the king of Assyria.

L/L' (32:13, 19): By way of comparison to I/I', this pair also shares frequent vocabulary that is possibly clustered. The cluster of ארץ ("land"), derivative root עשה ("to do, make"), and יד ("hand, power") may seem unusual, but the combination actually occurs approximately twenty-six times in the OT, three of which are in 2 Chronicles—twice through this pair and once in

---

35. Whether Sennacherib's representation of Yahwism reflects ignorance or an intentional deception, his accusation remains misleading.

36. Cf. 1 Chr 29:11–19, a passage that Braun considers paradigmatic for the theology of Chronicles. For further discussion, see Braun, "Significance," 84–85.

37. For further discussion, see David Toshio Tsumura, "שמים," in *NIDOTTE* 4:160–66, esp. 163–65, citation from 163; J. A. Soggin, "שמים," in *TLOT* 3:1369–72; Cornelis Houtman, *Der Himmel im Alten Testament: Israels Weltbild und Weltanschauung*, OTS 30 (Leiden: Brill, 1993).

2 Chr 13:9. Still, the combination is distinctive enough to suggest a correspondence between the two verses.

The distribution of shared terminology between these paired verses is as follows:

v. 13	a			עַמֵּי	הָאֲרָצוֹת	(לְכֹל)
	b	אֱלֹהֵי	גּוֹיֵ		הָאֲרָצוֹת	(הֲיָכוֹל יָכְלוּ)
	c				אֶת־אַרְצָם	(לְהַצִּיל)
v. 19	d	אֱלֹהֵי		עַמֵּי	הָאָרֶץ	(כְּעַל)

Verse 19d shares affinities beyond ארץ with each of the subverses of v. 13 (a's עמי; b's אלהי; d's likeness to c being that they do not have the absolute plural ending). Instead of listing specific nations, Sennacherib uses a general, sweeping term and reiterates it to denote Assyria's conquests in simple but memorable fashion—it is not just people that Assyria conquers, but arguably the most defining property of a people: their land. Thus in v. 19, within the immediate context of the verse, הארץ means "world" and alludes to the Assyrians' comparison between "the God of Jerusalem" and other gods.[38] At the same time, within the chiastic structure, הארץ also reminds the reader of the emperor's sweeping victory boasts in v. 13. The overall effect is twofold: to retroactively underline the Assyrians' implicit comparison in v. 13 of YHWH and other gods; for v. 19, to incriminate doubly (if not triply, with the city-bound epithet) the Assyrian rhetoric and so to doubly/triply distance the reader from the words and worldview of the Assyrians.

Sennacherib's emphasis in v. 13 on what עשיתי and his assertion that the gods of other nations were not able to deliver מידי are undermined by v. 19's observation that the gods of other nations—over which Assyria claims victory and which Assyria likens to YHWH—are merely מעשה ידי האדם. The God of Jerusalem will soon demonstrate he is otherwise.

M/M' (32:15, 17): These verses share similar content (Sennacherib defames Hezekiah/YHWH, likens YHWH to the gods of other nations, and asserts that YHWH will not be able to deliver Jerusalem from Sennacherib) and phraseology (לא־הצילו עמם מידי /להציל עמו מידי ;כאלהי גוי/כל־אלוה כל־גוי; לא־יציל אלהי יחזקיהו עמו מידי /אלהיכם לא־יצילו אתכם מידי).

Common phraseology serves to link vv. 15 and 17 and to emphasize Sennacherib's likening of YHWH to the gods of other nations, the Assyrian

---

38. In addition to the situation it describes, the comparison may be seen to achieve a further alienating effect between the reader and the Assyrians by using an OT-rare city-bound epithet—perhaps a deliberate evocation of the Assyrian worldview commonly attributing the mere domain of cities to deities. Consider discussion in Gordon, *Holy Land, Holy City*, 27–29.

argument of the inability of the nations' gods to deliver their people from Assyrian power, and the Assyrian insistence that therefore YHWH will not deliver his people. The Assyrian rhetorical rationale reinforces itself through the chiastic parallelism (which heightens the self-incriminating effects of that rationale).

Other relations may be found in the pairing of vv. 15 and 17. In v. 15, the Assyrian king denigrates Hezekiah on account of the Judean king's faith in YHWH; then in v. 17, the Assyrian king insults YHWH particularly. Thus, Sennacherib's accusation moves from representative to source, a strategic argumentative tactic in itself that also functions on the narrative level to heighten tension. The verses also evince a contrast: Sennacherib uses spoken rhetoric in v. 15 and written argumentation in v. 17. The result operates like that of a merismus—the Assyrians utilize every aspect of communication to dissuade the Jerusalemites' faith in YHWH and his representative, Hezekiah.

There is a brief observation to make at this point: notice that the main substance of Sennacherib's rhetorical argument is detailed and presented in direct speech in vv. 13–15. These verses structurally mirror vv. 17–19, which are also about the Assyrian rhetorical attack, but summarized by the narrator. While the narrator does not detail all the content of the Assyrian letters and speech, he provides enough clues and links to suggest that the arguments of vv. 17–19 were essentially the same as those of their counterpart, vv. 13–15.[39]

N (Pivot) (32:16): This verse has the central position in the chiasmus and comprises a self-contained chiasmus and consonantal assonance (ו, ד, ר, ב, ע). For these obvious reasons, its chiastic aspect is very high.

The self-contained chiastic structure is:

X (anacrusis) ועוד דברו

A עבדיו

B על-

C יהוה האלהים

B' ועל

A' יחזקיהו עבדו

---

39. Somewhat similarly, but basing his conclusions on content alone, is Ben Zvi, "When the Foreign," 219, which perceives the reinforcement of Sennacherib's speech (vv. 10–15) with the narrator's subsequent account in vv. 16–19.

The primary effect of this chiastic structure is to highlight יהוה האלהים and his central role in chapter 32. The effect of the assonance is to render the verse aesthestically-pleasing and hence attention-catching and memorable, as well as to reinforce the unity of v. 16's content.[40] Verse 16's structure conveys the message that YHWH is in control: in the midst of the conflict between the עבדים ("servants") of Sennacherib and the עבד ("servant") of YHWH[41]—and even in the midst of, ironically, Assyria's insults and attacks—YHWH is the determinative factor; he is the hinge on which everything changes and the circumstances make a turn for the better. Further, YHWH is at the centre of all the events of chapter 32, as the pivot indicates in its relation to the rest of the verses. Possibly the centrality of YHWH in the structure reflects the Chronicler's concern to uphold throughout his work the centrality of the cultus and exclusive worship of YHWH.[42]

The epithet יהוה האלהים is rare in the OT (41x) and unique within chapter 32.[43] With the few occurrences we have to consider, it may seem at first glance that "the use of 'YHWH [Ha]Elohim' is sporadic and does not seem to point to any particular intent or requisite context."[44] However, its use in chapter 32 appears to be more intentional than not, as האלהים occurs in 31:21; 32:16, 31, which are at the beginning, middle, and *near* (but not quite *at*) the end of the unit.

Even without recognizing the chiastic structure, Japhet writes concerning the significance of אלהים[ה]:

> The use of "Elohim" as the proper name for the god of Israel neutralizes any plural connotation the word might have and expresses the abstract idea of "godliness." The determinate form ("ha-Elohim") as a proper name suggests the fuller sentence "The Lord [is] God" (יהוה הוא האלהים).[45] Not only does it express an

---

40. Appreciation of the multiple effects of literary devices such as paronomasia and other consonantal wordplay was first brought to my attention by Isaac Kalimi, "The Contribution of the Literary Study of Chronicles to the Solution of its Textual Problems," *Biblical Interpretation* 3 (1995) 210–11.

41. עבד also occurs in v. 9 inconsequentially to the chiasmus here.

42. Consider esp. couplet K/K', vv. 12, 20, which explicitly concerns that issue.

43. Japhet, *Ideology of the Book*, 38 observes that the phrase appears twenty times in the story of the Garden of Eden (Gen 2:4—3:24), twelve times in Chronicles; and in the rest of the OT, nine times (mostly in Psalms).

44. Japhet, *Ideology of the Book*, 41.

45. Schmidt draws out the exclusiveness implied in this sentence more clearly, translating and scripturally explicating the confession "Yahweh is (the true, only) God." See W. H. Schmidt, "אלהים," in *TLOT* 1:115–126, esp. 124.

abstract understanding of the divine essence, it also emphasises *God's qualities of uniqueness and exclusiveness*. The increased use of the determinate form testifies to *a stronger awareness of God's exclusiveness* and may be seen as a theological-linguistic development typical of late biblical literature, including the book of Chronicles. [emphasis mine][46]

Japhet's conclusions above concerning the use of [ה]אלהים are reinforced by my observation, based on the chiastic structure of 2 Chr 32, that one of the chapter's dominant implicit messages is that YHWH alone is God. Further, the Chronicler's combining of האלהים with יהוה in v. 16 to emphasise YHWH's uniqueness, exclusiveness, and determinative power seems to affirm Japhet's proposal that the determinate form (האלהים) suggests "The Lord [is] God."

The chiastic structure of v. 16 also contrasts Sennacherib's servants (עבדיו) with YHWH's servant, Hezekiah (עבדו).[47] In many respects, the battle in chapter 32 is staged between these two representative parties, though the "servants" cannot be separated from their masters in this situation.[48] Bearing in mind that the role of Sennacherib's ambassadors and King Hezekiah is likened to that of faithful representatives, to counter the 'servant' is to counter the servant's master.

Hezekiah's exceptional status as the only king besides David to be designated in Chronicles as the servant of YHWH by a voice other than his own is no small honour, and the Chronicler's awareness of this is probably reflected in the placement of the servant-title in this central verse. The use of עבדו in v. 16 impresses upon the reader the dependence, favoured status, and faithful fulfillment of commissioned task(s) by Hezekiah.[49] Further-

---

46. Schmidt, "אלהים," 30.

47. This is to correct the perception that the Chronicler conveys the conflict as occurring primarily between Hezekiah and Sennacherib, e.g., as in Troy D. Cudworth, *War in Chronicles: Temple Faithfulness and Israel's Place in the Land*, LHBOTS 627 (London: Bloomsbury T. & T. Clark, 2016), 87. Rather, the battle is between Sennacherib's servants and YHWH's servant, as elucidated by the chiastic structure in v. 16 as well as the content of 2 Chr 32.

48. Relatedly, Childs, *Isaiah and the Assyrian*, 110 observes by way of comparison with the 2 Kings//Isaiah accounts: "The Chronicler does not allow the enemy for a moment to play Hezekiah off against Yahweh as B² had pictured. Their positions are identical throughout and the issue of faith is clear-cut between God with his servant Hezekiah and the Assyrian threat."

49. See H. Ringgren, U. Rütersworden, and H. Simian-Yofre, "עבד," *TDOT* 10:376–405, esp. 395; R. Schultz, "Servant, Slave," *NIDOTTE* 4:1183–1198, esp. 1190–93; C. Westermann, "עבד," *TLOT* 2:819–832, esp. 826–29; E. Carpenter, "עבד," *NIDOTTE* 3:304–9, esp. 306–7.

more, the strength of the theology inherent in the use of עָבֵד with YHWH as genitive object (namely, that the "servant" of YHWH acknowledges his/her dependence upon and service to YHWH, and that YHWH assumes a degree of ownership and responsibility for his servant) reinforces the polarization between Hezekiah and Sennacherib's ambassadors. The status of the two parties is not just a matter of representation, but of lordship.

Conclusion

Overall, I would rate the chiastic aspect of 2 Chr 32 as above average. In addition to the strong chiastic aspect of several individual pairs, the impressive maintenance of chiastic symmetry across 34 verses contributes to its strength. Emphases, nuances, contrasts, and reinforcements of literary elements are highlighted by varying degrees throughout the chiasmus. Some of the more salient ways by which recognition of the narrative chiasmus proves informative, if not necessary, to our reading of the text are: emphasis of the symbolic centrality of YHWH, identification of the conflict as being between the representatives of YHWH and the Assyrian king, literary affirmation of the historical text (the case of מגנים in vv. 5 and 27 being an eminent example), and delineation of the narratival unit, which includes vv. 24–33 by way of the structural balance and meaning it contributes to vv. 1–23 through the chiasmus.

The attention evidenced by the Chronicler in arranging chapter 32 as a chiasmus suggests several intents. To structure such a sizable length of text at the end of a kingly account signals more than closure to a section. The chiasmus gives a sense of unity to otherwise disparate parts. As well, chiastic structures contribute an aesthetic quality of balance and craftsmanship, which themselves often serve to highlight the chiastically-arranged text. Further, as we have seen, the primary emphases of the chiasmus are indispensably relevant for understanding the pericope and have proven to coincide with known aspects of the Chronicler's ideology (e.g., the centrality and exclusivity of YHWH-worship). These emphases of the chiasmus, in turn, may be seen to create thematic connections at least between the chapters concerning Hezekiah, if not the whole of the book.

When its chiastic structure is taken into account, 2 Chr 32 accomplishes too much to be regarded as a mere summary or minimized report of the 2 Kings//Isaiah account. Rather, the passage's chiastic structure may be seen to highlight Hezekiah's handling of the Assyrian attack and its aftermath. Possibly the chiastic structure marks the events of 2 Chr 32 as climactic in relation to the other features of Hezekiah's reign. At the very least, this narrative chiasmus distinguishes the situation between Hezekiah and the Assyrians as deserving of attention.

One final note is that the final redactor of Chronicles apparently maintained and/or crafted the chiastic structure as part of his work. The narrative chiasmus of 2 Chr 32 highlights themes that are consistent with the Chronicler's emphases elsewhere, which strongly suggests that the chiastic structure is the Chronicler's own creation.

THE NARRATIVAL-LINEAR CHARACTERIZATION OF THE ASSYRIANS IN 2 CHRONICLES 32

Introduction

In contradistinction to the first section, which investigated the portrayal of the Assyrians through poetics (particularly the chiasmus),[50] the particular contribution of this section is chiefly that of 2 Chr 32's narrational characterization, defined here as characterization arising from the reader's experience of a linearly-presented text. As Berlin is careful to qualify, narrative is linear, but the reading of it is not. "The reader holds the entire picture in his mind, adding to its various parts until the end of the narrative." Using the example of the Book of Ruth, she continues, "we unconsciously read back into earlier scenes information received in later ones."[51] Thus, in analyzing 2 Chr 32's narrational characterization of the Assyrians, our general approach to the pericope will take into account its linear nature and the ways the Chronicler moves throughout and plays within it.

Narratival-Linear Analysis

When Assyria first appears in 2 Chr 32, the reader encounters a tension. On the one hand, Hezekiah has already been characterized as an ideal king and opposite in all relevant respects to Ahaz (cf. 2 Chr 28); the reader is prepared to expect an outcome for Hezekiah's reign opposite to that of Ahaz's. On the other hand, there is the reappearance of Assyria, which had presented a test for Judah's previous king and had reflected YHWH's

---

50. My use of the term "poetics" is synonymous with that of "poetic devices." This also accords with the primary definition presented in *Webster's New World Dictionary, Third College Edition*, ed. Victoria Neufeldt (New York: Simon and Schuster, 1988), 1042 // "poetics: . . . the theory or structure of poetry." Contra Berlin, *Poetics and Interpretation*, 15, who describes poetics as "the science of literature."

51. Berlin, *Poetics and Interpretation*, 98–99.

judgment and punishment on that king. Still further, brief allusion to Assyria in Hezekiah's speech in 30:6 had suggested that Assyria is not wholly in control of the actual, transcendental reasons for its invasions on Judah. Reading "linearly," one is prompted to ask whether Hezekiah will pass the test, whether this new Assyrian invasion will prove to be a deserved punishment from YHWH,[52] and whether Hezekiah's mature theology regarding Assyria, as intimated in 30:6, will prove true.

Sennacherib's proper name and title introduce him—he is a different personage from Tiglath-Pileser III, but still a king of Assyria, which immediately associates him with Chronicles' developing typology of "the kings of Assyria." In relation to Hezekiah's idealized characterization and the reader's expectations so far, Sennacherib's entrance is a consequential statement unto itself: "came Sennacherib king of Assyria." After the narrator allows that significant new circumstance to sink in, he elaborates "and he came against Judah and encamped against its fortified cities" (v. 1b). Lest the reader be unclear about Sennacherib's intents, the narrator provides an inside view: "and he intended to conquer them for himself" (v. 1c; "The construction *'amar* followed by the infinitive construct + *le* states the intention of the thinking subject to do this or that").[53]

Sennacherib's arrival in Judah and his hostile determination against Jerusalem ("his face [was set] for war against Jerusalem") is apparent to King Hezekiah (v. 2).[54] Generally, the setting or turning of the face in a direction denotes decision and intention. Van Rooy's further assertion regarding the use of this expression is suggestive: "with the prepositions *'el* and *'al* the word gets a menacing meaning (Ezek 6:2)."[55] This is not a matter of simply extracting tribute (cf. 28:20–21) or carrying away exiles (30:9), but of the imperial enemy being determined to inflict hard-hitting, ugly war.

---

52. At the same time, recall that reading chiastically one is assured of Hezekiah's approved status before YHWH.

53. Siegfried Wagner, "אמר," *TDOT* 1:328–45, 333. Consider also Isa 10:7 ("He does not plan thus nor does he intend it, for he has it in mind to destroy and eliminate nations—not a few"), though the passage's *Sitz im Leben* and intentional relation to 2 Chr 32 are difficult to discern.

54. For further discussion of this idiom, see Scott Layton, "Biblical Hebrew 'To Set the Face,' in Light of Akkadian and Ugaritic," *Ugarit-Forschungen* 17 (1986) 169–180, see esp. 175–76, 177–80 (unfortunately Layton provides no examples of *le* as "against," but there are examples of *le* used otherwise and "against" conveyed through other prepositions); H. Simian-Yofre, "פנים," in *TDOT* 11:589–615, 602; Aubrey R. Johnson, "Aspects of the Use of the Term פנים in the Old Testament," in *Festschrift Otto Eissfeldt zum 60. Geburtstage 1 September 1947*, ed. Johann Fück (Halle: Niemeyer, 1947), 155–59, esp. 156 and 156n28–157n28; Harry F. van Rooy, "פנים," *NIDOTTE* 3:637–40.

55. Van Rooy, "פנים," 638.

In verses 2–8, characterization of the Assyrian forces is conveyed not only by what other characters' words say about them, but also by what other characters' actions indicate about them. Hezekiah's large-scale preparations—redirection of waterways, repair of the city wall, construction of a second wall and other defensive structures, production of military weapons—indicate that Hezekiah was preparing Jerusalem for a battle that would exceed its usual capacity and experience. The empire presents a new military challenge for Jerusalem that surpasses anything the current structures have known or prepared for. Hezekiah's anticipation of the Assyrians is shared by the leadership and the people, who themselves articulate the reason for their work: "Why should the kings of Assyria come and find many waters?" (v. 4). This is the third and final occurrence in Chronicles of the plural in reference to the kings of Assyria. As with the first two occurrences, the pluralization has a typologizing effect that further benefits from previous instances. The people perceive Sennacherib not just as one particularly powerful king, but as part of a historical entity that has invaded fruitful lands for generations. Their typologized view of the Assyrian leaders affirms on a general level to the reader Hezekiah's typologization of the Assyrian leadership and the associations he made with it (30:6–9); on the characters' level, this instance of typology conveys the people's acceptance of Hezekiah's ideological view of Assyria.[56] The confident vigor with which the people and Hezekiah prepare for the onslaught of "the kings of Assyria" also suggests an increasingly confident, faith-motivated ideological raising of Judah to the level of Assyria, such that Jerusalem is ready to confront the Assyrian power. Additionally, the people's typologizing of "the kings of Assyria" may be seen to carry the type into the sphere of the future, if indeed the people perform an action that is intended for permanence.[57]

---

56. Cf. Willi, *Die Chronik als Auslegung*, 164n214, which asserts "die Stelle II 32, 4 ist in dieser Hinsicht nicht deutlich" in contrast to 30:6. I argue, however, that 30:6 informs the occurrence of the plural form in 32:4 (this contention can stand on its own merit, though one may add that typologizations by nature generally build on successive occurrences).

57. See J. Simons, *Jerusalem in the Old Testament: Researches and Theories* (Leiden: Brill, 1952), 177, 187–88; L.–Hugues Vincent, *Jérusalem de l'ancien Testament: Recherches d'archaéologie et d'historie*, illustr. M.–A. Steve (Paris: J. Gabalda, 1954), 283; consider also Yigal Shiloh, "Jerusalem's Water Supply—The Rediscovery of Warren's Shaft," *BARev* 7/4 (1981) 24–39 (37, 39); similarly idem, "The Rediscovery of the Ancient Water System Known as 'Warren's Shaft,' " in *Ancient Jerusalem Revisited*, ed. Hillel Geva, 46–54 (Jerusalem: Israel Exploration Society, 1994), 54. Scholars subsequent to Parker and Vincent, Weill, Kenyon, Simons, and Shiloh (who themselves take into account Bliss-Dickie and Warren) tend to synthesize their reports and conclude similarly (e.g., W. Harold Mare, *The Archaeology of the Jerusalem Area* [Grand Rapids: Baker, 1987], 106–07; G. J. Wightman, *The Walls of Jerusalem: From the Canaanites to the Mamluks*,

Ackroyd has suggested that the "kings" typologization in 32:4 reaches the level where "the Hezekiah-Sonnacherib [sic] event becomes a type of the frustrating of the rulers of the nation who set themselves against Jerusalem,"[58] combining this "kings" typology with a universalizing of springs and a cosmic mythological reference to "many waters." Matters concerning "the springs" are best explained simply in a historical, plain sense—especially since the text reads as relatively dispassionate narrative in vv. 3–4a. In an analogous way, v. 4b is speech and its generalizations and rhetorical inquiry are consistent with the oft-made observation that the Chronicler's addresses tend towards a heightened rhetorical style,[59] and thus we may more reasonably expect in this genre hyperbole, typologization, etc. Typologization, if it occurs at all in v. 4, should be expected to derive meaning both vertically (i.e., from the characters' perspectives to the narrator and readers') and horizontally (through the corpus' successive occurrences). Thus if "many waters" is typologized, it seems less plausible that its typological reference is from aNE mythology (which is not evoked at all elsewhere in the text), as Ackroyd asserts, and more likely that it derives from the sacred, primeval associations of Jerusalem's water system (which clearly feature in the passage)—namely, the Gihon spring and the Siloam Channel and/or the channel's outflow. Among more direct associations are the shared name of the Eden headwater (Gen 2:13) with the Jerusalemite spring and Solomon's anointing (1 Kgs 1:33–40, though the precise significance of the Gihon is not stated).[60] Eising forwards that 'the fact that Gihon is a proper name shows that a spring was of great importance to a city' and it is often observed that "Gihon" etymologically derives from the root גיח, "to burst/gush forth."[61] That this is a distinctive characteristic of the karst spring (which gushes intermittently)[62] may underline the miraculous and/or sa-

---

Mediterranean Archaeology Supplement 4 [Sydney: Meditarch, 1993], 55, 58).

58. Ackroyd, "Chronicler as Exegete," 11.

59. E.g., Japhet, *1 and 2 Chronicles*, 36–38; Mason, *Preaching the Tradition*, 139.

60. Consider discussions in Gordon, *Holy Land, Holy City*, 7, 70; Jon D. Levenson, *Sinai and Zion: An Entry into the Jewish Bible* (Minneapolis: Winston, 1985), 130–31, cf. 159; and Vincent, *Jérusalem de l'ancien Testament*, 283. Cf. Isa 8:6. A thorough presentation and evaluation of various possible indirect references to the water systems' components as symbolic or sacred is beyond the purposes of this study; for further discussion see Tuell, "Rivers of Paradise"; and H. Eising, "גיחון," *TDOT* 2:466–68.

61. Eising, "גיחון," 466.

62. Simons, *Jerusalem in the Old Testament*, 163n2 states that "the frequency of the phenomenon is dependent on the rainfall and varies with the seasons, from four or five times a day in the rainy period and lasting about 40 minutes to once or twice towards the end of the long rainless summer"; Shiloh, "Rediscovery of the Ancient," 53, reckons "roughly forty minutes every six to eight hours"; Jerome Murphy-O'Connor, *The Holy*

cred attributes attested in later literature for the spring and its waters.[63] That the characterization of the Gihon reached its later-attested hagiographic and portentous proportions by the time of Hezekiah cannot be stated with certainty.[64] Rather, it seems the case that the waterworks components in 2 Chr 32 are depicted as abundant and important since fresh water sources in general were indispensably valued in the dry desert climate, the Gihon's name is specified in v. 30, and the waters flowing from it receive considerable attention from Hezekiah in the text. However, that the Gihon and its distributaries are esteemed in a prodigious, miraculous manner beyond cannot necessarily be said of the characters who engage with it in 2 Chr 32.[65] Reading narratively, the reference to "many waters" in v. 4 is primarily that of the Siloam Channel and/or its outflow and the channel's "springs";[66] reading chiastically (i.e., v. 4 in relation to v. 29), a secondary emphasis is that of abundance. Archaeological evidence indicates that the Siloam Channel's flow was significantly lessened after the installation of Hezekiah's Tunnel and that this change was more or less permanent.[67] Hence, if the waters

---

Land: An Archaeological Guide from Earliest Times to 1700, 3rd ed. (Oxford: Oxford University Press, 1992), 118 forwards that the spring "pours out a tremendous quantity of water for some 30 minutes and then almost dries up for between 4 and 10 hours."

63. See Simons, *Jerusalem in the Old Testament*, 163–64; Menasche Har-El, *Landscape, Nature and Man in the Bible: Sites and Events in the Old Testament*, trans. David Strassler and Yehudit Elgavi (Jerusalem: Carta, 2003), 51 (note: this work does not appear to be vigorously researched; for example, Har-El asserts that the Gihon spring provided water "sufficient for the drinking and cooking needs of 120,000 people"; cf. Murphy-O'Connor, *Holy Land*, 118, which estimates that the spring "could support a population of about 2,500").

64. I agree with Gass' general suggestion that characters may be entities other than people. Characterization is not just a matter of attributes, but also of degree. See William H. Gass, "The Concept of Character in Fiction," in *Essentials of the Theory of Fiction*, eds. Michael J. Hoffman and Patrick D. Murphy (Durham: Duke University Press, 1988), 267–76 (272). That said, the characterization of the Gihon in 2 Chr 32 does not appear to include a significant mystique.

65. This is not to negate the possibility that the Gihon spring had religious and/or mythological significance at other times or to other peoples (cf. Bruno Meissner, *Babylonien und Assyrien*, Kulturgeschichtliche Bibliothek [Heidelberg: Carl Winters Universitätsbuchhandlung, 1925], 87, which asserts the Mesopotamian sacred-ceremonial esteem of springs). I am currently skeptical, however, of attributing a "sacred" status to the Gihon for the initial reigns of the monarchy (contra J. Schreiner, "עין," *TDOT* 11:44–50 [46]). It seems possible that instances such as 1 Kgs 1:9, 33, 38 are political statements of a would-be ruler asserting his authority at a foundational site. "Of course, the spring was the primary given; it came first. The settlement was secondary; it came later" (Schreiner, "עין," 46).

66. E.g., Simons, *Jerusalem in the Old Testament*, 177; and Williamson, *2 Chronicles*, 381.

67. This simply has to do with a difference between the two watercourses with

of the Siloam Channel are to be considered mytho-cosmic, the permanent termination of those waters does not contribute to a heightened view of the channel, itself not named in the text. Possibly the outflow was a temporary change, but the characters' approach to "the river that overflowed through the land" (v. 4b) does not suggest a mytho-cosmic perspective, either.[68] For these several reasons I cannot support Ackroyd's hypothesis, which is attractive on the surface for its potential allusions to Gihon-Edenic ideology, but these associations are neither evident nor necessary in the text. Furthermore, to assume a mytho-cosmic typology for the "many waters" requires disregarding the meaning conveyed by the narrative (if anything, the latter should contribute to the former, but that is not the case in 2 Chr 32). In its narrational context, "many waters" does seem hyperbolic, exalting the hydric plentitude of the land-in-the-midst-of-the-desert,[69] but to assert that the imagery transcends this in a mytho-cosmic direction is unsubstantiated by the text.

The blocking of the exposed water resources of the city accomplishes several objectives in relation to the Assyrians: 1) the Assyrians would be dissuaded from destroying the Siloam Channel, which was still useful for irrigation of the Kidron Valley; 2) the Assyrians would underestimate the resources available to the besieged city (cf. v. 10); and 3) the Assyrians themselves would not have ready access to water for either physical or braggadocian purposes (2 Kgs 19:24//Isa 37:25).[70] All this assumes on the part of Hezekiah an Assyrian ignorance of his underground tunnel. The Assyrian empire may be a conqueror, but it remains an outsider to the inner workings of Jerusalem (similarly, v. 12). Perhaps this contributes to the shock of v. 18, in which the Assyrians demonstrate familiarity (albeit imperfect) with an intimate aspect of Judahite identity.

Hezekiah's speech in vv. 7–8 communicates explicitly and implicitly a view of the Assyrians that is generally consistent with his courageous and determined preparations in vv. 2–6—basically, that the Assyrians are a serious, but not irresistible, threat to Jerusalem. Hence, we may assume that

---

regard to depth.

68. Similarly, the diversion of the waters of the Gihon spring itself was commemorated without any reverence or particular attributes mentioned of the spring in the extrabiblical "Siloam Inscription" found in Hezekiah's Tunnel; see *COS* 2:145–46//2.28.

69. Selman, *2 Chronicles*, 510, proposes a literary sense along similar lines: "Mention of the stream and the springs may well be a double allusion, to God's special provision for Jerusalem (cf. Ps. 46:4) and to Sennacherib's boast to have personally dried up Egypt's streams (2 Ki. 19:24; Is. 37:25)." As well, the chiasmus contributes further to this sense.

70. Agreeing in this respect with Ackroyd, "Chronicler as Exegete," 11–12; Williamson, *1 and 2 Chronicles*, 381; and Selman, *2 Chronicles*, 510.

vv. 7–8 reflect Hezekiah's own perspective of the Assyrians, which itself contributes to the overall narrative's depiction of the Assyrian empire (recall that Hezekiah is usually presented by the narrator as exemplary, thus Hezekiah's words gain authoritative status in the world of the narrative). At the same time, Hezekiah's speech contributes uniquely to the culminating portrayal of the Assyrians in the story.

After evoking the historic language of Moses, Joshua, and David, Hezekiah refers obliquely to "the king of Assyria." In a compact and vigorous speech inclusive of precise historical allusions, rhetorical features, and the distinct name of Israel's God ("YHWH our God"), omission of Sennacherib's PN is noteworthy, suggesting a deliberate avoidance of the emperor's distinctive identity. Hezekiah does not allow Sennacherib the effectiveness that comes with distinctiveness and personalized identification (in contrast, "YHWH our God" is not only personally named, but identified as one with whom the people have a special relationship).[71] Furthermore, all the devastation and power with which Sennacherib's name has come to be associated are suppressed. Sennacherib is reduced to his function, "the king of Assyria," and the mighty Assyrian army is disparagingly referred to as "all the horde that is with him."[72] The abilities of Assyria are minimized to the finitude of human flesh (stated in two words, זרוע בשר), to be overwhelmed/outdone by the divine resources of YHWH (in five words, יהוה אלהינו לעזרנו ולהלחם מלחמתנו). Hezekiah further deflects attention away from Assyria by focusing the issue on neither Assyria nor Judah, but on *who is with each party/entity*. In this respect, Assyria is help-less, while Jerusalem is not. Bearing in mind the motif of YHWH being "with someone" as a sign of godliness in Chronicles,[73] the attentive reader is also subtly reminded of Hezekiah's righteous status before YHWH (and Assyria's unrighteous position, by way of contrast), and thus it

---

71. For the significance of a suffix with אלהים, see Helmer Ringgren, "אלהים," *TDOT* 1:267–84 (280); and W. H. Schmidt, "אלהים," *TLOT* 1:115–26 (120). It appears that this particular view of YHWH is especially associated with Hezekiah, in that "YHWH our God" occurs only twice in chapter 32 and both times in relation to King Hezekiah (vv. 7, 11).

72. The word translated "horde" is המון, which carries a sense of noise and tumult. As A. Baumann, "המה," *TDOT* 3:414–18 (415) puts it: "The verb *hamah* and its derivatives cannot be dissociated from the concrete representation of a confused mixture of noise and movement." Similarly, W. R. Domeris, "המה," in *NIDOTTE* 1:1041–43 (1042):

> In contrast to *qôl*, which plays a key role in the divine theophanies, the terms *hmh* and *hamôn* are rarely used of the voice of God, and when applied to humans may better be rendered as noise than voices. The emphasis is on *hmh* as a loud roaring noise rather than as an intelligible sound.

73. This was brought to my attention by Braun, "Significance," 176. E.g., 2 Chr 1:1; 13:12; 17:3; 15:9.

is intimated that one should expect Hezekiah's success somehow to actualize despite the unpromising material circumstances.

The theme of help in v. 8a is further developed by way of contrast to a pericope already noted for other comparisons it provides for chapter 32: 2 Chr 28:16–21, in which the envelope figure emphasizes by way of the root עזר the futility of Ahaz's dependence on Assyria instead of YHWH for help. Ahaz's dependence on Assyria instead of YHWH for help resulted in Assyria's oppression of Israel; as Hezekiah asserts the city's dependence on YHWH for help (and against none other than Ahaz's desired ally), the reader is prepared by the contrasts to expect an outcome for Hezekiah's situation that will be the opposite of 28:16–21. For the sake of maintaining some clarity in discussing the rich and complex characterizations in this chapter, it is worth appreciating now that the narrative will demonstrate later that this is indeed the case. The outcome in 28:16–21 was successful oppression by the Assyrians and futile dependence on the empire by Ahaz; in 32:21–23, it is disgraceful defeat of the Assyrians and rewarded dependence on YHWH by Hezekiah. In both cases Assyria emerges as a tyrannical imperial power intent on bringing trouble to Israel/Judah. By way of contrast, in 28:16–21 the details of the Israelite king's help-seeking and the Assyrian manner of oppression are withheld, composing characterizations mostly by way of general circumstances and impressions; in chapter 32 details are given of speech, action, thought, circumstance (e.g., Hezekiah's speech [vv. 6–8] and prayer [v. 20] for help; Assyrian intent to oppress [v. 2, 18] and failure [v. 21]), rendering the characterizations of 2 Chr 32 as more lifelike and memorable—round, full characters, as some may put it.[74]

Observe that Hezekiah perceives YHWH Elohim as in a position to directly meet the challenge of Sennacherib in that Hezekiah had seen that Sennacherib was intent on "war (מלחמה) against Jerusalem" (v. 2b), but now the king of Judah declares that YHWH Elohim is with Jerusalem "to help us fight our battles (מלחמתנו)" (v. 8). While in v. 2 the reader may have surmised fear and shock in Hezekiah with the unexpected introduction of Sennacherib in the land and in the text, v. 8 indicates a courageous and faith-filled development of Hezekiah in response to the Assyrian threat. Likewise, the people follow Hezekiah in gaining confidence (v. 8b).[75] Note

---

74. E.g., consider the description of character types in Berlin, *Poetics and Interpretation*, 23ff.

75. Perhaps the people gain confidence not only on the basis of the content of Hezekiah's speech, but also from the illocutionary aspects of Hezekiah's speech—i.e., the fact that Hezekiah asserted his authority as leader and YHWHistic representative, Hezekiah's boldness in declaring the weakness of mighty Assyria relative to invisible YHWH.

that in vv. 1–8 the Assyrians themselves have not changed (as far as the narrative is concerned), but Hezekiah and the people's perspective of the Assyrians has undergone a subtle transformation.[76] From the perspectives of both Hezekiah and the people, the Assyrians have positionally lowered from that of determined invader and conqueror (vv. 1–2) to imperial—but not indefeatable—historic force under the sovereignty of YHWH (vv. 3–5) to brute, creaturely enemy fatally opposed to the sovereign God who is known and embraced by an increasingly confident Jerusalem (vv. 6–8). As the Assyrians are ideologically lowered, the Jerusalemites ideologically rise, and thus the tension in their conflict tightens as their opposition becomes level.

After such a marked minimization of Sennacherib, the narrator renews the Assyrian king's identity with a new scene in v. 9. As well, the specific descriptors of Sennacherib clearly identify him in v. 9 as both military and ideological antagonist to Judah. The subtle rhetorical slant employed in Hezekiah's use of כל־ההמון אשר־עמו ("all the horde that is with him," v. 7) is retroactively highlighted by the narrator's description of the same object as וכל־ממשלתו עמו ("all his royal military forces with him," v. 9). At the same time, the reality of the Assyrian army's sway is suggested by the narrator's choice of the term ממשלה. Sennacherib continues to act against (על, 3x in v. 9; cf. vv. 1–2) Hezekiah and Judah. The narrative depicts Sennacherib and his great army as being physically distant, but psychologically near. As Williamson suggests, the implied author's depiction in this way may have been to avert any possible logistical difficulties arising from the presence of the Assyrian army before Jerusalem (2 Kgs 18:17//Isa 36:2) and the prophecy that the Assyrian king (and presumably his accompanying forces) would not besiege the city (2 Kgs 19:32//Isa 37:33).[77] As well, this brief report of Sennacherib's message delivery serves to direct attention on the message to follow. Along with v. 10a, v. 9 focuses on vv. 10–15 as being from one individual, Sennacherib king of Assyria (in comparison to 2 Kgs//Isa's detailed

---

76. Hezekiah and the people's approach toward the nations may have a second transformation inner-biblically, as perhaps indicated through the rare Niphal occurrence of סמך (Qal: "to support, lean"; Niphal: "to lean against, trust in"; 6 instances of the Ni. in the OT—see Heinz-Josef Fabry, "סמך," *TDOT* 10:278–86 [285]). 2 Kgs 18:21//Isa 36:6 draws out the metaphor inherent in the Niphal use of the root; 2 Chr 32:8 apparently builds further on that use of the metaphor. While in 2 Kgs 18:21//Isa 36:6 Judah's reliance was self-condemning, in 2 Chr 32:8 its reliance is ideal (and thus implicitly praiseworthy). The difference in the two circumstances is the object of Judah's סמך. See Mason, *Preaching the Tradition*, 113, for other discussion on 2 Chr 32:8's ironic use of the term, based on its usage in the 2 Kgs//Isa accounts.

77. Williamson, *1 and 2 Chronicles*, 383; similarly (though without concern for 2 Kgs 19:32), Childs, *Isaiah and the Assyrian*, 109.

inclusion of intermediates such as the Rabshakeh, 2 Kgs 18:17, 27–28; 19:8–9). Throughout the 2 Chr 32 account, responsibility for Assyria's invasion and attacks, whether in physical or rhetorical form, is accredited unambiguously to the empire's supreme representative, Sennacherib, king of Assyria.

Sennacherib's speech relies heavily on rhetoric to convey his basic point that Judah's god is unable to rescue Jerusalem from Assyria's attack. The Assyrian king accomplishes this thematically as well, beginning his address by challenging the object of the Jerusalemites' trust. The remainder of his speech attempts to undermine that trust and polarize the people from Hezekiah and their God, YHWH. Sennacherib also never directly acknowledges YHWH as God, or even as a god. In Sennacherib's perspective, "YHWH our God" is only a construct in the ideology of Hezekiah (v. 11a; cf. v. 7), hence Sennacherib thereafter (in a manner analogous to Hezekiah's avoidance of Sennacherib's PN) refers obliquely to the God of Israel (vv. 12, 14, 15, 17; possibly v. 19). The Assyrian king ironically tries to portray Hezekiah as the villain/harmful one to the Jerusalemites (v. 11), but he does so on obviously faulty grounds (v. 12, in which Sennacherib confuses true YHWH worship with the pluralistic worship Hezekiah outlawed), thus incriminating himself to the reader. The incrimination increases when one considers the wider context of chapters 29–31, in which Hezekiah's reforming activity and centralization of the cultus is positively affirmed by the narrator.[78] Thompson points out that in vv. 11–12, Sennacherib quotes truths spoken by Hezekiah, but thinks (or at least portrays) them as lies.[79] Thus, the irony is heightened and Sennacherib's errors in judgment are almost comical.

For the remainder of the speech (vv. 13–15), Sennacherib's allusions to history,[80] his generalized terminology,[81] and his triple reference to "my fathers" serve to generalize the Assyrians' previous successes such that Assyria is depicted as unfailing in its military power, and Jerusalem is viewed as fated to be undeliverable. Possibly this self-portrayal on the part of the Assyrians further contributes to the typologization of Assyria to the reader. Japhet suggests that "for the Chronicler, then, 'Assyria' is not one single king, but an existential threat to the world of nations."[82] It should be qualified that this is distinctly only the Assyrians' view, and that the Chronicler

---

78. As Childs, *Isaiah and the Assyrian*, 110 puts it: "In Chronicles the reform is used by the enemy to show that Hezekiah cannot be trusted. Naturally for the reader the effect is just the opposite since he has been taught to value the reform as Hezekiah's greatest act of faithfulness."

79. Thompson, *1,2 Chronicles*, 363.

80. Ibid., 363; and Ackroyd, *1 and 2 Chronicles*, 193 also observe this.

81. For detailed discussion, see Japhet, *1 and 2 Chronicles*, 987–88.

82. Japhet, *1 and 2 Chronicles*, 988.

uses that self-portrayal to contribute to the ongoing characterization and typologization of Assyria through not a wholesale adoption of the Assyrian view, but an ironic defeat of it. In the worldview of the implied author, Sennacherib has an exaggerated perspective of himself and the might of Assyria. Thus, the generalized Assyrian self-description renders them to the reader as self-deceived, arrogant, and boastful to a ludicrous degree. Ben Zvi's assertion that a common aNE *topos* is employed here, preparing the reader to expect Assyria's downfall in challenging the one true God (YHWH) reinforces the narrator's ironic use of Sennacherib's speech in vv. 13–15: "There is more than a hint of the long ancient Near Eastern tradition of describing the enemy as a hubristic king or a person who challenges the will of the gods and against all reason thinks that they can be successful in their endeavor. Of course, the *topos* is well-known, and when readers find it, they have the clear expectation that the offending character will be punished and their endeavor fail."[83]

Further, the more Sennacherib counters Hezekiah and YHWH (v. 15), the more he distances the reader from himself and the empire he represents.[84] Verses 16–17 draw this out as the narrator explicitly states Sennacherib and his officials' verbal assaults towards "YHWH the God" (v. 16) and "YHWH, the God of Israel" (v. 17), the PN of God making clear the target of Sennacherib's affronts, and the determinate forms of "God" making equally clear the supremacy of YHWH as God and his special relationship with Israel—hence, the futility and foolishness of Assyria's attacks. I do not agree with Japhet that the epithets "the God of Hezekiah" (v. 17b) and "the God of Jerusalem" (v. 19) contribute to a fourfold specification through vv. 16–19 that "this major threat [i.e., Assyria] to the people of Israel, to king Hezekiah, and to the city of Jerusalem, will come to nothing because the Lord is very specifically their God." The general concept applies aptly to "YHWH the God" (v. 16) and "YHWH, the God of Israel" (v. 17a), but vv. 17b, 19 are directly and indirectly more evocative of Assyrian rhetoric within the world of the text. It is difficult to view Japhet's proposal as applying even in an ironic way because the proposed sense would not be exploiting the plain sense of the epithet in the mouths of the Assyrians. The Assyrians' epithets

---

83. Ben Zvi, "When the Foreign Monarch," 220.

84. Ibid. perceives that "Sennacherib's speech serves not only to characterize Sennacherib and to shape an 'anti-Sennacherib,' but also to characterize Hezekiah in a way similar to that anti-Sennacherib figure." This seems correct for the passage to a degree, but one should bear in mind that other characterizations and contrasts are developed as well. Sennacherib and Assyria are posited against YHWH, for example. I am wary of simplistic explanations of characterization in 2 Chr 32, especially regarding primary characters—the Chronicler's skill has proven thus far to be much more nuanced and masterful than previously assumed.

for God in vv. 17b, 19 are better explained in contrast to the narrator's epithets—YHWH is not personally recognized, nor is the extent of YHWH's sovereignty acknowledged by the Assyrians.[85]

Sennacherib is relentless in his verbal assault against YHWH and Hezekiah. The king of Assyria uses spoken and written communication and the advantages of different languages to reiterate incessantly his point that YHWH is ineffective and unable to rescue Jerusalem (vv. 17, 19). While vv. 10-15 displayed the Assyrian rhetorical skill and psychological insidiousness (and folly), vv. 16-19 describe the Assyrian strategy in such as way as to convey the breadth and height of their intellectual resources at work. Literacy and polyglottalism added to the demonstrated Assyrian sophistry contribute an intimidatingly educated and intellectualistic—but theologically misled—dimension to the overall Assyrian characterization in Chronicles.[86]

The presentation of the Assyrians in 2 Chr 32 is intense. Their rhetoric is vigorous, their intent is insidious and destructive, and their verbal attack is sustained without interruption for eleven verses (vv. 9-19). Hezekiah and YHWH's responses have been long withheld, increasing the reader's anticipation of how Hezekiah will withstand the challenge and how YHWH will deal with both Assyria and Judah. When Hezekiah finally acts, it is not to address the Assyrian leadership; he turns instead to YHWH. It is a decisive moment in the conflict, continuing in a way Hezekiah's reversal of Ahaz's fatal appeal to Assyria instead of YHWH in 28:16-21. Though some perceive a paragon of faith in Hezekiah's response in v. 20,[87] this should not preclude urgent concern on the part of both the king and prophet who "cried out (ויזעקו) to heaven about this." זעק denotes a cry for help from a person in acute distress; it designates an "emotion-laden utterance" of both pain and plea.[88] While Hezekiah does not give Assyria the benefit of a response, Hezekiah and Isaiah evidently have urgently distressed responses that they direct to YHWH. Hence, the reader is indirectly informed that, at the characters' level, the psychological and military belligerency of the

---

85. Japhet, *1 and 2 Chronicles*, 989.

86. Possibly Sennacherib's citations of Hezekiah, his imperfect attempt to demonstrate and manipulate knowledge of Judean reforms, and the Assyrians' unexpected use of the Judean tongue (vv. 11-12, 17) were intended to insinuate that Assyrian "intelligence" forces (i.e., spies) had already penetrated the capital. See Dubovsky, *Hezekiah and the Assyrian Spies*, esp. 253. Concerning vv. 11-12, Selman, *2 Chronicles*, 512 observes that "detailed knowledge of the internal affairs of other countries is often paralleled in contemporary Assyrian letters."

87. Ackroyd, *1 and 2 Chronicles*, 194. Similarly, Japhet, *1 and 2 Chronicles*, 989.

88. G. Hasel, "זעק," *TDOT* 4:112-22 (115); see also R. Albertz, "זעק," *TLOT* 3:1088-93, esp. 1089; Leon J. Wood, "זעק," *TWOT* 1:248; and A. H. Konkel, "זעק," *NIDOTTE* 1:1131-32 (1131).

Assyrian leaders has had a serious effect on the Judean leadership, but Hezekiah's faith persists (presumably with the support of Isaiah the prophet, who appears in the Chronicles account only in v. 20; cf. v. 32).

YHWH is the one who responds to Sennacherib's hostilities. Sennacherib's aggressive sending (שלח) of his servants from Lachish to Jerusalem (v. 9) retrospectively gains significance and is returned by YHWH's sending (שלח) of his own "messenger/angel" to Lachish (apparently) on behalf of Jerusalem (v. 21). Whereas Sennacherib's servants delivered mere words, YHWH's angel delivers destruction and, implicitly, judgment.[89] In contrast to the 2 Kgs//Isa accounts, which vividly imply with numbers and description that the entire Assyrian camp was annihilated (2 Kgs 19:35//Isa 37:36), 2 Chr 32:21 more objectively reports the destruction of "all the mighty warriors, leaders, and officers in the camp of the Assyrian king." It is unclear as to whether the Chronicler intended to list only the leaders (in contrast to the entire encamped army, "petty soldiers" included) or whether he accumulates leaderly nouns to convey the impressiveness of YHWH's annihilation of them. At any rate, the Assyrian military forces included mighty and authoritative warriors who nonetheless could not resist the judgment of YHWH. The defeat is most acutely depicted in the royal Assyrian head and representative, Sennacherib, who heretofore has been portrayed as the source of the Assyrian imperial aggression. Hence, the reader may find it appropriate that it is Sennacherib who bears the greatest signs of defeat, shame being more than a private experience, but also a political and public humiliation.[90]

The next scene is unexpected as the narrative telescopes twenty years ahead to link Sennacherib's later death with YHWH's earlier judgment. The environment is also surprising because it depicts Sennacherib as a religious person (at least, by Assyrian standards) in a self-subordinate position. As Ben Zvi points out, the Assyrian king had made no allusion to the Assyrian gods during appropriate opportunities in his speech. "Sennacherib . . . seems to believe that he and the previous Assyrian kings—rather than the Assyrian gods—have achieved victories over (non-Assyrian) gods and

---

89. The reader may be aware that, previously in 1 Chr 21:15, it was *God's* (determinate: האלהים) angel who wrought destruction and judgment on Jerusalem, the terminology in that verse perhaps highlighting the sovereign, universal, more distant and abstract notions of God. In 2 Chr 32:21, however, the epithet is "YHWH," and the more personal epithet combined with the immediate context suggests that this time the judgment will be executed on behalf of YHWH's personal relationship with the people who know him by name. Consider Umberto Cassuto, *A Commentary on the Book of Genesis, Part One: From Adam to Noah*; *Genesis 1–6:8*, trans. Israel Abrahams (Jerusalem: Magnes, 1961), 86–88; and Helmer Ringgren, "אלהים," *TDOT* 1: 267–84 (284).

90. Consider Philip J. Nel, "בוש," *NIDOTTE* 1:621–27 (622–24).

will surely overcome YHWH's opposition . . . ."[91] No explanation is given for Sennacherib's sudden demonstration of religiosity (be it his encamped army's former defeat, old age, or rumored conspiracy plans—or simply the Chronicler's withholding of such a view of Sennacherib so it could effectively contribute an impression of growing subordination in the end),[92] but his self-diminishment is suggested by way of contrast with his self-reliant and self-exalting characterization in the previous verses. Despite the subtle indication of humility, Sennacherib apparently remains unjustified in his antagonistic relation to YHWH, in which case the Assyrian king is finally defeated in the house of his own god (who is unnamed in the Chronicles account, the emphasis being not on the precise identity of Sennacherib's god, but on the fact that Sennacherib is in the place he would consider safest). This is a double victory for YHWH (over both Sennacherib and "his god") and a double disgrace for Sennacherib (who is killed in the supposed safety of his god's "house" and by his own flesh-and-blood).[93] Note that both the Assyrian army and Sennacherib are depicted as experiencing with particularity what has been developed in Chronicles generally—that the Assyrians are formidable enemies to Israel/Judah but still subject to the sovereign will and power of YHWH.

Concerning vv. 22-23, it is worth observing that "Sennacherib king of Assyria" is fully identified with PN and title in v. 22, and thus recognized as fully defeated by YHWH. The significance of YHWH's victory over Assyria (and, implicitly, the seriousness of the threat Assyria posed) is indicated by way of the extension of the victory being also "from the hand of all [their enemies]." Given the typologizing tendencies of 2 Chr 32 and the semi-conclusive function of vv. 22-23, this generalization operating as hyperbole and/or typological consequence would be appropriate—Ackroyd's admittedly "conjectural" addition rendering "from the hand of all his army" reads as awkwardly pedantic.[94] As Williamson interprets, the extension from Assyria to all Hezekiah's enemies effectively "is to turn the foregoing narrative into an exemplary account which, it is implied, can be repeated for all who share Hezekiah's faith."[95] The very specific situation in 2 Chr 32 of

---

91. Ben Zvi, "When the Foreign Monarch," 220.

92. Given the well-known prevalence of religion (at least as a formality and institution) in the aNE, I lean towards the last explanation that the late indication of Sennacherib's religiosity in the Chronicles narrative is purely a literary device.

93. ומיציאו מעיו is literally "those coming forth from his insides." De Vries, *1 and 2 Chronicles*, 391 qualifies this as "a mocking term for his sons"—I am unaware so far as to how one may support this interpretation.

94. Ackroyd, *1 and 2 Chronicles*, 194.

95. Williamson, *1 and 2 Chronicles*, 385.

Sennacherib king of Assyria provides an example of what may be generally expected of all strong and intimidating enemies of God's people. Relative to all such opposition, YHWH is superior, sovereign, and will ultimately save and give rest to his people, those who call on him by name.

CONCLUSION

The portrayal of the Assyrians in 2 Chronicles 32 is a rich subject drawing on the many aspects that compose the nature of narrative. In this chapter, I have limited my focus to chiastic and linear readings of the passage.

As we saw in Section One, the chiastic structure of 2 Chr 32 is self-attested and contributes meaning and clarity to the text. Emphases, nuances, contrasts, anticipations, and explanations are some of the results of chiastic pairing within 2 Chr 32. As well, parts of the text that previously seemed anomalous and awkward now may be seen to comport well at least in the context of the chiasmus. The centrality of YHWH (despite the Assyrian rhetoric and taunts), identification of the conflict as being between the representatives of YHWH and the Assyrian king, the seriousness of the Assyrian challenge for Jerusalem, and the subtle undermining or incriminating reinforcement of the Assyrian rhetoric are some of the ways appreciation of 2 Chr 32's chiastic structure contributes to the portrayal of the Assyrians. Other poetic devices operate within 2 Chr 32, as noted throughout the analusis.

Section Two applied the classic approach of literary theory for a "linear" reading of the narrative. Thus, reading from beginning to end not only 2 Chr 32:1–23, but also the developing characterizations of the Assyrians and Hezekiah that precede in Chronicles, one perceives the contrasting portraiture of Sennacherib and Hezekiah, the growing typologization of the Assyrians, and the careful and select use of epithets, description, and detail by both narrator and characters. These combine to develop a full, round, particularized characterization of Sennacherib while at the same time aid to typologize that characterization into that of the Assyrians, which in turn at last (or, to be precise: in v. 22) is typologized into the imperial enemy oppressor of YHWH's people.

8

A Unique Chiasmus and the Assyrians as the Pivotal Intensifying Factor and Instrument of YHWH (2 Chronicles 33:1–20)

THE MOST EVIDENT SIGN of the Assyrians in the Chronicles account of Manasseh's reign is obviously in 2 Chronicles 33:11. Naturally, to more fully understand what is occurring in v. 11, one must consider it within its context—especially so for this passage. That context is the whole of vv. 1–20, and its distinctive structure is worth explicating and appreciating here.

CHIASMUS AND ANALYSIS

To my knowledge, there has been no extensive treatment of the chiastic structure of 2 Chr 33:1–20, the pericope concerning Manasseh. Japhet, Smelik, and Abadie all present basic chiastic outlines of 2 Chr 33:1–20.[1] None goes beyond general content in identifying and describing their chias-

---

1. Based on Japhet, *1 and 2 Chronicles*, 1001:
   - (a) Introduction: Manasseh is king (v. 1)
     - (b) Manasseh's transgressions (vv. 2–8)
       - (c) Punishment: exile to Assyria (vv. 10–11)
         - (d) Repentance and delivery (vv. 12–13)
       - (e) Manasseh's earthly enterprises (v. 14)
     - (f) Religious restoration (vv. 15–17)
   - (g) Conclusion: death and burial (18–20)

muses (Abadie's work offers the only possible exceptions in that it contrasts Manasseh's deportation to Babylon in v. 11 with his restoration of Jerusalem in v. 14); all three perceive that the pivotal center involves Manasseh's repentance and delivery (vv. 12–13; Smelik adds vv. 10–11, and hence Manasseh's refusal to listen to YHWH).

It seems to be the case, however, that the structure of 2 Chr 33:1–20 is more intentionally and particularly delineated. As well, the pivot of the chiasmus concerns not so much vv. 12–13, but v. 11.

On the basis of repeated words and phrases, as well as content, 2 Chr 33:1–20 appears to have the following complex structure. Correspondences are matched by number, and those within a subunit are connected by a solid, curved line, while those uniting the overall passage are connected by straight, dashed lines. Though incidental to our discussion, the frequent occurrences of בנה are italicized):

Based on Smelik, "Portrayal of King Manasseh," 170:

  Part I (v. 1)
    Part II (vv. 2–8)
      Part III (v. 9)
        Part IV (vv. 10–13)
      Part V (v. 14)
    Part VI (vv. 15–17)
  Part VII (vv. 18–20)

Based on Philippe Abadie, "From the Impious Manasseh (1 Kings 21) to the Convert Manasseh (2 Chronicles 33): Theological Rewriting by the Chronicler," in *The Chronicler as Theologian: Essays in Honor of Ralph W. Klein*, eds. M. Patrick Graham, Steven L. McKenzie and Gary N. Knoppers (London: T. & T. Clark, 2003), 96:

  A Manasseh is king (v. 1)
    B The religious *infidelities* of Manasseh (vv. 2–9)
      C In punishment, Manasseh is deported to Babylon (vv. 10–11)
        D Repentance of the king, following his deliverance (vv. 12–13)
      C' Manasseh restores Jerusalem (v. 14)
    B' The religious *reforms* of Manasseh (vv. 15–17)
  A' The end of the reign. Amon is king (vv. 18–20)

A UNIQUE CHIASMUS 201

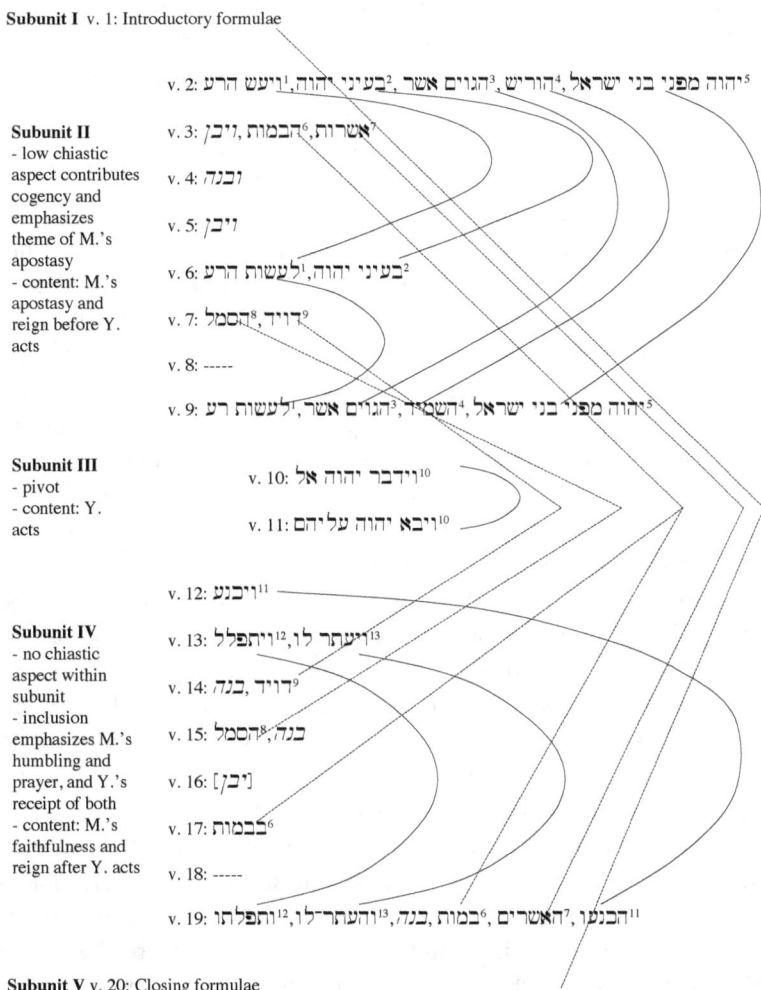

Subunit I is the beginning of a standard introductory formula (cf. v. 2), naturally paired with unit V, which features the end of a standard concluding formula (cf. v. 18).

Subunit II contains the thrice-repeated combination עשה + רע in vv. 2, 6, 9. Though it is a phrase, it is also a technical term, or idiom, that occurs elsewhere in Chronicles—notably, eleven times in 2 Chronicles; and even a fourth time in chapter 33, in v. 22. Still, 27% of the total occurrences of עשה + רע in 2 Chronicles are in subunit II. The combination that follows, בעיני יהוה, also is an idiom appearing fairly frequently in Chronicles (19 times; 18 of which are in 2 Chronicles). The repeated idioms and distinctive locations of vv. 2, 6, 9 contribute some chiastic aspect. An envelope figure, or inclusio, is strongly made between vv. 2 and 9's verse-ending phraseology of הגוים אשר³–(Verb in the Hiphil Perfect 3ms)⁴–יהוה מפני בני ישראל⁵.

The remainder of subunit II lacks further chiastic aspect. The overall chiastic aspect for the subunit is low, and its function appears to be simply that of emphasizing 1) the cogency of vv. 2–9 as its own subunit, and 2) the overall theme of subunit II as the apostasy of Manasseh.

Subunit III is composed of two verses, both of which begin with the construction (*wayyiqtol* 3ms form) + יהוה + (guttural-לְ preposition), which is generally unexceptional in biblical literature. However, being that the constructions here are chapter-unique, parallel, and centrally-located in the pericope, they distinguish vv. 10–11 as the pivot. (This differs from the more subjective, content-based conclusions of Smelik, Japhet, and Abadie, all of whom include at least vv. 12–13 in the pivot, shifting the centre's emphasis to Manasseh's action and condition instead of YHWH's action.) Further, vv. 10–11 convey and seem more theologically resonant with the emphases of the Chronicler (e.g., the sovereignty of YHWH and the decisive quality of His intervention in the course of history).²

Moving on to subunit IV, we bear in mind that כנע is frequent vocabulary in Chronicles. כנע occurs 19 times in Chronicles, 16 of which are in 2 Chronicles. The verb also occurs later in chapter 33, in v. 23, and nearby, in 32:26. On its own, the repetition of this root could be coincidental. However, the clustering in subunit IV of כנע with forms derived from root פלל and the more unique occurrences of וֹ + לְ + עתר strengthens its distinctive use here.³ The parallel aspect for subunit IV's beginning and end (i.e., vv. 12–13 and v. 19), which suggests an inclusio, may not seem to be strong at first because of the distance between elements in vv. 12 and 13. It could be argued that vv. 12 and 13 belong together, especially since they share similar content and are distinguished from the rest of subunit IV by the ואחרי־כן that begins v. 14. No other inner-subunit features are present. In terms of content, vv. 12–19, along with the formulaic conclusion of v. 20 (i.e., subunit V), share the subject of Manasseh's reign *after* YHWH acts.

Thus far repetitions have formed inclusios and appear to delineate subunits. Taking a look now at the general structure of 33:1–20, we may recall that subunit I includes a standard introductory formula, naturally placed in counterposition to subunit V, which features a standard concluding formula. Subunit II has shared phraseology at the beginning, centre, and end (vv. 2, 6, 9), which demarcates the boundaries of that unit while also emphasising

2. For further discussion, see Japhet, *Ideology of the Book*, 62, 125–136.

3. In addition to these unique occurrences of עתר + לוֹ, it is worth noting that עתר occurs twenty-four times in the OT, of which three are in Chronicles, of which two are in 2 Chronicles (namely, in these verses).

its primary motif of Manasseh's apostasy against YHWH. In contrast to the focus on Manasseh by the overwhelming majority of verses, subunit III (i.e., the pivot; vv. 10–11) emphasises a different subject: YHWH. In both verses of this pivot, YHWH appears immediately after the initial verb and before a guttural-ל preposition. As we observed, this is *not* unusual for the OT. However, the constructions gain distinction here as the only chapter-wide occurrences, and the verse pair overall is reinforced as a subunit by their central location and parallel positioning. Subunit IV is marked by an inclusio of shared vocabulary between vv. 12–13 and v. 19. While the repeated words and roots underline the key changes in Manasseh's behaviour to which God responded and thus enabled the king's recovery in subunit IV, the lack of repetition at the centre of subunit IV (which one might expect, in correspondence to subunit II) may be because the emphases of other significantly-located verses (i.e., the subunit's inclusio) also do not entirely reflect the general content of its subunit. Or, this situation may simply be because the portrayal of the reinstated Manasseh is more complex (cf. v. 17; 2 Kgs 21:10–16). At any rate, subunits II and IV clearly present a contrast of 'before' and 'after' the events of the pivot, Manasseh's apostasy and recovery.

Considering the unit as a whole, there do appear to be some chiastic elements functioning across it.[4] In particular, note the occurrences of במות, אשרים/אשרות, and הסמל. במות occurs 106 times in the OT, 17 times in 2 Chronicles. In 2 Chr 33, במות occurs in vv. 3 and 19, which are generally equi-distant of the pivot. However, במות also occurs in v. 17, which lowers its chiastic potential. That said, במות also appears in vv. 3 and 19 with the only chapter-wide occurrences of אשרים/אשרות. This combination of במות and אשרים/אשרות occurs 10 times in the OT, in the books of Kings and 2 Chronicles alone. Of its six occurrences in 2 Chronicles, two are here in vv. 3 and 19. I would rate the chiastic aspect of vv. 3 and 19 as low. While the pairs of words are, as I pointed out, fairly equi-distant, it is not clear that the clustering of cultic technical terms במות and אשרים/אשרות is significant, nor that במות's multiple occurrences are not merely dependent on the message of the content. Our third cultic reference, סמל, is not a technical term, though it is rare.[5] סמל occurs a total of five times in the OT, two times in

---

4. Possibly these chiastic elements suggest a second structure operating in tandem with the chiastic structure outlined above. However, whilst these other chistic elements do appear to be deliberate, the relative infrequency of them and the minor nature of their subject matter indicate, rather, that their function is to tighten the whole together. By linking individual parts of two large and clearly demarcated units together, those separate units gain more of a sense of cogency as part of one large pericope concerning Manasseh.

5. See Butterworth, *Structure and the Book*, 60, regarding the importance of rare words and relative un-importance of technical terms in discerning chiastic structure.

2 Chronicles (those two occurrences being vv. 7 and 15), and is attested outside the OT only in Phoenician and Punic inscriptions.[6] Further, the combination ה + סמל occurs in the OT only in 2 Chr 33:7 and 15. Even more distinction is added when it becomes apparent that the Chronicler deliberately chose הסמל in place of האשרה in his Kings *Vorlage* (cf. 2 Kgs 21:7).

Looking at other scholars' work on this matter, the chiastic relationship between vv. 7 and 15 has heretofore not been observed, though the marked change by the Chronicler of אשרה to סמל in v. 15 has been undeniable. Scholars since McKay, *Religion in Judah*, usually explain the change as reflecting specification of an idol type, probably Phoenician:

> It would therefore seem more probable that the word *semel* entered the Hebrew language through the Phoenician. From the Phoenician inscriptions it appears that a *semel* was an anthropomorphic idol. It could be dedicated to gods and goddesses, or could be erected to the memory of the dead, and it was at least sometimes cast in bronze.[7]

Hadley makes a different suggestion: סמל in chap. 33 emphasizes a sense of image, in contrast to a being. She remarks that the use of סמל "may suggest that סמל is specifically the goddess Asherah, but it is more likely that the Chronicler wished to remove any suggestion that an existent deity was involved, and asserted it was merely an image."[8] Either or both of McKay and Hadley's proposals may be operative for סמל in 2 Chr 33. It seems to me, however, that a chiastic relationship best explains both unique occurrences of הסמל. It is possible to harmonize the theories and suggest, for example, that the Chronicler wished to emphasise through the chiastic pairing the foreign, Phoenician nature of the Asherah that Manasseh erected. Being that the etymological evidence for סמל remains inconclusive, however, I hesitate to advocate such theories. What one can more confidently forward is the strong presence of chiastic aspect through הסמל in 32:7 and 15,[9] which functions structurally to emphasize the chiastic pairing between the two major parts of the Manasseh pericope and thus to unite the Manasseh pericope overall (vv. 1–20). Possibly the chiastic use of במות, אשרים/אשרות,

---

6. John W. McKay, *Religion in Judah under the Assyrians. 732–609 BC* (SBT 26; London: SCM, 1973) 21–22. The other three uses of סמל are in Deut 4:16; Ezek 8:3, 5.

7. Ibid., 22. Similarly, Williamson, *1 and 2 Chronicles*, 391; Japhet, *1 and 2 Chronicles*, 1007; Dillard, *2 Chronicles*, 268.

8. J. M. Hadley, "סמל," *NIDOTTE* 3:271–72.

9. See "סמל," *HALAT* 3:717. For further discussion on the term סמל itself, see Christoph Dohmen, "Heißt סֶמֶל 'Bild, Statue'?" *ZAW* 95 (1984) 263–66.

and הסמל functions to underline Manasseh's idolatry, though the frequent use of such terms may be coincidental to the content, which focuses heavily on Manasseh's apostasy and restoration.

Less certain, though perhaps worth mentioning is the appearance of דויד in vv. 7 and 14. דויד occurs in Chronicles 261 times; in 2 Chronicles, 74 times. Its only appearances in chapter 33 are in these two verses, but given the high concentration of דויד instances in 2 Chronicles—such that a chance double occurrence of דויד in any one chapter of 2 Chronicles is more likely than not—I consider the chiastic aspect of vv. 7 and 14 as very low. Another weak connection may be between vv. 4–5 and v. 17. With regard to content, the contrast between vv. 4–5 (in which pagan worship is conducted in YHWH's temple) and v. 17 (in which YHWH worship happens at pagan sites) is striking. Still, given the subjective nature of this correlation and the absence of clearer "signals," the chiastic aspect of vv. 4–5 and 17 is relatively insignificant.

The general infrequency of these chiastic elements and the relatively minor role of their subject matter suggest that their function is simply to tighten the whole together. By linking individual parts of two large and clearly demarcated subunits together (that is, subunits II and IV), the whole gains more of a sense of cogency as one large unit concerning Manasseh. The seven occurrences of keyroot בנה serve no apparent chiastic function, though their relatively high frequency here serves to unite the passage further.[10]

Now, with respect to our particular verse of interest, v. 11, it is important to recall that v. 11 functions within the pivot, subunit III. Subunit III is indeed the hinge upon which all turns—both plot and the characterization of Manasseh undergo a dramatic change as a result of unit III. Its two verses are distinguished and well-paired, with both featuring initial *wayyiqtol* forms followed by יהוה, emphasizing YHWH's initiative. In terms of overall content, v. 10 presents YHWH's first opportunity to Manasseh and the people to repent, but they refuse and hence, the narrative implies, the events of v. 11 were necessary. There is a movement between vv. 10 and 11 that is akin to that of poetic parallelism: verse 10 presents an opportunity from YHWH for repentance, v. 11 presents the same basic situation one step further and intensified. Note that the intensifying factor in the case of v. 11 is the Assyrian army and their brutal ways of captivation.

---

10. בנה, "to build," occurs sixty-one times in 2 Chronicles. Its various uses in 33:1–20 may be seen to draw attention to Manasseh's dramatic change in relation to his political and religious building projects.

Where a secular perspective would have seen the Assyrians controlling the action, the narrative makes it clear that YHWH is the primary actor and initiator of Assyria's action towards Manasseh.[11] The syntax places "the commanders of the army of the king of Assyria" in a medial position between the primary actor, YHWH, and the recipient (clearly indicated by the DDO, אֶת־), Manasseh. It is striking that the Chronicler selected such an unwieldy nominal phrase to refer to the Assyrian commanders. Elsewhere in Chronicles, the Assyrian forces are represented simply under the rubric of the Assyrian king, his officers (e.g., 32:9, 16), or the more general entity of the Assyrian kings (28:16; 30:6; 32:4). The phrase in 33:11 is a unique description of Assyrian authority and power in Chronicles, though it may have a parallel in Isa 10:8, in which the Assyrian king is poetically depicted as boasting, "Are not my commanders all together kings?" This intertextual echo reinforces attention to the might of the Assyrian forces, especially that of the commanders. At the same time, the syntax places the commanders between YHWH, the subject causing the bringing (ויבא) of the army leaders, and the king of Assyria, who merely has a passive role in that the army belongs to him (אשר למלך אשור). Thus, 33:11 implies that the Assyrian commanders may indeed be like kings, but they are more under the rule of YHWH than of the king of Assyria. Further, the Assyrian commanders are neither the beginning nor the end of the action in v. 11, but serve as means for YHWH to affect Manasseh. Relative to YHWH and Manasseh, Assyrian power has a secondary role. Though the historical, "on the ground" view of events may have had Assyria at the forefront of Manasseh's exile, the biblical perspective in chapter 33 drastically reduces Assyria's role to that of a YHWH-ordained agent towards Manasseh. That the Assyrians participated in an event of critical influence concerning Manasseh is not denied—they are, after all, featured in the pivot. Concurrently, it is necessary to observe that the Assyrians feature explicitly *only* in the pivot, and not elsewhere in the chapter, nor is the Assyrian action elaborated upon beyond v. 11. Thus, the Assyrian presence, carefully regulated by YHWH, comes at a critical juncture in biblical history, performs its duty (as it were), then disappears from the purview of the narrator, its fortunes and follow-up of no concern

---

11. Similarly, Steven James Schweitzer, *Reading Utopia in Chronicles*, LHBOTS 442 (London: T. & T. Clark, 2007), 113:

> It is worth noting that Manasseh does not revolt against the foreign power of Assyria to regain his kingdom; the impetus for his restoration to the throne comes solely from God in response to Manasseh's change of heart.... Thus, the Chronicler certainly does not use the example of Manasseh to illustrate the violent overthrow of the foreign power in an attempt to restore the Davidic Monarchy...

to the remainder of the Chronicler's account. In this, the Chronicler evidently remained steadfastly committed to his ideological perspective and intent, resisting significant attention towards or commentary regarding the empire that ruled and had even carried out the momentous international actions in vv. 10–13. Yet, to the Chronicler, the actions of true consequence and import were in the hearts and expressions of YHWH, Manasseh, and the people of Judah.

The Assyrians employ non-remarkable means of capture: "hooks" (חחים) and binding with bronze fetters (ויאסרהו בנחשתים). While "hooks" may have simply denoted the original historic situation to which the Chronicler attests,[12] innerbiblical allusions to the Kings/Isaiah tradition (2 Kgs 19:28//Isa 37:29) would have been unavoidable for the post-exilic reader, and indeed may have been intended by the Chronicler. In those oracular verses, YHWH turns the Assyrian captivity device on itself, in asserting that "I will put my hook in your nose and my bit between your lips and I will make you return by the way which you came." As well, prophetic references to "hooks" in Ezekiel recognize the standard capture technique and, more dramatically and metaphorically, depict YHWH as applying the punishment to his enemies (see Ezek 19:4, 9; 29:4; 38:4). Hence, the connotative result for the post-exilic reader of 33:11 would have been one that acknowledged the heavy and humiliating exile of Manasseh, but also was reminded of YHWH's mastery over his enemies by such means. Manasseh may be captured in humiliating fashion, but not in a way apart from the sovereignty of YHWH. Assyria's imperial military seizure abilities may be recognized, but with the same allusion YHWH's supremacy does as well.

Modern scholarship, from as early as Schrader to as recently as Rainey,[13] has been intrigued by the destination of "Babylon" instead of the capital city Nineveh (though Selman uniquely asserts simply that "Manasseh's presence in *Babylon* is not surprising, since Assyria had had a long interest in Babylon").[14] In general, scholars either try to explain the

---

12. See also *ANEP*, 154 (plate 447).

13. Eberhard Schrader, *The Cuneiform Inscriptions and the Old Testament*, vol. 2, tr. Owen C. Whitehouse, fr. the 2nd enlarged German ed. (London: Williams and Norgate, 1888), 55; Anson F. Rainey, "Manasseh, King of Judah, in the Whirlpool of the Seventh Century B.C.E.," in *kinattutu sa darati: Raphael Kutscher Memorial Volume*, no. 1 (Tel Aviv: Institute of Archaeology of Tel Aviv University, 1993), 147–64 (160). Also articulated more recently in Smelik, "Portrayal of King Manasseh," 187, and Abadie, "From the Impious Manasseh," 96. See also summary in William M. Schniedewind, "The Source Citations of Manasseh: King Manasseh in History and Homily," *VT* 41 (1991) 450–61 (452, esp. n11).

14. Selman, *2 Chronicles*, 522. It should be added that this was an especial interest on Assyria's part, as well as a tumultuous history/relationship during Neo-Assyrian

Babylon destination historically or typologically. As discussed more fully in the Excursus (below), the most solid historical explanation is that concerning Ashurbanipal's suppression of Shamash-shum-ukin's rebellion. There tends to be an even more confident assertion of the typological nature of the Babylon reference—e.g.: "It takes little imagination to see that Manasseh is a type of the post-exilic community."[15] Taking into account not only the post-exilic situation and the broader continuation of the theme of immediate retribution in chapter 33 (which was a timely theology for the Chronicler's audience), but also the more detailed observations that ויאסרהו בנחשתים להליכו בבלה is repeated verbatim in 36:6 and that 33:11 contains similar content to 36:10 and Ezek 19:9 (the latter apparently/allegedly referring to Jehoiachin), the popular scholarly interpretation of Manasseh's situation in 33:11 as an anticipation of the Babylonian exile is not unwarranted.[16] It is important to note that neither explanation, whether historical or literary, precludes the other. In terms of the literary understanding and our particular focus on Assyria's role, I would further observe that the shift from Assyria to Babylonia as the archetypal imperial enemy in Chronicles is intimated in this perhaps unexpected appearance of בבל at the end of v. 11. After v. 11, Assyria no longer explicitly appears in Chronicles, and the next world power, described with language and content reminiscent of this verse, is clearly Babylon (36:6, 10).[17]

---

times.

15. William M. Schniedewind, "Prophets and Prophecy in the Books of Chronicles," in *The Chronicler as Historian*, eds. M. Patrick Graham, Kenneth G. Hoglund and Steven L. McKenzie, JSOTSup 238 (Sheffield: Sheffield Academic, 1997), 204–24 (223).

16. E.g., "The chronicler's inclusion of Manasseh's sin, deportation, repentance, and restoration is most instructive for it serves as a foreshadowing in microcosm of the Judean captivity itself" (Eugene H, Merrill, *Kingdom of Priests: A History of Old Testament Israel* [Grand Rapids: Baker, 1987], 435–36 [quotation from 435]); Thompson, *1, 2 Chronicles*, 369; Williamson, *1 and 2 Chronicles*, 389, 393; Dillard, *2 Chronicles*, 268 (see also 265); Peter R. Ackroyd, "The Theology of the Chronicler," in *The Chronicler in his Age* (Sheffield: Sheffield Academic, 1991), 273–89 (278); repr. from *LTQ* 8 (1973) 101–16; idem, *1 and 2 Chronicles*, 198; Abadie, "From the Impious Manasseh," 102–4; Smelik, "Portrayal of King Manasseh," 188; Mosis, *Untersuchung zur Theologie*, 193.

17. Possibly there is a faint comparison suggested between the restoration of Manasseh and the deliverance of Jerusalem in the previous chapter. Cudworth, *War in Chronicles*, 181:

> It certainly would not make sense to read any type of truce or friendship between [Manasseh and the Assyrians] in vv. 12–13 since the Chronicler would never have Yahweh reward such behavior. After all, the Chronicler had just pictured the Assyrians as completely hostile to Yahweh in the reign of Hezekiah (32:10–19). For this reason, Manasseh's return from captivity looks as miraculous as Judah's victory over the Assyrians in Hezekiah's time, when Yahweh sent an angel to kill their vast army (32:21).

EXCURSUS: MANASSEH'S EXILE TO BABYLON

Much has been written in scholarly debate concerning the historical situation behind Manasseh's exile and return. Numerous rebellions and campaigns that occurred in the region during Manasseh's 55-year reign have been proposed, such as the rebellion of Abdimilkutte king of Sidon during the reign of Esarhaddon in 677 BC,[18] Esarhaddon's punitive campaign against the Cushite Tarharqa and his allies in 671-669 BC,[19] the rebellion of Baal king of Tyre during the reign of Ashurbanipal in 668-667 BC,[20] the rebellion of Psammetichus I in 655 BC,[21] Ashurbanipal's capture of Ushu near Tyre in 645,[22] and the rebellion of Shamash-shum-ukin against his brother Ashurbanipal in 652-648.[23] As Cogan points out,[24] since Schrader's original proposal,[25] most scholars correlate Shamash-shum-ukin's rebellion and defeat with Manasseh's exile in v. 11 (e.g., Rudolph, Rainey, McKay, Japhet, Williamson, Dillard, Selman, Oded, Ehrlich, and Kelly; similarly, Nelson).[26] This hypothesis is attractive because it not only accounts for Manasseh's being exiled, but it also best explains why Manasseh was exiled *to Babylon.* Babylon first came under Ashurbanipal's direct control upon

---

The historical situation may not have been as simple as Cudworth assumes, but this interpretation is worth considering.

18. See *ANET*, 290-91.

19. Supported by Cogan, *Imperialism and Religion*, 69. See sources and discussion in Rainey, "Manasseh, King of Judah," 152-57.

20. *ANET*, 295-96; see sources and discussion in Rainey, "Manasseh, King of Judah," 158.

21. See sources and discussion in Rainey, "Manasseh, King of Judah," 158.

22. *ANET*, 300c.

23. See sources and discussion in Rainey, "Manasseh, King of Judah," 159.

24. Cogan, *Imperialism and Religion*, 68.

25. Schrader, *Cuneiform Inscriptions*, 58, concludes: "On all these grounds I do not hesitate to connect with this attempted insurrection of Samas-sum-ukin the treasonable act of Manasseh which, though not openly proclaimed, was resolutely planned." See also 53-57.

26. Rudolph, *Chronikbücher*, 316-17; Rainey, "Manasseh, King of Judah," 159-61; McKay, *Religion in Judah*, 25-26; Japhet, *1 and 2 Chronicles*, 1009; Williamson, *1 and 2 Chronicles*, 391-92; Dillard, *2 Chronicles*, 265; Selman, *2 Chronicles*, 521-22; Oded, "Judah and Exile," 455; Ernst Ludwig Ehrlich, "Der Aufenthalt des Königs Manasse in Babylon," *TZ* 21 (1965) 281-86 (284); Brian E. Kelly, "Manasseh in the Books of Kings and Chronicles (2 Kings 21:1-18; 2 Chron 33:1-20)," in *Windows into Old Testament History: Evidence, Argument, and the Crisis of "Biblical Israel,"* eds. V. Philips Long, David W. Baker, and Gordon J. Wenham (Grand Rapids: Eerdmans, 2002), 131-46 (141-42); and Richard Nelson, "*Realpolitik* in Judah (687-609 B. C. E.)," in *Scripture in Context 2: More Essays on the Comparative Method*, eds. William W. Hallo, James C. Moyer, and Leo G. Perdue (Winona Lake, IN: Eisenbrauns, 1983), 177-89 (182).

defeating his brother Shamash-shum-ukin in 648 BC. While evidence is lacking as to whether or how long Ashurbanipal may have stayed in residence in Babylon thereafter, "there is good reason . . . for thinking that a rebellious or suspect vassal could have been brought before the Assyrian king in Babylon (rather than in Nineveh) around 648 or later, during Manasseh's reign."[27] Despite Cogan's (and similarly, Ben Zvi's) "serious objection" that Ashurbanipal's punitive action was "limited to territories east of the Jordan River,"[28] McKay offers a counterargument in that disaffection in the time of Shamash-shum-ukin spread further to Syria-Palestine.[29] The conditions surrounding the rebellion led by Shamash-shum-ukin were ripe for suspecting other rulers of treason and bringing them for interrogation and/or punishment to wherever Ashurbanipal's current residence was located. As Ehrlich points out, the degree of one's guilt may not have been a significant factor in determining whether or not one was forced to appear before the victorious Ashurbanipal: "Dabei mag es unwesentlich gewesen sein, ob Manasse bei der Verschwörung eine besonders active Rolle gespielt hatte oder nur insgeheim mit Assurbanipals Gegner im Bunde stand."[30] One may further extend Ehrlich's point and posit that even if Manasseh had been completely innocent of Shamash-shum-ukin's rebellion, various other factors may have made him suspect (e.g., geographical proximity to other rebels, alliances with other rebels).

It has been duly noted that our present Assyrian sources only show a loyal and submissive Manasseh.[31] Dillard, Williamson, and Japhet all concede this. Selman interprets that Manasseh is "a rather unwilling vassal forced to provide supplies for Assyria's building and military enterprises."[32] On the other hand, Ben Zvi and Nielsen insist that the current Assyriological evidence begs for consistency, and hence that the biblical depiction of Manasseh contradicts that of the Assyrian record.[33] Both Ben Zvi and Nielsen appear to prefer the present Assyrian record as historical, but this is

---

27. Kelly, "Manasseh in the Books," 142.

28. Cogan, *Imperialism and Religion*, 69. Similarly, Ehud Ben Zvi, "Prelude to a Reconstruction of the *Historical* Manassic Judah," *BN* 81 (1996) 31–44 (40n37).

29. McKay, *Religion in Judah*, 25.

30. Ehrlich, "Der Aufenthalt des Königs," 284. See also Rainey, "Manasseh, King of Judah," 160–61.

31. See *ANET*, 291b, 294b.

32. Selman, *2 Chronicles*, 521.

33. See Ben Zvi, "Prelude to a Reconstruction," 40–41, and Eduard Nielsen, "Political Conditions and Cultural Developments in Israel and Judah during the Reign of Manasseh," in *Fourth World Congress of Jewish Studies: Papers*, vol. 1 (Jerusalem: World Union of Jewish Studies, 1967), 103–06 (throughout, though note esp. 104).

a presumption that is problematic on two counts: 1) the Assyrian literature is shaped as much by its authors' particular agenda as the biblical literature is. It could be well argued that the seventh-century royal Assyrian inscriptions are more propagandistic than the biblical Chronicles accounts; and 2) the known corpus of extra-biblical texts involving Manasseh is extremely thin. Two mentions, both in lists, are all that compose the present extra-biblical evidence. In comparison, the biblical account evidently provides a more direct, detailed, and developed depiction of Manasseh.

Wiseman, Frankena, and Williamson forward a mediating view: Manasseh was taken not as a prisoner, but as a loyal vassal to Babylon to swear an oath of allegiance to the crown prince, Ashurbanipal, in 672 BC.[34] While this event indeed may have occurred, the difficulty in correlating it with 2 Chr 33:11 is simply that the latter describes a hostile exiling of Manasseh, implying a misdemeanour on his part,[35] not a privileged summons to royal enthronement and treaty ceremonies.

Finally, it should be noted that pardon by Ashurbanipal to repentant insurgents is historically-attested, and thus the pardon of Manasseh by the Assyrian throne is not as farfetched an event as the modern reader may be initially inclined to assume. Oded observes that Ashurbanipal displayed lenient treatment "towards the king of Tyre, the Egyptian ruler Necho I, and Psammetichus I [which] would parallel the type of treatment reportedly given Manasseh."[36]

MANASSEH WAS NOT "PRO-ASSYRIAN": A MORE NUANCED UNDERSTANDING OF MANASSEH'S APPROACH TOWARDS ASSYRIA

A few comments on how the narrative does *not* reflect the Assyrians are appropriate here. On the basis of Cogan and McKay's works proposing a correction to the traditional view that the Assyrians imposed their religion upon all conquered peoples, Evans and Nelson have contributed to the greater discussion essays re-evaluating Judah's foreign policy in the seventh

---

34. D. J. Wiseman, "The Vassal-Treaties of Esarhaddon," *Iraq* 20 (1958) 1–99 (3–4); R. Frankena, "The Vassal-Treaties of Esarhaddon and the Dating of Deuteronomy," *OTS* 14 (Leiden: Brill, 1965), 122–54 (151–52); and Williamson, *1 and 2 Chronicles*, 392.

35. This was first brought to my attention by Selman, *2 Chronicles*, 521–22.

36. Oded, "Judah and the Exile," 455. Similarly, Ehrlich, "Der Aufenthalt des Königs," 285. See *ANET*, 294d–295b; 295c–96a, cf. 297b; sources and discussion in Rainey, "Manasseh, King of Judah," 158.

century BCE (Evans also discusses the eighth century).[37] Cogan emphasizes the difference in treatment by the Assyrians towards provincial territories and vassal states. Only provincial territories had "Ashur's weapon" (*kakki Aššur*) formally imposed on them, and were still apparently allowed some liberality in assimilating diverse and various deities into a cultus that recognized Ashur's supremacy.[38] Vassal states like Judah were likely required to invoke and swear upon the names of Assyrian deities,[39] but enforced formal adoption of the Assyrian cultus is thus far unattested, however likely it was that vassal states sometimes *voluntarily* adopted the imperial religion.[40]

More recently, Steven W. Holloway's massive *Aššur is King!* sifts through a prodigious amount of Neo-Assyrian material, reaching a similar conclusion to that of Cogan (and, since then, most Assyriologists) in that the Assyrians were selective and strategic in the imposition of their religion on conquered states. At the same time, in contrast to Cogan, Holloway perceives no difference between Assyria's approaches between "client" (i.e., vassal) and provincial states *per se*. Further and more importantly, Holloway emphasizes the fluidity and political motivation in Assyrian religious impositions. Regarding the much-discussed *kakki Aššur*, Holloway asserts that by the time of the Neo-Assyrian empire, the term had become a "shorthand convention" "for the military standards of the Assyrian state pantheon" used in *ade* (i.e., loyalty)-oaths.[41] Hence the *kakki Aššur*, in the eighth-century, had a primarily *political*, administrative function, though this is not to deny the term's origins in ancient, Old Assyrian and Old Babylonian cultic and juridical traditions.[42] The applicability of procedures involving the *kakki Aššur* to Manasseh's situation may be further removed than biblical scholars have assumed. As Holloway observes, the evidence for the *kakki Aššur* is scant—a mere "seven times in published Assyrian royal inscriptions, all instances limited to a fifty-year span (745–696),"[43] which notably does not include the reigns of Esarhaddon and Manasseh. Holloway makes the suggestion, which is worth considering, that "the imposition of the *kakki Aššur*

---

37. Carl D. Evans, "Judah's Foreign Policy from Hezekiah to Josiah," in *Scripture in Context: Essays on the Comparative Method*, eds. Carl D. Evans, William W. Hallo, and John B. White, PTMS 34 (Pittsburgh: Pickwick, 1980), 157–78.

38. Cogan, *Imperialism and Religion*, 53–55, 112.

39. McKay, *Religion in Judah*, 62–64.

40. Ibid., 65. See also 66–70.

41. E.g., Holloway, *Aššur is King!*, 176–77.

42. Ibid., 160–61.

43. Ibid., 261.

was inaugurated by Tiglath-Pileser III and abruptly discontinued early in the reign of Sennacherib."[44]

Thus, the traditional view that Manasseh was generally "pro-Assyrian" and that all his religious policies were direct responses to Assyrian imposition in cultic matters cannot necessarily be sustained:[45]

> In other words, the cultic measures of Ahaz and Manasseh, which the biblical historiographers deemed detrimental to true Yahwism, can no longer be explained simply as the religious price of Assyrian allegiance, nor can the cultic reforms of Hezekiah and Josiah be understood simply as the religious expression of a defiant anti-Assyrian political stance. Rather, the religious fluctuations must be explained in other ways.[46]

McKay, in re-evaluating the biblical record concerning Manasseh, emphasizes Phoenician and Arabic influence (in addition to the evident Canaanite infiltration and in contradistinction from Assyrian/Mesopotamian influence) on Manasseh's reign and the Judahite cultus. Cogan focuses more on the possible assimilation of Mesopotamian religious elements and concludes that the few discernible instances of Mesopotamian religious elements in Judahite cultic practices "seem to have gained entrance into Judah through Aramaean mediation, only after having merged with local Palestinian pagan traditions."[47] Cogan and Robinson take a further step by suggesting that Manasseh's re-establishment of local pagan sites (v. 3; cf. v. 17) was an attempt to re-assert what was perceived to be "traditional" Judean religion (in contradistinction to the supposedly increasingly present Assyrian/Mesopotamian religious elements):

> He may have felt, as many in Judah certainly did feel, that these shrines were legitimate centres of the worship of Yahweh, and that even Hezekiah had no right to overthrow them. Not a few must have traced the calamities which befell the land during Sennacherib's invasion to Hezekiah's sacrilege, and have welcomed the restoration of the old ways.[48]

---

44. Ibid., 161n261.

45. For an example of the traditional view, see Myers, *2 Chronicles*, 197–99.

46. E.g., Evans, "Judah's Foreign Policy," 158. Similarly, Nelson, "*Realpolitik* in Judah," 177–78 (quotation from 177): "Manasseh's religious policies cannot automatically be taken as indications of subservient vassalage nor Josiah's reformation as a declaration of political independence from Assyria."

47. Cogan, *Imperialism and Religion*, 88. See also 95.

48. Theodore H. Robinson, *A History of Israel*, vol. 1, *From the Exodus to the Fall of Jerusalem, 586 B.C.* (Oxford: Clarendon, 1932), 403. Cogan, *Imperialism and Religion*,

Neither the portrayal of Manasseh in Chronicles nor Chronicles' *Vorlage* of a Kings tradition depicts the monarch himself with such naivety, however. The people are perhaps naïve (cf. v. 17), but Manasseh is depicted as opposing YHWH's ways thoroughly—in deed and heart, the latter of which is central to Manasseh's change of behaviour and fortunes (vv. 12, 19; note the significance of Manasseh's being humbled [הכנעו]).

Nelson critiques the simplistic notion of the popular traditional terminology "anti-Assyrian" and "pro-Assyrian," sensibly articulating that:

> To modern ears these terms carry the implication of ideological loyalty, in the sense of "pro-Palestinian" or "pro-America." Of course no Lydian, Egyptian, or Judean was ever likely to be pro-Assyrian in that sense. Being pro-Assyrian could have meant nothing more than the belief that, in the ever-changing arena of international politics, this year at least the nation's best interests are served by subservience to Assyria. Are we to believe that any king of Judah was ever pro-Assyrian in the sense that he would go one single step beyond the national self-interest in supporting Assyrian policy?[49]

He also helpfully further captures the political nuance and emphasis of Manasseh's probable approach towards Assyria:

> Manasseh may have been the very model of the good vassal, but hardly for reasons of ideological attachment. He may have seen Assyria as a stabilizing element in Palestine which worked to Judah's advantage. He may have valued Assyrian trade contacts. He may have found in Assyrian suzerainty protection from hostile domestic elements. Nor could he forget that half a day's journey north of his capital was the Assyrian imperial border or that at about the age of seven he himself had lived through Sennacherib's siege of Jerusalem. He may have wished to avoid being flayed, impaled, or put in a dog collar to guard the gate of Nineveh. Yet to call him pro-Assyrian seems to invite misunderstanding....
>
> In 672, Esarhaddon moved to regularize the succession, requiring renewed vassal oaths from his subjects. There is Biblical evidence that Manasseh was one of those forced to pledge support for this plan of succession....
>
> We may affirm ... that Manasseh's decision [concerning participation in Shamash-shum-ukin's rebellion], whatever it may

---

95–96, affirms this view.

49. Nelson, "*Realpolitik* in Judah," 178.

have been, was conditioned by the realities of power politics and not by some unsubstantiated pro-Assyrian attitude.⁵⁰

In distinguishing politics from general ideology, Nelson effectively limits the applicability of his historical reconstruction of the relationship between Assyria and Judah during Manasseh's reign to vv. 11–14, for the remainder of vv. 1–20 involves religious ideology and, implicitly, Manasseh's heart-orientation (as observed before, הכנע, vv. 12, 19), but not so much political ideology and events. That said, while it is quite possible that Manasseh's building works were either in anticipation of an Assyrian attack or to assist Assyria by strengthening Judah's function as a buffer against Egypt,⁵¹ such motivations are of little relevance to the presentation in v. 14. To begin, the verse functions in a context in which all other verses clearly concern and contribute to a theme of Manasseh's restoration (unit IV, vv. 12–19). It may be appreciated that v. 14 itself also functions this way when one recalls that "building activities and especially fortifications are usually an expression of divine blessing in Chronicles."⁵² The empire and threat it could pose may factor in the historical background, but the Chronicler makes no explicit allusion to this possible aspect of the building projects. The resincribing is clearly intentional: here, as in vv. 10–13, the metanarrative of Assyria and its power is minimized despite its significant historical role, so that the more-indigenous values and ideology of Israel could come to the fore and preserve the community perspective and narrative (and, with it, its sense of community identity). Thus, it is the fact of the building projects themselves and their implicit indication of divine favour that is presented by v. 14.

CONCLUSION

After establishing the complex and unique chiasmus concerning the reign of Manasseh in 2 Chr 33:1–20—including the "before" and "after" functions of subunits II and IV, and the structural and content-related roles of terms such as סמל in the unit—we focused on the pivot (subunit III) and

---

50. Ibid., 178, 180, 182.
51. E.g., ibid., 181; Myers, 2 Chronicles, 199.
52. Ehud Ben Zvi, "The Chronicler as a Historian: Building Texts," in Graham, Hoglund, and McKenzie, Chronicler as Historian, 132–49 (142; see also 148–49). See also Peter Welten, Geschichte und Geschichtsdarstellung in den Chronikbüchern, WMANT 42 (Neukirchen-Vluyn: Neukirchener, 1973), 1–78; intimated in Nadav Na'aman, "The Date of 2 Chronicles 11:5–10—A Reply to Y. Garfinkel," BASOR 271 (1988) 74–77 (76d).

particularly, because of its explicit inclusion of the Assyrians, v. 11. Notably, the pivot of 2 Chr 33:1–20 functions as the hinge for both events and the characterization of Manasseh. Verse 11 presents an intensification of the situation in v. 10, and the element instrumentally causing that intensification are the Assyrian military commanders and their capture of Manasseh. The syntax surrounding the phrase "the commanders of the army of the king of Assyria," the precise word order within this unwieldly phrase, and the Assyrians' use of "hooks" are analyzed for their innerbiblical allusions and immediate contributions to meaning.

The restriction of the Assyrians in the overall unit to only the pivot (in contrast to the historical, "on the ground" perspective) reflects an ideological evaluation of Assyria as playing a literally pivotal role, but also an emphatically boundaried and limited one that was clearly subservient to YHWH and His purposes. After Assyria performs its YHWH-ordained task, it disappears from the narrative and is no longer of concern to the remainder of the Chronicler's account. Quite possibly Manasseh's exilic destination of "Babylon" is an indication of a wider typological shift in history and Chronicles from Assyria to Babylonia, but it could also be historically explained (Ashurbanipal's suppression of Shamash-shum-ukin's rebellion is the strongest explanation, if this is the case).

Finally, a couple popularly hypothesized ways in which the unit does *not* actually reflect the Assyrians are discussed. Judah's vassal-state status would not have required the imposition of the Assyrian cultus (nor does it appear that the *kakki Aššur* have been in effect during Manasseh's time). The situation is not without nuance, however, in that vassal states sometimes voluntarily adopted the imperial religion. The assertion that Manasseh was "pro-Assyrian" is critiqued for its misleadingly simplistic connotation in view of the complex international politics with which Manasseh was forced to engage.

9

Conclusions

WHILE THE INTENTION OF this work is primarily to offer a compendium of individual literary analyses of biblical texts involving the Assyrians in Kings and Chronicles, there are several overall observations worth noting within the books themselves. After presenting general conclusions for Kings and Chronicles, I will summarize the most salient findings for each kingly account in this study with regard to the narratological characterization of the Assyrians, and then will close with a broader, discursive summary comparing the characterizations of the Assyrians in Kings and Chronicles.

IN KINGS

While in reality, the Assyrian presence during the events in the vast majority of our passages in Kings would have been undeniable and enormous to an unprecedented extent for any people group up to that time in aNEn history, within the world of Kings, Assyria is a controllable and contained power under the active sovereignty of YHWH. The Kings author often indicates the secondary nature of Assyria by minimizing its presence through withholding of details about Assyria (e.g., 2 Kgs 17; 21:14; 23:29), omission of Assyrian kings' personal names (esp. 2 Kgs 16), explicit commentary that the reason for the Assyrian devastation was Israel/Judah's apostasy and wicked practices (in contradistinction to Assyria's active choice to conquer; e.g., 2 Kgs 15; 2 Kgs 17), and explicit statements of YHWH's superiority, rule, and victory over the Assyrians (2 Kgs 18–20).

Also, Assyria contributes to a number of types in Kings. An obvious type for Assyria is that of the instrument of YHWH, while the many and various nuanced ways by which that instrument also worked out of its own volition and the vicissitudes of history are woven into these texts, which never lose strong sight of the sovereignty of YHWH in all. The development of this type in Kings focuses more on the sovereignty of YHWH over the Assyrians as instrument rather than the strength of that instrument, the latter being more pronounced in the book of Isaiah.

Another key type is that of Assyria as the foreign superpower oppressor over the people of God. This new entity quietly but quickly arrives on the Kings scene as Israel is rapidly degenerating. Its presence and threat result in several situations in which the Israelites/Judahites are challenged to respond and know their hearts. Until Hezekiah, the Kings author reports failure in this on the part of Israel/Judah. Hezekiah's faithfulness ushers in the power of YHWH over His instrument and this so-called superpower. YHWH's clear, miraculous demonstration of His sovereignty and victory over Assyria in 2 Kgs 18–20 is followed by a literary demise of Assyria in 2 Kgs 21:14 and 23:29 as Babylon rises to supersede it (e.g., 2 Kgs 20; 24).

Relatedly, the arrival of the new superpower known as Assyria presents a challenge in being an "alternative" to YHWH. This characterization of Assyria is so prevalent in Kings and basic to the wider biblical corpus that it is arguably its own type. We see this intimated in Menahem's reign in 2 Kgs 15, and especially expressed in the account of Ahaz in 2 Kgs 16. The challenge to idolatry of Assyria is present in 2 Kgs 18–19, and Hezekiah overcomes it. However, when seeds are sown for a new superpower on the rise (2 Kgs 20), Hezekiah's response compromises the impact of his victory.

It is also worth noting that in Kings (as well as in Chronicles), several regnal accounts omit or severely minimize the influence of the Assyrians to such a degree that rejection of the imperial agenda and support and embrace of the subaltern metanarrative are reflected in texts. These include: 1 Kgs 16:21–28; 16:29—22:40; 19:16–17; 2 Kgs 9–10; 14:23–29; 21:1–18; 21:19–26; 22:1—23:30; 2 Chr 33:21–25; and 34–35.

Let us now review the conclusions of the individual reigns in Kings concerning the Assyrians:

Menahem's Reign (2 Kings 15:13–22)

In 2 Kings 15, Assyria is an inimical influence on Israelite king Menahem, not simply by way of "distracting" Menahem from reliance on YHWH, but by giving Menahem a military example and resources for oppressing others

CONCLUSIONS   219

(in this case, his own people, the Israelites). Assyria also provides a foil for Menahem with regard to the destruction and oppression that he inflicts and his overall characterization in the pericope as the ultimate negative power entity against the Israelites.

The passage also reflects the sobering proximity of the Assyrian threat, geographically, politically, and militarily. This threat is portrayed as an intimidatingly powerful and threatening enemy to Israel, and the narrative indicates that Israel would do best not to align itself with Assyria and its demands.

From a post-colonial perspective, Assyria offers the metanarrative to which Menahem submits himself, with unavoidable consequences for the people he rules. In particular, Assyria provides the means by which Menahem becomes an intermediary colonizer on Assyria's behalf towards the Israelite people.

Pekah's Reign (2 Kings 15:25–31, 37; 16:5–9)

Assyria has an instrumental role in the Pekah pericope as an agent of YHWH's warning to Israel. Interestingly, though, Assyria's instrumental role is less influential in 2 Kings 15 than that of Pekah and Ahaz. Assyria continues to invade the land, conquering and exiling significant portions of the northern kingdom, and now the empire is also on the brink of invading the narrative in the abstract sense—Assyria will soon replace Israel and Aram in their role of divinely-ordained oppressor of Judah (cf. 16:8, 18; 19:25–26).

Ahaz's Reign (2 Kings 16)

In 2 Kings 16, Assyria itself is not featured, but its emperor, Tiglath-Pileser III—who effectively represents the empire—plays a significant role. To begin, distance and a sense of "otherness" is created between the reader and Tiglath-Pileser III by way of repetitive use of Tiglath-Pileser III's title alone and selective use of his personal name when it is mentioned. Such means of literary minimization deny the Assyrian emperor and his empire the dominance of their imperial metanarrative in the interest of bringing forth the Kings' author's subaltern perspective, which places more responsibility for the events of 2 Kings 16 on Judahite king Ahaz. That said, Tiglath-Pileser III still appears to take Ahaz's agenda several steps further in that the Assyrian empire not only delivered Jerusalem from Aram and Israel as requested, but also put an end to Aram and its king and exiled part of Israel (15:29). Through his action of military protection and support for Ahaz and his passive role of recipient of Ahaz's cultic and son-father deferences, the Assyrian emperor is the means by which Ahaz abandons devotion to YHWH and increases the efficacy of his destructive agenda. Thus, events, actions, and terminology all combine for these aspects of Tiglath-Pileser III's narratological role.

Interestingly, a comparison of the role of Aram/Damascus and the role of Assyria/Tiglath-Pileser III in 2 Kings 16 demonstrates the strength of Aram's age-old relations with Judah-Israel, which even overshadows momentarily (vv. 10b–16) the ominous new relation between Assyria and Judah. Assyria disappears into the background of the account of the Damascene altar, a last vestige of Aram's influence on Judah. When that report is finished and the old arch-enemy is indeed a thing of the past, Assyria re-enters the picture (v. 18b), soon to be the new dominant foreign power with which Judah-Israel engages.

Hoshea's Reign, the Assyrian Exile, and the Resettlement (2 Kings 17)

As Israel is conquered by Assyria, Hoshea defeated by Shalmaneser, 2 Kgs 17:1–6 reflects this literarily as Hoshea's name quickly ceases from mention (apart from an incidental chronological reference in v. 6) and the Assyrian emperor is the sole subject for the remainder of vv. 1–6. Furthermore, Shalmaneser's forceful and significant power is indicated by the eight verbs of conquest used to describe him in this short passage (in contrast to the relatively passive verbs that describe Hoshea). The narrative not only telescopes here, but characters do as well, as Shalmaneser and Sargon II are apparently fused together under the title "king of Assyria."

This narratological rise of the Assyrian king in 2 Kgs 17:1–6 contrasts to the Assyrian king's relatively passive role in 2 Kings 16, heightening the sense of danger and warning that accompanies mention of the king of Assyria and indicating the serious level of threat to which Assyria has now grown.

In the theological reflection that follows, Assyria does not make an explicit appearance until the pericope's final statement on YHWH's response to the northern kingdom (v. 23b). In this statement, Assyria is merely incidental to the more consequential action of YHWH in determining to remove Israel from his presence (v. 23a). Thus, Assyria is primarily characterized in a sense by what it is not—it is not Israel's homeland, and so it is a concrete reminder of YHWH's judgment upon Israel.

We also proposed a slight adjustment and expansion of Goldstein's theory that vv. 7–9 include Assyrianisms, which would reflect a source that could encompass vv. 7–23 or part of it and that was initially composed as an ideological response to the typically braggadocian Assyrian perspective of their conquests. In vv. 24–28, the issue of who follows the agenda of whom elucidates that the king of Assyria wields influence over his jurisdiction of people, conquered nations, and officers, but also must and does concede that the land, the lions, and the god(s) over these things are beyond his power. The overall depiction of the Assyrian king in this passage is that of a very competent and effective imperial leader in command of his people throughout his empire and, in the manner of a good leader, aware that his power has limitations. By way of comparison, the king of Assyria is portrayed here mildly positively while the Israelites themselves are the ones who fail to respond to YHWH's warnings (cf. vv. 14ff). The omission of Sargon II's personal name throughout the narrative weakens the impact of this character who, on the ground historically, had an extremely strong persona as one of the most powerful Assyrian conquerors in history.

The Assyrian characterization in the last part of 2 Kings 17 includes not only the king of Assyria, but also the new settlers and the people who report to the Assyrian king in v. 26 and who are given orders by the king in v. 27. Based on their locations and the fact that they are forced to resettle on the periphery of the empire, the new settlers are seen as Assyrian citizens of such low rank that it endows them with a sort-of hybrid quality. Note that the Assyrian settlers do not function in 2 Kings 17 as a foil for the displaced Israelites, but rather as a confirmation of the universal failure of human societies to be devoted and faithful to YHWH. The third party to constitute the Assyrian characterization in the chapter are evidently Assyrian officials who act as intermediaries between the emperor and the people, bringing the interests of the empire to the far reaches of its conquered lands at an intimate level. The most unifying factor of the three parties comprising the Assyrian characterization here, in addition to their commitment and subservience to the Assyrian empire, are their syncretistic perspective and limited respect for and knowledge of "the god of the land."

In considering the overall treatment of the Assyrian exile in Kings, it is striking to note the contrast between the lengthy, theological-parenetic reflection of the Assyrian exile in 2 Kings 17 and the absence of such a reflection regarding the Babylonian exile. Adopting Cross' theory and expanding on Viviano's conclusion, I conclude that the reason for this difference is because Judah still had a future at the time of the Dtr[1]'s reflection on the Assyrian exile, while the Babylonian exile did not offer the same hope of avoiding an exile as had the Assyrian exile.

Hezekiah's Reign (2 Kings 18–20)

The characterization of Assyria develops through the Hezekiah Narratives of 2 Kings 18–20. In 2 Kgs 18:1–12, Assyria enters the narrative as one entity among others providing a challenge to Hezekiah's trust (v. 6). The threat of Assyria quickly grows, both in the world of the story and in the focus given to it in the text (vv. 9–12). This leads to the introduction of a new Assyrian king—and, in a sense, a renewal of the Assyrian threat (v. 13). Sennacherib is immediately characterized by his actions, which are aggressive and highly threatening (v. 13). He also brings to the Assyrian king type a new level of hostility by introducing in the world of the narrative the Assyrians' first wartime betrayal (vv. 14–17). Arriving unexpectedly in the story (v. 17), the Assyrian forces' actual invasion is further narratologically emphasized by the unusual repetition of verbs and phrases in v. 17 that accumulate to the confrontative root עמד.

The Assyrian delegation's members are described in vv. 17–18 with the following elements: 1) they are described mostly, if not entirely, with Akkadian-derived terminology; 2) they are each preceded by the direct object marker (את-), emphasizing their high status; 3) they are identified by title only; 4) they are radically more militarily experienced and powerful than the Judean delegation; and 5) they are accompanied by a large force. All these factors increase the empathetic distance between the Assyrian delegation and the reader.

The Rab-šaqeh proceeds to deliver a speech in which Hezekiah is referred to by personal name without title while Sennacherib is referred to with titles only, thus denigrating Hezekiah and emphasizing his humanity while elevating Sennacherib and emphasizing his position in language reminiscent of that used for YHWH. The Assyrians are shown to keenly recognize that the issue is trusting YHWH, and they continue to present relentless challenges to it as the narrative continues. Meanwhile, the long-distance presence of Sennacherib is minimized as the Rab-šaqeh shifts between speaking in first person and third person, blurring the distinctions between the messenger and the sender, himself at the gates of Jerusalem and his master on the battlefield at Lachish. The Rab-šaqeh's first speech has tones of negativity, sarcasm, and claims that confuse, all of which are intended to contribute to deflating the recipient's confidence. His second speech continues a sense of negativity and increases psychological aggression and intimidation in an effort to evoke fear and to marginalize and ultimately silence the voice of Hezekiah and his officers. In both, the Rab-šaqeh attempts to identify with the values and language of the Jerusalemites (albeit falsely, without integrity) and then smoothly proceeds to question the sacred, defining elements of the Judahite collective identity and to offer to the Jerusalemites an alternative collective metanarrative by surrendering to the Assyrian empire. In addition to actions and motives evidenced in the character of the Assyrians thus far in this passage, explicit and implicit claims contribute to their self-portrayal and overall narratological portrayal. The Assyrian officials imply that Assyria and its king are trustworthy and superior to other alternatives, that the empire outshines all others because of its abundant military resources, that the Rab-šaqeh/Sennacherib have "omniscient" eyes (though the narrative exposes their erroneous "vision"), that YHWH himself is with Sennacherib and not actually with Hezekiah (the narrative is clear that this is false), and that the Assyrians are faithful servants of YHWH (again, the narrative is clear that this is a falsity on the part of the Assyrians, which reinforces that they are deceptive and not trustworthy). In the third Assyrian speech (19:10–13), the Assyrians add to this list the presumption of having godlike abilities and status, and thus the ability to defeat YHWH.

Isaiah's prophecy depicted Sennacherib as self-exalting, a characteristic emphasized by the many first-person references in vv. 23b–24 (9x in 6 cola). Notably, it is not Sennacherib's strength and accomplishments that are condemned, but his raging, arrogant attitude towards YHWH (v. 28a). Sennacherib's defeat in the narrative is quietly marked by a sudden cease of verbal activity on the Assyrians' part and the quick, non-verbal response of Sennacherb thereafter (v. 36).

In 2 Kings 20, the Assyrians function in the first half of the chapter as providing an occasion for YHWH to demonstrate his faithfulness to himself and David, as well as to give an opportunity for Hezekiah's character to be upheld. In the second half of chapter 20, the background consisting of the previous events concerning the Assyrians supplies a contrast between the outcome of Hezekiah's faithfulness to the Davidic covenant and the consequences of Hezekiah's complacency towards the covenantal relationship with YHWH. The motif of tribute and foreign nations (in particular, Babylon) in 2 Kgs 20:12–19 recalls that of Hezekiah and the Assyrians in 2 Kgs 18:14–16. Again, an implicit comparison is established, and the Assyrians as the challenge that Hezekiah stumbles on are superseded by Babylon, anticipating the eventual takeover by that rising superpower.

IN CHRONICLES

Given the more retrospective and reflective approach of Chronicles, the texts explicitly or implicitly involving the Assyrians are generally tighter with words, but also denser with meaning. Out of this and in contrast to Kings, Chronicles presents a unique set of characterizations of the Assyrians. Key aspects of this include: narratival structures, an emphasis on the covenantal relationship for which Assyria is an intermediary, a slightly more enticing portrayal of Assyria in the first half of the Chronicles passages concerning that empire, and a stronger development of the basic foreign enemy oppressor type that progresses from Assyria to Babylon.

A unique distinctive for Chronicles that was discovered through the course of this research is the unusually high presence of chiasmus in texts involving the Assyrians. Interestingly, one of the chief, consistent ways these chiasmuses contributed meaning to the texts and the characterization of the Assyrians was to emphasize and literally illustrate the important, but secondary role of the Assyrians to that of YHWH (2 Chr 28:16–21; 31:20—32:33; 33).

Assyria's instrumental role is emphasized in Chronicles with particular respect to the covenantal relationship between YHWH and His people. We see this especially with the theme of the Israelites' מעל (1 Chr 5:25; 2 Chr 28:16; 29:9; 30:7; cf. 33:19) and YHWH's response of giving them into the hands of the Assyrians. In Chronicles, with its strong emphasis on Hezekiah, this trajectory does not end with punishment, but often with Israelite repentance and return to YHWH, which then results in deliverance from the Assyrians (e.g., 2 Chr 32; 33; cf. 2 Chr 29:9–10; 30:6–9). Again, the significance of Hezekiah in Chronicles shapes the characterization of the Assyrians in that the focus on his reforms and re-establishment of convenantal institutions is the context in which we see much of this pattern expressed involving the Assyrians.

On a different note, whereas in Kings Assyria is often associated with violence, emotionless brutality, and apostasy, in Chronicles we are shown more the allure of Assyria, from its ambiguous introduction (1 Chr 1:17) to Ahaz's seemingly naïve beseeching of Assyrian help (2 Chr 28:16–21) to the return of captives possibly by the Assyrians (2 Chr 30:9).

In contrast to Kings and Isaiah, the typological development of Assyria as the oppressive enemy from a foreign land is more pronounced in Chronicles, no doubt aided in this by the benefit of retrospective post-exilic perspective. Assyria is introduced among a virtual parade of eponymous ancestors, which anticipates its power to come, while its moral-ideological ambiguity keep it from immediate classification (1 Chr 1:17). Soon enough, however, Assyria will define herself as a new phenomenon on the scene—a distant empire that suddenly takes over the land. That said, the narrator makes clear that it is actually YHWH who has defined and given power to Assyria, and the instrumental function of Assyria is explicitly stated (1 Chr

5:25–26). In 2 Chr 30:6–9, "the kings of Assyria" are presented as something of an historical phenomenon, while in 2 Chr 32, the Assyrians are given a voice and details that round out the characters of Sennacherib and his officers. Both the instrumental element and the inimical aspect of this imperial enemy type are reinforced in 2 Chr 33:11.

Also, the progression of this type from Assyria to Babylon is indicated more in Chronicles than in Kings through 1) similar vocabulary, phrases, and themes in 1 Chr 5:25–26 and 2 Chr 36:13b–20; 2) the gradual broadening of the type of foreign enemy oppressor from Assyria alone to a generalized entity in 2 Chr 29:9; 30:9; 3) the movement from Assyria to Babylon as foreign danger in 2 Chr 32; and 4) the association of the king of Assyria with Babylon in 2 Chr 33:11 (cf. 2 Chr 36:6, 10), which is the last explicit mention of the Assyrians in Chronicles.

With this broader understanding in mind, we will now summarize the conclusions of individual narratives and passages in Chronicles:

The Eponymous Ancestry of Assyria (1 Chronicles 1:17)

Within the genealogy of 1 Chronicles, the eponymous ancestor אשור endows the overall character of Assyria with a mixed heritage alluding back to Genesis 10 and associations with Shem, the Hamites, Nimrod, and Cush. This creates suspense for the reader concerning the Assyrians and how their character will unfold as the overall narrative of Chronicles continues.

Also, this early appearance of אשור places the Assyrians in the "human family," but within that context its place is secondary and defined in relation to Israel—the origin of Assyria is defined here not by the Assyrian empire's metanarrative but by the subaltern "metanarrative" of Chronicles' Judean originary account.

Assyria Within the Account of the Transjordanian Tribes (1 Chronicles 5:6, 22b–26)

Assyrian emperor Tiglath-Pileser III is portrayed as having conducted a significant action (exiling the Reubenites), but more as a function of the will of YHWH than as that of Tiglath-Pileser III. The grammatical combination עור (in the Hiphil) + רוח (as object) reinforces this relationship between YHWH and Tiglath-Pileser III with theological nuance and depth, which is further discussed in this study. The use of two names for Tiglath-Pileser III in 1 Chr 5:26 may allude to Tiglath-Pileser III's imperial influence in both Mesopotamia and Palestine.

The Chronicler maintains a focus on the Transjordanian tribes throughout 1 Chr 5, relegating Assyria and events concerning the Assyrians to those that impinge on the Israelite tribes and broader themes of his concern (e.g., exile and restoration). That said, the gravity of Tiglath-Pileser III's actions towards the Transjordanian tribes is not denied, and the two-verse account of this Assyrian exile (vv. 25–26) contributes to a wider contrast with the account of the Babylonian exile ahead (cf. 2 Chr. 36:13b–20). By all counts in the narrative, this Assyrian exile is mild compared to the Babylonian one—the circumstances surrounding the Babylonian exile are more extreme than those of the Assyrian exile of the East Bank, and the description of Nebuchadnezzar and the Babylonian exile render them as far more egregious than Tiglath-Pileser III and this Assyrian exile.

Though explicit references to Assyrians in 1 Chr 5 are few, they are meaningful, multi-functional, and well-integrated in a complex history presented in this chapter and beyond.

The Reign of Ahaz (2 Chronicles 28)

2 Chronicles 28 focuses on the stubborn unfaithfulness of king Ahaz and the contrasting penitence of the Israelites, thus yet again keeping Assyria in the background. Though it is a secondary player in the narrative, Assyria functions within the chiastic structure of vv. 16–21 as the object by which Ahaz's appeals for help apart from YHWH prove futile, as a foreign enemy among others that pose a threat to Israel, and as an option competing with YHWH for the Judahite king's trust. Assyria and Tiglath-Pileser III are implied by the narrative to be the agents of YHWH's retributive humbling of Judah. מלכי אשור (v. 16) likely functions as a typologization for the Assyrian empire and its demonstrated power through history, though not from the perspective of the narrator so much as from the perspective of Ahaz. Select verbs describing the actions of Tiglath-Pileser III in v. 20 briefly but effectually convey his hostile approach towards Ahaz.

The overall characterization of Assyria in these verses develops from that of a fairly neutral recipient of Ahaz's request to that of a duplicitous, unreliable, opportunistic, intimidating superpower that is likewise able to impair Judah through the dual role of tempter and oppressor.

A Possible Allusion to the Assyrians in the Narrative of Hezekiah Reestablishing the Temple (2 Chronicles 29:9)

The Assyrians are not explicitly mentioned in this verse, but are most likely the agents behind the captivity to which Hezekiah alludes. This narratival evasion of specification regarding Assyria minimizes the attention that would normally be drawn to such an impressive worldly superpower as well as facilitates the broadened application of Hezekiah's speech to circumstances contemporaneous with the Chronicler's initial audience.

Brief References to Assyria in the Narrative of Hezekiah Celebrating the Passover (2 Chronicles 30:6–9)

For the second time in Chronicles, מלכי אשור occurs, pluralizing power into the abstract and elevating the Assyrian threat from being associated with any particular Assyrian monarch to being a typologized entity. Here, the Chronicler uses Hezekiah's authoritative voice to establish further the typologization of the Assyrian threat through this phrase.

It is clear in this passage the enemy foreign nations—and imperial Assyria in particular—are depicted by the Chronicler as wholly serving the purposes of YHWH. Assyria is simply portrayed in the mouth of Hezekiah as one among other captors who are peripheral agents of the will of YHWH.

The Deliverance of Jerusalem from Assyrian Attack and the Conclusion of Hezekiah's Reign (2 Chronicles 32)

A Chiastic Reading

After a brief discussion of chiastic structure and "chiastic aspect," 2 Chr 31:20—32:33 is identified as a narratival chiasmus. The chiastic pairs within this particular chiasmus extend from A/A' to M/M' with N being the pivot. Among the various highlights regarding the characterization of the Assyrians through the chiasmus are: the A/A' inclusio (31:20–21; 32:32–33) situates the account of the Assyrian threat within the narrative about the faithfulness of Hezekiah; the C/C' (32:3, 30) occurrences of the fairly rare root סתם, "to shut, stop," combined with references to springs reinforce the importance of Hezekiah's blockage of the springs to dissuade the Assyrians, in addition to elucidating how Hezekiah prevents the Assyrians from exploiting one water supply while Jerusalem can be maintained by another; the E/E' (32:5, 27–28) occurrences of מגנים, "shields," lay to rest interpretive textual controversy regarding the term's appearance in v. 27, as well as reflect the before-and-after states of warfare preparation and peace surrounding the Assyrian attack; the F/F' (32:6, 26) shared vocabulary of לבב/לב, "heart," emphasizes the strong degree of fear induced in Jerusalem by the Assyrian threat; the pairing of K/K' (32:12, 20) draws attention to the concept that the sovereignty of YHWH is far beyond the limited vision of Sennacherib; the shared cluster of ארץ, עשה, and יד in L/L' (32:13, 19) reinforce the relationship between the two verses and result in a statement–rebuttal dynamic between the claims of Sennacherib and the reality that undermines those claims; the common phraseology in M/M' (32:15, 17) emphasizes the Assyrian rhetorical rationale, exposes Sennacherib's strategic argumentative tactic in moving from accusation of the representative to accusation of the source, and creates a merismus-like relation between the Assyrians' use of speech and writing, conveying the sense that the Assyrians utilized every form of communication possible to try to dissuade the Jerusalemites' faith in YHWH and his representative, Hezekiah; and the central position of N (32:16, the pivot), its self-contained chiasmus, and its consonantal assonance (ו, ד, ר, ב, ע) highlight יהוה האלהים and his predominantly key role in 2 Chronicles 32—that even in the midst of the conflict between the עבדים, "servants," of Sennacherib and the עבד, "servant," of YHWH, YHWH is the hinge on which everything changes and the circumstances make a turn for the better. Also, the use of the distinctive epithet יהוה האלהים at the beginning, middle, and *almost*-end of the narrative chiasmus draws attention to its theological use here, emphasizing YHWH's uniqueness, exclusiveness, and determinative power with the sense that "YHWH [is] God."

The arrangement of the narrative of 2 Chr 31:20—32:33 as a chiasmus may be seen, in relation to the remainder of the account of Hezekiah's reign in 2 Chr 29–31:19, as highlighting Hezekiah's dealing with the Assyrian attack and its aftermath, possibly marking these events as the climax of Hezekiah's reign, and bringing an aesthetic sense of closure to the account of Hezekiah's reign.

A Narratival-Linear Reading

The linear structure of 2 Chronicles 32 introduces Sennacherib by way of his proper name (PN) and title, immediately building on Chronicles' developing typology of "the kings of Assyria." The statements—and especially verbs—used to introduce Sennacherib are succinct, but effective in conveying an aggressive and hostile intruder in the land (v. 1). In vv. 2–8, the Assyrian forces are characterized by both what other characters say about them and how other characters' actions respond to them; it can be seen that the Assyrian empire presents a military challenge for Jerusalem at a superlative level as the city prepares for the attack with new defensive strategies and a superlative level of trust in YHWH and king Hezekiah. At the same time, the "kings of Assyria" (the typologization of which continues, v. 4), remain ignorant outsiders to the inner workings of Jerusalem (i.e., Hezekiah's underground tunnel, but see also v. 12) and Hezekiah's speech in vv. 7–8 expresses that the Assyrians are a serious, but not irresistible, threat to Jerusalem. Hezekiah's omission of Sennacherib's PN in v. 7 suggests a deliberate avoidance of the Assyrian emperor's distinctive identity, while by way of contrast YHWH our God in v. 8 is personally named and noted for having a personal and special relationship with the people. The mighty Assyrian army is disparagingly referred to as "all the horde that is with him" (v. 7), and Sennacherib's abilities are minimized to the finitude of two short words—זרוע בשר "human flesh"—while YHWH's provisions in the same sentence overwhelm with five words (v. 8). The theme of help in v. 8a functions in part as a comparative allusion to the Ahaz–Assyria passage in 2 Chr 28:16–21; whereas the Assyrians successfully oppressed the Judahites and Ahaz's dependence on Assyria proved futile, the empire is disgracefully defeated at the gates of Jerusalem and Hezekiah's dependence on YHWH is rewarded—in both cases, Assyria is depicted as a tyrannical power intent on bringing trouble to Judah. In vv. 1–8 overall, Hezekiah and the people's perspective of the Assyrians undergoes a subtle transformation (note also that all the while, the Assyrians themselves have not significantly changed). The empire is increasingly lowered from being perceived as a determined conqueror (vv. 1–2) to being an imperial, but not indefeatable, force still under the sovereign rule of YHWH (vv. 3–5) to being a brute, human enemy fatally opposed to YHWH (vv. 6–8). Meanwhile, as Assyria's ideological position lowers, Jerusalem's rises, heightening the tension in the narrative.

With the new scene in v. 9, Sennacherib is clearly depicted as a military and ideological antagonist to Judah by way of an allusion back to Hezekiah's rhetorical slant of the Assyrian army and the narrator's select terminology. The focus of the message delivery scene on the source (in contrast to the deliverer) of the message in vv. 10–15 renders a sense of Sennacherib and his great army as being psychologically near, though actually in part physically distant. Sennacherib's message exposes his beliefs—he never directly acknowledges YHWH as God, or even as a god; he avoids use of the PN YHWH; and he considers "YHWH our God" to be only a construct in the mind of Hezekiah. At the same time, Sennacherib demonstrates an exaggerated perspective of himself and of the power of Assyria, evoking a common aNE *topos* where the reader is to expect the downfall of the hubristic Assyrian king and his forces.

The response of Hezekiah and Isaiah in v. 20 reflect the serious effect that the psychological and military belligerency of the Assyrian leaders has had on the Jerusalemites (cf. v. 18). Verse 21 brings a reversal in the battle, as YHWH sends (שלח) his own messenger/angel to defeat Sennacherib's forces; the use of שלח contrasts with Sennacherib's sending (שלח) of his servants to attempt to conquer Jerusalem in v. 9.

In vv. 22–23, Sennacherib is identified with both PN and title. Consistent with the select and meaningful use of PNs and titles in this narrative, such usage here also conveys consequential meaning: Sennacherib is fully identified in person and position, and thus is recognized as fully defeated as well.

The Reign of Manasseh (2 Chronicles 33:1–20)

The Assyrians only feature in one verse, v. 11, in this chapter. However, it is the pivotal verse in the chiastic structure of 2 Chr 33:1–20, and the details in this verse convey meaning.

To begin, where a secular perspective would have viewed the Assyrian leaders as controlling the action, the narrative here makes it clear that YHWH is the primary actor. The phrase "the commanders of the army of the king of Assyria" is an unusually unwieldy construction and may be an innerbiblical allusion to Isa 10:8 ("Are not my commanders all together kings?"). Further, the phrase is syntactically in a medial position between YHWH and the recipient Manasseh (clearly marked as such by the DDO, את־), reflecting the instrumental role of the Assyrian leaders.

The Assyrians employ חחים, "hooks," and נחשתים, "bronze [bindings]," in capturing the the Judahite king, creating an unavoidable innerbiblical allusion with 2 Kgs 19:28//Isa 37:29 in which YHWH uses the Assyrian captivity device of hooks against the Assyrians themselves. More generally in Ezekiel, YHWH uses hooks as punishment to his enemies (Ezek 19:4, 9; 29:4; 38:4), and echoes of these passages may also have been present for the post-exilic audience of Chronicles. Through allusions to both passages, the reminder is of YHWH's mastery over such conquests.

While a precise historical explanation for the destination of בבל (instead of the Assyrian capital city of Nineveh at the time) remains indefinite, there is a literary intimation of the wider shift in Chronicles from Assyria to Babylonia as the archetypal imperial enemy. After 2 Chr 33:11, Assyria no longer explicitly appears in Chronicles, and Babylon is the next world power to rise—with language and content reminiscent of this verse.

On the one hand, the Assyrian participation in an event of consequence here is not denied, as reflected in their appearance in the pivot of 2 Chr 33:1–20. On the other hand, the Assyrians feature only in the pivot and not elsewhere in the passage, demonstrating the limited power granted to them. The Assyrians arrive at a critical juncture in events, perform their duty, and then disappear from the purview of the narrative, literally becoming history and no more.

It is also worth observing that the Assyrians do *not* feature in 2 Chr 33:1–20 with regard to supposedly required religious elements of the Assyrian cultus and possible "anti-Assyrian" or "pro-Assyrian" positions.

A LAST COMPARATIVE LOOK AT THE CHARACTERIZATION OF THE ASSYRIANS IN KINGS AND CHRONICLES

Some general observations comparing the characterization of the Assyrians in Kings and Chronicles are apropos here. In Kings, with its detailed, predominantly narratival-linear approach, the Assyrians occupy more space on the page and receive more explicit description in comparison to Chronicles, the style of which appears more succinct and the literary structures that include the Assyrians more rigorous as form contributes meaning where words might not—and thus the Assyrians are sparingly explicitly referred to in Chronicles apart from 2 Chr 32, but the theologically and structurally profound contexts in which they appear communicate beyond mere words and call for deeper engagement and analysis of the texts. Likely the differences in circumstances and theological development between the exilic and post-exilic periods contributes in part to these general differences in the books' styles. The exilic audience was closer to the events and thus better served by straightforward accounts and more political-religious details; the post-exilic audience was closer to the restoration of the temple and the people in the land, and so details concerning either of those topics were of especial interest to the Chronicler. As well, the Chronicler had the opportunity for more retrospective contemplation of events than did the Kings author, thus he presents subtler, complex, and theologically thoughtful allusions and literary structures.

Kings' attention to both sides of the divided monarchy does explain on a practical level much of those books' wider interest in Assyria, whether it is recounting the Assyrian involvement in the reigns of the later kings of Israel and the nation's downfall or tellingly avoiding or minimizing the Assyrian presence in the reigns of influential kings.[1] While the Kings omission and minimization of Assyria in the accounts of select kings is consistently an evident prioritization of the subaltern narrative, ideology, and values over the imperial metanarrative that the Assyrians would have attempted to impose on Israel and Judah, the Chronicles absence of Assyria is less marked because of its already streamlined focus on the southern kingdom and its nuanced and narratologically sophisticated defiance of Assyria's influence in the references, details, and motivations that the authors chose to bring to the fore (or, likewise, leave in the background). Having said this, there remain three major subjects for which both books include the Assyrians, and thus lend themselves to worthwhile comparison: the Assyrian exile, Ahaz's reign, and Hezekiah's reign.

The Assyrian exile, in both role and depiction, differs between the two books. In Kings, the Assyrian exile basically serves as a theological-parenetic example by Dtr^1 to future, obviously pre-Dtr^2/pre-exilic generations. Hence, the Kings account of the Assyrian exile is lengthy, detailed, and dramatic in 2 Kgs 17. This is in contrast to the absence of such an account in Kings for the Babylonian exile, which is presented relatively straightforwardly and without theological reflection. While this might seem surprising at first, it is easily explained by the fact that the Babylonian exile did not allow the same level of hope for survival for Dtr^2 that the Assyrian exile did for Dtr^1. Thus, in Kings, the Assyrian exile stands independent of the Babylonian exile as a costly and profound warning to the Judeans. There is no literary advantage to placing the Assyrian exile out of chronological sequence with the rest of the regnal accounts, and so it follows directly after the reigns of Ahaz and Hoshea.

In Chronicles, the Assyrian exile serves a wholly different purpose. It is essentially an anticipation of the Babylonian exile ahead, and as such, it helps link the genealogical history at the beginning of Chronicles[2] with the Babylonian exile and Persian-era restoration at the end. This is indicated structurally in the MT by the conclusion of 1 Chr 5, which is 5:41 (= 6:15 in LXX and most English translations) and the first clear mention of the Babylonian exile in Chronicles. Also, similar vocabulary, phrases, and themes link the two-verse account of the Assyrian exile in 1 Chr 5:25–26 to the longer and more vivid account of the Babylonian exile and its hopeful resolution under Cyrus and Persia in 2 Chr 36:13b–23. While for Kings'

---

1. Regarding the latter, see Appendix 3.

2. This is an ingenious move on the part of the Chronicler, in that this maintains a sense of chronological order while effectively placing his brief account of the Assyrian exile at the beginning of the book.

exilic audience, the aftermath of the Assyrian exile was more hopeful, for the Chronicles' post-exilic audience, hope had emerged through Cyrus. The Assyrian exile is a mild foreshadowing of the more egregiously-rendered Babylonian exile, and the prosperity-unfaithfulness-exile pattern of both exiles is more pronounced for the Babylonian exile—partly because, by a similar extreme under which the Judeans experienced the Babylonian exile, they also experienced the hope of return under the Persians. The resolution of the God of Israel's "stirring of the spirit" (את־רוח ... עור) of Assyran emperor Tiglath-Pileser III is not a similar action towards Babylonian emperor Nebuchadnezzar, but towards Persian emperor Cyrus (2 Chr 36:22) when he worshipfully proclaims the name of YHWH and decrees the restoration of the temple and people to Jerusalem.³ Thus, Chronicles can afford to recognize the depth of the Babylonian exile's tragedy and the Judahites' contribution to that—because virtually in the same breath (2 Chr 36:20–23, esp. here v. 20B), the Chronicler demonstrates his awareness of the hope of restoration that can arise even despite such formerly bleak difficulties. By way of comparison, the Assyrian exile in Chronicles is merely a precursor and anticipation of these things.

Another shared topic that includes the Assyrians is that of the reign of Ahaz in 2 Kgs 16 and 2 Chr 28. In both, the point is Ahaz's unfaithfulness towards YHWH. In Kings, Assyria is more complicit and influential in Ahaz's apostasy than in Chronicles, which makes a few subtle and noticably vague mentions of Assyria. This difference is best explained by the differing emphases of each book's account of Ahaz. Kings demonstrates more through the extent of Ahaz's political-religious decisions how he deserved punishment, while Chronicles presents more YHWH's evaluative punishment on Ahaz during that king's reign. Ahaz's actions are shown to have effect (albeit negative effect) in Kings; in Chronicles, Ahaz is depicted for the most part as having defeat after defeat. Since, during Ahaz's reign, Assyria participated more in Ahaz's deleterious actions than in his defeats, it is naturally featured more in the Kings account of Ahaz's reign than in the Chronicles one.

As restoration is a stronger theme in Chronicles than in Kings, so Chronicles devotes two additional chapters concerning Hezekiah's religious-cultic reforms to its Hezekiah Narrative. In confronting the degree to which Israel has fallen and Judah has become endangered, an allusion to the Assyrians is unavoidable (2 Chr 29:9) and helpful within the clear

---

3. עור ... את־רוח occurs only three times in Chronicles: 1 Chr 5:26; 2 Chr 21:16; and 2 Chr 36:22. Note that in all three cases the subject is "the God of Israel" or "YHWH" and he "stirred"/"aroused" the spirit of a foreign enemy that serves in each case as his agent of punishment or restoration towards his people.

boundaries of the YHWH-centric ideology that Hezekiah calls the people to re-espouse (2 Chr 30:6–9). The focus remains on the relationship between the Israelites/Judahites and YHWH in these chapters, and so Assyria's instrumental punitive-restorative role in these cases is emphasized by content stating explicitly this dynamic and by the relative minimization of Assyria's appearance in the text, even with its developing typologization in 2 Chr 30:6–9.

Far more comparison is to be seen between the Kings and Chronicles accounts of the Assyrian attack on Jerusalem (2 Kgs 18–20; 2 Chr 32). However, contrary to popular scholarly comparative literary approaches to these two accounts, the differences are not to be reckoned so much between the Kings and Chronicles accounts as linear readings, but rather between the Kings account as primarily linear and the Chronicles account as primarily chiastic. In this way, the two accounts read entirely differently, with the Kings narrative recounting the details of the events, emphasizing the issues of trust and lordship, and presenting the Assyrians conveniently along the way as these things unfold. As a result, the Assyrians are characterized through multiple angles and techniques—in the past, from hundreds and thousands of miles away, at the gates of Jerusalem, through writing, through messengers, in various languages, through their own words, through Hezekiah's words, through the words of Isaiah, through the narrator's words, through circumstances, in the future. In Chronicles, the same events are condensed to one simple, but highly important point around which all the remainder of the narrative is shaped: YHWH is sovereign and remains in control in the midst of a battle between Sennacherib's servants and YHWH's servant, Hezekiah. All else in the passage effectively serves this message, and so, while the chiasmus develops and emphasizes numerous details about the Assyrians and their approach towards the Jerusalemites and YHWH, in comparison to the details concerning the Assyrians in 2 Kgs 18–20, the details about the Assyrians in the 2 Chr 32 read as much more secondary and incidental.

Finally, I would like to note that, from a yet broader perspective, both Kings' and Chronicles' various portrayals of the Assyrians contribute to the biblical-theological view of human kingship. The portrayals in the Historical Books tend to explore with nuance and depth-of-character the issues and internal states of the Israelite and Judahite kings with regard to the evaluations of their reigns and the ideal standards of human kingship and its place in relation to YHWH and the people. By way of contrast, the Assyrians kings, on these issues, are depicted in Kings and Chronicles with broader brushstrokes. On the one hand, elaboration on the Assyrian emperor's internal condition and relationship with YHWH is generally unattended to;[4] on the other, the expressions and dangers of human kingship when the institution moves beyond appropriate boundaries (in particular, worship of and service to YHWH) are shown in bold relief, a natural demonstration of the negative extremes that human kingship can develop (e.g., as an alluring temptation, idol, and "alternative" to YHWH; a devastating, out-of-control superhuman power that must be contained or destroyed; oppression and tyranny; over-reliance on provisional leadership) when it dismisses the divine rulership of YHWH the King.[5]

The presence of the Assyrians in Kings and Chronicles hopefully has demonstrated itself to be a worthy and engaging topic for study and contemplation. In this work, we have considered the depiction of the Assyrians from atomic matters such as narratological alliteration and nuanced Assyrianisms to various levels of select vocabulary and phraseological usage to historical and interpretive debates to the inner workings of chiastic aspect and other poetic and narratological devices to overall observations and discursive discussion on the characterization of the Assyrians in Kings and Chronicles, and much, much more. And yet, where questions may remain or have arisen from the studies in this book, I would be glad, for it proves the sophistication and complexity of these texts and suggests the inexhaustible inquiries and discoveries that engagement with these texts offers. Though the Assyrians no longer roam the land, through the ancient Hebrews' apprehension of them in their sacred Scriptures, their influence (and "non-influence," from an imperialist perspective) lives on.

---

4. Obviously, this would partly be because it was widely understood that Assyrian kings did not pursue worship of YHWH. However, a close look at the internal character and relationship of an Assyrian emperor towards YHWH is of clear value in Isaiah. E.g., see Isa 10:5–19 and discussion in Hom, *Characterization of the Assyrians in Isaiah*, 36–44.

5. Many thanks to J. G. McConville, R. P. Gordon, and P. S. McClure for thought-provoking discussion regarding kingship in Deuteronomy–Kings. Also: McConville, *God and Earthly Power*, 126–29, 165–67, 172–73.

Appendix 1
The "Twenty Years" Reign of Pekah in 2 Kings 15:27

REGARDING THE FIGURE OF "twenty years" for the reign of Pekah, it seems to be a scholarly given that an actual official twenty-year reign for Pekah in Samaria is impossible.[1] For this reason, the length of Pekah's reign often is approached as "the first of the notorious chronological difficulties in the history of Israel and Judah from now until Hezekiah's time,"[2] and that Pekah's reign is the beginning of "the period [which] bristles with difficulties, both internal and external. It is here that the most baffling problems of Hebrew chronology are found."[3] Theories abound, the most commonly-cited ones being those of Thiele, Cook, and Oded. Tracing back to Lederer the basic idea that Pekah set up a rival kingdom commencing the same year as Menahem's ascent to the throne,[4] Thiele and Cook forward detailed arguments to that effect. Thiele proposes that Pekah's rival reign was in Gilead/Transjordan and possibly included a time of peace with Pekahiah, which earned him a high military post that Pekah subsequently exploited at an opportune time for the coup.[5] According to this theory, a later hand was not aware of the fact of Pekah's rival reign and attempted to synchronize subsequent reigns accordingly, with mixed results.[6] Cook asserts that the

---

1. Frequently observed, e.g. see Cook, "Pekah," 121–23; Wiseman, *1 and 2 Kings*, 256; Edwin R. Thiele, "Pekah to Hezekiah," *VT* 16 (1966) 88; and idem, *The Mysterious Numbers of the Hebrew Kings: A Reconstruction of the Chronology of the Kingdoms of Israel and Judah* (Exeter, UK: Pasternoster Press, 1965), 123, 124n6.

2. Gray, *1 and 2 Kings*, 626.

3. See Thiele, *Mysterious Numbers*, 118–19.

4. Carl Lederer, *Die biblische Zeitrechnung: vom Auszuge aus Agypten bis zum Beginne der babylonischen Gefangenschaft* (Speier: F. Kleeberger, 1888), 135–38.

5. Thiele, *Mysterious Numbers*, 124–26; idem, "Pekah to Hezekiah," 85–106.

6. Thiele, "Pekah to Hezekiah," 106.

northern kingdom was more clearly divided and that three kingdoms vied for a time: Judah, Israel, and Ephraim. When Pekah assumed the Samarian throne, then Gilead and the remnant of the north were reunited with Samaria, and thereafter Hosea uses "Ephraim" to denote the entirety of Israel (what was left of it, that is) and also resumes using it interchangeably, on occasion, with "Israel."[7] Kuan follows a similar trajectory, but proposes a syncronically earlier start for Pekah's rival reign, with an emphasis on the role of Rezin of Aram: Pekah seized the Transjordan and Galilee from Israel with the collaboration of Rezin and began his rival rule (albeit as "puppet" under Rezin) during the twilight years of Jeroboam II.[8] Along with Cook and Thiele, Kuan supports a start date of 752 BCE for Pekah's rival reign; however, Kuan emphasises the synchronism of Pekah's reign with part of that of Jeroboam II.[9] With a slight departure from all these, Oded suggests that Pekah "ruled over northern Transjordania on behalf of the king of Israel, cut his ties with Samaria and, voluntarily or perforce, surrendered to Rezin northern Transjordania, in return for being placed on the throne in Samaria."[10] It appears that Oded hypothesizes that Pekah had a governor-like jurisdiction over northern Transjordania under the rule of Samaria. Pekah then rebelled and submitted to Rezin of Damascus instead—apparently in order to secure the Samarian throne for himself at the cost of relinquishing northern Transjordania to Rezin. Hobbs criticizes the persistent contradictions of these theories with the text (e.g., 15:27 clearly states that Pekah's twenty-year reign was in Samaria) and questions why such "partisan" dating on behalf of Pekah would have been in the records used by the Kingly historian.[11] Wiseman appears to uphold the possibility that Pekah led a rival faction (in a grassroots manner similar to the situation of Omri

7. Cook, "Pekah," 133–34. Thiele later proposes Assyrian evidence to support this notion, observing that Tiglath-Pileser III uses "Samaria" for the domain of Menahem but "Bit Humri" for that of Pekah. Edwin R. Thiele, "Coregencies and Overlapping Reigns Among the Hebrew Kings," *JBL* 93 (1974) 195. See *ANET*, 283a, 284a.

8. Jeffrey Kah-Jin Kuan, *Neo-Assyrian Historical Inscriptions and Syria-Palestine: Israelite/Judean-Tyrian-Damascene Political and Commercial Relations in the Ninth-Eighth Centuries BCE* (Alliance Bible Seminary: Hong Kong, 1995), 127–33.

9. See ibid., esp. 127, 128, 132–33. Lederer, *Die biblische Zeitrechnung*, 135–36, may allow for this in that he highlights that Jeroboam II's death and Menahem's reign fall on the same year (749, supposedly). Lederer also asserts that Menahem must have had a power base established *before* Jeroboam II's death, and that Pekah was an opponent of Menahem's *"von Anfang."* It is not clear whether Lederer meant the outset of Menahem's official reign, or the outset of Menahem's "power base" in Israel. If the later, then Lederer, as well as Kuan, perceives Pekah's power and/or reign to have begun during Jeroboam II's later years.

10. Oded, "Historical Background," 162–63.

11. Hobbs, *2 Kings*, 201.

and Tibni after Zimri's suicide, 1 Kgs 16:15–22), but he does not support that the rival faction reached the level of a distinct kingdom and reign.[12] Another theory is that Pekah began his rival reign after Menahem began his own, then after Pekah assumed the Samarian throne, he back-dated his "official" commencement (this was the initial conclusion of Thiele, though he has since abandoned it.[13] Reade makes the novel suggestion that Pekah is the same person as Pekahiah.[14] Obviously, Reade's theory poses numerous difficulties (such as how the Kingly author came to mistake one person as two—and moreover, as one person who apparently served, assassinated, and succeeded himself!), none of which is addressed.

Any serious reading of Kings as literature must consider that the numbers in Kings may serve an ideological purpose. This is not to deny possible direct historical referents, but it is to question whether the Kingly author prioritizes recording precise linear temporal data (which, it should be noted, is more often a modern Western emphasis than an aNE one)[15] or ideological representation. As Provan puts it in the "Introduction" to his commentary on 1 and 2 Kings,

> It has long been recognized by scholars, for example, that certain names in the MT have been deliberately corrupted, apparently in order to express disgust for them . . . and that the large numbers of the MT are not necessarily to be understood as actual historical numbers. The use of smaller numbers also raises questions, however. The immediate successors of kings who receive news of impending judgment on their royal house, for example, characteristically reign for "two years" in Kings (1 Ki 15:25; 16:8; 22:51; 2 Ki 21:19). Are we really being told exactly how long they reigned, or are we to see this as an example of narrative art, linking these kings together and inviting reflection upon them as a group? And what are we to make of the highly schematic ending to the book, where the last four kings of Judah are described as reigning successively for three months; eleven years; three months; and eleven years (2 Ki 23:31—24:20)? One wonders whether some of the attempts to resolve the enormous problems connected with the chronology of the MT Kings—e.g. E. R. Thiele, *The Mysterious Numbers of the Hebrew Kings* . . .— would have been quite so tortuous if the scholars concerned had

---

12. Wiseman, *1 and 2 Kings*, 256–57, 256n2.
13. Thiele, "Pekah to Hezekiah," 88–89.
14. Reade, "Mesopotamian Guidelines," 4–6, 8; note also 6n15.
15. See Hobbs, *2 Kings*, xl–xli.

paused to ask how the various numbers concerned were *meant* to be taken.[16]

In the case of 15:27, "twenty years" may denote an actual length of twenty years and/or suggest a comparison with other kings who are attributed the same length or comparable ones. One must also consider the synchronizations in 15:27, 32; 16:1. The author may have employed the synchronizations as a way of demonstrating the overall unity of the two kingdoms' histories and, implicitly, YHWH's purposes in history.[17] Obviously, the synchronizations may reflect actual dates as well. Note also that "twenty" occurs frequently at the beginning of Kings regarding details of Solomon's reign.

The only other such proposal I am aware of (beyond that of Provan) is that of Hughes, which is problematic in its assumptions and conclusions. Pekahiah and Pekah's stated reigns of 10 (in the LXX^{AL}) and 20 and are described with "schematic round numbers," both of which involve "exactly proportional" schematic increases—albeit, in inverse directions—between actual and "rounded" figures.[18] While identification of these figures as "round numbers" comports reasonably with the ideological nature of this literature, Hughes' assumption that the figure of "two years" may not also be a "round number" betrays a misunderstanding of how numbers may be used in the Bible. As well, the assertion that the figures for Pekahiah and Pekah are "exactly proportional" involves too many exceptions to evidence a solid or deliberate relationship posited between figures. If anything, these very specific figures *may* provide *one* example of ancient historians preferring proportions of five.

In conclusion, the most sensible interpretation regarding Pekah's reign of "twenty years" in 2 Kgs 15:27 is that the figure is ideological, possibly suggesting a comparison with other temporally-immediate kings (esp. Menahem and Pekahiah, cf. 15:17, 23) or an irony with the more YHWH-worshipping, prosperous, healthy reign of Solomon at the beginning of 1 Kings.

---

16. Provan, *1 and 2 Kings*, 18–19.

17. On this possibility, I happen to agree with Reade, "Mesopotamian Guidelines," 6.

18. The proportions perceived by Hughes are 2 (actual): 10 (rounded, LXX^{AL}) for Pekahiah; and 4 (actual): 20 (rounded) for Pekah. See Jeremy Hughes, *Secrets of the Times: Myth and History in Biblical Chronology*, JSOTSup 66 (Sheffield: Sheffield Academic Press, 1990), 201, 205.

Appendix 2
Diagram for the Relational Complex in 2 Chronicles 30:6–9

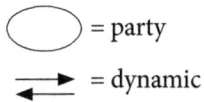 = party

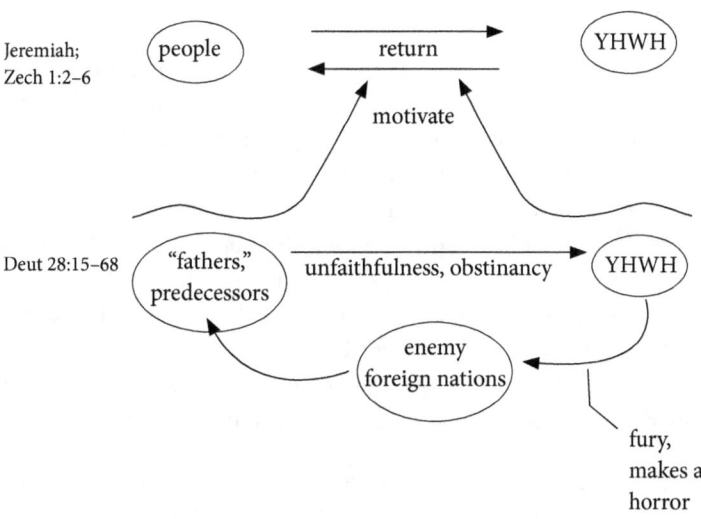 = dynamic

Appendix 3
The Absence and Minimization of Assyria in Kings and Chronicles (1 Kings 16:21–28; 16:29—22:40; 19:16–17; 2 Kings 9–10; 14:23–29; 21:1–18; 21:19–26; 22:1—23:30; 2 Chronicles 33:21–25; 34–35)

OMRI'S REIGN (1 KINGS 16:21-28)

THE ACCOUNT OF OMRI's reign in 1 Kgs 16:21–28 evades any mention of Assyria (and Chronicles does not present Omri's reign at all, let alone any Assyrian presence or influence during Omri's reign). Historically, this may seem surprising, given Omri's evident political impact, which was recognized internationally and for generations to come. The Mesha Inscription from Moab describes Omri as a long-time oppressor of that nation,[1] and several Assyrian emperors' royal accounts refer to Israel as the "house of Omri" (*bīt-ḫumrî* / *bīt-ḫumria*).[2] However, the Kings author refers to none of this. Instead, the formal description of Omri's reign highlights 1) the humble establishment of Samaria as a city and capital; and 2) the thus-far superlative evil committed by the Israelite king.[3] The only other distinctive

---

1. See discussion in van der Deijl, *Protest or Propaganda*, 304–39, esp. 310, 338–39.

2. The reigns of Shalmaneser III, Tiglath-Pileser III, and Sargon II all use this epithet. E.g., see COS 2: 267, 268, 270, 286, 288, 291, 292, and 297. For further discussion regarding the variants of Omri's name in Akkadian, see Ran Zadok, *On West Semites in Babylonia During the Chaldean and Achaeenian Periods: An Onomastic Study* (Jerusalem: H. J. & Z. Wanaarta, 1977), 148–49, section 11250 and esp. 306, the note regarding section 11250.

3. This is also well-put by Provan, *1 and 2 Kings*, 129:

factor presented regarding Omri's reign are the reports preceding the main body of the account of his reign (1 Kgs 16:16–19, 21–22); they describe the bloodshed and factionalism surrounding Omri's rise to the throne. Again, his international conquests and relations—including anything that might involve Assyria—are not a priority to the text. In this, the Kings author demonstrates an ideology that expresses itself in a metanarrative that distances itself from then-popular perceptions of power and value regarding Moab, the Israelite king himself, and likely also the expanding Assyrian empire. Thus, one may see that, despite pressures from multiple sources that would have wielded and applied dominating presence and power, the biblical author maintains his traditional Yahwistic vision, values, and standards.

AHAB'S REIGN (1 KINGS 16:29—22:40)

The account of the reign of Ahab in Kings reports several events, ranging from the personal to the public. On the subject of battles and international relations, there is an emphasis on Israel's on-again/off-again relationship with Aram (and the consequences thereof) with considerable ink spilt describing, in particular, two separate battles between Ahab and Ben-Hadad along with the prophetic voice commenting on those events. The biblical historical accounts do not give attention to any other battles during Ahab's reign. However, the Assyrian accounts—most famously, the Kurkh Monolith[4]—record a great battle at Qarqar that involved both Ben-Hadad and Ahab as part of the leadership of a coalition of eleven kings:

> I departed from the city of Arganâ. I approached the city of Qarqar. I razed, destroyed and burned the city of Qarqar, his royal city. 1,200 chariots, 1,200 cavalry, (and) 20,000 troops of Hadad-ezer (*Adad-idri*) of Damascus; 700 chariots, 700 cavalry, (and) 10,000 troops of Irhulēni, the Hamathite; 2,000 chariots, (and) 10,000 troops of Ahab, the Israelite (*Sir'alāia*); 500 troops of Byblos; 1,000 troops of Egypt; 10 chariots (and) 10,000 troops of the land of Irqanatu (Irqata); 200 troops of Matinu-ba'al of

---

The only event of Omri's reign that is described is his purchase of the hill of Samaria and his building of the new northern capital there. His life as king, too, is simply subsumed under the heading "idolater" (vv. 25–26). He took the throne; he sinned; he died. Almost everything else (and extra-biblical evidence suggests there was quite a bit) is unimportant.

4. See K. Lawson Younger, "Kurkh Monolith," *COS* 2: 261; and discussion in Shigeo Yamada, *The Construction of the Assyrian Empire: A Historical Study of the Inscriptions of Shalmaneser III (859–824 BC) Relating to His Campaigns to the West*, CHANE (Leiden: Brill, 2000), 143–63.

> the city of Arvad; 200 troops of the land of Usanatu (Usnu); 30 chariots (and) [ ],000 troops of Adon-ba'al of the land of Šianu (Siyannu); 1,000 camels of Gindibu' of Arabia; [ ] hundred troops of Ba'asa, (the man) of Bīt-Ruhubi, the Ammonite — these 12 kings he took as his allies.
> They marched against me [to do] war and battle. . . .[5]

Not only does it appear that the battle of Qarqar truly occurred, but a close reading past the propagandistic tendencies of the Assyrian kingly annals along with an analysis of Shalmaneser III's subsequent victories and expansion limitations in Syria indicate that the anti-Assyrian coalition at that time was successful at impeding the advance of Shalmaneser.[6] And yet, the biblical accounts regarding Ahab do not present this victory or Assyria at all. The closest mention and best hint that such an event—or rather, such an alliance leading to such an event—could have occurred is in 1 Kgs 22:1 (TNIV): "For three years there was no war between Aram and Israel." Surprisingly, the Kings account is not interested here in massive battles with the empire—not even one which Ahab and his allies won. Israel's memory of Assyria is stubbornly subordinated to its memory of more intimate battles with neighbor Aram and the moral-ideological implications that accompanied those battles.

It is difficult to tell whether the Kings authors intended to subvert directly the Assyrian presence during Ahab's reign by not including Assyria in that account. What is clear is that the Kings authors were concerned with significant moral-ideological decisions made by Ahab regardless of the nature of the event (e.g., whether it be the unjust murder of one man or a military battle involving hundreds of thousands) and particularly those decisions that led to the demise of him and his lineage. In a way, whether intentional or not, the Kingly author's ability to perceive the reign of Ahab as independent of any significant influence by the Assyrians is already a subversion of the Assyrian empire's claim to sovereignty, influence, and conquest. This subaltern perspective continues to dominate, to the noticeable exclusion of the imperial metanarrative or any hint of its presence. Again, this was likely not the primary intent of the Kings author, but the related eschewing of any mention of Assyria's activity during the reign of Ahab—especially the battle of Qarqar—suggests an intentional effort on the part of the author to resist the imperial influence.

---

5. Younger, "Kurkh Monolith," *COS* 2: 263-64.

6. See Yamada, *Construction of the Assyrian Empire*, 163; and Younger, "Kurkh Monolith," 264n35.

While the subversion of the Assyrian empire appears to be an implicit action that is secondary to the author's primary purposes for the passage, by way of contrast, the narrative explicitly condemns Ahab's more intimate international relations—in particular, his marriage to Jezebel, the daughter of the Sidonian king (1 Kgs 17:30–33). Ahab's intermarriage with a Canaanite is understood to directly violate the traditional Yahwistic community's boundaries and their distinctive relationship with YHWH (e.g., Deut 7:3–6; 1 Kgs 11:1–6). It thus appears that the Kings author was more concerned with the community's own maintenance of their ideology, values, and identity than he was with an extermal entity (i.e., Assyria) attempting to suppress that ideology and related aspects of personhood.

JEHU'S REIGN (1 KINGS 19:16-17; 2 KINGS 9-10)

One generation and usurper after Ahab, Jehu reigns in Israel while Shalmaneser III continues as emperor over Assyria. The Kings account details Jehu's anointed calling under the prophet Elijah, his avenging destruction of the house of Ahab (along with Ahaziah of Judah), his annihilation of Baal worship in the land, his compromise with regard to righteousness and keeping the law of the LORD, and the reduction of the size of Israel at the hands of Hazael king of Aram (1 Kgs 19:16–17; 2 Kgs 9–10). Various aspects of Jehu's leadership at both the intra-national and international level come into play in the narrative, but Israel's dealings with Assyria is not one of them.

Meanwhile, the Black Obelisk of Shalmaneser of Assyria depicts Jehu of Israel in obesiance to the Assyrian emperor along with a caption briefly describing the tribute Jehu gave to Shalmaneser.[7] As well, previous recensions, along with that of the Black Obelisk, designate Jehu as of "the house of Omri,"[8] which recalls the former political power of Israel under that king. So, the depiction of Jehu here is not necessarily entirely negative.[9] However, this

---

7. As translated by K. Lawson Younger, "Black Obelisk," *COS* 2: 270: "I received the tribute of Jehu of Bīt-Humrî: silver, gold, a golden bowl, a golden goblet, golden cups, golden buckets, tin, a staff of the king's hand, javelins."

8. In addition to the Black Obelisk, see K. Lawson Younger, "Annals: Calah Bulls," *COS* 2: 267; and idem., "Annals: Marble Slab," *COS* 2: 268.

9. Nadav Na'aman, "Jehu Son of Omri: Legitimizing a Loyal Vassal by His Lord," in *Ancient Israel and Its Neighbors*, vol 1: *Interaction and Counteraction: Collected Essays* (Winona Lake: Eisenbrauns, 2005), 13–15, suggests that the epithet was Shalmaneser's way of expressing his favour towards Jehu and legitimizing the usurper's reign (and, relatedly, his submissive policy towards Assyria). See also discussion and other interpretive possibilities in Younger, "Annals: Calah Bulls," 267n5, especially that: "The Assyrians often denoted countries by the name of the founder of the ruling dynasty at the time of their first acquaintance with it (e.g., 'Bīt Bahiani, Bīt Agusi, Bīt Humri'),

element, along with the remainder of the depiction on the obelisk, serves to elevate the image of the empire. As Younger observes, the inclusion of Jehu's submission, representing the southwesternmost part of the empire, along with that of Sūa of Gilzānu, representing the easternmost part, "creates a pictorial merism stressing the gigantic extent of Shalmaneser's Assyrian empire."[10] Thus, while Jehu is featured by Assyria in order to express the breadth and expanse of the Assyrian empire, the biblical accounts are completely silent with regard to this politically strategic relationship. Smaller, less powerful kingdoms and their impact on Israel are acknowledged (e.g., Aram in 2 Kgs 10:32–33), but the Assyrian giant is not allowed to carry her boast or even her presence into the biblical accounts. Note that the biblical text is explicit in its censure of Jehu's failure by way of the persistent worship of the golden calves (2 Kgs 10:29, 31), but his alliance with Shalmaneser—which surely also would have been perceived as negative by the biblical authors—receives no comment.

As far as Kings (and Chronicles) are concerned, the Assyrian empire during the reign of Jehu had no significant influence (or is allowed none)—in this case, the value and consequences of that powerful political alliance pales in comparison to internal strife and more geographically-localized moral-ideological compromise, according to the values and perspective of the biblical author. The Assyrian monument may use Jehu to demonstrate the empire's greatness, but the Israelite literature ignores Shalmaneser to focus instead on other aspects under the kingdom's autonomy. Again, while it is difficult to tell to what degree subversion of the empire is intentional in the biblical accounts, the fact of the matter is that it is clearly present and that, in light of the historical circumstances, such a sustained perspective without inclusion of the Assyrian presence or influence evidences a remarkable depth, awareness, and ability on the part of the biblical authors to persist and therefore preserve the distinctive ideology and metanarrative of Yahwistic Israel.

It is also worth noting that, while the biblical authors did not *explicitly* counter the imperial colonizers, they did explicitly describe and appear to favour a more localized subversion of oppressive leadership and power. Ahab, Jezebel, and their supporters technically may not have been colonizers, but in the biblical authors' perspective, their imposition of their religious culture and values against what was understood to be the indigenous Yahwistic faith and values—to the point that Ahab and Jezebel had the innocent Naboth murdered for the sake of taking his Yahwistically-granted

---

regardless of which dynasty was currently in power."

10. Ibid., 269.

inheritance (1 Kgs 21)—renders them colonizers on a regional level. Such oppression may be understood as more egregious than that of an externally-imposed empire, since a more localized oppression that is borne out of the nation itself can be more immediate, more intimate, more threatening—and because of all this—makes it more damaging and difficult to disentangle oneself from the regional colonizer's ideology. Indeed, part of the power of the story of Jehu's rise in Kings (1 Kgs 19:16-18; 2 Kgs 9) is that the traditional Yahwistic ideology lived on despite Ahab and Jezebel's tyranny and that it both outlived and triumphed over those oppressors and their imposed perspective. This noteworthy elevation of the suppressed Yahwistic ideology is depicted as not simply a happenstance of the vicissitudes of history, but also as an intentional subversion both by YHWH (which the narrative introduces about halfway through the section that includes Ahab's reign and well before Jehu is introduced in the overall narrative, see 1 Kgs 19:16-17) and the people (2 Kgs 9, esp. vv. 1–10, 13, 18–19, 32–33; 2 Kgs 10:15).[11]

JEROBOAM II'S REIGN (2 KINGS 14:23-29)

Jeroboam II held the longest reign of all the kings of the northern kingdom. Though he was evidently a politically successful king, the account is notably brief concerning his achievements. Indeed, it presents Jeroboam II's success in a somewhat subversive manner—it was not simply Jeroboam II's work, but YHWH's decision and work though the agency of Jeroboam II. It is, in fact, the direction and authoritative rule of YHWH that is literally and literarily the central point (2 Kgs 14:25–27) of the pericope. This is preceded by an introductory evaluative summary of Jeroboam II's reign as a moral-religious failure (רע, "evil"; 2 Kgs 14:24) and preceded by a concluding comment on his remarkable recovery of former Israelite territory (2 Kgs 14:28). The overall effect is to recognize the most salient accomplishments of Jeroboam II's governance, but to also contextualize it within the broader cosmic perspective of traditional Yahwistic ideology.

Meanwhile, the absence of Assyria in the passage suggests another subversion. The puzzling recovery by Jeroboam II of territory as far north as Hamath is best explained (bearing in mind the current lack of documentation in scholarship for that period and region) by either a power vacuum in

---

11. Regarding the subversion by the people, see also perhaps 2 Kgs 10:4–7, 9–11, 24–27, though these responses may have been motivated by a fear of Jehu—given his death threats to the remaining palace and temple staff in the interest of dispensing with the previous regional "colonizers."

the peripheral regions of the empire or a submissive and cooperative alliance to Assyria. The former explanation has been popular because a conspicuous power vacuum did exist in the Assyrian empire in the early eighth century BCE.[12] That said, it is also possible that Assyria still held enough influence in Syria that Jeroboam II's conquest of Damascus "was conducted with the assent of the Assyrian kings."[13] Tadmor explains the political rationale for this on the part of a relatively weak, but still influential Assyrian empire:

> In the light of Urartean interference in the North-Syrian league, it is no wonder that the King of Assyria had to accept the *status quo* in Southern Syria and to acknowledge Israelite suzerainty over Aram. A larger Israel, which could not dispute Assyrian influence in the area of Carchemish and the Upper Euphrates, was much safer than the revival of Aramaean hegemony, which would form a single block of northern and southern Syrian states.[14]

Reinforcing the possibility that Jeroboam II secured Hamath and Damascus because of an alliance with the Assyrian empire is Aster's in-depth analysis of the Nimrud Wine Lists.[15] In particular, NWL 4 may reflect that Samarian emissaries regularly visited the royal palace as part of the *ṣerāni*, who annually presented themselves for a generously hosted visit in the capital palace. Moreover, Aster finds that the period of these Samarian emissaries' visits "corresponds largely to the beginning of the reign of Jeroboam II (790–749)."[16] These visits would have been a key part of the Assyrian strategy to communicate, ingratiate, inculcate, and centralize Neo-Assyrian imperial ideology to peripheral territories. As Aster puts it:

> To understand the process of transmission of Assyrian claims of empire to vassal states, it is important to understand how the *ṣerāni* were treated in Assyria. As Postgate notes, they were fed at the state's expense and were given presents of clothing and

---

12. William W. Hallo, "From Qarqar to Carchemish: Assyria and Israel in the Light of New Discoveries," *The Biblical Archaeologist* 23/2 (1960) 33–61, see 44, 46. Despite the claim of Haran, "Rise and Decline," 279, that Jeroboam II's expansion would have been most likely when "the region was *completely* free of any Assyrian influence," see Cogan and Tadmor, *2 Kings*, 163–64.

13. Hayim Tadmor, "Azriyau of Yaudi," *SH* 8 (1961) 232–71, see 240.

14. Ibid., 240–41. Tadmor adds that this situation of Aramaean hegemony was exactly what had preceded Jeroboam "in the latter half of the ninth and early years of the eighth century."

15. Shawn Zelig Aster, "Israelite Embassies to Assyria in the First Half of the Eighth Century," *Biblica* 97/2 (2016) 175–98.

16. Ibid., 189.

shoes for their journeys, as well as silver and gold rings. Not only the ṣerāni themselves but also their servants received valuable gifts. These gifts were not part of the usual traditions of hospitality, but rather were intended by Assyria as incentives to the ṣerāni to undertake the journey again and to be punctual in the bringing of tribute. The incentives made the ṣerāni into eager tribute-bearers, who had a personal stake in promoting Assyrian royal ideology. Given sufficient incentives, the ṣerāni would convince their kingdoms to remain loyal to Assyria, and they would bring the tribute which was important to the Assyrian treasury. Thus, these ṣerāni would be turned into vehicles for the propagation of Assyrian claims of empire. . . .

The encounter in the Assyrian palaces was the most effective way of conveying this ideology to foreign kingdoms, and this profoundly influenced the elite of these states. . . . Sidall notes that although discussions of the diffusion of Assyrian royal ideology include "the reliefs on walls, stelae, cliff faces, sculpture and cylinder seals," "access to all of these media was not universal," and the empire aimed to convey royal ideology primarily to the elite of society who entered the palaces. . . . Morrow concludes that diplomatic contacts were the most important channel for communicating Assyrian claims of empire to Judah. Thus, the palace audiences emerge as the key vehicle leading to the knowledge of Assyrian royal ideology in the courts of client states, including Israel and Judah. Assyrian royal ideology, therefore, was known in the kingdom of Israel from the late ninth century and on through the early eighth century.[17]

In this way, the Assyrians attempted to convince the peripheral populations to embrace and adopt the imperial ideology, values, and interests. If Aster's analysis is correct, this was done during the time of Jeroboam II primarily through representatives of the peripheral populations. These representatives of the periphery were encouraged and expected to transition into representatives of the empire—it was a transition that was effectively imposed by the Assyrian imperial culture. In this sense, it was not a true liminal space, though one may posit that liminal space existed for those members of the periphery who had more freedom to wrestle with and negotiate between peripheral ideology and imperial ideology and what those ideologies claimed regarding identity.

As to the content of this Assyrian royal ideology in the late-ninth and early-eighth centuries, Aster forwards that:

17. Ibid., 181, 193.

> Assyrian royal ideology underwent limited changes in the course of the late ninth and eighth centuries, from the end of the reign of Shalmaneser III to the time of Tiglath-Pileser III. The central themes which remain constant included: the religious legitimacy of the king as leader of the Ashur cult (expressed by the epithets *šangu* and *iššiaku*); the king as military leader responsible for expanding the empire (*šarru dannu, šarru rabû, šar kiššati*); the universal nature of the empire; and the doctrine of Assyrian invincibility. Many of the motifs found in royal inscriptions of Adad-Nirari III are also found in those of the late eighth-century kings. These include the king going to war by the command of Ashur, and the enemy overwhelmed by the *melammu* of Ashur. In his discussion of "continuity and innovation" in ninth-century Neo-Assyrian royal ideology and in that of Adad-Nirari III, Sidall emphasizes the continuity of each of these kings with the themes and ideology of their predecessors. Each of these kings sought to portray themselves as part of a strong tradition of dynastic continuity. Expressions are modified to correspond to the particular achievements of each king, but there is no evidence of large-scale shifts in the ideology expression royal inscriptions.[18]

Thus, it appears that the Assyrian imperial ideology during the reign of Jeroboam II was generally consistent during that period as well as broadly consistent with the imperial ideology of the period which followed, that of Tiglath-Pileser III and the reigns described in 2 Kgs 15–16. At the same time, in our attention to the Kings account of Jeroboam II's reign, it should be noted that none of these Assyrian royal themes or motifs are present. One could construct a case for mimicry, for example, in that there are motifs of YHWH and Jeroboam II as leading and conducting warfare instead of Aššur or his Assyrian representative. However, the account of Jeroboam II in Kings does not present itself to be thematically different from previous accounts in Kings—in other words, the motifs of leadership, warfare, and so on in 2 Kgs 14:23–29 are best explained as simply a result of consistency with the themes and ideology of the whole of Kings. In maintaining that focus to the exclusion of Assyrian ideology, the Kings author may have intentionally allowed a natural, consequential countering or subversion of the empire's ideology. Still, it must be emphasized that such a subversion of Assyria and its ideology was a secondary, consequential result of a primary agenda to promote the traditional Yahwistic metanarrative and ideology, in this case with regard to the reign of Jeroboam.

18. Ibid., 193.

MANASSEH'S REIGN (2 KINGS 21:1-18)

Interestingly, Assyria is *not* mentioned at all in the Manasseh pericope in 2 Kgs 21:1-18. The absence of Assyria is especially striking in consideration of the clear historical circumstance of Manasseh's loyal vassalage to Assyria, as evidenced in the Assyrian inscriptions;[19] his imprisonment by Assyria, as recorded in 2 Chr 33:11-13, an incident and account of which the Kings author was surely aware; the mention in the passage of other foreign entities (i.e., the Amorites, v. 11; the former northern kingdom, v. 13; Egypt, v. 15); and according to some studies, the adoption of Assyrian gods and their culture under an imperialist requirement or more vague, imperialist cultural pressure to assimilate and gain more favor with the Assyrian empire during its apex.[20]

Concerning the last point, it has been demonstrated more recently that the Assyrian empire actually did not officially require vassals to adopt Assyrian religious practices and that, in fact, the gods and practices described in 2 Kgs 21:2-16 are much more descriptive of Canaanite, Sidonian, and Arabian religions, some parts of which had been present in the land long before the Israelites invaded.[21] However, it must be acknowledged that the pressure of assimilation to the powerful Assyrian empire must have had an effect on Manasseh's and the Judean people's preferences, including in the area of worship. What the effect was precisely is impossible to tell, but I would agree with McKay and Jones that probably some elements of Assyrian religion that had adopted earlier Canaanite practices were embraced more readily in Manasseh's Judah because of their acceptance by the empire's dominant religious culture.[22]

Meanwhile, the first three points remain concerning the evident impact of Assyria on Manasseh and the Kings author's international awareness,

---

19. See *ANET*, 291, 294.

20. Martin Noth, *The History of Israel*, 2nd ed. (London: Adam & Charles Black, 1960), 266, 272; John Bright, *A History of Israel*, 4th ed. (Louisville: Westminster John Knox Press, 2000), 312; Herrmann, *History of Israel*, 259-60. Consider also Hermann Spieckermann, *Juda unter Assur in der Sargonidenzeit* (Göttingen: Vandenhoeck & Ruprecht, 1982), 271-73.

21. For further discussion, see Cogan, *Imperialism and Religion*, 56, 84-85, 88; McKay, *Religion in Judah*, 25, 96-97; Cogan and Tadmor, *2 Kings*, 272; Jones, *2 Kings*, 592-96.

22. See Cogan, *Imperialism and Religion*, 88-95, esp. 95; McKay, *Religion in Judah*, 59; Jones, *2 Kings*, 595; somewhat Bright, *History*, 312n5. I agree with McKay, *Religion in Judah*, 59, that the indigenous cults gained popularity in Judah likely because of, to a degree, Assyrian cultural influence, but even more because of Judahite disillusionment with the Yahwistic cultus.

and they underscore the absence of Assyria in this passage. The narratival focus on Manasseh's apostasy remains at the fore throughout 2 Kgs 21:1–18, and the potential distractions of not only Manasseh's return and restoration to the LORD, but also the active engagement of the Assyrian empire during his reign are not permitted to confuse or cloud the literary message that the author was intent to communicate: Manasseh completely reversed the reforms of his father Hezekiah, and, as presented in 2 Kgs 21:1–18, provides an anticipatory literary foil to elevate the forthcoming reign, reforms, and character of his grandson Josiah.[23] Recalling that other foreign entities are named in 2 Kgs 21:1–18 while Assyria—which was evidently active and influential during that time—is not, suggests the powerful effect the mere mention of the empire would have on the narrative. The history and connotations (simply put, the "baggage") that would have accompanied an explicit or extensive implicit reference to Assyria would have been both too pagan and too significant to maintain the literary impact of the portrayal of Manasseh's apostasy and moral-ethical failures.

Thus, the activity of the empire is relegated to a mere and vague implication that ideologically situates Assyria under the sovereignty of YHWH: v. 14 implies that Assyria forms part—if not the entirety—of the "enemies" to whom the "remnant," which YHWH had previously defended (cf. 19:30–31), would be handed over as plunder and spoil. It is unclear to what degree Assyria is part of the "enemies" or if the events of 2 Chr 33:11–17 are implied, though the location of this implication within the pericope naturally alludes to that. In a deft subversion of Assyria during one of its seasons of strength, the narrative denies the empire significant acknowledgement and clearly places any possible existence of Assyria in this passage under the power of YHWH, for whom these enemies such as Assyria are simply instruments of his will.

And so, the Kings' Manasseh pericope is an instance of Assyria not being allowed a role in the narrative because its presence would distract too much from the biblical author's focus—in this case, a focus on the grave apostasy of Manasseh, which forms a literary contrast to the positive portrayal of Josiah while providing a religio-moral-ethical explanation for the eventual downfall of Judah (cf. 23:26; 24:3–4).

---

23. McKay, *Religion in Judah*, 26; Cogan and Tadmor, *2 Kings*, 271; Hobbs, *2 Kings*, 309.

AMON'S REIGN (2 KINGS 21:19-26)

Amon, son of Manasseh, had a brief reign of two years. The account of his reign in Kings is equally brief, presenting the distinctives of Amon's reign as 1) his moral-religious apostasy, continuing in the ways of his father Manasseh; and 2) the complex of murders related to his assassinations. Although both 1) and 2) evidently involved more details of a peculiar nature, the Kings author maintains a minimum of words and seems intent on reporting simply the facts without denying a complex historical event that had occurred (vv. 23-24). The result is to simply emphasize the negative reign of Amon and the state of chaos and factionalism among the leadership and people of Judah—all of which, the text strongly implies, resulted in his death. On this literary note, the reader has been poised to expect the worst to follow, which renders the success of Josiah's reign all the more striking and impressive.

Similar to the Kings account of Manasseh, the mention of Assyria is curiously missing from the account of Amon, and the reason is probably similar to that concerning the Manasseh account—that is, that Assyria had such a significant presence during the reign of Manasseh that explicit reference to it would communicate circumstances and an imperial presence that would distract from the literary intent of the passage. The literary intent of the passage is to convey the moral-religious failure of Amon and broken state of the kingdom of Judah at the eve of Josiah's reign. The consequences of human volition and the will of God are brought to the fore in the account; the influence of Assyria is not. In light of the historical fact of a strong Assyrian presence throughout most of the ancient Near East at that time, this is suggestive of an intentional disregard of the empire and its boastful influence, despite Assyria's dominance. Though Assyria may overshadow on the historical stage, on the ideological one here it is not allowed even a role.

Malamat suggests that Amon was assassinated because of a pro-Assyrian stance which was challenged by an anti-Assyrian contingent among the officials but reinforced by עַם־הָאָרֶץ ("the people of the land"):

> The murder of Amon was doubtless an anti-Assyrian repercussion of his foreign policy, since the Bible unequivocally presents him as a loyal satellite of the Assyrian regime....
>
> We may assume that the coup d'état in Jerusalem was aimed against the pro-Assyrian policy of Amon and that the conspirators wanted to join the general uprising against Ashurbanipal. However, upon the approach of the Assyrian army to Syria and Palestine and its initial successes against the rebels, those forces in Judah who wished to prevent a military encounter with

Assyria gained the upper hand. Thus a counter-revolution was achieved and the nobles, who had wished to throw off the yoke of Assyrian rule, were exterminated. It was a stitch in time, and it seems to have placated the Assyrians, for we hear of no punitive action being taken against Judah by their army.[24]

As we have seen above, it is not defensible that Kings *unequivocally* presents Manasseh—and, likewise, Amon—as loyal vassals of Assyria to the extent that Malamat presumes. However, his general point that Amon had a pro-Assyrian policy that was violently (and fatally, for Amon) countered by an anti-Assyrian faction which itself was countered by a broader pro-Assyrian population remains possible and worth considering. Building on Cho and Malamat, Kim suggests that "[w]hether Amon died simply because of his pro-Assyrian policy or because of the factional infighting, it was Judah's location within the Assyrian hegemony that resulted in the assassination of Amon and the killing of the assassins."[25] This broadens more subtly but just as relevantly the suggestion that Amon was dethroned and murdered as a result of a complication of imperialism that subaltern or transitional "colonies" may experience. In other words, Judah's transitional position within the Assyrian empire may have contributed to the end of Amon and the political disarray surrounding that. Having said that, one should bear in mind Amon's own role in choosing and navigating through the various options he had while Judah was in that transitional position. "The system" of the empire may have given Amon a disadvantage, but Amon himself still had consequential decisions of his own (both politically and moral-religiously) that helped shape his relations with his officers, the wider population of Judah, and Assyria and its leadership. And yet, to the extent that the empire did play a role in the self-destruction (or, at least, superficial self-destruction, if one gives more responsibility to imperial structures and pressures) of Judean leadership, the Kings author's suppression of Assyrian influence in Judean ideological history is even more pronounced.

---

24. See A. Malamat, "The Historical Background of the Assassination of Amon, King of Judah," *IEJ* 3 (1953) 26–29, quote from 26–27. See also Noth, *History of Israel*, 272; and Frank M. Cross, Jr. and David Noel Freedman, "Josiah's Revolt Against Assyria," *JNES* 12 (1953) 56–58, esp. 56. Malamat has been followed in this by others, e.g., Bright, *History of Israel*, 316; E. W. Nicholson, *Deuteronomy and Tradition* (Oxford: Basil Blackwell, 1967), 11; Eun Suk Cho, *Josianic Reform in the Deuteronomistic History: Reconstructed in the Light of Factionalism and Use of Royal Apology* (n. p.: YN Press, 2013; Kindle edition); Kim, *Decolonizing Josiah*, 217–18.

25. Kim, *Decolonizing Josiah*, 219.

JOSIAH'S REIGN (2 KINGS 22:1–23:30)

The account of Josiah in 2 Kgs 22:1–23:30 greatly minimizes the presence of Assyria in the narrative. Apart from one merely incidental mention of Assyria in 2 Kgs 23:29, Assyria is not mentioned anywhere in the account. While this situation is similar to that of the Kings accounts of Manasseh and Amon's reigns, the likely explanation for this phenomenon in the account of Josiah's reign is different if one considers the particular historical circumstances at that time. Whereas Manasseh and Amon operated under a still-powerful Assyrian empire, Josiah is shown in the Kings text to have instituted his seminal reforms as Assyrian influence was on a rapid decline.[26] Thus, in applying an imperialism-intent hermeneutic, the absence of Assyria in this passage is not so much because of a secondary concern on the part of the Kings author to minimize the distracting presence of a powerful Assyria, but more because of a historically actual, decreasing presence of Assyria on the Judean scene. In other words, there simply was less of Assyria around to distract from the historical circumstances and the text that reflects aspects of that.

This is not to deny, however, the likely historical role of Assyria in encouraging aspects of the foreign cults that were introduced into Judah, as seen during the reigns of Manasseh and Amon and inherited by Josiah's generation (2 Kgs 22:16–17; 23:4–16, 19–20, 24, 26). Further, Assyria's increasing absence would likely have encouraged Josiah in his reforms that reached even into the Assyrian provinces (Samaria, 2 Kgs 23:19–20)[27] and his confrontation towards Neco in Megiddo, a former Assyrian stronghold (cf. 2 Kgs 23:29–30). Clearly, the withdrawal of Assyrian power and presence in Palestine during Josiah's reign politically and geographically eased the path for Josiah to re-expand the kingdom and his activities. As Cross and Freedman articulate,

> Whether Josiah's action is taken as an open break with Assyrian authority or, as seems more likely, as an internal reorganization within the framework of nominal Assyrian suzerainty (i.e.,

---

26. The precise dates and subsequent synchronisms of reigns and events may be debated, but the general decline of the Assyrian empire and its change in leadership coinciding with the overall time of the rise and reforms of Josiah still indicates a historical correlation. For further discussion, see Cross and Freedman, "Josiah's Revolt," 56–58; Cogan and Tadmor, 2 Kings, 298; Jones, 1 and 2 Kings, 607.

27. The capital city of Samaria was, expectably, part of the territory reorganized by the Assyrians into the province of Samerina. As Simon Wiesgickl, "Vom Vasallenstaat zum ‚Informal Empire'. Postkoloniale Theorien und ihre Bedeutung für die alttestamentliche Exegese," BZ 59/1 (2015) 17–38 (26), observes, "Eroberte Städte wurden als Ausdruck assyrischen Herrschaftsanspruchs umbenannt."

maintaining the legal fiction of Assyrian control, since Josiah was a vassal king), it is clear that a drastic change in the Palestinian situation had taken place. Assyria was losing effective control both of Judah and of the northern provinces; at the same time Josiah was making good the ancient claim of the house of David to these territories.[28]

Unfortunately, as the text assesses, Josiah's increased confidence in the historical circumstances of his national reforms, the decrease of Assyria in his region, and a perceived need to counter Egyptian support to Assyria, still could not counter the sovereign will of YHWH (2 Kgs 23:26–27, 29–30).

On that point, 2 Kgs 23:29 has the book of Kings' last explicit reference to Assyria. "The king of Assyria" plays an unusually trivial narratological role as he is simply part of the circumstantial explanation for why Neco was headed north, and thus why Josiah made the decision—the precise nature of which the Kings author is not concerned to fully explain—to confront Neco in battle. Historically, Assyria's power was on the wane, so the threat was likely more felt from Egypt than Assyria at that juncture in time. Indeed, Neco did soon take control of the Levant (cf. 2 Kgs 23:33–35) despite his failed attempt in the north to conquer Haran.[29] Thus, perhaps the reduction of the Assyrian presence in the text to being merely an incidental explanation in v. 29 reflects and marks the departure of Assyria from the Judean scene. Both historically and literally, Assyria has fast faded from the ongoing story of Kings.

It should be noted that a few additional parallels have been suggested regarding the foreign cults described in the Kings account of Josiah and Assyrian religion. This is especially the case in Cogan and Tadmor's discussion of this passage (especially regarding the horses dedicated to the sun in 2 Kgs 23:11; the slaughtering of idolatrous people, cf. 2 Kgs 23:20).[30] While these correlations may have been historically possible, it is impossible to determine the exact origins and influences of various aspects of the foreign cults in 2 Kgs 23. Assyrian religion may have played a role in the development of these specific aspects, but just as well other ancient Near Eastern religions and regions evidenced many of these practices.[31] Interestingly, Cogan and

---

28. Cross and Freedman, "Josiah's Revolt," 57.

29. Yohanan Aharoni, Michael Avi-Yonah, Anson F. Rainey, and Ze'ev Safrai, *The Carta Bible Atlas*, 4th ed. (Jerusalem: Carta, 2002), 122.

30. Cogan and Tadmor, *2 Kings*, 288, 290.

31. For further discussion with regard to horses and worship specifically, one may begin with the commentary in Jones, *1 and 2 Kings*, 622–23.

Tadmor observe a distinctive of the community pledge in 2 Kgs 23:1–3 in the light of its contrast with Assyrian loyalty oaths:

> Now, the description of the entire community undertaking an oath of loyalty to YHWH is literarily similar to the descriptions of oath ceremonies in Assyria during the days of Sennacherib, Esarhaddon, and Ashurbanipal. So, for example, in order to insure the undisturbed transfer of rule from father to son, Ashurbanipal reports that his father "gathered the people of Assyria, young and old, from the upper and the lower seas, and had them take an oath by the gods and enforced the(ir) obligations." In addition, as has been shown in several studies, there is a distinct affinity between some of the curses which conclude the covenant in the book of Deuteronomy and those in the "vassal treaties" of Esarhaddon. . . . The loyalty oath in Sargonid Assyria concerned itself with the newly appointed successor and in this respect can be compared to the covenant undertaken by the people to protect the succession of Johoash (2 Kgs 11:17). But there is no parallel anywhere in the ancient Near East to an entire community swearing allegiance to its God as depicted in 2 Kgs 23:1–3. Josiah's act and the biblical concept of a covenant made between God and people remain unique.[32]

Finally, one must consider Kim's insightful suggestion that the discovery of the Book of the Law during Josiah's reign was a "the catalytic event that launched Josiah's reform and, at the same time, began the recovery of forgotten or overwritten 'inscriptions' during Assyrian domination."[33] Thus, the Book of the Law sparked a wider recovery of Judean history and memory that may have been lost and/or suppressed by an overbearing Assyrian empire.[34] Following this train of thought, the Deuteronomistic History is an attempt to reinscribe the social memory and identity of the Judeans in Josiah's day. It is a provocative and possible scenario, though if it was the case, it probably did not carry a subversive agenda that was as strong as Kim posits. Kim asserts that Judah was

> firmly rooted in the hegemony imposed by Assyria and other imperial forces [and that] Josiah and his court ignored Assyria and other imperial forces . . . the story of Josiah can be understood as an attempt to write "a history of their own" independent from the framework of the imperial powers. Thus there is no

---

32. Cogan and Tadmor, *2 Kings*, 296–97.
33. Kim, *Decolonizing Josiah*, 227.
34. Ibid., 229. See also McConville, *God and Earthly Power*, 99.

mention of Assyria or Egypt. It was a subversive strategy to give the agency to the colonized—to imagine one's own history and destiny apart from the empire, an alternative view of the world.[35]

This is supportable if adjusts Kim's hypothesis *mutatis mutandis* in that Assyrian hegemony had greatly loosened by the time Josiah began his reforms, including his response to the discovery of the Book of the Law. This is not to deny that there was an element of subversion and rebellion against the Assyrian empire in Josiah's reforms, but it is to nuance the extent of it.[36] Further, it is also to recognize that overthrowing the social memory that had been formed in Judah under the Assyrian empire during its days of strength was a necessary and related, but secondary, priority to the primary priority of regaining Judah's own social memory and identity—a re-inscribing of the re-inscribing, so to speak.

AMON'S REIGN (2 CHRONICLES 33:21-25)

As observed earlier concerning 2 Kgs 21:21–26, the very brief reign of Amon draws little attention from the biblical authors apart from brief narratives in which the distinctive elements are Amon's moral-religious apostasy and a complex of murders related to his assassination. Regarding the former element, Amon may have been motivated in part to adopt foreign cults because of the political expediency of such, especially in his relationship to the Assyrian empire. That said, as has also been argued earlier, Assyria did not impose official requirements on vassal states to adopt Assyrian religions, though doubtless there was a natural pressure from the imperial power imbalance to curry favour by doing so. At the very least, the imperial nature of the ancient Near East at the time lent itself to a liberality and plurality of religious perspectives, which would have been attractive to an oppressed and fractured Judah that was disenchanted with its ancient Yahwistic religion.

Since Chronicles includes the repentance and restoration of Manasseh, it also sets up a contrast between Manasseh and Amon. Whereas in Kings, Amon was like an extension of Manasseh's reign in all its apostasy, in

---

35. Kim, *Decolonizing Josiah*, 242.

36. Once again, one bears in mind Cogan and Tadmor, *2 Kings*, 297–98, but also Jones, *1 and 2 Kings*, 607:

> The acceptance of Cogan's contention that it was not Assyrian policy to impose the worship of its own gods on conquered peoples does not demand the acceptance of his further conclusion that the reforms of Hezekiah and Josiah were not acts of rebellion against Assyria . . . Any move to centralize power in the king and to assert his authority in Jerusalem had political implications . . .

Chronicles, the reign of Amon presents itself as an example of what happens when a king does not turn back to YHWH. In Kings, the brevity of Amon's reign reads as a consequence of a leadership and nation that were severely broken politically and moral-religiously; in Chronicles, the quick end to Amon's reign contextually appears as more of a necessary truncation of increasing and superlative damage from the Judean throne (2 Chr 33:23). In either case, the absence of imprisonment or humbling oppression by Assyria (cf. 2 Chr 33:11) to move Amon towards repentance is not missed nor presented as a factor in his lack of humility. The Chronicler does not consider the determinative factor to be external circumstances, regardless of the pervasive influence of the empire at that time, whether it be imprisonment or non-imprisonment by Assyria, or a so-called pro-Assyrian or anti-Assyrian policy on the part of Judah. Rather, it was the inward, desperately humble posture of the Judean king that turned the tide in the case of Manasseh, and the lack of such that, likewise, led to the self-destruction ahead for Amon's leadership (2 Chr 33:24-25). Yet again, the community narrative with its values and ideology are impressively maintained in the Chronicler's account of Amon while resisting the influence of the Assyrian metanarrative.

JOSIAH'S REIGN (2 CHRONICLES 34-35)

The issues regarding the absence of Assyria in Chronicles' account of the reign of Josiah are similar to those concerning the minimization of Assyria in Kings' account of Josiah. Thus, I will not redundantly repeat my analysis of the Kings report, but focus here on two distinctives involving Assyria in the Chronicles version.

The first is that, though the extent of Josiah's reforms as far away as Samaria (2 Kgs 23:19-20) is not included in the Chronicles narration, his foray into "Manasseh, Ephraim and Simeon, as far as Naphtali" is (2 Chr 34:6). Especially with the mention of Naphtali, the geographical reach of Josiah's work is described as exceeding even that of the former Samerina in 2 Kgs 23:19-20. Moreover, the reference to these geographical locations by their ancient Judean tribal names—and thus, their ancient Judean span, boundaries, and organization—immediately reclaims on the ideological level not just the described land areas, but the formative narrative that gave not only Judah, but the whole of Israel their sense of a right to the land and nationhood. It is a clear reminder of the foundational days of Israel's nationhood and its golden era as a united monarchy.[37] At the level of the text, this

---

37. Similar to and building further from Noth, *History of Israel*, 274; and Cross and

selective use of descriptors could be understood, at least in part, as a retort to the Assyria's attempts to erase the Judean/Israelite metanarrative with the empire's own metanarrative. Again, recall that, as Wiesgickl observes, "Eroberte Städte wurden als Ausdruck assyrischen Herrschaftsanspruchs umbenannt."[38] The Chronicler's response to this imperial imposition is that the Assyrian designations for imperial western provinces are shunned in favour of distinctively Judean epithets. Whether these regions were designated so by Josiah is impossible to know with complete certainty, but it would be the interpretation that is most consistent with the portrayal of Josiah in Chronicles and clearly it was the author's purpose in using these terms to convey that Josiah's intention and spirit, at the very least, were along these lines.

Secondly, though Assyria played a political role in the movement of Neco to Carchemish—and thus Josiah's motivation to confront Neco at Megiddo—this role is so minimized that not only is Assyria not mentioned, but Neco himself is described as puzzled at Josiah's confrontation. Whereas the Kings version gives a faint attention to the role of Assyria in Josiah's last battle, the Chronicles version interprets that there was no reasonable reason to fight at Megiddo and that, moreover, God himself was against the action and the fear that motivated it (2 Chr 35:21–22). In other words, the Assyrian threat at that point was so weak in the opinion of Neco and so subject to the sovereignty of YHWH that it was no real threat in the eyes of either, and this view is reflected in the text as well. Similar to the Kings version, the Chronicles account of Josiah's battle at Megiddo strangely does not explain the Judean king's reasons for pressing on with his campaign. The best explanation for this intentional omission would be that the author did not want to draw attention to Josiah's reasons for battle. Whether Josiah was inspired by his success in reforming and restoring part of Israel, lured by pride, or provoked by fear of the Assyrians, his reasons were apparently considered so contrary to the expressed intent of God (2 Chr 35:21–22) that they are not at all presented. What matters to the Chronicler is not Josiah's excuse, but that Josiah did not discern the voice of God in the situation and take heed. Even if the threat of the empire revived in the form of Neco joining Aššur-uballit at Carchemish, the subaltern perspective, with its elevation of YHWH, needed to take precedent. Unfortunately, in 2 Chr 35:20–25, Josiah failed to do this, to his own tragic demise. Possibly the Chronicler shaped the account this way to emphasize the importance of sustaining the subaltern perspective of the Judah over the imperial metanarrative.

Freedman, "Josiah's Revolt," 56.

38. Wiesgickl, "Vom Vasallenstaat zum ‚Informal Empire'," 26.

Bibliography

Abadie, Philippe. "From the Impious Manasseh (1 Kings 21) to the Convert Manasseh (2 Chronicles 33): Theological Rewriting by the Chronicler." In *The Chronicler as Theologian: Essays in Honor of Ralph W. Klein*, edited by M. Patrick Graham, Steven L. McKenzie, and Gary N. Knoppers, 89–104. JSOTSup 371. London: T. & T. Clark, 2003.

Ackroyd, Peter R. *1 and 2 Chronicles, Ezra, Nehemiah: Introduction and Commentary*. Torch Bible Commentaries. London: SCM, 1973.

———. "The Biblical Interpretation of the Reigns of Ahaz and Hezekiah." In *In the Shelter of Elyon: Essays on Ancient Palestinian Life and Literature in Honor of G. W. Ahlström*, edited by W. Boyd Barrick and John R. Spencer, 247–59. JSOTSup 31. Sheffield: JSOT Press, 1984.

———. "The Chronicler as Exegete." *JSOT* 2 (1977) 2–32.

———. "An Interpretation of the Babylonian Exile: A Study of 2 Kings 20, Isaiah 38–39." *SJT* 27 (1974) 329–52.

———. "The Theology of the Chronicler." In *The Chronicler in His Age*, 273–89. Sheffield: Sheffield Academic, 1991. Reprinted from *LTQ* 8 (1973) 101–16.

Aharoni, Yohanan. *The Land of the Bible: A Historical Geography*, rev. and enl. ed. Translated by A. F. Rainey. Philadelphia: Westminster, 1979.

———. "The Use of Hieratic Numerals in Hebrew Ostraca and the Shekel Weights." *BASOR* 184 (1966) 13–19.

Aharoni, Yohanan, and Michael Avi-Yonah. *The Macmillan Bible Atlas*. New York: Macmillan, 1968.

Aharoni, Yohanan, Michael Avi-Yonah, Anson F. Rainey, and Ze'ev Safrai. *The Carta Bible Atlas*. 4th ed. Jerusalem: Carta, 2002.

Allen, Leslie C. *1, 2 Chronicles*. Communicator's Commentary. Word: Waco, 1987.

———. "Aspects of Generational Commitment and Challenge in Chronicles." In *The Chronicler as Theologian: Essays in Honor of Ralph W. Klein*, edited by M. Patrick Graham, Steven L. McKenzie, and Gary N. Knoppers, 123–32. JSOTSup 371. London: T. & T. Clark, 2003.

Ashcroft, Bill, Gareth Griffiths, and Helen Tiffin. *The Empire Writes Back: Theory and Practice in Post-Colonial Literatures*. 2nd ed. London: Routledge, 2002.

Auld, A. Graeme. "What Was the Main Source of the Books of Chronicles?" In *The Chronicler as Author: Studies in Text and Texture*, edited by M. Patrick Graham and Steven L. McKenzie, 91–99. JSOTSup 263. Sheffield: Sheffield Academic, 1999.

Axskjöld, Carl-Johann. *Aram as the Enemy-Friend: The Ideological Role of Aram in the Composition of Genesis-2 Kings.* CBOT 45. Stockholm: Almqvist & Wiksell, 1998.
Bailey, Benjamin. "Switching." *Key Terms in Language and Culture*, edited by Alessandro Duranti, 238-40. Malden, MA: Blackwell, 2001.
Baker, David W. "Further Examples of the *Waw Explicativum*." *VT* 30 (1980) 129-35.
Balentine, Samuel E. *Prayer in the Hebrew Bible: The Drama of Divine-Human Dialogue.* OBT. Minneapolis: Fortress, 1993.
Beal, L. M. W. *1 and 2 Kings.* Apollos Old Testament Commentary 9. Nottingham, England: Apollos, 2014.
Beentjes, Pancratius C. *Tradition and Transformation in the Book of Chronicles.* Studia Semitica Neerlandica 52. Leiden: Brill, 2008.
Becking, Bernhard Engelbert Jan Hendrik [Bob]. "De ondergang van Samaria: Historische, exegetische en theologische opmerkingen bij II Koningen 17." ThD diss., Utrecht. Meppel: Krips, 1985.
Ben Zvi, Ehud. "The Chronicler as a Historian: Building Texts." In *The Chronicler as Historian*, edited by M. Patrick Graham, Kenneth G. Hoglund, and Steven L. McKenzie, 132-49. JSOTSup 238. Sheffield: Sheffield Academic, 1997.
———. "A Gateway to the Chronicler's Teaching: The Account of the Reign of Ahaz in 2 Chr 28,1-27." *SJOT* 7 (1993) 216-49.
———. "Prelude to a Reconstruction of the *Historical* Manassic Judah." *BN* 81 (1996) 31-44.
———. "The Secession of the Northern Kingdom in Chronicles: Accepted 'Facts' and New Meanings." In *The Chronicler as Theologian: Essays in Honor of Ralph W. Klein*, edited by M. Patrick Graham, Steven L. McKenzie, and Gary N. Knoppers, 61-88. JSOTSup 371. London: T. & T. Clark, 2003.
———. "When the Foreign Monarch Speaks." In *The Chronicler as Author: Studies in Text and Texture*, edited by M. Patrick Graham and Steven L. McKenzie, 209-28. JSOTSup 263. Sheffield: Sheffield Academic, 1999.
———. "Who Wrote the Speech of Rabshakeh and When?" *JBL* 109 (1990) 79-92.
Ben Zvi, Ehud, and Michael H. Floyd, eds. *Writings and Speech in Israelite and Ancient Near Eastern Prophecy.* SBL Symposium Series 10. Atlanta: SBL, 2000).
Benzinger, I. *Die Bücher der Könige.* Kurzer Hand-Commentar zum Alten Testament. Freiburg: Mohr/Siebeck, 1899.
Berg, Evert van den. "Fact and Imagination in the History of Hezekiah in 2 Kings 18-20." In *Unless Someone Guide Me . . . Festschrift for Karen A. Deurloo*, edited by J. W. Dyk, P. J. Midden, K. Spronk, et al., 129-36. Amsterdamse Cahiers voor Exegese van de Bijbel en Zijn Tradities Supplement Series 2. Maastricht: Shaker, 2000.
Berlin, Adele. *Poetics and Interpretation of Biblical Narrative.* Bible and Literature Series 9. Sheffield: Almond, 1983.
Billig, Michael. *Arguing and thinking: A rhetorical approach to social psychology.* 2nd edition. Cambridge: Cambridge University Press, 1996.
Bostock, David. *A Portrayal of Trust: The Theme of Faith in the Hezekiah Narratives.* Milton Keynes, UK: Paternoster, 2006.
Braun, Roddy. *1 Chronicles.* WBC 14. Waco: Word, 1986.
———. "The Significance of 1 Chronicles 22, 28, 29 for the Structure and Theology of the Work of the Chronicler." ThD thesis, Concordia Seminary, St. Louis, May 1971.

Breck, John. "Biblical Chiasmus: Exploring Structure for Meaning." *BTB* 17 (1987) 70–74.

———. *The Shape of Biblical Language: Chiasmus in the Scriptures and Beyond.* Crestwood, NY: St. Vladimir's Seminary Press, 1994.

Bright, John. *A History of Israel.* 4th ed. Louisville: Westminster John Knox Press, 2000.

Brinkman, J. A. *A Political History of Post-Kassite Babylonia, 1158–722 B. C.* AnOr 43. Rome: Pontificium Institutum Biblicum, 1968.

Brueggemann, Walter. *1 and 2 Kings.* Smyth and Helwys Bible Commentary. Macon, GA: Smyth & Helwys, 2000.

———. "Isaiah 37:21–29: The Transformative Potential of a Public Metaphor." *HBT* 10 (1988) 1–32.

Budde, Karl. "The Poem in 2 Kings 19:21–28 (Isaiah 37: 22–29)." *JTS* 35 (1934) 307–13.

Burke, Kenneth. *A Rhetoric of Motives.* Berkeley: University of California Press, 1969.

Burney, C. F. *Notes on the Hebrew Text of the Books of Kings: With an Introduction and Appendix.* Oxford: Clarendon, 1903.

Bush, Frederic W. *Ruth, Esther.* WBC 9. Dallas: Word, 1996.

Butterworth, Mike. *Structure and the Book of Zechariah.* JSOTSup 130. Sheffield: Academic, 1992.

Campbell, Edward F. *Ruth: A New Translation with Introduction, Notes and Commentary.* AB 7. New York: Doubleday, 1975.

Cassuto, Umberto. *A Commentary on the Book of Genesis.* Part One, *From Adam to Noah; Genesis 1–6:8.* Translated by Israel Abrahams. Jerusalem: Magnes, 1961.

Chapman, Cynthia R. *The Gendered Language of Warfare in the Israelite-Assyrian Encounter.* HSM 62. Winona Lake, IN: Eisenbrauns, 2004.

Childs, Brevard S. *Isaiah and the Assyrian Crisis.* SBT 2/3. London: SCM, 1967.

———. "A Study of the Formula, 'Until This Day.'" *JBL* 82 (1963) 279–92.

Cho, Eun Suk. *Josianic Reform in the Deuteronomistic History: Reconstructed in the Light of Factionalism and Use of Royal Apology.* N. p.: YN Press, 2013. Kindle edition.

Clements, R. E. *Isaiah and the Deliverance of Jerusalem: A Study of the Interpretation of Prophecy in the Old Testament.* JSOTSup 13. Sheffield: JSOT Press, 1980.

Coats, George W. "Self-Abasement and Insult Formulas." *JBL* 89 (1970) 14–26.

Cogan, Mordechai. *1 Kings: A New Translation with Introduction and Commentary.* AB 10. New York: Doubleday, 2001.

———. *Imperialism and Religion: Assyria, Judah and Israel in the Eighth and Seventh Centuries B.C.E.* SBLMS 19. Missoula, MT: Scholars, 1974.

———. "'Ripping open Pregnant Women' in Light of an Assyrian Analogue." *JAOS* 103 (1983) 755–57.

———. "Tyre and Tiglath-Pileser III: Chronological Notes." *JCS* 25 (1973) 96–99.

Cogan, Mordechai, and Hayim Tadmor. "Ahaz and Tiglath-Pileser in the Book of Kings: Historiographic Considerations." *Bib* 60 (1979) 491–508.

———. *2 Kings: A New Translation with Introduction and Commentary.* AB 11. Garden City: Doubleday, 1988.

Coggins, R. J. "The Old Testament and Samaritan Origins." In *Annual of the Swedish Theological Institute* 6, edited by Gillis Gerleman et al., 35–48. Leiden: Brill, 1968.

Cohen, Harold R. (Chaim). *Biblical Hapax Legomena in the Light of Akkadian and Ugaritic.* SBLDS 37. Missoula, Mont.: Scholars, 1978.

———. "Neo-Assyrian Elements in the First Speech of the Biblical Rab-šāqê." *Israel Oriental Studies* 9. (1979) 32–48.

Cohn, Robert L. *2 Kings*. Berit Olam. Collegeville: Liturgical, 2000.
Cook, H. J. "Pekah." *VT* 14 (1964) 121–35.
Cross, Frank Moore. *Canaanite Myth and Hebrew Epic: Essays in the History of the Religion of Israel*. Cambridge: Harvard University Press, 1973.
———. "Epigraphic Notes on Hebrew Documents of the Eighth-Sixth Centuries B.C.: II. The Murabbaʿat Papyrus and the Letter Found Near Yabneh-Yam." *BASOR* 165 (1962) 34–46.
Cross, Frank M., and David Noel Freedman. "Josiah's Revolt against Assyria." *JNES* 12 (1953) 56–58.
Cudworth, Troy D. *War in Chronicles: Temple Faithfulness and Israel's Place in the Land*. LHBOTS 627. London: Bloomsbury T. & T. Clark, 2016.
Deijl, Aarnoud van der. *Protest or Propaganda: War in the Old Testament Book of Kings and in Contemporaneous Ancient Near Eastern Texts*. Studia Semitica Neerlandica 51. Leiden: Brill, 2008.
De Odorico, Marco. *The Use of Numbers and Quantifications in the Assyrian Royal Inscriptions*. State Archives of Assyria Studies 3. Helsinki: University of Helsinki Press, Neo-Assyrian Text Corpus Project, 1995.
De Vries, Simon J. *1 and 2 Chronicles*. FOTL 11. Grand Rapids: Eerdmans, 1989.
———. *1 Kings*. WBC 12. Waco: Word, 1985.
Dietrich, Walter. *Prophetie und Geschichte*. FRLANT 108. Göttingen: Vandenhoeck & Ruprecht, 1972.
Dillard, Raymond B. *2 Chronicles*. WBC 15. Waco: Word, 1987.
Dohmen, Christoph. "Heißt סֶמֶל 'Bild, Statue'?" *ZAW* 95 (1984) 263–66.
Dray, Carol A. *Translation and Interpretation in the Targum to the Books of Kings*. Studies in the Aramaic Interpretation of Scripture 5. Leiden: Brill, 2006.
Driver, Godfrey Rolles. "Affirmation by Exclamatory Negation." *JANES* 5 (1973) 107–14.
———. "The Modern Study of the Hebrew Language." In *The People and the Book: Essays on the Old Testament*, edited by Arthur S. Peake, 73–120. Oxford: Clarendon Press, 1925.
Peter Dubovsky. *Hezekiah and the Assyrian Spies: Reconstruction of the Neo-Assyrian Intelligence Services and its Significance for 2 Kings 18–19*. BibOr 49. Rome: Editrice Pontificio Istituto Biblico, 2006.
———. "Neo-Assyrian Warfare: Logistics and Weaponry During the Campaigns of Tiglath-Pileser III." In *Arms and Armour through the Ages: From the Bronze Age to the Late Antiquity: Proceedings of the International Symposium:*, edited by M. Novotna et al., 61–67. Trnava: Trnavská Univerzita, Filozofická Fakulta, 2006.
———. "Ripping Open Pregnant Arab Women: Reliefs in Room L of Ashurbanipal's North Palace." *Orientalia* 78 (2009) 394–419.
———. "Why Did the Northern Kingdom Fall according to 2 Kings 15?" *Bib* 95 (2014) 321–46.
Duke, Rodney K. *The Persuasive Appeal of the Chronicler: A Rhetorical Analysis*. Bible and Literature Series 25. Sheffield: Almond, 1990.
———. "A Rhetorical Approach to Appreciating the Books of Chronicles." In *The Chronicler as Author: Studies in Text and Texture*, edited by M. Patrick Graham and Steven L. McKenzie, 100–136. JSOTSup 263. Sheffield: Sheffield Academic, 1999.

Duranti, Alessandro. *Key Terms in Language and Culture*. Malden, MA: Blackwell, 2001.
Ederer, Matthias. "Der Erstgeborene ohne Erstgeburtsrecht 1 Chr 5, 1–2 als Schlüsseltext für die Lektüre von 1 Chr 5,1–26." *Bib* 94 (2013) 481–508.
Ehrlich, Ernst Ludwig. "Der Aufenthalt des Königs Manasse in Babylon." *TZ* 21 (1965) 281–86.
Ellul, Jacques. *The Politics of God and the Politics of Man*. Edited and translated by Geoffrey W. Bromiley. 1972. Reprint, Eugene, OR: Wipf & Stock, 2012.
Erlandsson, Seth. "Några exempel på Waw Explicativum." *Svensk exegetisk årsbok* 41–42 (1977) 69–76.
Evans, Carl D. "Judah's Foreign Policy from Hezekiah to Josiah." In *Scripture in Context: Essays on the Comparative Method*, edited by Carl D. Evans, William W. Hallo, and John B. White, 157–78. PTMS 34. Pittsburgh: Pickwick, 1980.
Evans, Paul S. *The Invasion of Sennacherib in the Book of Kings: A Source-Critical and Rhetorical Study of 2 Kings 18–19*. VTSup 125. Leiden: Brill, 2009.
Fewell, Danna Nolan. "Sennacherib's Defeat: Words at War in 2 Kings 18:13—19:37." *JSOT* 34 (1986) 79–90.
Fishbane, Michael. *Biblical Interpretation in Ancient Israel*. Oxford: Clarendon, 1985.
Frankena, R. "The Vassal-Treaties of Esarhaddon and the Dating of Deuteronomy." *OTS* 14. (1965) 122–54.
Friedman, Richard Elliott. *The Exile and Biblical Narrative: The Formation of the Deuteronomistic and Priestly Works*. HSM 22. Chico, CA: Scholars, 1981.
Fritz, Volkmar. *1 and 2 Kings: A Continental Commentary*. Translated by Anselm Hagedorn. Minneapolis: Fortress, 2003.
Gass, William H. "The Concept of Character in Fiction." In *Essentials of the Theory of Fiction*, edited by Michael J. Hoffman and Patrick D. Murphy, 267–76. Durham: Duke University Press, 1988.
Gelb, Ignace J. *A Study of Writing*. Rev. ed. Chicago: University of Chicago Press, 1963.
Gervais, Marie-Claude, Nicola Morant, and Gemma Penn. "Making Sense of 'Absence': Towards a Typology of Absence in Social Representations Theory and Research." *Journal for the Theory of Social Behaviour* 29 (1999) 419–44.
Gevaryahu, Haim. "Isaiah and Hezekiah: Prophet and King." *Dor le-Dor* 14/2 (1987–1988) 78–85.
Goldstein, Ronnie. "A Suggestion Regarding the Meaning of 2 Kings 17:9 and the Composition of 2 Kings 17:7–23." *VT* 63 (2013) 393–407.
Gordon, Robert P. *Holy Land, Holy City: Sacred Geography and the Interpretation of the Bible*. Carlisle, UK: Paternoster, 2004.
Graham, M. Patrick, Kenneth G. Hoglund, and Steven L. McKenzie, eds. *The Chronicler as Historian*. JSOTSup 238. Sheffield: Sheffield Academic, 1997.
Graham, M. Patrick, and Steven L. McKenzie, eds. *The Chronicler as Author: Studies in Text and Texture*. JSOTSup 263. Sheffield: Sheffield Academic, 1999.
Graham, M. Patrick, Steven L. McKenzie, and Gary N. Knoppers, eds. *The Chronicler as Theologian: Essays in Honor of Ralph W. Klein*. JSOTSup 371. London: T. & T. Clark, 2003.
Gray, John. *1 and 2 Kings: A Commentary*. 2nd ed. OTL. Philadelphia: Westminster, 1970.
Grayson, A. K. *Assyrian and Babylonian Chronicles*. Locust Valley, NY: Augustin, 1975.

Greenfield, Jonas C. "Aspects of Aramean Religion." In *Ancient Israelite Religion: Essays in Honor of Frank Moore Cross*, edited by Patrick D. Miller, Jr., Paul D. Hanson, and S. Dean McBride, 67–78. Philadelphia: Fortress, 1987.

———. "Some Aspects of Treaty Terminology in the Bible." *Fourth World Congress of Jewish Studies: Papers*. Vol. 1. Jerusalem: World Union of Jewish Studies, 1967.

Greenstein, Edward L. "Some Developments in the Study of Language and Some Implications for Interpreting Ancient Texts and Cultures." In *Israel Oriental Studies 20; Semitic Linguistics; The State of the Art at the Turn of the Twenty-First Century*, edited by Shlomo Izre'el, 441–79. Winona Lake, IN: Eisenbrauns, 2002.

Gunn, David M. *The Story of King David: Genre and Interpretation*. JSOTSup 6. Sheffield: JSOT Press, 1978.

Hallo, William W. "From Qarqar to Carchemish: Assyria and Israel in the Light of New Discoveries." *BA* 23/2 (1960) 33–61.

Hallo, William W., and William Kelly Simpson. *The Ancient Near East: A History*. 2nd ed. Orlando: Harcourt Brace, 1998.

Haran, Menahem. "The Rise and Decline of the Empire of Jeroboam Ben Joash." *VT* (1967) 266–97.

Har-El, Menasche. *Landscape, Nature and Man in the Bible: Sites and Events in the Old Testament*. Translated by David Strassler and Yehudit Elgavi. Jerusalem: Carta, 2003.

Hayes, John H., and Jeffrey K. Kuan. "The Final Years of Samaria (730–720 BC)." *Bib* 72 (1991) 153–81.

Hayes, John H., and J. Maxwell Miller, eds. *Israelite and Judaean History*. OTL. Philadelphia: Westminster, 1977.

Herrmann, Siegfried. *A History of Israel in Old Testament Times*. Rev. ed. Translated by John Bowden. Philadelphia: Fortress, 1981.

Hjelm, Ingrid. *Jerusalem's Rise to Sovereignty: Zion and Gerizim in Competition*. JSOTSup 404. London: T. & T. Clark, 2004.

Hobbs, T. R. *2 Kings*. WBC 13. Waco: Word, 1985.

Holladay, William L. "Form and Word-Play in David's Lament over Saul and Jonathan." *VT* 20 (1970) 153–89.

———. *The Root Šûbh in the Old Testament: With Particular Reference to Its Usages in Covenantal Contexts*. Leiden: Brill, 1958.

Holloway, Steven W. *Aššur is King! Aššur is King! Religion in the Exercise of Power in the Neo-Assyrian Empire*. CHANE 10. Leiden: Brill, 2002.

Hom, Mary Katherine Y. H. *The Characterization of the Assyrians in Isaiah: Synchronic and Diachronic Perspectives*. LHBOTS 559. New York: Bloomsbury, 2012.

———. "Chiasmus in Chronicles: Investigating the Structures of 2 Chronicles 28:16–21; 33:1–20; and 31:20–32:33." *AUSS* 47/2 (Autumn 2009) 163–179.

———. "'. . . A Mighty Hunter before YHWH': Genesis 10:9 and the Moral-Theological Evaluation of Nimrod." *Vetus Testamentum* 60 (2010) 63–68.

———. "Significant Vocabulary Pertaining to the Davidic-Solomonic Ideal in Chronicles." *Evangelical Journal* 35 (2017) 10–17.

———. "'To' or 'Against': The Interpretation of יבא על in 2 Chr 28:20." *VT* 60 (2010) 560–64.

House, Paul R. *1, 2 Kings*. NAC. Nashville: Broadman and Holman, 1995.

Houtman, Cornelis. *Der Himmel im Alten Testament: Israels Weltbild und Weltanschauung*. OTS 30. Leiden: Brill, 1993.

Hubbard, David Allan. *Hosea: An Introduction and Commentary*. Downers Grove, IL: InterVarsity, 1989.
Hubbard, Robert L. *The Book of Ruth*. NICOT. Grand Rapids: Eerdmans, 1988.
Hughes, Jeremy. *Secrets of the Times: Myth and History in Biblical Chronology*. JSOTSup 66. Sheffield: Sheffield Academic, 1990.
Hull, John H. "Hezekiah—Saint and Sinner: A Conceptual and Contextual Narrative Analysis of 2 Kings 18–20." PhD diss., Claremont Graduate School, 1994.
Hyman, Ronald T. "The Rabshakeh's Speech (2 Ki 18–25): A Study of Rhetorical Intimidation." *JBQ* 23 (1995) 213–20.
Irvine, Stuart A. *Isaiah, Ahaz, and the Syro-Ephraimitic Crisis*. SBLDS 123. Atlanta: Scholars, 1990.
Janzen, David. *The Necessary King: A Postcolonial Reading of the Deuteronomistic Portrait of the Monarchy*. HBM 57. Sheffield: Sheffield Phoenix, 2013.
Japhet, Sara. "Female Names and Gender Perspectives in Chronicles." In *The Writings and Later Wisdom Books*, edited by Christl M. Maier and Nuria Calduch-Benages. The Bible and Women: An Encyclopaedia of Exegesis and Cultural History, 33–53. Atlanta: SBL, 2014.
———. *1 and 2 Chronicles: A Commentary*. OTL. Louisville: Westminster John Knox, 1993.
———. *The Ideology of the Book of Chronicles and Its Place in Biblical Thought*. Translated by Anna Barber. Beiträge zur Erforschung des Alten Testaments und des Antiken Judentums. Frankfurt: Lang, 1989.
Johns, C. H. W. *Assyrian Deeds and Documents: Recording the Transfer of Property; Including the so-called private contracts, legal decisions and proclamations preserved in the Kouyunjik Collections of the British Museum; Chiefly of the 7th Century B. C.* Vol. 1, *Cuneiform Texts*. 2nd ed. Cambridge: Deighton, Bell and co., 1924.
Johnson, Aubrey R. "Aspects of the Use of the Term פנים in the Old Testament." In *Festschrift Otto Eissfeldt zum 60. Geburtstage 1 September 1947*, edited by Johann Fück, 155–59. Halle: Niemeyer, 1947.
Johnstone, William. *1 and 2 Chronicles*. Vol. 1, *1 Chronicles 1–2 Chronicles 9: Israel's Place among the Nations*. JSOTSup 253. Sheffield: Sheffield Academic, 1997.
———. *1 and 2 Chronicles*. Vol. 2, *2 Chronicles 10–36: Guilt and Atonement*. JSOTSup 254. Sheffield: Sheffield Academic, 1997.
Jones, Gwilym H. *1 & 2 Chronicles*. Old Testament Guides. Sheffield: Sheffield Academic, 1993.
———. *1 and 2 Kings*. Vol. 1, *1 Kings 1—16:34*. NCBC. London: Marshall, Morgan & Scott, 1984.
———. *1 and 2 Kings*. Vol. 2, *1 Kings 17:1—2 Kings 25:30*. NCBC. Grand Rapids: Eerdmans, 1984.
Kalimi, Isaac. "The Contribution of the Literary Study of Chronicles to the Solution of Its Textual Problems." *Biblical Interpretation* 3 (1995) 210–211.
———. *The Reshaping of Ancient Israelite History in Chronicles*. Winona Lake, IN: Eisenbrauns, 2005.
Kartveit, Magnar. *Motive und Schichten der Landtheologie in I Chronik 1–9*. ConBOT 28. Stockholm: Almqvist & Wiksell International, 1989.
Kalluveettil, Paul. *Declaration and Covenant: A Comprehensive Review of Covenant Formulae from the Old Testament and the Ancient Near East*. Analecta Biblica 88. Rome: Biblical Institute Press, 1982.

Kelly, Brian E. "Manasseh in the Books of Kings and Chronicles (2 Kings 21:1-18; 2 Chron 33:1-20)." In *Windows into Old Testament History: Evidence, Argument, and the Crisis of 'Biblical Israel,'* edited by V. Philips Long, David W. Baker, and Gordon J. Wenham 131-46. Grand Rapids: Eerdmans, 2002.

Kessler, Karlheinz. *Untersuchungen zur historischen Topographie Nordmesopotamiens nach keilschriftlichen Quellen des 1. Jahrtausends v. Chr.* Beihefte zum Tübinger Atlas des Vorderen Orients 19. Wiesbaden: Reichert, 1980.

Kim, Uriah Y. *Decolonizing Josiah: Toward a Postcolonial Reading of the Deuteronomistic History.* Bible in the Modern World 5. Sheffield: Sheffield Phoenix, 2005.

King, Philip J. "Warfare in the Ancient Near East." In *The Archaeology of Jordan and Beyond: Essays in Honor of James A. Sauer*, edited by Lawrence E. Stager, Joseph A. Greene, and Michael D. Coogan, 266-76. Winona Lake, IN: Eisenbrauns, 2000.

Klostermann, August. *Die Bücher Samuelis und der Könige.* Kurzgefasster Kommentar zu den heiligen Schriften Alten und Neuen Testamentes sowie zu den Apokryphen. Nördlingen: Beck'schen, 1887.

Knoppers, Gary N. *1 Chronicles 1-9: A New Translation with Introduction and Commentary.* AB 12. New York: Doubleday, 2003.

———. "Treasures Won and Lost: Royal (Mis)appropriations in Kings and Chronicles." In *The Chronicler as Author: Studies in Text and Texture*, edited by M. Patrick Graham and Steven L. McKenzie, 181-208. JSOTSup 263. Sheffield: Sheffield Academic, 1999.

———. *Two Nations under God: The Deuteronomistic History of Solomon and the Dual Monarchies.* Vol. 2, *The Reign of Jeroboam, the Fall of Israel, and the Reign of Josiah.* HSM 53. Atlanta: Scholars, 1994.

Kooij, Arie van der. "The Story of Hezekiah and Sennacherib (2 Kings 18-19): A Sample of Ancient Historiography." In *Past, Present, Future: The Deuteronomistic History and the Prophets*, edited by Johannes C. de Moor and Harry F. van Rooy, 107-19. Leiden: Brill, 2000.

Kselman, John S. "Semantic-Sonant Chiasmus in Biblical Poetry." *Bib* 58 (1977) 219-23.

Kuan, Jeffrey Kah-Jin. *Neo-Assyrian Historical Inscriptions and Syria-Palestine: Israelite/Judean-Tyrian-Damascene Political and Commercial Relations in the Ninth-Eighth Centuries BCE.* 1995. Reprint, Eugene, OR: Wipf & Stock, 2016.

Kutscher, Eduard Yechezkel. *A History of the Hebrew Language.* Edited by Raphael Kutscher. Leiden: Brill, 1982.

Layton, Scott. "Biblical Hebrew 'To Set the Face,' in Light of Akkadian and Ugaritic." *Ugarit-Forschungen* 17 (1986) 169-80.

Lederer, Carl. *Die biblische Zeitrechnung: vom Auszuge aus Agypten bis zum Beginne der babylonischen Gefangenschaft.* Speier: Kleeberger, 1888.

Levenson, Jon D. "The Last Four Verses in Kings." *JBL* 103 (1984) 353-61.

———. *Sinai and Zion: An Entry into the Jewish Bible.* Minneapolis: Winston, 1985.

Levine, Louis D. "Menahem and Tiglath-Pileser: A New Synchronism." *BASOR* 206 (1972) 40-42.

Linebarger, Paul M. A. *Psychological Warfare.* Washington, D.C.: Combat Forces Press, 1954.

Long, Burke O. *2 Kings.* FOTL 10. Grand Rapids: Eerdmans, 1991.

Loretz, O., and W. Mayer. "Pulu-Tiglatpileser III. und Menahem von Israel: nach assyrischen Quellen und 2 Kön 15, 19-20." *UF* 22 (1990) 221-31.

Louis, Kenneth R. R. Gros. "The Difficulty of Ruling Well: King David of Israel." *Semeia* 8 (1977) 15–33.

Luckenbill, Daniel David. *Ancient Records of Assyria and Babylonia*. Vol. 2, *Historical Records of Assyria: From Sargon to the End*. Chicago: University of Chicago, 1927.

Machinist, Peter. "The Rab Šāqēh at the Wall of Jerusalem: Israelite Identity in the Face of the Assyrian 'Other.' " *Hebrew Studies* 41 (2000) 151–68.

MacIntyre, Alasdair. *Three Rival Versions of Moral Enquiry: Encyclopaedia, Genealogy, and Tradition; Being Gifford Lectures Delivered in the University of Edinburgh in 1988*. London: Duckworth, 1990.

Malamat, Abraham. "The Historical Background of the Assassination of Amon, King of Judah." *IEJ* 3 (1953) 26–29.

———. "A Political Look at the Kingdom of David and Solomon and Its Relations with Egypt." In *Studies in the Period of David and Solomon and Other Essays: Papers Read at the International Symposium for Biblical Studies, Tokyo, 5–7 December, 1979*, edited by Tomoo Ishida, 189–204. Winona Lake, IN: Eisenbrauns, 1982.

Mare, W. Harold. *The Archaeology of the Jerusalem Area*. Grand Rapids: Baker, 1987.

Marriott, John, and Karen Radner. "Sustaining the Assyrian Army among Friends and Enemies in 714 BCE." *JCS* 67 (2015) 127–43.

Mason, Rex. *Preaching the Tradition: Homily and Hermeneutics after the Exile*. Cambridge: Cambridge University Press, 1990.

———. "Some Echoes of the Preaching in the Second Temple?: Tradition Elements in Zechariah 1–8." *ZAW* 96 (1984) 221–35.

Mastin, B. A. "Was the SALIS the Third Man in the Chariot?" In *Studies in the Historical Books of the Old Testament*, edited by J. A. Emerton, 125–54. VTSup 30. Leiden: Brill, 1979.

Mathias, Dietmar. " 'Levitische Predigt' und Deuteronomismus." *ZAW* 96 (1984) 23–49.

Mattila, Raija. *The King's Magnates: A Study of the Highest Officials of the Neo-Assyrian Empire*. State Archives of Assyria Studies 11. Helsinki: Neo-Assyrian Text Corpus Project, 2000.

Mazar, Benjamin. "The Aramean Empire and its Relations with Israel." *BA* 25 (1962) 98–120.

McCarthy, Dennis J. "Notes on the Love of God in Deuteronomy and the Father-Son Relationship between Yahweh and Israel." *CBQ* 27 (1965) 144–47.

McConville, J. G. *God and Earthly Power: An Old Testament Political Theology*. LHBOTS 454. London: T. & T. Clark, 2006.

McKay, John W. *Religion in Judah under the Assyrians, 732–609 BC*. SBT^2 26. London: SCM, 1973.

McKenzie, Steven L. "The Chronicler as Redactor." In *The Chronicler as Author: Studies in Text and Texture*, edited by M. Patrick Graham and Steven L. McKenzie, 70–90. JSOTSup 263. Sheffield: Sheffield Academic, 1999.

———. *1 and 2 Chronicles*. Abingdon Old Testament Commentaries. Nashville: Abingdon, 2004.

Meissner, Bruno. *Babylonien und Assyrien*, Kulturgeschichtliche Bibliothek. Heidelberg: Winters, 1925.

Merrill, Eugene H. *Kingdom of Priests: A History of Old Testament Israel*. Grand Rapids: Baker, 1987.

Miglio, Adam E. "The Literary Connotations of Letter-Writing in Syro-Mesopotamia and in Samuel and Kings." *BN* 162 (2014) 33–46.

Millard, A. R. "Assyrians and Arameans." *Iraq* 45 (1983) 101–08.
Montgomery, James A. "Archival Data in the Book of Kings." *JBL* 53 (1934) 46–52.
———. *The Books of Kings*. ICC. Edinburgh: T. & T. Clark, 1951.
Mosis, Rudolf. *Untersuchungen zur Theologie des chronistischen Geschichtswerkes*. Freiburger theologische Studien 92. Freiburg: Herder, 1973.
Murphy-O'Connor, Jerome. *The Holy Land: An Archaeological Guide from Earliest Times to 1700*. 3rd ed. Oxford: Oxford University Press, 1992.
Myers, Jacob M. *2 Chronicles: Translation and Notes*. AB 13. Garden City, NY: Doubleday, 1965.
Na'aman, Nadav. "The Date of 2 Chronicles 11:5–10—A Reply to Y. Garfinkel." *BASOR* 271 (1988) 74–77.
———. "The Deuteronomist and Voluntary Servitude to Foreign Powers." *JSOT* 65 (1995) 37–53.
———. "The Historical Background to the Conquest of Samaria (720 BCE)." *Bib* 71 (1990) 206–25. Reprinted in *Ancient Israel and Its Neighbors: Interaction and Counteraction: Collected Essays*, 1:76–93. Winona Lake, IN: Eisenbrauns, 2005.
———. "Jehu Son of Omri: Legitimizing a Loyal Vassal by His Lord." *IEJ* 48 (1998) 236–38. Reprinted in *Ancient Israel and Its Neighbors: Interaction and Counteraction: Collected Essays*, 1:13–15. Winona Lake, IN: Eisenbrauns, 2005.
Nam, Roger S. *Portrayals of Economic Exchange in the Book of Kings*. Biblical Interpretation Series 112. Leiden: Brill, 2012.
Nelson, Richard D. "The Altar of Ahaz: A Revisionist View." *Hebrew Annual Review* 10 (1986) 267–76.
———. *First and Second Kings*. Interpretation. Atlanta: John Knox, 1987.
———. "*Realpolitik* in Judah (687–609 B. C. E.)." In *Scripture in Context 2: More Essays on the Comparative Method*, edited by William W. Hallo, James C. Moyer, and Leo G. Perdue, 177–89. Winona Lake, IN: Eisenbrauns, 1983.
Neufeldt, Victoria, ed. *Webster's New World Dictionary, Third College Edition*. New York: Simon & Schuster, 1988.
Nicholson, E. W. *Deuteronomy and Tradition*. Oxford: Basil Blackwell, 1967.
Nielsen, Eduard. "Political Conditions and Cultural Developments in Israel and Judah during the Reign of Manasseh." *Fourth World Congress of Jewish Studies: Papers*, 1:103–6. World Union of Jewish Studies. Jerusalem: World Union of Jewish Studies, 1967.
Ninow, Friedbert. "Approaches to Typology." Chapter 1 in *Indicators of Typology within the Old Testament: The Exodus Motif*. Frankfurt: Lang, 2001.
Noth, Martin. *The Deuteronomistic History*. JSOTSup 15. Sheffield: JSOT Press, 1981.
———. *The History of Israel*. 2nd ed. Translated by P. R. Ackroyd. London: Adam & Charles Black, 1960.
———. "The Nature of the Composition." In *The Chronicler's History*, translated by H. G. M. Williamson, 75–81. JSOT Sup 50. Sheffield: Sheffield Academic, 1987.
Oded, B[ustenay]. "The Historical Background of the Syro-Ephraimite War Reconsidered." *CBQ* 34 (1972) 153–65.
———. "Judah and the Exile." Pages 436–37 in *Israelite and Judaean History*. Edited by John H. Hayes and J. Maxwell Miller. London: SCM, 1977.
———. "Observations on Methods of Assyrian Rule in Transjordania after the Palestinian Campaign of Tiglath-Pileser III." *JNES* 29 (1970) 177–86.

Olley, John W. " 'Trust in the Lord': Hezekiah, Kings and Isaiah." *TynBul* 50 (1999) 59–77.
Olmstead, A. T. *History of Assyria*. New York: Scribner, 1923.
Oren, Mikhal. "Interference in Ancient Languages as Evidenced by Governed Prepositions." *JSS* 58 (2013) 1–11.
Östreicher, Theodor. *Das Deuteronomische Grundgesetz*. Beiträge zur Förderung christlicher Theologie 4/27. Gütersloh: Bertelsmann, 1923.
Owen, David I. "An Akkadian Letter from Ugarit at Tel Aphek." *Tel Aviv* 8 (1981) 1–17.
Paul, Shalom M. "Sargon's Administrative Diction in 2 Kings 17:27." *JBL* 88 (1969) 73–74.
Perdue, Leo, and Warren Carter. *Israel and Empire: A Postcolonial History of Israel and Early Judaism*. Edited by Coleman A. Baker. London: Bloomsbury, 2015.
Perri, Antonio. "Writing." In *Key Terms in Language and Culture*, edited by Alessandro Duranti, 272–74. Malden, MA: Blackwell, 2001.
Person, Raymond F. *The Deuteronomic History and the Book of Chronicles: Scribal Works in an Oral World*. Ancient Israel and Its Literature 6. Atlanta: SBL, 2010.
Plöger, Otto. *Aus der Spätzeit des Alten Testaments: Studien zu seinem 60. Geburtstag am 27.11.1970 herausgegeben von Freunden und Schülern*. Göttingen: Vandenhoeck and Ruprecht, 1971.
Pongratz-Leisten, Beate. "All the King's Men: Authority, Kingship, and the Rise of the Elites in Assyria." In *Experiencing Power, Generating Authority: Cosmos, Politics, and the Ideology of Kingship in Ancient Egypt and Mesopotamia*, edited by Jane A. Hill, Philip Jones, and Antonio J. Morales, 285–309. PMIRC 6. Philadelphia: University of Pennsylvania Museum of Archaeology and Anthropology, 2013.
Pope, Marvin H. *Song of Songs: A New Translation with Introduction and Commentary*. AB. New York: Doubleday, 1977.
Porter, Barbara Nevling. *Images, Power, Politics: Figurative Aspects of Esarhaddon's Babylonian Policy*. Philadelphia: American Philosophical Society, 1993.
———. "Language, Audience and Impact in Imperial Assyria." In *Israel Oriental Studies 15: Language and Culture in the Near East*, edited by Shlomo Izre'el and Rina Drory, 51–72. Leiden: Brill, 1995.
Press, Michael D. " 'Where Are the Gods of Hamath?' (2 Kings 18.34 // Isaiah 36.19): The Use of Foreign Deities in the Rabshakeh's Speech." *JSOT* 40/2 (2015) 201–23.
Provan, Iain W. *1 and 2 Kings*. NIBC. Peabody, MA: Hendrickson, 1995.
Radner, Karen. "Abgaben an den König von Assyrien aus dem In- und Ausland." In *Geschenke und Steuern, Zölle und Tribute; Antike Abgabenformen in Anspruch und Wirklichkeit*, edited by H. Klinkott, S. Kubisch, and R. Müller-Wollermann, 213–30. CHANE 29. Leiden: Brill, 2007.
———. "The Assyrian Army." *Assyrian Empire Builders*. University College London 2012. http://www.ucl.ac.uk/sargon/essentials/soldiers/theassyrianarmy/.
———. "Royal Decision-making: Kings, Magnates, and Scholars." In *The Oxford Handbook of Cuneiform Culture*, edited by Karen Radner and Eleanor Robson, 358–79. Oxford: Oxford University Press, 2011.
———. "Tiglath-pileser III, King of Assyria (744–727 BC)." *Assyrian Empire Builders*. University College London, 2012. http://www.ucl.ac.uk/sargon/essentials/kings/tiglatpileseriii/.
———. "Urartu, Assyria's northern archenemy." *Assyrian Empire Builders*. University College London, 2013. http://www.ucl.ac.uk/sargon/essentials/countries/urartu.

Rainey, Anson F. "Manasseh, King of Judah, in the Whirlpool of the Seventh Century B.C.E." In *kinattutu sa darati: Raphael Kutscher Memorial Volume*, no. 1, 147–64. Tel Aviv: Institute of Archaeology of Tel Aviv University, 1993.

Reade, Julian. "Mesopotamian Guidelines for Biblical Chronology." *Syro-Mesopotamian Studies* 4/1 (May 1981) 1–9.

Rendsburg, Gary A. *Israelian Hebrew in the Book of Kings*. Occasional Publications of the Department of Near Eastern Studies and the Program of Jewish Studies, Cornell University, 5. Bethesda, MD: CDL, 2002.

———. "Linguistic Variation and the 'Foreign' Factor in the Hebrew Bible." In *Israel Oriental Studies 15: Language and Culture in the Near East*, edited by Shlomo Izre'el and Rina Drory, 177–90. Leiden: Brill, 1995.

———. "Morphological Evidence for Regional Dialects in Ancient Hebrew." In *Linguistics and Biblical Hebrew*, edited by Walter R. Bodine, 65–88. Winona Lake, IN: Eisenbrauns, 1992.

Revell, E. J. *The Designation of the Individual: Expressive Usage in Biblical Narrative*. CBET. Kampen: Kok Pharos, 1996.

Robinson, Theodore H. *A History of Israel*. Vol. 1, *From the Exodus to the Fall of Jerusalem, 586 B. C.* Oxford: Clarendon, 1932.

Rad, Gerhard von. "The Levitical Sermon in 1 and 2 Chronicles." In *The Problem of the Hexateuch and Other Essays*, translated by E. W. Trueman Dicken, 267–80. Edinburgh: Oliver and Boyd, 1966.

Rogers, Robert William. *Cuneiform Parallels to the Old Testament*. 2nd ed. New York: Abingdon, 1926.

Rudman, Dominic. "Is the Rabshakeh also among the Prophets? A Rhetorical Study of 2 Kings 18: 17–35." *VT* 50 (2000) 100–110.

Rudolph, Wilhelm. *Chronikbücher*. HAT. Tübingen: Mohr/Siebeck, 1955.

Saggs, H. W. F. "The Assyrians." In *Peoples of Old Testament Times*, edited by D. J. Wiseman, 156–78. Oxford: Clarendon, 1973.

———. "The Nimrud Letters, 1952—I: The Ukin-zer Rebellion and Related Texts." *Iraq* 17 (1955) 21–56.

Šanda, Albert. *Die Bücher der Könige: Übersetzt und Erklärt*. Vol. 2, *Das zweite Buch der Könige*. EHZAT. Münster: Aschendorffsche, 1912.

Schniedewind, William M. "Prophets and Prophecy in the Books of Chronicles." In *The Chronicler as Historian*, edited by M. Patrick Graham, Kenneth G. Hoglund, and Steven L. McKenzie, 204–24. JSOTSup 238. Sheffield: Sheffield Academic, 1997.

———. "The Source Citations of Manasseh: King Manasseh in History and Homily." *VT* 41 (1991) 450–61.

Schrader, Eberhard. *The Cuneiform Inscriptions and the Old Testament*. Vol. 2. Translated by Owen C. Whitehouse. London: Williams & Norgate, 1888.

Schweitzer, Steven James. *Reading Utopia in Chronicles*. LHBOTS 442. London: T. & T. Clark, 2007.

Segovia, Fernando F. *Decolonizing Biblical Studies: A View from the Margins*. Maryknoll, NY: Orbis, 2000.

Seitz, Christopher R. "Account A and the Annals of Sennacherib: A Reassessment." *JSOT* 58 (1993) 47–57.

Selman, Martin J. *1 Chronicles: An Introduction and Commentary*. TOTC. Leicester, UK: Inter-Varsity, 1994.

———. *2 Chronicles: A Commentary*. TOTC. Leicester, UK: Inter-Varsity, 1994.

Shiloh, Yigal. "Jerusalem's Water Supply—The Rediscovery of Warren's Shaft." *BARev* 7/4 (1981) 24–39.

———. "The Rediscovery of the Ancient Water System Known as 'Warren's Shaft.'" In *Ancient Jerusalem Revisited*, edited by Hillel Geva, 46–54. Jerusalem: Israel Exploration Society, 1994.

Siddall, Luis Robert. "Tiglath-pileser III's Aid to Ahaz: A New Look at the Problems of the Biblical Accounts in Light of the Assyrian Sources." *ANES* 46 (2009) 93–106.

Simons, J. *Jerusalem in the Old Testament: Researches and Theories*. Leiden: Brill, 1952.

Sivan, Gabriel A. "The Siege of Jerusalem: Part I: Assyria the World Power." *JBQ* 42/3 (2015) 83–92.

———. "The Siege of Jerusalem: Part II: The Enigmatic Rabshakeh." *JBQ* 43/3 (2015) 78–85.

Smelik, Klaas A. D. "The New Altar of King Ahaz (2 Kings 16): Deuteronomistic Re-Interpretation of a Cult Reform." In *Deuteronomy and Deuteronomic Literature: Festschrift C. H. W. Brekelmans*, edited by M. Vervenne and J. Lust, 263–78. BETL 133. Leuven: Leuven University Press, 1997.

———. "Portrayal of King Manasseh: A Literary Analysis of 2 Kings 21 and 2 Chronicles 23." In *Converting the Past: Studies in Ancient Israelite and Moabite Historiography*, 129–89. OTS 28. Leiden: Brill, 1992.

———. "The Representation of King Ahaz in 2 Kings 16 and 2 Chronicles 28." In *Intertextuality in Ugarit and Israel*, edited by Johannes C. de Moor, 142–85. OTS 40. Leiden: Brill, 1998.

Smend, Rudolph. "Das Gesetz und die Völker: Ein Beitrag zur deuteronomistichen Redaktionsgeschichte." In *Probleme biblischer Theologie: Gerhard von Rad zum 70. Geburtstag*, edited by Hans Walter Wolff, 494–509. Munich: Kaiser, 1972.

Spieckermann, Hermann. *Juda unter Assur in der Sargonidenzeit*. Göttingen: Vandenhoeck & Ruprecht, 1982.

Stade, Bernhard, and Friedrich Schwally. *The Books of Kings: Critical Edition of the Hebrew Text*. In *The Sacred Books of the Old Testament: A Critical Edition of the Hebrew Text*. Edited by Paul Haupt. Leipzig: Hinrichs, 1904.

Stökl, Jonathan. "Divination as Warfare: The Use of Divination across Borders." In *Divination, Politics, and Ancient Near Eastern Empires*, edited by Alan Lenzi and Jonathan Stökl, 49–63. ANEM 7. Atlanta: SBL, 2014.

Stuart, Douglas. *Hosea–Jonah*. WBC 31. Waco: Word, 1987.

Sugirtharajah, R. S. *The Bible and the Third World: Precolonial, Colonial and Postcolonial Encounters*. Cambridge: Cambridge University Press, 2001.

———. *Exploring Postcolonial Biblical Criticism: History, Method, Practice*. Malden, MA: Wiley-Blackwell, 2012.

———. *Postcolonial Criticism and Biblical Interpretation*. Oxford: Oxford University Press, 2002.

Sweeney, Marvin A. *1 and 2 Kings: A Commentary*. OTL. Louisville: Westminster John Knox, 2007.

Tadmor, Hayim. "Azriyau of Yaudi." *Scripta Hierosolymitana* 8 (1961) 232–71.

———. *The Inscriptions of Tiglath-Pileser III, King of Assyria: Critical Edition, with Introductions, Translations and Commentary*. Jerusalem: Israel Academy of Sciences and Humanities, 1994.

———. "Monarchy and the Elite in Assyria and Babylonia: The Question of Royal Accountability." In *The Origins and Diversity of Axial Age Civilizations*, edited by Shmuel N. Eisenstadt, 203–26. New York: State University of New York Press, 1986.

———. "On the Role of Aramaic in the Assyrian Empire." In *Near Eastern Studies: Dedicated to H. I. H. Prince Takahito Mikasa on the Occasion of His Seventy-Fifth Birthday*, edited by Masao Mori, Hideo Ogawa, and Mamoru Yoshikawa, 419–26. Wiesbaden: Harrassowitz, 1991.

Thiele, Edwin R. "Coregencies and Overlapping Reigns Among the Hebrew Kings." *JBL* 93 (1974) 174–200.

———. *The Mysterious Numbers of the Hebrew Kings: A Reconstruction of the Chronology of the Kingdoms of Israel and Judah*. Grand Rapids: Eerdmans, 1965.

———. "Pekah to Hezekiah." *VT* 16 (1966) 83–107.

Thomas, Benjamin J. *Hezekiah and the Compositional History of the Book of Kings*. FAT 2/63. Tübingen: Mohr/Siebeck, 2014.

Thompson, J. A. *1, 2 Chronicles*. NAC. Nashville: Broadman & Holman, 1994.

Thompson, Michael E. W. *Situation and Theology: Old Testament Interpretations of the Syro-Ephraimite War*. Prophets and Historians Series 1. Sheffield: Almond, 1982.

Throntveit, Mark A. "The Chronicler's Speeches and Historical Reconstruction." In *The Chronicler as Historian*, edited by M. Patrick Graham, Kenneth G. Hoglund, and Steven L. McKenzie, 225–45. JSOTSup 238. Sheffield: Sheffield Academic, 1997.

———. "The Relationship of Hezekiah to David and Solomon in the Books of Chronicles." In *The Chronicler as Theologian: Essays in Honor of Ralph W. Klein*, edited by M. Patrick Graham, Steven L. McKenzie, and Gary N. Knoppers, 105–21. JSOTSup 371. London: T. & T. Clark, 2003.

———. *When Kings Speak: Royal Speech and Royal Prayer in Chronicles*. SBLDS 93. Atlanta: Scholars, 1987.

Tuell, Steven S. *First and Second Chronicles*. IBC. Louisville: John Knox, 2001.

———. "The Rivers of Paradise: Ezekiel 47:1–12 and Genesis 2:10–14." In *God Who Creates: Essays in Honor of W. Sibley Towner*, edited by William P. Brown and S. Dean McBride Jr., 171–89. Grand Rapids: Eerdmans, 2000.

Tur-Sinai, N. H. *The Book of Job: A New Commentary*. Jerusalem: Kiryath Sepher, 1967.

Vaux, Roland de. *Ancient Israel: Its Life and Institutions*. Translated by John McHugh. 1961. Reprint, Biblical Resource Series. Grand Rapids: Eerdmans, 1997.

Vater, Ann M. "Narrative Patterns for the Story of Commissioned Communication in the Old Testament." *JBL* 99 (1988) 365–82.

Villard, Pierre. "La notion de famille royale à l'époque néo-assyrienne." In *La famille dans le Proche-Orient ancien: réalités, symbolismes, et images: Proceedings of the 55th Rencontre Assyriologique Internationale at Paris; 6–9 July 2009*, edited by Lionel Marti, 515–23. Winona Lake, IN: Eisenbrauns, 2014.

Vincent, L.-Hugues. *Jérusalem de l'ancien Testament: Recherches d'archaéologie et d'historie*. Illustrated by M.-A. Steve. Paris: Gabalda, 1954.

Viviano, Pauline A. "2 Kings 17: A Rhetorical and Form-Critical Analysis." *CBQ* 49 (1987) 548–59.

Waltke, Bruce K., and M. O'Connor. *An Introduction to Biblical Hebrew Syntax*. Winona Lake, IN: Eisenbrauns, 1990.

Watson, Wilfred G. E. *Classical Hebrew Poetry: A Guide to Its Techniques*. JSOTSup 26. Sheffield: JSOT Press, 1984.

———. *Traditional Techniques in Classical Hebrew Verse*. JSOTSup 170. Sheffield: Sheffield Academic, 1994.

Weippert, Helga. "Die 'deuteronomistischen' Beurteilungen der Könige von Israel und Juda und das Problem der Redaktion der Königsbücher." *Bib* 53 (1972) 301–9.
Welten, Peter. *Geschichte und Geschichtsdarstellung in den Chronikbüchern*. WMANT 42. Neukirchen-Vluyn: Neukirchener, 1973.
Wenham, Gordon. "The Coherence of the Flood Narrative." *VT* 28 (1978) 336–48.
———. *Genesis 1–15*. WBC 1. Waco: Word, 1987.
Wiesgickl, Simon. "Vom Vasallenstaat zum 'Informal Empire': Postkoloniale Theorien und ihre Bedeutung für die alttestamentliche Exegese." *BZ* 59/1 (2015) 17–38.
Wightman, G. J. *The Walls of Jerusalem: From the Canaanites to the Mamluks*. Mediterranean Archaeology Supplement 4. Sydney: Meditarch, 1993.
Willi, Thomas. *Die Chronik als Auslegung: Untersuchungen zur literarischen Gestaltung der historischen Überlieferung Israels*. Göttingen: Vandenhoeck & Ruprecht, 1972.
Williamson, H. G. M. *Ezra, Nehemiah*. WBC 16. Waco: Word, 1985.
———. *1 and 2 Chronicles*. NCBC. London: Marshall, Morgan & Scott, 1982.
———. *Israel in the Books of Chronicles*. Cambridge: Cambridge University Press, 1977.
Wiseman, Donald J. *1 and 2 Kings: An Introduction and Commentary*. TOTC. Downers Grove, IL: InterVarsity, 1993.
———. "The Nimrud Tablets." *Iraq* 15 (1953) 135–60.
———. "Some Historical Problems in the Book of Daniel." In *Notes on Some Problems in the Book of Daniel*, by D. J. Wiseman, T. C. Mitchell, et al., 9–18. London: Tyndale, 1965.
———. "The Vassal-Treaties of Esarhaddon." *Iraq* 20 (1958) 1–99.
Wolff, Hans Walter. *Hosea*. Translated by Gary Stansell. Hermeneia. Philadelphia: Fortress, 1974.
Wright, Jacob L. "Surviving in an Imperial Context: Foreign Military Service and Judean Identity." In *Judah and the Judeans in the Achaemenid Period: Negotiating Identity in an International Context*, edited by Oded Lipschits, Gary N. Knoppers, and Manfred Oeming, 505–28. Winona Lake, IN: Eisenbrauns, 2011.
Wright, John W. "The Fight for Peace: Narrative and History in the Battle Accounts in Chronicles." In *The Chronicler as Historian*, edited by M. Patrick Graham, Kenneth G. Hoglund, and Steven L. McKenzie, 150–77. JSOTSup 238. Sheffield: Sheffield Academic, 1997.
Würthwein, Ernst. *Die Bücher der Könige: 1. Kön. 17–2. Kön. 25: Übersetzt und Erklärt*. Göttingen: Vandenhoeck & Ruprecht, 1984.
Xella, Paolo. "Sur la nourriture des morts: Un aspect de l'eschatologie mésopotamienne." Pages 151–60 In *Death in Mesopotamia: XXVIe Rencontre assyriologique internurnational*, edited by Bendt Alster, 151–60. Mesopotamia 8. Copenhagen: Akademisk, 1980.
Xenophon. *Anabasis*. Translated by Carleton L. Brownson. LCL 90. London: Heinemann, 1980.
Yadin, Yigael. "Ancient Judaean Weights and the Date of the Samaria Ostraca." *Scripta Hierosolymitana* 8 (1961) 9–25.
Yamada, Shigeo. *The Construction of the Assyrian Empire: A Historical Study of the Inscriptions of Shalmaneser III (859–824 BC) Relating to His Campaigns to the West*. CHANE 3. Leiden: Brill, 2000.
Younger, K. Lawson. "The Deportations of the Israelites." *JBL* 117 (1998) 201–27.
———. "The Fall of Samaria in Light of Recent Research." *CBQ* 61 (1999) 461–82.
Zadok, Ran. *On West Semites in Babylonia during the Chaldean and Achaemenian Periods: An Onomastic Study*. Jerusalem: Wanaarta, 1977.

Index of Subjects

Ahaz, 29, 31–47, 49–51, 63–64, 115, 139–51, 153–54, 157, 159, 184, 191, 195, 213, 218–20, 224, 226, 229, 232–33, 245
Aram(ean), 16, 29, 32–35, 38–39, 41–42, 44, 46–48, 50, 63, 141–42, 146, 151, 159, 213, 219–20, 238, 243–46, 248
Aramaic/Aramaism, 23, 78
archaeology, 15, 16–17, 82, 186–88, 207
Assyrian exile, 14, 29, 59, 61, 64, 125–28, 132, 134–41, 220–21, 226, 232–33
Assyrian oaths (loyalty, *ade-*), 212, 214, 257
Assyrian palace reliefs, 16, 52

Babylon, 20, 56, 69, 118, 119, 120, 121, 122, 137, 162, 169, 171, 200, 207–11, 216, 218, 223–25, 231
Babylonia, 20, 68, 72, 125, 133, 136, 216, 230
Babylonian exile, 59, 60, 61, 136, 137, 138, 152, 221, 226, 232–33
Babylonians, 1, 117, 118, 119, 121, 159, 170
Bethel, 56–57

Chronicler, 125, 128–41, 146–47, 149–65, 170, 175–76, 181–84, 187, 189, 193–94, 196–97, 202, 204, 206–8, 215, 216, 226–27, 231–33, 259–60

chiasmus, 4, 12–13, 101, 142, 163–84, 189, 198, 200–216, 224, 227–28, 234
chiastic aspect, 101, 122, 165–68, 171, 173–75, 177, 180, 183, 201–5, 227, 235
chronology, 10, 113, 237–40
covenant(al), 12, 36, 37, 40–42, 53, 57–58, 66, 90, 108, 109, 116–18, 121, 130, 149, 152, 153, 155–56, 158, 162, 223–24, 257

Damascene, 43–47, 64, 220
Damascus, 33, 42, 44, 46, 142, 146, 220, 238, 243, 248
David(ic), 10–12, 60, 66, 108, 109, 116–18, 121, 129–30, 135, 140, 151, 153, 158, 161, 173, 176, 182, 190, 206, 223, 256
death, 9, 83, 86, 95, 96–97, 109, 113, 122, 168, 177, 196, 199, 238, 247, 253
Dtn/Deuteronomic, 114, 115, 116, 129
Dtr1, 60, 61, 221, 232
Dtr2, 60, 232
DtrH/Deuteronomistic Historian, 5, 60, 61, 79, 156, 257

Egypt, 78, 80, 88, 102–3, 162, 173, 189, 215, 243, 251, 256, 258
Egyptians, 1, 48, 50, 106, 112, 114, 211, 214
Euphrates, 17, 56, 248

INDEX OF SUBJECTS

faith(ful)(ness), 58, 64, 66, 67, 69, 80, 88, 90, 116–18, 127, 130–32, 137, 168–69, 170, 174, 176, 178, 180, 182, 186, 191, 193, 195–97, 201, 218, 221, 223, 227–28, 246
faithless(ness)/unfaithful(ness), 40, 59, 121, 128, 129, 139, 142, 147, 149–50, 153, 157–58, 160, 170, 226, 233, 241

Gihon, 187–89
Greek, 6, 15–16, 173

Hamath(ite), 56, 243, 247–48
Hezekiah, 3, 4, 10, 39, 65–70, 73–81, 83–86, 88–89, 91–99, 103–4, 106–22, 136, 144, 149–55, 157–62, 168–74, 176–80, 182–98, 208, 212–13, 218, 222–24, 227–30, 232–34, 237, 239, 252, 258
hybrid(ity), 56, 221

idol(s)/idolatrous, 51, 57, 142, 157, 203–5, 218, 235, 243, 256

Jeroboam, ways of, 10–11, 13, 15, 18, 27, 30, 45, 58, 238, 247–50
Josiah, 4, 11, 44, 60, 81, 136, 213, 252, 253, 255–58, 259–60

kingship, 72, 82, 97–98, 114, 234, 235
kakki Aššur, 212, 216
kiṣir šarri, 70, 71

land, 14, 18, 20, 21, 23, 25, 26, 27–28, 31, 38, 43, 48–49, 52–61, 67, 72, 73, 80, 81, 86–88, 96, 97, 99, 102, 107–8, 110, 111, 112, 119, 125, 126, 127–32, 136–37, 144, 154, 160–62, 168, 169, 173, 178–79, 186, 187–89, 191, 213, 219, 220–21, 224, 228, 231, 235, 243–44, 245, 251, 253, 259
lion(s), 54, 56, 69, 129, 221

Menahem, 12, 13, 14, 15–29, 30–32, 34, 63, 133, 218–19, 237, 238, 239, 240

Merodach-Baladan, 117
Metanarrative, 22, 35, 86, 91, 109, 125, 215, 218–19, 223, 225, 232, 243–44, 246, 250, 259–60
military, 15–18, 25–27, 29, 30, 38, 40, 42, 66, 68, 71–73, 80, 82, 90, 92, 97–98, 100–101, 111, 114, 120, 132, 141, 144, 146, 161, 168, 173, 174, 176, 177, 186, 192–93, 195–96, 207, 210, 212, 216, 218, 219, 223, 229–30, 237, 244, 250, 253

name, 6, 15, 19–21, 35, 38–39, 41–42, 46, 49, 50, 55, 57, 64, 76, 82, 84, 93, 98–99, 109, 111, 122, 126, 127–29, 130, 132–33, 146, 150, 158, 170, 175, 181, 185, 187–90, 196–98, 212, 217, 219–22, 225, 228–29, 233, 239, 242, 245, 252, 259
Nineveh, 16, 69, 113, 207, 210, 214, 230

Persia(n), 6, 53, 150, 162, 232–33
Phoenicia(n), 204, 213
politics/political, 11, 29, 37–40, 42, 43, 45–47, 50–51, 63, 72, 74, 81–82, 95, 117, 132, 141, 146, 161, 188, 196, 205, 212–16, 219, 231, 233, 238, 242, 245–48, 254, 255, 258–60

Rab-šaqeh, 70, 72–75, 76–91, 92–93, 94–97, 106, 222, 223
rebellion, 80, 133, 208, 209–10, 214, 216, 258
representative, 3, 22, 28, 42, 55, 57, 85, 93, 112, 121, 126, 134, 144–45, 153, 158, 180, 182, 183, 191, 193, 196, 198, 228, 249–50

Sargon II, 50, 52–55, 71–73, 75, 88, 141, 221, 242
Samaria, 15, 19, 27, 32, 48–51, 53–59, 87–88, 140
Sennacherib, 3, 66–70, 72–77, 79–82, 84, 86, 88–91, 93–106, 108–16,

INDEX OF SUBJECTS   279

118, 121–22, 125, 168–70, 173, 174–83, 185–86, 189, 190–98, 213–14, 222–23, 225, 228–30, 234, 257
Shalmaneser, 19, 20, 48–50, 55–56, 64, 71, 72, 88, 141, 220, 242–44, 245–46, 250
Siloam Channel, 187–89
Solomon(ic), 44–45, 47, 85, 115, 122, 129, 140, 150, 153, 158, 161–62, 173, 176, 187, 240

Tartan, 70, 71–73, 111
Temple/temple, 35, 37, 39–40, 42–47, 63–64, 68–69, 116, 137, 149–50, 154, 158, 176, 178, 205, 227, 231, 233, 247
Tiglath-Pileser III, 16, 18–21, 26–28, 32–48, 50, 63, 71, 73, 88, 113, 125–28, 131–34, 136–38, 141–42, 145–47, 151, 185, 213, 219–20, 225–26, 238, 242, 250
typological/typologization/typologize/typology, 1, 69, 122, 143–44, 159–60, 162, 172, 185–87, 189, 193–94, 197, 198, 208, 216, 224, 226, 227, 228–29, 234

Urartu, 72–73

violence, 12, 15–17, 29, 63, 224

wall, 84, 106, 137, 186, 249
worship, 43–47, 56–60, 64, 79, 91, 127–129, 140, 158, 161, 178, 181, 183, 193, 205, 213, 233, 235, 240, 245–46, 251, 256, 258

Index of Hebrew Terms

בטח, 65–66, 76–77, 78, 79, 87, 88, 120, 127, 176
בנה, 200, 201
גלה, 61, 64, 126, 127, 133
זהב, 69
חזק, 145–47
חיל, 22, 24–27
חפא, 62–63, 64
חרם, 99
חרף, 98–99, 101, 106
יצא, 22–24
ישע, 37–38

מגנים, 168–69, 173, 227
מעל, 129–30, 136–37, 142–44, 149, 154, 157, 224
נצל, 88–89
סתם, 168–69, 171, 172, 227
עמד, 70, 84, 122
עשה, 168–69, 172, 178–79, 201, 228
שוב, 48, 95, 97, 106, 109, 111–13, 155–57, 159, 162
שחד, 39–41
שלח, 31, 96, 230
שמע, 41, 58, 94–95, 99, 104, 118

Index of Ancient Documents

ANCIENT NEAR EASTERN DOCUMENTS

Amarna Letters
36

Aššur Ostracon
19

Babylonian Chronicle (Shalmaneser V)
20, 21, 56

Babylonian King List A
19, 20, 21

Black Obelisk
52, 245

Calah Annals (Tiglath-Pileser III)
27–28

Calah Bulls (Shalmaneser III)
245

Cylinder Inscription (Sargon II)
52

Grant of Aššuretel-ilani
72

Great "Summary" Inscription (Sargon II)
52

Iran Stela
27–28

Kurkh Monolith
243–44

Marble Slab (Shalmaneser III)
245

Mesha Inscription
242

Nimrud Prisms D and E
52, 53, 54

Nimrud Tablets
27

Nimrud Wine Lists
248

Royal Inscriptions (Adad-Nirari III)
250

Royal Inscriptions (Sargon II)
52, 242

Royal Inscriptions
(Shalmaneser III)   242

Royal Inscriptions
(Tiglath-Pileser III)   242

Samaria Ostraca   27

Siloam Inscription   68

Small "Summary" Inscription   52

Summary Inscription 4
(Tiglath-Pileser III)   32

OLD TESTAMENT/ HEBREW BIBLE

Genesis

2:13	187
2:4–3:24	181
2:10–14	172
9:23–27	124
10	124
10:8–12	124, 125
10:22–23	7
10:22	124, 125
15:16	129
24:53	173
26:14–15	173
26:18	173

Exodus

8:17	31
34:6–9	158

Leviticus

26:22	31
27:8	22
27:12	22
27:14	22

Numbers

32:38	127

Deuteronomy

3:9	129
4:16	204
7:3–6	245
8:7–9	86
17:16–17	114
28	150
28:15–68	241
28:52	145

Joshua

1:14	24
6:2	24
8:3	24, 25
10:7	24
13:8–32	7
13:17	127

Judges

2:12	130
3:1–6	129, 130
3:3	129
3:4	129, 130
3:6	130
3:7	129
6:12	24
11:1	24, 25

Ruth

2:1	24, 25
2:8	104

1 Samuel

8:3	39
9:1	24, 25
16:18	24

2 Samuel

2:8–4:2	135
7:5–16	11
11–19	135

INDEX OF ANCIENT DOCUMENTS 285

1 Kings

1–2	135
1:9	188
1:11	104
1:33–40	187
1:33	188
1:38	188
4:20–25	85
8	11, 150, 162
8:23–53	162
8:37	145
8:50	162
8:64	44
11:1–6	245
11:7	115
11:12–13	11
11:28	24
11:34	11
11:36	11
12:15	13
12:24	13
12:28–13:32	56
12:31–13:5	11
13:24–32	54
13:33–34	11
14:9	11
14:15b–16	11
14:15	78
14:23	51
15	44
15:4–5	13
15:11–15	40
15:16–21	45
15:16–20	40
15:17	15
15:15	50
15:18	40
15:19	39, 40
15:21	15
15:25	239
15:29–30	13
15:33	15
16:1–4	13
16:8	15, 239
16:15–22	239
16:15	15
16:16–19	243
16:21–28	2, 5, 218, 242–43, 242
16:21–22	243
16:23–24	15
16:25–26	243
16:29–22:40	2, 5, 218, 243–45
16:34	13
17:30–33	245
18:36	158
19:16–18	247
19:16–17	5, 218, 245–47, 245, 247
20:35–36	54
21	247
22:1	244
22:51	239

2 Kings

3:9	173
3:16–20	173
3:25	173
19:24	173
5:1	24
6:25	83
8:9	13, 36
8:12	16, 17
8:13	36
9–10	2, 5, 218, 245–47, 245
9	247
9:1–10	247
9:13	247
9:18–19	247
9:32–33	247
10:4–7	247
10:9–11	247
10:15	247
10:24–27	247
10:29	246
10:30–32	13
10:30–31	13
10:30	9
10:31	9, 246
10:32–33	246
11:17	257
12:12	22
13:2–3	9
13:14	36
14:23–15:38	35
14:23–29	2, 5, 218, 247–50, 250
14:24	9, 247
14:25–27	247

2 Kings (continued)

14:26–27	13
14:28	247
15–17	9–64, 13, 63
15–16	11, 250
15	2, 5, 11, 12, 18, 31, 35, 217, 218
15:1–7	12
15:5	13
15:8–15	12
15:8–12	9
15:8	9
15:10	12, 30
15:11–15	40
15:12	9, 12, 13, 14, 15
15:13–17:6	13
15:13–22	218–19
15:13–16	15–18
15:13	11
15:14–22	14
15:14	12, 15, 30
15:15	12
15:16–22	12
15:16	13, 15, 17
15:17–22	18–29
15:17	240
15:18	18, 29
15:19–20	12, 13, 18, 19, 20, 21, 28, 37, 134
15:19	17, 18, 20, 21, 22, 29, 67, 133, 134
15:20	18, 22, 24, 25, 26, 28, 29
15:22	29
15:23–31	12, 30–35, 219
15:23	240
15:25	12, 30
15:27–31	14
15:27	11, 30, 237–40, 238, 240
15:29–30	19, 32
15:29	9, 12, 18, 30, 32, 33, 34, 37, 39, 40, 41, 45, 67, 126, 134, 135, 139, 140, 141, 219
15:30	12, 48, 139
15:32–16:20	10
15:32–37	30–35
15:32–38	12
15:32	240
15:37	31, 33, 35, 219
16	2, 3, 5, 11, 29, 33, 35–48, 35, 41, 46, 51, 63, 217, 219–20, 233
16:1–8	41, 64
16:1–3	35
16:1	240
16:2–20	7
16:2–4	31, 45
16:3–4	35
16:4	51
16:5–9	30–35, 32, 33, 37, 40, 139, 146, 219
16:5–6	35
16:5	30, 34, 50
16:6	36
16:7–9	26, 33, 42, 44, 45, 46, 146
16:7–8	45, 47, 50
16:7	36, 37, 38, 42, 126
16:8	32, 39, 40, 63, 219
16:9–12	46
16:9	42, 46
16:10–18	41, 43, 45, 46
16:10–17	41, 46
16:10–16	44, 46, 47, 220
16:10	42, 43, 46, 47, 126
16:13	47
16:14–18	115
16:15	47, 51
16:18	32, 43, 46, 47, 48, 50, 219, 220
17	2, 11, 48–63, 48, 50, 53, 58, 59, 60, 61, 62, 64, 67, 146, 217, 220–1, 232
17:1–6	14, 49, 220
17:1–7aa	5
17:1–4	49
17:2	48
17:3–7	41
17:3–6	19, 48, 51, 53, 55, 139
17:3	32, 48, 50, 67, 140
17:4	49, 50
17:5	49, 50
17:6	14, 49, 50, 51, 52, 61, 134, 135, 140, 220
17:7ab–41	5
17:7–23	11, 13, 14, 29, 48, 51, 52, 53, 54, 59, 221
17:7–22	12, 13
17:7–21	58

INDEX OF ANCIENT DOCUMENTS 287

17:7–17	51, 60	17:40	57, 58, 59
17:7–9	53, 221	17:41	57
17:7–8	54	18–20	2, 65–123, 121, 217, 218, 234
17:7	13, 14		
17:9–10	51	18–20:11	5
17:9	62	18–19	3, 65, 80, 104, 111, 116, 119, 122, 222–23
17:11	61		
17:13	11, 13, 51, 58	18	97, 101
17:14–17	58	18:1–16	121
17:14	58, 59, 221	18:1–12	65, 222
17:15	58	18:1–8	13
17:16	60	18:1–2	65
17:17	51	18:3	65
17:18–23	51, 55, 79	18:4	65, 78
17:18–22	13	18:5–6	65, 68
17:18–20	11	18:5	66, 76
17:18	14, 52	18:6	222
17:18a	5	18:7–8	66
17:20	13, 14, 52	18:7	66, 68
17:21–34a	5	18:9–12	41, 66, 67, 88, 135, 140, 222
17:21–23	13, 52	18:9–11	139
17:23	14, 52, 54, 58, 61, 220	18:9–10	67
17:24–41	45, 48, 53, 58, 59	18:9	67
17:24–40	58	18:10–12	79
17:24–33	53, 54	18:11	67, 134
17:24–28	54, 55, 221	18:12	13
17:24–27	55	18:13–20:21	7
17:24	50, 54, 57, 87, 88, 161	18:13–19:37	3, 75
17:25	54, 41	18:13–19:36	67
17:26	50, 55, 59, 61	18:13–16	66–70, 68, 69, 70
17:27–28	54	18:13–15	19
17:27	50, 54, 55, 59, 61, 221	18:13	66, 67, 74, 222
17:28	55, 61	18:14–17	222
17:29–34	58	18:14–16	68, 223
17:29–32	58	18:14	67, 69, 70, 111
17:29–30	57	18:15–16	68, 69
17:30–31	57, 88	18:16	69
17:32	57	18:17–19:37	70
17:33	57, 61	18:17–19:36	122
17:34–41	53, 57, 88	18:17–18	70–75, 222
17:34–40	57, 58	18:17	66, 70, 71, 84, 96, 112, 115, 120, 192, 193, 222
17:34–39	57		
17:34	57, 58, 88	18:18–25	84
17:35	57	18:18	71, 75
17:36	57	18:19–25	76–83, 82
17:37	57	18:19	76, 80, 84
17:38	57	18:20	78, 80
17:39	57	18:21	78, 80, 192

INDEX OF ANCIENT DOCUMENTS

2 Kings *(continued)*

18:22	76, 78, 79, 82
18:23–24	115, 116
18:23	78, 80
18:24	80, 111
18:25	78, 79, 80, 82, 105
18:26–19:28	75
18:26–28	84
18:26–27	79, 84
18:26	82, 84
18:27–35	83–91
18:27	83, 84, 85, 108
18:27–28	84, 193
18:28–37	89
18:28–35	89
18:28	76, 82, 84, 85, 102
18:29–35	102
18:29	76, 84, 88, 89
18:30	76, 85, 88, 89, 97
18:31–32	82, 108
18:31	76, 86, 91
18:32–35	97
18:32	76, 86, 88
18:33	88, 89, 98
18:33–34	88
18:34–35	87
18:34	56, 87, 88, 89, 95, 105
18:35	88, 89, 98, 115
18:36–19:5	91–94
18:36	79, 85, 91, 92, 223
18:37	85, 93
19	88, 97
19:1–21	94–99
19:1–16	94
19:1–5	93
19:1–4	97
19:1–2	96
19:1	85, 93
19:2	75
19:3	93, 94
19:4	50, 94, 106
19:6–13	96
19:6	94, 97, 106
19:7–9	97, 104, 106
19:7	94, 95, 97, 106, 111, 115
19:8–9	94, 95, 96, 97, 111, 193
19:8	96, 111
19:9	78, 95, 96, 97, 110, 111
19:10–13	95, 97, 98
19:10	89
19:11–13	95
19:11–12	98
19:11	88, 94, 98, 104
19:12–13	87, 105
19:12	88
19:13	87, 95
19:14–19	96
19:14–16	97
19:14–15	97
19:14	89, 110
19:15–19	108, 112
19:16–17	98
19:16	95, 98, 106
19:17	98, 99
19:18	89, 98
19:19	89, 98
19:21–34	99–109
19:21–28	99
19:21	99–100, 108, 109
19:22–23	101
19:22	76, 106
19:23–24	102–3, 105
19:23	89, 103, 106, 110, 115, 116
19:24–25	103
19:24	99, 102, 103, 189
19:25–28	103, 104, 105
19:25–26	32, 104, 219
19:25	104
19:26	89, 105, 108
19:27	105
19:28	105, 106, 109, 111, 207, 230
19:29–31	107
19:29	107, 108
19:30–31	108, 252
19:31	107
19:32–33	109
19:32	100, 109, 192
19:33–34	100
19:33	100, 109, 111
19:34	108, 109, 116
19:35–37	109–14, 117
19:35–36	113
19:35	109, 111, 196
19:36–37	115
19:36	112, 113
19:37	99, 109, 113, 116

INDEX OF ANCIENT DOCUMENTS 289

Reference	Pages
20	116, 121, 218, 223
20:1–19	116–21, 122
20:1–11	116, 117, 170
20:3	120
20:6	116
20:12–20	118
20:12–19	5, 68, 118, 119, 120, 223
20:13–15	119
20:13	121
20:16–18	69, 119
20:18	120
20:19	119–20
20:20	115
21	3
21:1–18	2, 7, 218, 251–52, 251, 252
21:1–7	5
21:2–16	251
21:3	60
21:7	204
21:8–16	5
21:10–16	203
21:10–15	13
21:14	217, 218, 252
21:17–18	5
21:19–26	2, 5, 7, 218, 253–54
21:19	239
21:21–26	258
21:23–24	253
22:1–23:30	2, 7, 218, 255–58, 255
22:1–14	5
22:15–20	5
22:16–17	255
23	256
23:1–15	5
23:1–3	257
23:4–16	255
23:11	256
23:16–18	5
23:19–25	5
23:19–20	255, 259
23:20	256
23:24	255
23:25–27	13
23:26–30	5
23:26–27	256
23:26	252, 255
23:27	60
23:29–30	255–56
23:29	2, 217, 218, 255, 256
23:31–24:20	239
23:33–35	256
23:35	22
24:2–4	13
24:3–4	252
24:12	91
24:13	13
24:14	24, 25, 61
24:15	61
24:20	13
25	61
25:11	61
25:21	60, 61
25:27–30	60

1 Chronicles

Reference	Pages
1	138
1:1–2:2	125
1:1–23	124
1:17	2, 7, 124–25, 124, 138, 224, 225
2–9	158
2:1	125
4:41	174
5	125, 126, 127, 128, 131, 135, 137, 138, 226, 232
5:1–6	127
5:3–16	128
5:5	127
5:6	2, 7, 126, 127, 137, 155, 225–26
5:8–10	127
5:8	127
5:10	131
5:18–22	129, 131
5:19–22	127
5:20	127, 132
5:22b–26	2, 7, 225–26
5:22	132, 137
5:22b	127
5:22c	127, 128
5:23–26	128, 138
5:23–24	128
5:23	128, 129, 130, 131
5:24	24, 129, 131
5:25–26	127, 132, 134, 137, 155, 224–25, 226, 232
5:25	129, 130, 131, 137, 224

1 Chronicles (continued)

5:26	21, 126, 128, 131, 132, 134, 137, 141, 226, 233
5:27–41	137
6:15	232
7:2	24
7:5	24
7:9	24
7:11	24
7:14–19	128
7:40	24
8:30	127
8:40	24
9:1	125
9:13	24
9:36	127
11:26	24
12:8	24
12:21	24
12:25	24
12:28	24
12:30	24
15	151
21:15	196
26:6	24
26:31	24
28:1	24
29:6	24
29:11–19	178
29:18	158

2 Chronicles

1:1	190
2:10–15	124
6	150, 162
6:14–42	162
6:18	178
6:21	178
6:28	145
6:39–40	162
7:13–15	162
7:14	162
9:8	124
9:15–16	173
10–36	161
13:3	24
13:4–12	161
13:12	190
13:19	179
14:8	24
15:9	190
16:1–10	40
17:3	190
17:13	24
17:14	24
17:16	24
17:17	24
20:1–30	176
20:17–30	176
21:3	173
21:16	131, 132, 233
23	3
25:6	24
26:12	24
28	2, 3, 7, 139–48, 139, 140, 141, 142, 149, 150, 151, 152, 154, 184, 226, 233
28:1	149
28:1–15	142
28:2–4	142
28:5–21	146
28:5(b)–8	135, 140, 141, 142
28:5–6	139
28:5(a)	141, 142, 146, 150, 151, 159
28:6–15	7
28:6	130, 140, 141, 150
28:8(b)–15	140, 141, 142
28:8	140. 152
28:9–15	33
28:11	33
28:12–21	141
28:12–15	135, 140
28:12	135, 139, 140, 151
28:14–15	150
28:15	33
28:16–27	142
28:16–21	3, 140, 141, 142, 143, 144, 147, 148. 151, 191, 195, 224, 226, 229
28:16	142, 143, 144, 145, 147, 148, 154, 159, 206, 224, 226
28:17–18	143, 145, 147, 159
28:17	146, 150, 151
28:18	151
28:19–21	145

INDEX OF ANCIENT DOCUMENTS

28:19	135, 140, 141, 142, 143, 144, 147, 149, 157	30:9	151, 152, 157, 158, 160, 162, 185, 224, 225
28:20–21	147, 151, 154, 185	30:10–12	155
28:20	126, 142, 143, 145, 146, 147, 195, 226	30:10	136
		30:17–20	172
28:21	142, 143, 144, 145, 146, 147, 148, 151	30:17–19	153
		30:18	155
28:22–25	142	30:20	162
28:22–23	141, 142	30:23	153
28:22	145, 149, 157	30:24	153, 174
28:23	140	30:25–31:1	172
28:24	149	30:25	161
28:26–27	142	30:26	153
28:26	140	30:27	162, 178
28:27	140	31:1	155
28:32	47	31:4–10	172
29–31	161, 176, 193	31:20–32:33	167, 168–69, 224, 227, 228
29–31:19	228	31:20–21	168, 170, 227
29:9	2, 7, 149–52, 149	31:20–32:2	170
29:5–11	149, 154	31:21	162, 181
29:6–9	149, 157	32	2, 3, 7, 143, 151, 162, 163–98, 163, 164, 165, 167, 170, 171, 174, 175, 181, 182, 183, 184, 185, 188, 189. 191, 193, 195, 197, 198, 202, 224, 225, 227–30, 228, 231, 234
29:6–7	149		
29:7	149		
29:8–9	150, 151		
29:8	150, 151		
29:9–10	224		
29:9	150, 152, 224, 225, 227, 233	32:1–32	170
29:10–11	149	32:1–23	170, 183, 198
29:10	162	32:1–8	192, 229
29:36	172	32:1–2	168, 171, 192, 229
30–32	162	32:1	174, 175, 185, 228
30–31	162	32:2–8	176, 186, 228
30:1–31:1	152	32:2–6	189
30	152, 153, 161, 162	32:2	175, 185, 191
30:1–13	172	32:3–5	192, 229
30:1	154, 155	32:3–4	187
30:5–11	136, 152	32:3	168, 171, 173, 227
30:5	136, 155	32:4	143, 144, 159, 168, 171–72, 186, 187, 188–89, 206, 229
30:6–9	2, 7, 134, 143, 144, 152–62, 153, 154, 157, 160, 161, 162, 186, 224, 227, 234, 241	32:5	168, 173, 183, 227
		32:6–8	191, 192, 229
30:5	153	32:6	168, 172, 173–74, 228
30:6	135, 136, 143, 151, 152, 154, 155, 157, 158, 159, 160, 162, 185, 186, 206	32:7–8	176, 189–90, 229
		32:7	168, 175, 176, 192, 193, 204, 229
30:7–8	157	32:8	168, 172, 174, 191, 192, 229
30:7	157, 160, 224	32:9–23	174
30:8	157, 162	32:9–19	195

1 Chronicles (continued)

32:9	168, 174, 175, 181, 192, 196, 206, 229, 230
32:10–19	208
32:10–15	180, 195, 229
32:10	168, 175–76, 189, 192
32:11–12	193, 195
32:11	168, 175, 177, 193
32:12	168, 178, 181, 189, 193, 228, 229
32:13–15	180, 193–94
32:13	168, 178–79
32:14	168, 193
32:15	169, 179–80, 193, 194, 204, 228
32:16–19	180, 194–95
32:16–17	194
32:16	169, 170, 180–3, 194, 206, 228
32:17–19	180
32:17	169, 179–80, 193, 194–95, 228
32:18	169, 176, 189, 191, 230
32:19	131, 169, 178–79, 193, 194–95
32:20	169, 176, 178, 181, 191, 196, 228, 230
32:21–23	191
32:21	24, 169, 177, 181, 196, 208, 230
32:22	169, 175–76, 197, 198
32:22–23	197, 230
32:23	169, 173, 174
32:24–33	170, 183
32:24–26	170, 171
32:24	169, 174
32:25	169
32:26	169, 172, 173–74, 202, 228
32:27–30	170
32:27–28	169, 173, 227
32:27	173, 183
32:29	169, 171–72, 188
32:30	127, 169, 171, 188, 227
32:31–33	170
32:31	169, 170, 171, 181
32:32–33	169, 170, 227
32:32	7, 130, 196
32:33	172
33	162, 201, 204, 205, 206, 208, 224
33:1–20	2, 3, 7, 199–216, 200, 202, 205, 215–16, 230–1, 230–1
33:1	199, 200, 201
33:2–9	200, 201, 202
33:2–8	199, 200
33:2	201, 202
33:3	201, 203. 213
33:4–5	205
33:4	201
33:5	201
33:6	201, 202
33:7	201, 204, 205
33:8	201
33:9	200, 201, 202
33:10–13	200, 207, 215
33:10–11	199, 200, 201, 202, 203
33:10	201, 205, 216
33:11–17	252
33:11–14	215
33:11–13	251
33:11	106, 199, 200, 201, 205, 206, 207, 208, 209, 211, 216, 225, 230, 251, 259
33:12–19	201, 202, 215
33:12–13	199, 200, 202, 203, 208
33:12	145, 201, 214, 215
33:13	201, 251
33:14	199, 200, 201, 202, 205, 215
33:15–17	199, 200
33:15	201, 204, 251
33:16	201
33:17	201, 203, 205, 213, 214
33:18–20	199, 200
33:18	201
33:19	201, 202, 203, 214, 215, 224
33:20	201, 202
33:21–25	2, 7, 218, 258–59
33:23	202, 259
33:24–25	259
34–35	2, 7, 218, 259–60
34:6	136, 259
35:20–25	260
35:21–22	260
35:25	7
36:6	208, 225
36:10	208, 225
36:11–21	136

INDEX OF ANCIENT DOCUMENTS

36:13–23	232
36:13b–20	136, 225, 226
36:14–20	137
36:14	137
36:15–20	137
36:20–23	233
36:20	233
36:22–23	124
36:22	131, 132, 233

Ezra

	6
1:5	131, 132
8:17	22

Nehemiah

	6
2:1	74
11:14	24
12:26	74
13:6–7	74

Job

2:11	100
6:22	39

Psalms

22:4–5	88
25:1–2	88
28:7	88
31:14–15	88
42:6	128
46:4	189
47:3	76
69:21	100
86:2	88
89:12	128
94:9	104
95:3	76
103:19	178
133:3	128

Proverbs

20:26	156
21:14	39

Song of Songs

4:8	129

Isaiah

7	34
7:1	34
7:17	147
8:2	44
8:6	187
9:13	78
9:14	78
10:5–19	235
10:8	143, 206, 230
19:6	103
21:14	39
36–39	2, 7
36:2	192
36:4	76
36:6	192
36:12	83
36:13–14	76
37:25	189
37:26	104
37:29	207, 230
37:33	192
37:36	196
38:1–22	170
40:21	104
42:3	78
58:5	78

Jeremiah

3:12	155
3:14	155
3:22	155
8:4–5	155
10:18	145
15:4	7
15:19	155
18:16	100
29:10	61
29:18	150
39:18	88

Ezekiel

6:2	185
8:3	204

Ezekiel *(continued)*

8:5	204
14:13	31
16:33	39
19:4	106, 207, 230
19:9	207, 208, 230
27:5	129
29:4	207, 230
29:67	78
38:4	106, 207, 230
47:1–12	172
47:16	56

Daniel

6:29	133

Hosea

13:15–14:1	16
13:8	16, 17

Amos

1:13	16, 17
4:2	106
8:11	31

Zephaniah

1:17	145

Haggai

1:14	131, 132

Zechariah

1:2–6	155, 241

Malachi

1:14	76

ANCIENT VERSIONS

Greek (G)

15

Lucianic LXX (L)

6

LXX^{AL}

240

Syriac (S)

15

Targum (T)

15

APOCRYPHA

Sirach

6

DEAD SEA SCROLLS

$4QSam^a$

6

RABBINIC WRITINGS

b. Baba Bathra

15a	6

b. Sanhedrin

60a	74

GRECO-ROMAN WRITINGS

Anabasis (Xenophon)

17

Ptolemaic Canon

19

www.ingramcontent.com/pod-product-compliance
Lightning Source LLC
Chambersburg PA
CBHW061430300426
44114CB00014B/1622